Emiliano Zapata

SAMUEL BRUNK

EMILIANO ZAPATA

Revolution
& Betrayal
in Mexico

UNIVERSITY OF NEW MEXICO PRESS

Albuquerque

To Anne Perry

Library of Congress Cataloging-in-Publication Data

Brunk, Samuel, 1959–
Revolution and betrayal in Mexico : a life of Emiliano Zapata /
Samuel Brunk—1st ed.   p.   cm.
Includes bibliographical references and index.
ISBN 0–8263–1619–0. — ISBN 0–8263–1620–4 (pbk.)
1. Zapata, Emiliano, 1879–1919.   2. Mexico—Politics and
government—1910–1946.   3. Revolutionaries—Mexico—Biography.
I. Title.
F1234.Z37B78   1995
972.08′1′092—dc20
[B]   CIP 94–18742
© 1995 by the University of New Mexico Press
All rights reserved.
First edition

Designed by Linda Mae Tratechaud

Morelos

Zapata's Core Region

Morelos

Zapata's Core Region

Contents

Acknowledgments

THIS BOOK COULD NOT HAVE BECOME A REALITY without the help of many people. My research was funded by a Fulbright Grant from the United States Information Agency and by several awards from organizations at the University of New Mexico: a Graduate Achievement Award from the Office of Graduate Studies; Tinker/Mellon and Field Research grants from the Latin American Institute; and three grants from the Student Research Allocations Committee.

Special thanks are due to Linda Hall, who conceived of this project when I was her graduate student at the University of New Mexico, and then guided me every step of the way. Robert Himmerich y Valencia also provided the kind of support without which it is impossible to negotiate the perils of graduate school—as well as many invaluable suggestions about the manuscript. Aaron Mahr, too, has been an insightful critic, whose crash course on computers was indispensable. Enrique Semo, Nelson Valdés, and Paul Vanderwood read the entire work and contributed their excellent advice. Alberto Sandoval helped with Mexican colloquialisms. Much tested by my research demands, the staffs of the University of New Mexico's Zimmerman Library and the University of Nebraska-Lincoln's Love Library—and especially their respective Inter-Library Loan departments—have always risen to the occasion. David Holtby, Barbara Guth, and the rest of the employees at the University of New

Mexico Press have made this work infinitely better than it was when it first arrived at their door.

In Mexico I received support and instruction from Alicia Olivera, Laura Espejel, Carlos Barreto, Salvado Rueda, Eugenia Meyer, Mateo Zapata, and the Fulbright Office. Thanks are also due to Ana Buriano and the rest of the staff at the Instituto de Investigaciones, Dr. José María Luis Mora; María Esther González Hernández and her co-workers at the Centro de Estudios Sobre la Universidad at UNAM; as well as the employees of the Archivo General de la Nación, the Instituto Nacional de Antropología e Historia, the Hemeroteca Nacional, the Biblioteca Nacional, the Archivo Histórico de la Defensa Nacional, the Centro de Estudios de Historia de México (Condumex), and the libraries of the Universidad Panamericana and the Colegio de México. Víctor Raúl Martínez Vásquez and family, Luis Roberto Vera, and Lisa Sparaco gave me not only their thoughts about Zapata, but the occasional, much needed home-cooked meal or place to stay.

No words can possibly express my debt to my wife, Anne Perry, whose life this resurrection of Zapata has touched perhaps as deeply as it has mine, and not always in a positive way. This book is dedicated to her.

Introduction

THE LIFE OF MEXICAN REVOLUTIONARY EMILIANO ZA-
pata was the stuff that legends are made of. Born and
raised in a tiny village in the small south-central state of Morelos, in
1911 he led an uprising—one strand of the larger Mexican Revolution—against the regime of long-time president Porfirio Díaz. He
fought not primarily to fulfill personal ambitions, but for the
campesinos of Morelos, whose rights were being systematically ignored in Don Porfirio's courts. Expanding haciendas had been appropriating land and water for centuries in the state, but as the
twentieth century began things were becoming desperate. The via-
bility of village economies was threatened, and with it the cultural
survival of the Morelian peasantry.[1] Surprisingly, it was not long
before Díaz fell. But Zapata then discovered that other national
leaders—Francisco Madero, Victoriano Huerta, and Venustiano Carranza—would not put things right, and so he fought them too. He
fought for nearly a decade until, in 1919, he was gunned down in an
ambush at the hacienda Chinameca.

During his lifetime, Zapata was much loved and much hated.
For many of the campesinos he led he was *"el hombre"*—the man.[2]
He dazzled them in the local rodeos—called *jaripeos*—in which he
performed. He won their trust with his fairness and his persistent
pursuit of their well-being. His deep, dark eyes seemed to penetrate
their thoughts and plumb their hearts. When he entered a village, he

was received with church bells and fireworks. But much of the rest of Mexico never understood the attraction. With its dreams of Europe and of progress, Mexico City was, in many ways, light years away from the countryside that surrounded it. It was here in the city that the Morelian hacendados spent most of their time, and here that the products of Morelian land and labor were consumed. The haciendas, in other words, were devices that served the capital; they were its means of exploiting the campesinos of Morelos while keeping them out of sight. Zapata hated the city, and as it watched ominous Zapatista campfires burn in the mountains to its south, the city would grow to hate Zapata. Except for the short year in which Zapatistas occupied the capital, the Mexico City press consistently attacked Zapata while he lived, shaping national opinion in the process. For much of Mexico Zapata was a blood-soaked bandit, a killer of innocents, the Attila of the South.

Many of the peasants of Morelos were unable to accept Zapata's death. Some claimed the body that was presented to them as proof of his mortality lacked his distinctive birthmark. Others missed the mole they remembered, or wondered why the corpse included the finger Zapata lost years before in a roping accident. Zapata was not dead, they argued, a compadre who looked like him had taken his place on that fateful day, and Zapata was hiding in the mountains until they needed him again, or fighting in Arabia or for Hitler. For them he was too smart, too strong, too important, too symbolic of their cause to die, and in a sense they were right, for he lived on in their stories.[3]

But this was not the only way that myth grew up around Zapata. In 1920 the Zapatistas joined the rebellion against Venustiano Carranza that won the revolution for Alvaro Obregón. Obregón was a masterful politician who understood the demand of many of Mexico's rural rebels for land reform. He and his successors also understood that it was Zapata who had voiced that demand best. The figure of Zapata—once cleansed of certain troublesome realities—could thus be used to help firm up the new revolutionary coalition by holding the support of the campesinos. Thus Zapata became the intransigent of the revolution, an immaculate symbol of the emancipation of the rural masses. As a humble Indian clothed in sandals and the white cotton uniform of the Morelian peasantry, he was placed alongside his arch-enemy Carranza in the pantheon of revolutionary heroes, ironically serving as one of the founding fathers of a state that increasingly favored the city over the countryside.[4]

This vision of Zapata naturally demanded a written history, and many of his old advisors and secretaries—intellectuals in the eyes of the Zapatistas at least—were anxious to provide it. Though full of critically important material, the accounts of men like Gildardo Magaña, Antonio Díaz Soto y Gama, Serafín M. Robles, and Octavio Paz Solórzano were little concerned with separating reality from myth.[5] They were usually more about the movement than they were about Zapata, and when they did approach the man they generally found him a Robin Hood, a redeemer, a symbol of something larger than himself. Zapata was their most important asset in the new revolutionary order: they dressed him up because the more stunning a figure he cut, the better they themselves appeared.

But as one veteran of the movement put it, "Zapata fought so that the poor could have land, not for the fucking politicians."[6] Some people have tried to keep the record straight, among them historians Jesús Sotelo Inclán and John Womack.[7] Sotelo Inclán's *Raíz y razón de Zapata* (1943) was a thoughtful study of the long history of Zapata's village—Anenecuilco—and of Zapata's life prior to the revolution. A quarter of a century later, Womack's expansive and beautifully written *Zapata and the Mexican Revolution* gave Zapata's rebellion the full, critical coverage that it had previously lacked. Despite the biographical information that they included, however, neither of these authors was primarily concerned with Zapata. What interested them was the movement as a whole—its background, its contours, its successes and failures—and not the man, who was sometimes lost in the shuffle. In fact, both authors often minimized the importance of individual choices and actions, and tended to argue, as Womack put it at least once, that Zapata was "perfectly representative of his people's feelings."[8] Though now much more life-like, in other words, for both Sotelo Inclán and Womack, Zapata was something of a symbol still.

In failing to scrutinize Zapata's role as leader, Sotelo Inclán and Womack reflected the inclinations of a larger body of scholars. In recent decades many students of revolution have concluded that leadership, in general, is a factor of small consequence in the making of revolutions. Others have focused their attentions on leaders of national movements—usually urbanites of middle or upper class origins—whom they consider, at least implicitly, to be more important than peasant leaders as agents of revolutionary change. Although some empirical studies of the Mexican Revolution have recognized its fundamental personalism and included leadership within their purviews, even here repeated calls to understand peasants as conscious shapers of their own history have inspired few books that provide detailed, critical investigations of the role of leadership in a regionally-based, peasant rebellion like Zapatismo.[9]

Perhaps one reason that peasant leaders are often not considered especially significant as historical actors is that anthropologists have sometimes deemphasized individualism in peasant societies; indeed, some of those who have done so have done their field work in Morelos. In *Tepoztlán, A Mexican Village* (1930), Robert Redfield discovered a degree of communal solidarity in Tepoztlán, Morelos, that was unknown in his urban world, and in stressing that solidarity left a lasting imprint on the study of anthropology in the state. Taken to its logical conclusion—a conclusion reached by at least one recent student of Morelian village life—insistence on community makes the study of the individual in peasant societies unnecessary. For many anthropologists and other social scientists, however, Redfield's interpretation is now outdated. Much has been done since 1930, and the considerable body of data that anthropologists have now collected on Morelos demonstrates quite clearly—as do the documents of Zapatismo—that both intra- and intervillage conflicts have been common occurrences. It has become apparent that Morelian communities have been composed of individuals who have often had different interests or have simply failed to agree.[10] Moreover, the study of peasants elsewhere has led to similar conclusions. While it is true, then, that a degree of communal solidarity exists in peasant societies, and it is obvious that Zapatismo was essentially a communal movement, communalism has not been the only factor at play. A balance must be struck between tendencies to communalism, familialism, and individualism—a balance that leaves plenty of room for biographies of peasant leaders.[11]

While inquiry into the nuances of peasant leadership has undoubtedly also been limited by the fact that peasant rebellions often produce little documentation, there is a substantial amount of evidence available for this study. The Archive of Gildardo Magaña and the newspaper collection at the Hemeroteca Nacional, both in Mexico City, have been heavily mined by previous historians but remain wonderful sources of information. Other materials have been less well explored. In Mexico's National Archives there are more than forty boxes of relatively unused documents, primarily in the collections of Emiliano Zapata and Genovevo de la O. In addition, oral accounts of the revolution have been supplemented by the Programa de Historia Oral of the Instituto Nacional de Antropología e Historia, which in the 1970s recorded interviews with dozens of Zapatista veterans.

Still, the task of disentangling the real Zapata from his mythical twin is daunting, and there are limits to what a biographer can discover. Even with the best documentation the individual is elusive—motivations, for instance, are notoriously difficult to gauge—and in the case of Zapata this difficulty is enhanced by several factors. Most obviously, perhaps, the historical materials do not make it possible to trace his day-to-day movements like one might those of a modern American president. Furthermore, though one can make some general statements about the social psychology of the people of Morelos, too little is known about Zapata's childhood to put him on the analyst's couch, and so I have largely resisted the temptation to pursue psychological speculations.[12] Finally, much of the material on Zapata partially screens him from our view. There is no indication that any of the documents of the movement were given their definitive form by Zapata himself; they were written, instead, by the secretaries who swarmed around him throughout the revolutionary decade. Moreover, the mythification in which these secretaries indulged when they wrote the first books about Zapata means that these crucial, first-hand accounts, upon which the historian must somehow depend, are at times self-serving and often full of distortion. From our perspective, in other words, Zapata is encased in, and mummified by, his secretaries. It is very hard to get him alone. If there is much that we will probably never know about Zapata, however, there is much that we can know, too. By exercising caution in the attribution of motive and a healthy skepticism about his personal contribution to any given document, by reading between the lines of the documents and carefully comparing different kinds of evidence, I believe it is possible to produce a reasonable picture of Zapata's life.

The primary goal of this book, then, is to provide a much needed political biography of Zapata, and to demonstrate in the process that his choices and actions did have a historical impact. Zapata was, I will argue, an excellent leader on the local and regional levels. Able to balance different priorities and pressures in a practical fashion, he demonstrated a great understanding of the milieu in which he operated, and so did much to give his movement the ideology and organization it needed to maintain its coherence for many years, often against tremendous odds. One measure of his success within the region was that Zapatismo rose to national prominence in 1914 and 1915, a remarkable accomplishment for what was fundamentally an autonomous, regional peasant rebellion. But Zapata was unable to maintain a significant share of state power and see that power institutionalized, and I will contend that this was partly because his leadership was less successful in the national arena, especially with regard to interfactional diplomacy and the use of his urban advisors. Partly as a result of these shortcomings, after the middle of 1915 the movement entered into a decline that no amount of good leadership could reverse.

Emiliano Zapata

1 The Making of a Rebel

EMILIANO ZAPATA HAD SPENT A HARD SIX MONTHS when he left the front at Puebla just before Christmas in 1914. Six months earlier his troops had been besieging Cuernavaca, the last stronghold of the federal army in Morelos. They were still pressing Mexico City from the sierra of Ajusco, which rose between Morelos and the capital. And Zapata was still promising that there would be no peace "while the land is not distributed among those who know how and want to cultivate it."[1]

Five months earlier, in July, the dictator Victoriano Huerta had finally surrendered power and gone into exile, but the fighting continued against the government he left behind. It meant a lot of time on horseback. On July 19 Zapata took Topilejo, the next day Milpa Alta, and then San Pablo Actopan, chasing off small bands of federal troops. There was nothing the matter with time on horseback; one found a certain peace there, or found peace at least after dark, sleeping anonymously on the fringes of a mountain camp. The trouble lay more in a kind of frustration. In these villages of the Federal District, only a few miles south of the center of Mexico City, national power flitted just beyond Zapata's reach. Home, however, was close too, just over the mountains to the south, and the voices of home never stopped calling. Remigio Cortés made him the gift of a machete; Onecima Promera asked for money from her death bed; and at the

3

end of the month birthday wishes began to find him, along with news from Yautepec about a child of his that nearly died.[2]

Pursuing that elusive national power that might guarantee the change he sought for Mexico, in July and August Zapata had had several discussions with representatives of the other factions that had fought Huerta. If the fighting was bad, the talking generally felt worse. Dr. Atl, Antenor Sala, Manuel N. Robles, Guillermo García Aragón, Carmen Serdán, Lucio Blanco, Juan Sarabia, Antonio I. Villarreal, Luis Cabrera—the list of messengers, sycophants, profiteers could go on and on. Zapata tried to make it clear that peace was impossible unless everyone signed the Plan of Ayala, but it was sometimes hard to know if it was that simple, and Zapata got angry and perhaps even a little ill. By the end of August he had heard enough, at least, to make up his mind about the hacendado Venustiano Carranza, leader of the northern, Constitutionalist faction. Carranza was a man who could not be trusted; he was only in the revolution for himself.[3]

In September and October things had settled down a little. Carranza's emissaries stopped coming, and with the bloody fall of Cuernavaca in mid-August Zapata controlled all of Morelos. He could then respond to requests for money from his cousin Alberta Merino, and from his compadre Lucio Rios in Cuautla, who wanted fifty pesos to start a small business. Emigdio Alcalco had again raised the matter of a baptism at Tepalcingo, and Zapata had even found time to attend a saint's day celebration or two. Of course, there was no relaxing. Carranza had negotiated his way into Mexico City, bringing his forces face to face, in a precarious cease-fire, with those of Zapata in the southern Federal District.[4] Plus there was the question of a second prominent northern revolutionary—Francisco "Pancho" Villa—who had also come to hate Carranza and sought Zapata's support against him.

Sometime in October or November Zapata had decided to give Villa that support, and the war started again. On the night of November 24 Zapata's men penetrated to the center of Mexico City: a share of national power was finally theirs. Then, on December 4,

Zapata and Villa had met for the first time at Xochimilco in the Federal District. Like Zapata, Villa was a man of the people, but there the resemblance ended. A large, animated man, dressed in khaki, Villa was not exactly what Zapata had expected. Zapata quickly discovered, in fact, that his new ally did not even drink. Still the meeting went smoothly enough. Villa agreed to recognize the land reform goals of the Plan of Ayala and to send Zapata much needed arms and ammunition. And so on December 6, apparently of one mind and with their combined forces behind them, they rode into Mexico City together to the cheers of a wildly enthusiastic crowd.[5]

Zapata got through it all because there was so much at stake, but it had not been his kind of celebration. He hated Mexico City, both for what it was and what it stood for. On the ninth of December he gladly left to plan the attack on Puebla; on the sixteenth Puebla fell. Carranza was on the run, and it seemed that this round of fighting would soon be over. But there were difficulties. Zapata's intellectual advisors were already bickering with those of Villa and other nominal allies; nearly every night in the capital scores were being settled by assassination; and the discipline of many of Zapata's men was no match for the temptations of Mexico City. Ambitions and expectations were everywhere on the increase, and they raised doubts in Zapata's mind. Indeed, it was impossible to know who could be trusted. Surely the people of Mexico City would have cheered as loudly for anyone else who was winning; and why had Villa been so slow to send Zapata the artillery pieces he needed for the Puebla siege? There was no peace in this; there was no feeling in the victory in Mexico City or in Puebla, no remembering what the years of struggle and bloodshed had all been for, no knowing what, if anything, had been won.[6]

And so Zapata left the front at Puebla just before Christmas in 1914. As he crossed into Morelos the voices grew louder. The voices of the people who fought for him and the people he fought for, voices from the green valleys and dry hills of another Morelos winter. First down to Tlaltizapán, his new headquarters; then up into the mountains, to Quilamula. There, when he got up on a cloudless morning, he might put a chair outside under the fruit trees and sit among the chickens pecking through the dust, smell the horses, smoke a cigar. And when the birds stopped screeching long enough, he might hear the pat pat pat of palm against corn meal as Gregoria made the tortillas.[7] It would take only a few minutes of peace to remember the point and feel what was won, and when the cigar was finished he would try, as he always did, to find a way to answer the voices.

Zapata was born on August 8, 1879, in a two-room house of adobe walls and thatch roof in the village of Anenecuilco, Morelos. The ninth of ten children of Gabriel Zapata and Cleofas Salazar—both mestizos of campesino background—he was among only four or five who survived their childhood. The Zapatas worked a plot of village land, and owned some cattle and horses in which they traded. Gabriel also had ties to the nearby hacienda Hospital, from which he probably rented land upon occasion, and where he may have worked at times in a supervisory role. In relative terms, they were not especially poor: though luxuries and comforts were few, when it came to necessities—the tortillas, beans, and chile of everyday life—they did better than most of their neighbors.[8]

Although rural Mexican society did not put a premium on education, Zapata's father sent him to school at about age seven, "to get him out of the sun, and so he can learn a little." Classes were probably conducted at Villa de Ayala—the head village of the municipality of which Anenecuilco was a part—and attended by perhaps twenty-five children of various ages. Because work was the top priority, Zapata's schooling was irregular, but he did learn to read and write and may have developed an interest in Mexican history as well. The product of a haphazard country system with limited goals, his would have been considered a sufficient formal education by most of the villagers of Morelos.[9]

Zapata was probably not sorry to leave his school days behind, for the place where he grew up had many other attractions. Laced with irrigation canals and rock walls, Anenecuilco was a scattering of low-slung adobe houses much like his own. It was always warm there and often hot. In the winter, when it did not rain, the sky was a deep blue above the dry, stony hills that rose to the west of the village, and the valley glowed green with sugarcane. When the rains came in the summer the small homes of Anenecuilco nearly disappeared in a sea of foliage and flowers and fruit; and corn and other foodstuffs grew in the hills where irrigation did not reach. Zapata enjoyed the work of a campesino, especially when it involved animals. Though most of Anenecuilco's land was owned communally, each family farmed its own plot. The Zapatas hired extra labor when it was needed, but hiring labor was expensive. And so like other local boys Zapata began—by the age of eight or nine—to contribute to the family economy by hauling wood and fodder and helping with the livestock and planting. His life was increasingly dictated by the rhythms of sunup and sundown, of planting and harvest: preparing the ground in May, sowing the corn in June, three major weedings, and in November or December bringing in the crops. Zapata also helped an aunt who lived next door with her chores, and later cared for the cattle of a local Spaniard. Over time he accumulated animals of his own, often as a reward for his work: his father gave him a mule when he began school, and then a horse named "La Papaya"; and other relatives and employers made him similar gifts.[10]

Zapata was an energetic and perhaps a somewhat nervous child. One cousin tells of the time he mounted his Aunt Crispina's horse bareback and shot off through the underbrush at breakneck speed. When he returned tousled and torn a few minutes later, he merely bragged about having managed to hang on, as if oblivious to the danger he had put himself through. Of course, this riding ability was not innate; it was part of the informal education of the place. Gabriel Zapata was himself a good horseman, and he had Emiliano practicing jumps by the age of twelve. Because Gabriel knew the value of horsemanship on the local scene, the younger Zapata was not offered sympathy when he fell, but rather a scolding for his clumsiness. This harsh training, so the story goes, only inspired Emiliano. Accepting the challenge, he soon perfected his jumps over a nearby

stone wall, and was then taken out to the main street to demonstrate his talent in public.[11]

Another important skill for a local boy—the use of firearms—
was taught him by his uncle José Zapata on their deer hunting
expeditions together. From the same uncle and from another named
Cristino he heard stories to go with such lessons, and to flesh out his
more formal instruction in history. Some of these stories concerned
the exploits of his uncles on behalf of the Liberals during the battles
of the Reform era, battles that helped form the Mexican nation.
Others dealt with the forays of a group of outlaws called the Plateados. Led by a man named Salomé Plasencia who epitomized charro
elegance—embroidered shirts of Brittany cloth, wide sombreros,
splendid horses—these men raided haciendas and assaulted travellers in Morelos during the 1860s. But they failed to give their rebellion meaning to match its style, and so Cristino and other villagers
fought them, and saw Plasencia hang.[12]

Other stories still worth telling came from a time that Cristino
and José could not remember. Locals also helped make history during the War of Independence, when in the larger town of Cuautla, a
few miles to Anenecuilco's north, rebel José María Morelos y Pavón
was besieged for nearly three months in 1812 by troops loyal to the
Viceroy. Many Morelenses fought on the side of the rebels. The
most renowned of them was hacendado Francisco Ayala, who was
married to a Zapata from Anenecuilco. It was he who gave his name
to Villa de Ayala, as Morelos y Pavón eventually gave his own to the
state. Zapata's maternal grandfather played a smaller part during the
siege. Just a young boy at the time, he smuggled supplies past roy-
alist lines.[13]

Thus had Zapatas and Anenecuilcans provided sure evidence
that they were not averse to standing up for what they believed in.
They had fought for Independence and for the Liberal Constitution
of 1857. They had fought against the 1860s intervention of the
French, and against the clericalism and militarism of the Conservative party. In the process they had helped create and protect a national government. And though what was at stake for the villagers

of Morelos in the national politics of the nineteenth century was problematic enough that local campesinos could usually be found on both sides in any confrontation, they had demonstrated what kind of national government most of them wanted by consistently supporting politicians who favored a decentralized state that would largely allow them to govern themselves. In fact, the entire Cuautla region had become a bastion of Liberal and federalist feeling.

The campesinos of Zapata's world understood themselves, in other words, to be part of the Mexican nation—Anenecuilco was, after all, little more than fifty miles south of Mexico City. Still their immediate concerns were local, and as they always do for peasants, those immediate concerns centered around land. They liked politicians who promised to let them run things for themselves, but they also listened for another kind of appeal. Zapata's grandfather may have thought he heard it in the nebulous agrarianism of Morelos y Pavón. Later, during the 1870s, yet another Zapata certainly heard it during his personal conversations with a Liberal named Porfirio Díaz, who sought to gain the presidency through rebellion, and eventually did so. Anenecuilcans listened for any indication that a politician might demand that the land and water the haciendas of Morelos had stolen from the villages over the years be returned to their rightful owners. They listened, and they hoped, but they were always disappointed.[14]

Because land was so central to life in Anenecuilco, Zapata undoubtedly heard stories, as he grew, about the struggle against the haciendas. Morelos began to receive its modern form when the Spanish entered the area in 1521. Like many other settlements still around in 1900, Anenecuilco already existed when the Spanish arrived. But when they discovered that the lowlands of the region were wonderfully suited for growing sugar, the conquerors began to threaten the Indian villages by competing with them for resources. To produce sugar the new arrivals needed land and water, commodities that became increasingly available during the sixteenth century, as European diseases decimated the native population. The Spanish also needed labor, which they were able to secure through a variety of legal and economic coercions despite the demographic collapse. Near the end of the sixteenth century sugar boomed. Haciendas sprouted all around Cuautla just as the decline in Indian population began to slow. Pressure on communal resources grew. In fact, the very existence of Anenecuilco was already endangered in 1603, when the colonial government suggested that its shrinking population be combined with that of Cuautla.[15]

Meaning in Nahuatl "the place where the water rushes," Anenecuilco—land, water, and culture—seemed to its inhabitants worth fighting for. The result was what one observer called a "long continuous movement of resistance." In 1603 that resistance was successful, but in the long run it faced difficult odds. After a late seventeenth-century sugar recession decreased conflict for a time, the latter half of the eighteenth century brought better economic conditions for the industry, and the haciendas again used force and guile to push onto village holdings. No longer economically viable, many communities disappeared. While some legal recourse did remain, laws emanating from the sixteenth century that were designed to protect the Indians rarely worked as they were meant to, and legal procedures did little to stop the greedy hacendados. In the villages there was a growing malaise—some even dreamed of an Indian millennium, in which the Spanish were nowhere to be seen. Under these conditions it was only natural that many in the area chose the route of violence by welcoming the arrival of the independence leader Morelos.[16]

Though Morelos y Pavón never saw his program enacted, when independence was finally accomplished by a conservative coalition in 1821, it may have had some positive results for the campesinos. With it came a period of political discord and violence on the national level, as various caudillos fought for power. The political instability helped produce another interval of economic hardships for the haciendas, and again they ceased to expand. But if there was respite for the villagers it was of limited duration. Though political difficulties continued through much of the Reform era, by the middle of the century the economy began haltingly to improve, always a sign that more land grabs were forthcoming. It is no coincidence that in the late 1840s sometimes violent protest returned to Morelos. In the mid-1850s Anenecuilcans gathered together the documents necessary to defend their rights against the hacienda of Mapastlán. Soon a second José Zapata from Anenecuilco—not Emiliano's uncle, but perhaps his great-uncle—emerged to lead the community's struggle for land. In 1866–1867 he fought with Porfirio Díaz against the French-imposed Emperor Maximilian. Then, in exchange for the promise that Anenecuilco's land titles would be honored, he supported Díaz's efforts to achieve power in the early years of the following decade.[17]

But at about the time—in 1876—that Díaz realized his ambitions by capturing the presidency, José Zapata died. Left to his own devices, the new chief executive found he had more pressing concerns than fulfilling his promise to Anenecuilco. In fact, pronouncing for the positivist notion of order and progress that was then sweeping Latin America, he presided over the greatest onslaught of haciendas against villages that Morelos had ever seen.

In fairness to Díaz, the stage was already set. With the primary goal of breaking the economic power of the church, the 1857 Constitution had banned corporate landholding. A second target of this legislation was the land that peasant communities held in common. In the eyes of the Liberal reformers who wrote the Constitution, this kind of land tenure thwarted progress. With a communal safety net to fall back on and without the entrepreneur's drive for individual success, Mexico's villagers, they believed, were not using the land as efficiently as they might. For this reason they designed their proscription of corporate landholding to include communally held lands, in the hope that by insisting on an individualistic form of land tenure they could either imbue the peasantry with the spirit of progress or—by undermining communal defense mechanisms—facilitate the acquisition of its lands by hacendados who already possessed this ethic. The Díaz regime (1876–1911) merely elaborated on these Constitutional provisions with legislation of its own.[18]

Perhaps the most significant change that came with Díaz was

that the political and social turmoil that characterized postindependence Mexico finally came to an end. Order and progress reinforced each other, and in doing so allowed Mexico a new degree of involvement in the world economy. Foreign investment and trade were encouraged by increasing fiscal solvency, by lower tariffs, and by laws that favored private enterprise. Railroads were built with dizzying speed; mining and industry prospered; the domestic market expanded. For the hacendados of Morelos—who largely produced for this domestic market—conditions were ripe for progress, and they seized the initiative in a way that they had never done before. They brought the railroad to the state, undertook massive new irrigation projects, and invested in the most modern milling equipment. They had little choice: as other regions of the country increased their sugar output, competition was beginning to grow.[19]

For the planters the results were gratifying. Between 1905 and 1908 alone they increased production by over 50 percent, and still they hoped for more. But to do more, they needed more control—over land, water, and labor. Modernizing haciendas were now usurping village resources at an unprecedented rate, until, in 1909, 28 hacendados may have owned as much as 77 percent of the state's land. Many previously independent smallholders were forced to seek day labor on the growing estates, or even to become full-time hacienda peons. At the same time, however, the increasing mechanization of the sugar industry kept the demand for workers down, assuring those who had to depend on temporary labor agreements of low wages and considerable periods of unemployment. These changes gave the planters a decided advantage in labor relations and helped them keep production costs low, but the ancient, uncomfortable coexistence with the villages was finally breaking down. Most hacendados apparently did not care. Remnants of an arrangement that provided the estates with cheap, seasonal labor by giving the campesinos a place to go and land to work when the haciendas did not employ them, the troublesome independent communities increasingly seemed in the way. Perhaps they could finally be removed from the scene, giving the hacendados total control in the countryside. Indeed, strangled by the bleeding off of their resources and surrounded by hacienda lands, many towns and villages did stop growing, and again some disappeared. When the campesinos complained of the mounting insecurity, they were often met with brutal repression.[20]

Anenecuilco was naturally not immune to this Porfirian progress. After the train tracks reached it in 1881, Cuautla became the capital of the Morelos sugar industry, and during the first decade of Zapata's life the cane spread until it rustled against the outermost houses of his village. In fact, in 1887 the hacendado of Cuahuixtla took Anenecuilco's barrio of Olaque by force, its unlucky inhabitants losing not only their lands but their homes as well. Then Vicente Alonso—owner of the hacienda Hospital—began a new onslaught against the pueblo. Many Anenecuilcans had turned to livestock-raising to adjust to the loss of their most fertile lands. In response the hacendado started to complain about village livestock damaging his crops, and one day in 1895 Alonso's men sought to solve the dispute by appropriating some of Anenecuilco's pastures, killing the animals that were grazing there in the process.[21]

And so there were more than just accounts of old national wars in the air as Zapata grew up. There were stories about this longer and more elemental struggle against the hacendados, about the defense of a way of seeing the world. These stories remained important because while much had changed during the almost four centuries since the conquest—it was no longer, for instance, strictly a case of the Spanish against the Indians—one thing had remained the same: two cultures were colliding on the soil of Morelos, and the village culture that had been there first was under siege.[22]

Raised on this oral tradition, then, and on the realities that gave it shape, Zapata became conscious at a young age that injustice and inequality surrounded him. One oft-repeated story with an apocryphal ring concerns the fate of the barrio Olaque, which was stolen when Zapata was eight or nine. Arriving at the scene of this crime, Zapata found his father in tears and asked why. Gabriel explained that the hacienda had taken the village land, and that he was powerless to resist the incursion that hurt him so deeply. Full of noble indignation, Emiliano then promised to recover the lands when he was grown. However suspicious the story sounds—a bit like George Washington and the cherry tree—it does illustrate the fact that lands had been lost in Morelos within easy reach of individual memories when the revolution broke out, and that Zapata was not without such memories of his own.[23]

Zapata himself would later trace his personal rebellion back to around 1897, and perhaps he was thinking of events related to his brief arrest by local authorities during a fiesta on June 15 of that year. By this time both of his parents were dead—they had recently passed away in quick succession—so it was up to his brother Eufemio to come to his rescue. Powerfully built, raspy voiced, and something of a drinker, Eufemio was the kind of macho the campesinos both admired and feared. Some fifteen years older than Emiliano, he was already an experienced opponent of local officialdom. He now appeared with fellow rake Juan Sánchez and a small group of friends as a bound Emiliano was being led away. Drawing his pistol, he demanded that his brother be released; outnumbered, the arresting officers complied. Together the brothers fled to an exile in the state of Puebla, a typical way of escaping local law enforcement, which rarely bothered to track such fugitives down. There Emiliano found work—with the help of a friend from Cuautla—at the hacienda of Jaltepec in the district of Izúcar de Matamoros. This may have been his first experience as a full-time hacienda employee, but he was no lowly field worker. Rather, his experience with animals got him the job of caring for the horses.[24]

Why Zapata was arrested on this occasion is unclear. Some commentators remember him as a Mexican Robin Hood by this time, joining Eufemio to dole out rough justice against hacienda employees, officials, and bandits on the roads and in the villages of the area. Naturally this would explain his arrest, especially if his activities included, as they did in one account, gunning down soldiers in an ambush. Others argue a variation on this theme: that Zapata was already sufficiently implicated in the struggle for the return of Anenecuilco's land to justify his capture.[25]

More likely than either of these explanations is that he was simply known to the authorities, in a vague way, as someone to watch. Growing up in a world in which land rights were always in debate, Zapata was exposed at a tender age to insult and injury from hacienda employees when he entered land—perhaps to collect wood or to graze the family livestock—that one of the estates had claimed. As he grew he undoubtedly asserted himself in various ways against these employees and the officials who almost invariably supported them. Local life, in other words, was full of opportunities to earn a reputation as a troublemaker without any special effort. Already under some suspicion, then, it would have taken little to get him into trouble that day in Anenecuilco—nothing more significant, perhaps, than a drunken brawl. As the people of the village later put it: " 'Miliano was a brave man who would not take any crap; as a result, already during the time of peace, he was often in trouble."[26]

It was a year before family and friends could arrange a safe return home for Zapata, and it seems likely that he now chose to lie low. At any rate, we know nothing of his activities for several years. When we do hear of him again, his battle against the status quo had taken a more explicit path: he had become involved in legal efforts to defend the lands of Anenecuilco and neighboring villages against the large estates. Between 1902 and 1905 he may have played a small role in Yautepec's prolonged legal initiative against the hacienda of Atlihuayán. Linked to this nearby town by relatives on his mother's side of the family, it is even rumored that he was in attendance when a large commission spoke directly to Porfirio Díaz about the case. Though the Yautepec delegation received some encouragement from Díaz, in the spring of 1905 the hacendados cracked down. Many of those involved in the conflict were jailed and the town's leader, Jovito Serrano, was sent to work on the dreaded plantations of Quintana Roo. Like so many others held there for political reasons, he soon died of overwork and disease.[27]

While this series of events can hardly have encouraged anyone seeking a legal solution to a land dispute, there seemed no other recourse. As a result, in 1904 Anenecuilco set out to bring its grievances to the attention of the Porfirian bureaucracy by launching a search for land and water titles in the National Archives. Two years later this initiative had developed enough that Governor Manuel Alarcón assembled representatives of the hacienda Hospital, citizens of Anenecuilco and Villa de Ayala, and the *jefe político* of Cuautla to try to sort things out. This time Zapata was definitely present. When this meeting had no material results, Anenecuilco tried to complain to Díaz himself, who was in the area in February 1907 for health reasons. Though Díaz did not receive their call, he indicated through his subordinates that he would look into the matter. Then, in June of the same year, Anenecuilco's titles were submitted to Alarcón, who promised to give them his consideration. There, however, the petition stalled. The wheels of justice turned slowly, if at all; Zapata and his fellow villagers waited, with whatever hope they could maintain; and in December of 1908 the governor died, having said or done nothing about Anenecuilco in the interim.[28]

Meanwhile, Zapata was again in trouble with the authorities, and by this time part of the problem was surely his growing visibility in the battle for land. While some contend that he was forcibly inducted into the army in 1908, there is no good evidence for this. Instead it appears that he fled again, perhaps after spending a short time in jail. Again his destination was Puebla, where he found work as a horse trainer on an estate near Chietla and waited for things to blow over. But things would not blow over again. Though he was still nothing more than a minor troublemaker in the Porfirian scheme of things, Zapata had begun a fight to redeem his village and others like it that would end only with his death. In Morelos the threat of persecution would now hang permanently over his head.[29]

He did, however, make a quiet return to the state in late 1908 or early 1909, because it seemed that there was an opening in sight. In

the famous interview he gave to American journalist James Creelman in February 1908, Porfirio Díaz had announced that elections
would now be free of the usual engineering from above, and a number of people in Morelos and elsewhere were willing to take him at
his word, or at least to test it. Thus when Alarcón passed suddenly
from the scene, a heated race for governor ensued.

Much of the heat was due to the complete unacceptability of
Díaz's preferred candidate, Pablo Escandón, to the increasingly desperate campesinos. If Alarcón had failed the people of Anenecuilco,
he was not without some redeeming features. A native son of the
state who worked himself up from poverty, he possessed the common touch, leaving those who appealed to him with at least the
impression that he had listened. Escandón was of a completely different sort. Fundamentally a creature of Mexico City and Europe, he
lacked the political understanding to make even a show of appeasing
the locals. Moreover, his position was well known: he was the
owner of the hacienda of Atlihuayán that had recently expropriated
the lands of Yautepec. While the economic elite and government
officials had generally cooperated in the past, Escandón's election
would mean an intolerable new level of identification between the
two groups. His candidacy, in other words, was a gauntlet cast; it
was a signal that the state's worthies, who had lobbied for Escandón's selection, would no longer suffer even the appearance of compromise with the villages.[30]

Thus the pueblos had no choice but to field a candidate of their
own. Through democrats in Mexico City who found in Morelos a
convenient laboratory in which to analyze the electoral opening,
they first approached popular Reform-era general and ex-governor
Francisco Leyva. When he refused to run, they settled on his son
Patricio. Before long, Patricio Leyva's representatives had sounded
out their constituency and begun to hint at the possibility of land
reform. As the stakes rose, passions that had long remained beneath
the calm surface of the Porfiriato revealed themselves. There was
even a small riot in Cuautla on February 1, 1909, when villagers
hissed and threw rocks at the Mexico City orators Escandón had

imported, and the authorities tried in vain to assert the familiar Porfirian order.

Naturally Zapata was among those swept up in the campaign. In his first known political activity, on January 24 he enrolled in the Villa de Ayala branch of the Melchor Ocampo Club, an organ created to back Leyva. A few days later he and others signed a letter of protest—in anticipation of electoral fraud—that was printed in the national press. He may also have joined in the Cuautla rock-throwing. Still, his role was not a large one: in the act of formation of the local Leyvista club his name came far down on the list of signatures.[31] This was probably because Porfirian politics had become rather exclusive over the years. Though the old caudillos who had helped bring Díaz to power often still had political positions, the political sphere had become largely the province of the *científicos,* the hacendados, and their relatively educated brethren.[32] There was little room for people like Zapata, and perhaps even the campesinos had come to believe that politics was a game best left to the educated, at least on the state and national levels. And so it was not Zapata, but better-read locals like Luciano Cabrera and Pablo Torres Burgos—the thirty-two year old shopkeeper, sometime school-teacher, and amateur lawyer of Villa de Ayala—who served as the area's leading Leyvistas.

Of course, Zapata's participation in this campaign was to no avail. Evidently against the will of the people, Escandón was declared the winner of the February 7 elections and sworn in as governor on March 15. To make matters worse, the Leyvistas were eventually pressured to deny ever having promised land reform. Zapata cannot have avoided the conclusion that the justice he sought would not come soon through conventional politics. Not prominent enough to draw the wrath now unleashed by Escandón's government against people like Torres Burgos, he just returned to work. But there was new potential for action. Campesinos from all over the state were now more organized in a roughly political way than they had ever been before. They were even in touch with people in Mexico City who were also looking for change. Angrier now, with hopes that had again been raised and then dashed, Zapata and his fellow Anenecuilcans threw electoral politics onto their scrap-heap of discarded alternatives. They were, however, far from finished: it was merely time to explore other options.[33]

The elders in charge of village defense had recently run into trouble in Mexico City, where they were easy prey for a con-man who took from them much of the money that had been invested in their commission. Combined with the repeated frustrations of legal and electoral processes, this episode made them feel their ages. They decided it was time to elect new village leaders, and so on Sunday, September 12, 1909, they called a meeting. A different kind of politics was now at work. The matter was too solemn for campaigning, for visiting dignitaries, or for letters to the press. There was no angling for support; nor were there pompous orations of the kind that had sparked the Cuautla riot. There was just a short, tired speech from the outgoing president of the village council, José Merino, and then three young men were nominated to replace him. When the votes were counted, Zapata had received an impressive majority.

Personal history and village tradition had merged. The past activities of Zapata's family and its overall stature naturally played into the decision. So did Zapata's own efforts on behalf of village defense—his election was a mark of the seriousness he had displayed on the subject. But his reputation as something of a rebel must have been important as well, because this was a move of desperation. Young men were chosen to lead only in extraordinary times. Zapata's selection was a sign that the villagers wanted a man of action, who could do *whatever* it took to make sure Anenecuilco survived.[34]

As this meeting ended someone is said to have announced that the villagers only wanted "a man with *pantalones* on," to defend them.[35] Since pantalones—which Zapata had preferred since his childhood to the more common homemade, white cotton *calzones* of peasant dress—were a sign of status, this statement may have reflected a desire not only for a man of action, but also for a man of some success. At any rate, it is quite clear that Zapata was chosen in large part because of the admiration he aroused as an exemplary product of local life. Just turned thirty, over the years he had become one of the area's leading citizens. Building on the small plot of land he inherited from his father and the livestock he began to accumulate as a child, Zapata rented more land from surrounding haciendas to plant corn, beans, and watermelon. He also ran a mule-train business, hauling corn between the towns scattered through the valley south of Cuautla and lime—dug from the hillsides around Villa de Ayala—down to the hacienda of Chinameca for construction.

These economic activities demonstrate, in other words, that he was not a typical peasant. To obtain estate land to sharecrop one needed a certain amount of status, and it seems that Zapata had a personal relationship with Ignacio de la Torre y Mier, hacendado of Tenextepango and son-in-law of President Díaz. Furthermore, Zapata often hired people to work for him in his various enterprises. This made him a *patrón*, a standing that gave him certain obligations to the village—it is likely, for instance, that he often helped pay for fiestas. Still he was far from wealthy, but rather found a niche within the small rural middle class. "He was not what we would call rich," one fellow villager remembered, "he was poor, but he had a lot of livestock. From this he lived, as a campesino."[36]

While Zapata's measure of prosperity made him stand out, it was not enough to set him apart from the cultural milieu of his village. In fact, he thrived in that milieu, and his success reflected how Anenecuilco had changed over the centuries. As the sugar industry pulled the campesinos into the capitalist world, differences in wealth and occupation had grown. Some residents hired themselves out as day-laborers on nearby haciendas, others had a plot of their own land to farm, still others sharecropped or owned livestock or worked for their neighbors or ran a small shop. Like Zapata, most combined several activities to get by. In any case, individual initiative was important, and economic activity took place almost exclusively on an individual or family level, not a communal one.[37]

Zapata fit in in other ways as well. Like most young men, he

plunged enthusiastically into the events of market days and fiestas—the cockfights and card games and fireworks, the singing and
dancing and drinking—that were the best way the people knew to
break up the otherwise monotonous cycle of rural life. By all accounts one of the leading horsemen and judges of horses in the
state—thanks to Don Gabriel he excelled at the skills that country
people valued most—Zapata specialized as a bull-roper in the *jaripeos* of the region.[38] It was all part of the ethic of machismo that
helped shape the lives of men in his village. Machismo often involved a certain emotional constriction. Men like Zapata sometimes related best to their horses, and only felt comfortable with
others when they were drinking—something they did on a regular
basis. In this culture under pressure, where there was considerable
jealousy over differences of wealth and status, machismo and drinking could naturally lead to conflict. Indeed, the level of violence was
probably high, and there was a moral fatalism about male behavior:
it was understood that manhood meant drinking and fighting and
committing adultery, and it is doubtful that Zapata could have led
Anenecuilco had he not participated in these activities.

Anenecuilco was, in other words, a complicated place. Riven by
conflict and by the selfishness and suspicion of its inhabitants, it
was in large part a product of modern capitalism, and there was
plenty of room for individuals like Zapata to stand out. But when
Anenecuilcans came together to ask Zapata to lead them, they demonstrated that they could also act, in a profound sense, as a community. In fact, there was much that held them together. They were
united by a shared religiosity—by the religious landscape of shrines
and pilgrimages that surrounded them, and by a calendar full of
saint's days and other sacred occasions that brought them together
in celebration. They were united by their lasting tradition of owning
land and other economic resources in common. And, above all, they
were united by their long history of struggle to protect what they
owned against the insatiable haciendas.

What Anenecuilco got in Zapata, then, was a man who was both
one of them and one of their best. He must have reminded some

1. Emiliano Zapata (*Archivo General de la Nación, Mexico City, Archivo Fotográfico Díaz, Delgado y García*)

old-timers of the bandit Plasencia himself when he appeared at a fiesta in full charro regalia, astride a magnificent horse outfitted with the best gear a campesino could buy. In tight black pants with giant silver buttons along the outer seam of each leg, an embroidered leather or cotton jacket, a silk handkerchief tied loosely around his neck, silver spurs, a pistol at his waist and, to top it off, a wide felt sombrero with a flowered border, Zapata was impressive and clearly more than a little vain. Somewhat taller than the average villager and of a normal build, he had a long, thick moustache that curled up slightly at the ends, dark skin, dark eyes, and a penetrating gaze. He had the look of a man who—dandy or not—could be deadly serious. He wasted little time with talk; when he did speak his words— emerging in "rushes and sparks"—betrayed the nervous energy he had had since childhood. Though rather ignorant about things one learned in books, Zapata was an intelligent man who understood the world around him. He was fair, generous, and trustworthy. He was in control enough not to lose himself in drink as his older brother and many other villagers did. In 1909 Zapata was ready. Strong, angry, and charismatic, he was the kind of man who might lead a revolution.[39]

2 The Hacendado's Revolution

ZAPATA MOVED QUICKLY TO FULFILL THE DUTIES OF village president. He and his aides reviewed the land titles and supporting documents that had come to serve, during the nineteenth century, as almost sacred components of Anenecuilco's collective memory. Then, on September 27, 1909, he left for Mexico City as part of a commission sent to hire a lawyer. On the following Sunday the commission officially reported its success to the village council: Luis Ramírez de Alba, "a person of integrity," would come to Morelos as soon as possible to start work on their case against the hacienda Hospital.[1]

There were, of course, no immediate results of this initiative. Zapata could do little but return to his usual routine and wait. As he waited, trouble again found him. He did not have to become a revolutionary to dazzle many of the women of the area: his piercing eyes, his charro posture, and his small success were enough for that. The most serious of his several liaisons was with a Villa de Ayala woman named Inés Aguilar. By at least 1906—the year she bore him his first child, Nicolás—Zapata set up housekeeping with her, some say in Cuautla. In the years that followed they had two other children together. This was not a formal marriage, and perhaps because of that or because of Zapata's bad reputation, Aguilar's respectable family did not approve. When the relationship ended in early 1910, Remigio Alfaro—who was either her father or her uncle—saw the chance to have his revenge. Due to his complaint and the claim that Zapata was found "wandering in a state of drunkenness," Zapata was consigned on February 11 to an army regiment stationed in Cuernavaca. The drafting of troublemakers was one of the Porfirian system's most commonly used methods of repression. With Alfaro's help the authorities must have believed they could break the will of this small-town tough who kept making noise about land.[2]

By soliciting the aid of the well-connected hacendado of Tenextepango, Ignacio de la Torre y Mier, Zapata's friends and family managed to arrange his release the following month. Knowing Zapata to be a skilled trainer of horses, Torre y Mier had decided he could use him in his Mexico City stables. This, of course, would get him away from the unpleasantness in Morelos. But Zapata did not last long in the capital. For him Mexico City was the seat of all the world's wealth and hypocrisy. He resented the luxury in which the hacendado's horses lived, luxury that compared favorably to the living conditions of some of his Morelian neighbors. Furthermore, this job—which many campesinos would have considered the opportunity of a lifetime—weighed poorly in the balance against the green fields of home and the responsibilities to his village that he had assumed the fall before. He suffered the capital only briefly before returning to wrestle again with the problems of Anenecuilco.[3]

There the situation was growing worse. With Escandón safely ensconced in power, he and his landed supporters had begun to turn the pressure even higher, much as the campesinos had expected. In June 1909 a new real estate tax law was passed, a law that both lowered appraisals of hacienda worth—thus shifting more of the tax burden onto the shoulders of peasants and townsmen—and threatened to legitimize estate claims to lands they had recently acquired through dubious means.[4]

This is not to say that Escandón was an activist governor. With no vocation for politics and no appreciation of Morelian realities, he often found occasion to flee the provincial boredom of the state, leaving a secretary to govern in his place and the hacendados to do as they wished. True, Porfirio Díaz himself had asked the planters to settle their conflicts with the pueblos. The foolish Creelman interview of 1908 had inspired not only the Leyva campaign in Morelos, but an electoral challenge on the national level from a diminutive Coahuilan hacendado named Francisco Madero. While this challenge remained unresolved, Díaz preferred to minimize conflict. But Madero's presidential campaign, which hit full stride during the first months of 1910, also meant that Díaz had larger concerns than the land battle in Morelos, and was thus unlikely to force a compromise there. The hacendados pushed on.[5]

In anticipation of the summer rains of 1910, the citizens of Anenecuilco had already prepared land in dispute for planting when the hacienda Hospital, upset by their stubborn opposition to "progress," decided not to let them use it. Instead the hacienda agreed to rent it to the people of Villa de Ayala. On April 25 the villagers sent a letter imploring Escandón for help before the rains began. Desperate now, they offered to recognize whomever the courts decided was the true owner of the land in question, but one way or another they had to sow immediately. "Farming," they noted, "is what gives us life, from it we draw sustenance for ourselves and for our families." A week later came a bureaucrat's reply: which lands, it asked, did they mean? Though the campesinos tried to clarify, in the end the state government left it to the hacienda to declare its intentions, and the hacendado suggested that they "plant in a flower pot." As the villagers pondered this proposal it began to rain.[6]

Among those who had planted the land in question was Zapata, who came home from Mexico City just as this exchange of views was ending. Unless something was done quickly, he saw, Anenecuilco might lose its economic autonomy. With no land of their own, many more of the villagers would have to work for the haciendas, if they were lucky enough to find employment at all. With no land of its own, fiercely independent Anenecuilco might become a home for hacienda peons, or disappear altogether. And so Zapata took drastic action. Rounding up some eighty men, he rode out to where Villa de Ayalans were planting rows that Anenecuilcans had hoed, and after a brief discussion the Ayalans—and the hacienda's guard—retreated. When informed of the incident, Hospital's owner is said to have responded, "leave the lunatic alone." At any rate nothing happened. Whether this was due to pressure from Díaz, because the people at Hospital felt they had made their point, or because no one else was now willing to work the fields, it was a monumental blunder. Zapata's reputation quickly spread, until even the privileged of Cuernavaca, the state capital, knew his name.[7]

When harvest time came, however, Hospital did expect rent. At a meeting of local authorities, hacienda representatives, and campesinos near the end of the year, Zapata insisted that the villagers would not pay. A season of little rain had meant a bad harvest, and anyway the land was theirs. Though the jefe político suggested that the rent be paid the following year if possible, for the time being he backed Zapata.[8]

This remarkable decision reflected the increasingly unsettled times. Francisco Madero's electoral challenge to the Díaz regime had begun to blossom into something bigger. It was not just in Morelos that people were upset. In other parts of Mexico, too, they were angry about losing their land, about a lack of economic opportunity, about the failure of the Díaz regime to deliver the democracy that the Constitution of 1857 promised. And Madero's campaign against yet another Díaz reelection had stirred them up. Meanwhile, Díaz kept making mistakes that seemed to indicate that he had lost his political touch. He imprisoned Madero in the summer of 1910 while the elections were fixed; then, underestimating the challenge, he set him free. As a result, Madero was able to flee to San Antonio, Texas, in October. There he composed his Plan of San Luis Potosí, which announced his intention to fight. Initially planned for November 20, Madero's rebellion got off to a slow start, its strategy of forcing Díaz to his knees by taking a few crucial cities failing miserably. Still there was revolution in the air as 1910 ended, and unease in the hearts of such petty Porfirians as the jefe político of Cuautla.[9]

None of this was lost on Zapata. Though Madero had hardly

included them in his plans, Zapata and others in Morelos—like other potential rural revolutionaries around the country—were becoming convinced that Madero's crusade could help them. Zapata may have believed that simply getting rid of Porfirio Díaz would benefit the campesinos. After all, he was not old enough to remember what it was like when another man ruled the republic. More importantly, article three of the Plan of San Luis Potosí made allowances for returning stolen village lands. This was hardly a promise of massive social reform, but to Zapata it sounded good. In fact, it was all he really wanted: that the land the campesinos owned be returned to them, that the old balance of village and hacienda be restored. New to the business of even thinking about revolution, he had no idea yet how complicated it could become.[10]

By the end of 1910 Zapata's successful defiance of Hospital had won him the support of the inhabitants of Villa de Ayala—who had a long history of cooperating with Anenecuilco—and of nearby Moyotepec. In the last days of the year he began to assign disputed lands to these villages too. When a new jefe político named Eduardo Flores rode out to the fields with ten men to inspect Zapata's activities, he found him surrounded by more than a hundred adherents. Somewhat cowed, Flores announced that he had been told Zapata was up in arms. When Zapata responded that they were just dividing the land, Flores could only leave them to it. Power had shifted, largely because local authorities could not count on the federal government, increasingly occupied with Maderismo, to tip the balance in their favor. Still, Zapata was not the kind of man to rush headlong into a revolution. Instead, he planted watermelons on his portion of the recovered land and, celebrating his growing stature, threw a jaripeo for the old jefe político when that dignitary decided to leave the state. During another such celebration at Moyotepec, a bull wounded Zapata in the thigh.[11]

It was clear, however, that the local stand-off could not last indefinitely, and so a small group of conspirators began to gather in November to discuss the possibility of joining Madero. Despite his new reputation, Zapata did not automatically assume the leadership of this group. If anyone did, it was probably Pablo Torres Burgos, who was better educated than Zapata, and one of Villa de Ayala's most active participants in the Leyva campaign. At any rate it was Torres Burgos, with his experience in extra-local politics, who was sent to San Antonio in mid-December when the plotters decided it was time to contact Madero.[12]

While the folks around Villa de Ayala waited for Torres Burgos to return, other small groups of Morelian campesinos broke into open rebellion. In the mountains at the northwest corner of the state a man named Genovevo de la O began to fight in December 1910. Then on February 7, 1911, septuagenarian Gabriel Tepepa went on the warpath. Veteran of the Wars of the Reform and foreman on the Temilpa hacienda near Tlaltizapán, Tepepa had sometimes attended the meetings of the Ayala conspirators. Patience, however, was not one of his virtues, and now he moved north from the Jojutla area to take Tepoztlán before running out of initiative.

Outside Morelos, as well, the rural populace began to embrace Madero's cause, which was clearly picking up steam by early 1911. Still Zapata held his hand, believing it best to wait for the legitimacy that only Madero could confer. When Torres Burgos finally returned in mid-February, he brought the inevitable appointments. As the state's symbol of frustrated democracy, Patricio Leyva was to head its rebellion should he choose to do so. If not, leadership would devolve upon Torres Burgos himself. For Zapata and the others who gathered to hear their emissary's report, there were blank forms for commissions. Once those were filled out there was nothing else to do but get started, before the authorities had more time to prepare their defenses.[13]

On March 10 the conspirators met at the fair in Cuautla that marked the second of "the three Fridays" of Lent. Between the drinks and the cock-fights, and under cover of the cries of merchants hawking their holiday wares, Torres Burgos, Zapata, and Zapata's cousin Rafael Merino decided it was time to begin. They first rode down to Villa de Ayala, where on March 11 Torres Burgos read the Plan of San Luis Potosí aloud on the plaza to shouts of "Viva Madero" and "Death to Díaz" and the sound of firearms shot in the air. Then they organized a small guerrilla band of perhaps seventy men. Slowly picking up followers, they headed south along the Cuautla river to San Rafael Zaragoza. From there they sought the safety of the mountains of southern Puebla, where they took stock and sent messengers to other pueblos along the Morelos/Puebla border. In Cuernavaca the newspapers rumored that the Plateados were in arms again.[14]

Though some of the new *guerrilleros* had been victims of the draft, few had much military experience, and it seems likely that there was little strategy and that tactics were a matter of trial and error. Still, a week or so of waiting in the mountains apparently produced some disagreement between Zapata and Torres Burgos over such questions. Finally, Torres Burgos ordered the group divided into three bands—one led by himself, one by Zapata, and the third by Merino. Torres Burgos would take Tepepa—who had just joined them—and head toward the rich district seat of Jojutla, while Zapata was to cover the Morelos/Puebla border region, and Merino to operate around Jonacatepec. Briefly occupying one undefended village after another to collect followers, provisions, and arms, Zapata went from Jolalpan, Puebla back into Morelos at Axochiapan. At the train station there he engaged in his first skirmish, driving off a handful of federal troops.[15]

Meanwhile, Torres Burgos and Tepepa occupied Jojutla without resistance on March 24. Escandón himself had come down from Cuernavaca to make a show of defending the town, but when he realized the rebels actually meant to attack he began a flight that ended only when he reached the safety of Europe. In control of an important population center, the campesinos behaved as they would elsewhere. They freed the prisoners, drank the wine, destroyed telephone and telegraph lines, and availed themselves of arms, horses, and food. They also burned the local archives to make it harder to identify liberated prisoners and other fugitives. Much of this was simple necessity, but there was also an element of revenge. Led by Tepepa, who knew the area well, they sacked and burned the town's main businesses and public offices. They were especially destructive when it came to the property of Spaniards, who were popularly perceived as foreign oppressors.[16]

There were apparently no executions on this occasion, at least not in Jojutla proper. Still, the looting proved a bit much for Torres Burgos. While he may have been well-suited for diplomacy, he shared with Madero the belief that revolution should be orderly, and was unable to accept the misconduct that was inevitable in the wake of the uprising. Later in the day, when a junta at which Zapata was present would not condemn the actions of Tepepa's forces, Torres Burgos quit the movement in disgust. Alone on the road to Villa de Ayala, he and his two sons were shot the next afternoon by a federal patrol. Their bodies were taken to Cuautla, to be exhibited in the portal of the municipal palace.

That same day, probably still unaware of Torres Burgos's death, Zapata sat silently on his horse in southern Puebla while an impromptu council of campesino warriors chose him to assume the leadership of their revolt. Zapata was not far from Jojutla when the sacking occurred, and it is even possible that he took part. He was, at any rate, more realistic and less squeamish than Torres Burgos, and understood that what Torres Burgos had considered excesses most of his followers had considered rewards. Like many of the villagers of Morelos, he undoubtedly felt that violence and brutality were to be expected from human nature, especially in the context of a revolution. In fact, he was quite capable of brutal behavior himself. On the other hand, his anger burned more slowly than that of such other potential leaders of the movement as Tepepa and Juan Sánchez. In the heat of victory, when a town lay open to them, a peasantry in arms had shared in Tepepa's vengeful frenzy. But in the repose of the mountains of Puebla, where they hid from others bent on their *own* revenge, these same peasants wanted a leader who was not "one of the killers," a leader less likely to let anger cloud his thinking. A moderate man without the naiveté of Torres Burgos or the volatile impatience of Tepepa, Zapata was the logical choice.[17]

Continuing to raid along the Puebla/Morelos border, Zapata

gained further legitimacy in the eyes of his troops on April 4, when he met a former medical student from the city of Puebla named Juan Andrew Almazán. Claiming to be an emissary from Madero, Almazán endowed Zapata with official status as head of the revolution in Morelos—status that Zapata had already begun to seek by sending a messenger to the Maderistas in Mexico City almost as soon as he replaced Torres Burgos. Together Zapata and Almazán then took a half-hearted stab at capturing Jonacatepec before drifting back into Puebla to take Chiautla. There the citizens of nearby Huehuetlán convened to demand the blood of Chiautla's jefe político, whom they accused of a recent massacre. Joining Almazán in manufacturing the record of a trial in order to absolve himself of responsibility, Zapata allowed them their revenge. Almazán then moved west into the state of Guerrero with Gabriel Tepepa in tow.[18]

Later that month Zapata suffered his first significant loss in the environs of the important Puebla town of Izúcar de Matamoros, where more than a hundred of his followers died, including Rafael Merino. Otherwise the string of small victories continued, and Zapata's forces began to develop a style. The fields and the villages for which they were fighting were inevitably surrounded by hills and ravines where the revolutionaries could hide, and the ultimate security of the mountains was never far away. Poorly armed—some carried only machetes—and with little military experience, only their intimate knowledge of this complicated landscape worked in their favor. To maximize that single advantage they resorted—more from common sense than from theory—to the constant mobility of guerrilla warfare. "We were never in one place," recalled one veteran. "We were always running, not by choice, but of necessity." Fleeing from government troops whenever they were more than a handful, the rebels concentrated their attacks on lightly defended villages and haciendas, where they would spend a few hours commandeering arms and provisions, and then move on before the enemy arrived. When the federals split into smaller groups in an effort to track them down, the campesinos ambushed them from a hill, from a thick patch of underbrush, or from behind one of the ubiquitous stone walls of this countryside. To fighters trained in more conventional warfare this looked like cowardice. In fact, these tactics and the usual peasant dress caused the opponents of Zapata's men to call them *liebres blancas*—white hares—and Zapata himself was accused of a lack of bravery. But such accusations only revealed frustration. The tactics worked, and success drew more and more people to Zapata's side. By early April he led between 800 and 1000 men, and though the hacendados pressured the central government and recruited on their own, they could not keep up.[19]

Recognizing Zapata's success Francisco Leyva, recently appointed state military commander, invited him to Jonacatepec in an attempt to use the Leyva name to work out a compromise that would include choosing a new governor of the state. But the elections of 1909 were now a thing of the past, and Zapata was beyond compromising with Porfirians. He rejected Leyva's offer.[20] There were, however, other political challenges that he could not so lightly dismiss. Zapata was not the only revolutionary leader in the area. In northern and western Morelos and in the surrounding states there were other, similar, home-grown jefes whose ill-defined domains pushed up against his, and Zapata knew that his legitimacy depended not only on grass-roots support, but on coming to terms with these competitors for revolutionary power. Perhaps the strongest of these other chieftains was Ambrosio Figueroa, from Huitzuco, in northeastern Guerrero. Figueroa was interested in Morelos because fighting there, closer to the capital, could make him a more important factor on the national political scene. The leading lights of Maderismo, however, wanted their jefes to cooperate rather than compete with each other for territory. And so at the urging of a delegate of Madero's named Guillermo García Aragón, Zapata met Figueroa at Jolalpan, Puebla on April 22. There they signed the Pact of Jolalpan, which recognized Zapata—more convincingly than could Almazán—as chief revolutionary in his home state. Zapata and Figueroa also agreed to coordinate their activities for the good of the cause. When they fought together in Morelos, Zapata was to preside over operations; when they did so in Guerrero, Figueroa would lead.

To test these new arrangements they planned to attack Jojutla on the twenty-eighth.[21]

But these two men were not destined to get along. Though not too different in personal background—Figueroa was also a ranchero with a history as a local troublemaker—they were naturally jealous of each other's power. More importantly, they had different notions of what constituted a revolution. It was evident that Figueroa's goals were largely political rather than social and economic, in part because the land problem had not yet reached crisis proportions around Huitzuco. As a result, when Zapata heard disconcerting news from Jojutla he was inclined to believe it. His spies there reported that Figueroa's troops had penetrated as far as the suburbs of the town without a fight, and that the federal artillery now pointed to the east—the direction from which Zapata was supposed to attack. Figueroa had lived in Jojutla for years and had developed lasting ties there, especially with the prominent Ruiz de Velasco family. Now it looked as though he was drawing up a peace of convenience with them—and with the army garrison—rather than a plan of attack, and this peace seemed to include an ambush of Zapata. There was even word that an assassin had infiltrated Zapata's camp.

As Zapata collected evidence he grew increasingly uneasy. A suspected assassin was caught and executed. Meanwhile, Figueroa ignored orders to come explain himself at Zapata's mountain camp. Whether Zapata's information was true or not, the scenario his spies created was not as preposterous as it may sound: Figueroa's troops would soon succeed in ambushing and killing Gabriel Tepepa, and the revolution would prove itself a nest of similar intrigues. Furthermore, the spies were correct that peace was being discussed. In early May, after cordially arranging an armistice with the commander of the Jojutla garrison, Figueroa sent his brother Francisco to Mexico City to cut a deal with Díaz. Uncertain about how these conversations would affect the balance of power in Morelos, Zapata was enraged. He hated the idea of bargaining with the enemy, and in a letter to the Mexico City press he charged Figueroa with treason.

In the end little came from Figueroa's bid for an individual peace, except that it planted the seeds of a conflict with Zapata that would color the pivotal summer of 1911.[22]

Zapata seems now to have realized that big victories were necessary to keep Figueroa from winning the state. On the last day of April he stepped up the pace of his military campaign by besieging Jonacatepec, the most important settlement in southeastern Morelos. Defended by seventy to a hundred men holed up in the church and the municipal palace, Jonacatepec faced two thousand rebels, as Zapata brought to bear the kind of numbers he would always need to win a set battle against the army's superior firepower. On the fourth day of fighting the soldiers finally surrendered in the face of Zapata's threat to burn down the town if they did not. The victors then celebrated with the usual looting, and some claim they exacted revenge for their many dead by executing several soldiers. If this upset Zapata, he was apparently powerless to stop it.[23]

This was a huge achievement, especially when coupled with a simultaneous triumph at Yautepec by a loosely allied rebel band. The movement was beginning to peak. Growing short on resources, the federals were on the defensive—they would not, for instance, recover Jonacatepec. Zapata now climbed into the folds of the volcano Popocatepetl that loomed over the northeast corner of the state, and from there raided the textile factory at Metepec, Puebla to clothe his forces. But this was only a momentary diversion: it was time for the biggest battle of the campaign. Zapata began to call his guerrillas to join him at the village of Yecapixtla, above Cuautla. Cuautla, he had decided, would be the battle to settle their destiny.[24]

While Zapata was establishing himself in the field during the spring of 1911, Madero's forces in northern Mexico had also been hard at work. Now, as Zapata prepared to attack Cuautla, the northerners turned their attention to Ciudad Juárez, Chihuahua. An important port of entry on the United States border, Ciudad Juárez possessed great strategic value, for here the revolutionaries could more easily obtain arms and other crucial resources. On May 8

Madero's most prominent warriors, Pancho Villa and Pascual Orozco, launched their assault; on the tenth the border city fell. By far the biggest rebel victory yet, for the tottering old regime it was a decisive blow. Díaz sent negotiators north to discuss the transition of power. The bloodshed, it seemed, was almost over.

Zapata, however, had heard enough talk in Porfirian courts to know that one had to force the issue. The largest, most important town in eastern Morelos, Cuautla might serve the regime as a final object lesson—if he could take it. He would not hold off until a peace was concluded. Unfortunately, Cuautla was defended by about 350 troops of the famous Fifth Regiment, which boasted it had never been defeated. And in response to Zapata's request that the plaza be surrendered to protect civilian lives, Colonel Eutiquio Munguía swore to fight "as long as I have a soldier and a cartridge."[25]

To capture a town garrisoned this well and by this many men was a new challenge. In set battles Zapata generally relied on one cavalry charge after another, the horses bringing the attackers quickly to enemy lines—before the machine guns could cut them all down—and giving them mobility once they got close. Country skills would then come in handy—sharp-shooting hunters could pick the soldiers off, and champions of the jaripeo might even manage to lasso the machine guns. Wave after wave of attackers would eventually wear the opposing forces down. But at Cuautla the federals huddled behind barricades and the thick stone walls of colonial buildings. Against this kind of defense those waves of men would be less effective than usual. Zapata would also have to count on trickery—and on brutality. It would be a total war with limited means: the federal soldiers would have to be brought into the open, even if that meant burning down the town around them as Zapata had threatened to do at Jonacatepec.[26]

By May 12 Zapata's forces had encircled their objective: Cuautla's communications with the rest of the world were cut off by perhaps four thousand rebels. The next morning the shooting started, and on the fourteenth Zapata's men cut the water supply. On the fifteenth they launched a general assault, but were pushed back again and again. One problem was the soldiers perched in the heights of an aqueduct, from which they dominated the plain on the west side of town. To Zapata is credited the idea of pouring gasoline into the water that passed through this bulwark and lighting it. This created a curtain of fire that quickly brought federals, many aflame, tumbling down from otherwise impregnable positions.[27]

Though Zapata's casualties were much greater than those of the federals, by May 17 or 18 the enemy began to suffer from a shortage of food and munitions. Then the rebels thought of augmenting the incessant shooting, the war-cries, the explosions of home-made bombs lit with cigars, and the sounding of horns that came naturally to their siege by pounding on empty oil cans. Drenched by rain during sleepless nights and surrounded by rotting bodies, the soldiers of the mighty Fifth Regiment watched the vultures circle overhead and felt their morale weaken. Finally, Munguía decided it was time to get out. On the nineteenth his forces broke the circle and ran for Cuernavaca, where they arrived the next day.

On May 21 the negotiators of the old regime and Francisco Madero came to an agreement—the Treaty of Ciudad Juárez—which ended the fighting of Madero's revolution. Five days later Porfirio Díaz set sail for Europe, never to return to the country he had ruled for so long. In Morelos there were related events. On the twenty-first the capital, Cuernavaca, was evacuated, leaving the state entirely in rebel hands. On the twenty-sixth, at 4 o'clock on a bright Friday afternoon, Zapata rode triumphantly into that city at the head of four thousand troops. Waving images of the Virgin of Guadalupe overhead, these revolutionaries were a ragged lot in the eyes of the urbane. But to the throngs who greeted them—the common people of Morelos, the young girls with armfuls of bougainvillea—they were conquering heroes. That evening, small bands of village musicians took over the plaza with their countrified music, "sometimes wailing, sometimes riotous." For the moment Zapata must have felt that anything was possible. For the moment it must have seemed the beginning of better days for the peasants of Morelos.[28]

In reality, things were only becoming more complicated. By

pressing his attacks on Jonacatepec and Cuautla while Figueroa stalled and dickered, Zapata had played a critical role in forcing Díaz out. But he had not hurried to Cuernavaca—the natural focal point of state politics. Though he had threatened Francisco Leyva with death if he surrendered Cuernavaca to anyone else, Zapata may have failed to appreciate how critical state politics would be, or how quickly the political battle would be joined. Or perhaps he simply chose to postpone the politics and parades of the state capital for the much-deserved pleasures of a Cuautla homecoming. The result, at any rate, was that Zapata was not the first Maderista to reach Cuernavaca. That honor went instead to Manuel Asúnsolo, one of Figueroa's Guerreran chiefs, who occupied the city on the twenty-second; and by the time Zapata arrived trouble was already brewing.[29]

At Jojutla on May 25 one of Figueroa's jefes, Federico Morales, had executed Gabriel Tepepa after inviting him to dinner. Since Figueroa himself had been feuding with Tepepa, it only made sense that he was involved, and this naturally upset Zapata. But Zapata liked Asúnsolo, who seemed a reasonable man despite his ties to Figueroa, his aristocratic background, and his education in the United States. And Asúnsolo was able to calm him down. After all, Zapata himself had been ready to fight Tepepa on at least one occasion, and had probably sent him off with Almazán in April to get rid of him. It could not have been hard for him to believe charges that Tepepa had been running amuck around Jojutla. And so Zapata and Asúnsolo were quickly able to assure the new authorities in Mexico City that harmony reined in Cuernavaca.[30]

With one obstacle to peace among revolutionaries surmounted, however, other obstacles came quickly into view. While Zapata's communications to Mexico City on the selection of a provisional governor were repeatedly ignored, Asúnsolo suggested Juan N. Carreón for the job. Director of the Bank of Morelos and one of Cuernavaca's most prominent citizens, Carreón hardly seemed likely to meet Zapata's agenda. Indeed, in a letter to Madero's representative in Mexico City, Alfredo Robles Domínguez, which expressed his willingness to take the job, Carreón let it be known

where his sympathies lay. He complained that the "principal inhabitants" of Cuernavaca were alarmed because Asúnsolo planned to
leave the city in the hands of Zapata. In fact, he continued, seized by
a panic that was understandable in light of the fact that "General
Zapata cannot discipline his troops," the better class of Cuernava-
cans had already begun to flee.[31]

When Robles Domínguez asked him, on June first, to end the
"grave disorders" that were transpiring in Cuernavaca, Zapata
seems to have been bewildered. "I don't know what disorders today's message refers to," he replied, "[but] I will make sure that
there are none." Asúnsolo confirmed that everything was under
control. Far from creating chaos, in fact, Zapata remained anxious to
cooperate. He did his best to control the banditry that was perhaps
inevitable given the decentralized nature of rebellion in Morelos. He
also accepted Carreón as provisional governor, though probably
without enthusiasm, and perhaps without knowing that it was
Carreón who was bringing charges against him. He even refused,
apparently, to openly sanction land seizures, informing those who
solicited land that he was not empowered to act on the issue. Finally, when he heard that the cities of Durango and Chihuahua had
still not surrendered to the revolutionaries, he offered the help of his
troops. All of this added up to a remarkable display of good-will, of
trust, and of concern for national events. Zapata clearly believed, or
at least hoped, that it was *his* revolution that was now triumphing
around the country, that Mexico City would now dispense justice to
Morelos.[32]

Naturally he was anxious to go to Mexico City, where he could
find out from Madero himself if this was true, and where his troops
could help defend the revolution by protecting its leader. But as he
prepared to leave orders came that he, Asúnsolo, and Almazán—who
had recently joined them at Cuernavaca—were to stay where they
were. Always ambitious, Almazán snuck north anyway to explore
the new political terrain, but Zapata waited. As he did so more
disquieting news reached him: it was rumored that federal commander Arnaldo Casso López intended to intercept Zapata if he tried

to go north; and Robles Domínguez expressed the fear that the campesinos of Morelos were not disciplined enough for the capital. Within days of its victory a revolution that had once seemed black and white had become a confusion of grays.[33]

Finally, on June 6, Zapata was allowed to make the trip north with a small group of advisors and confidants. In the early hours of the next morning—the day of Madero's arrival—a strong earthquake shook the delegation from Morelos awake. It must have seemed a reassurance that their hopes would not be in vain. Later that morning Zapata and thousands of others waited at the train station for the conqueror of Porfirio Díaz, and then followed him for hours on his way to the National Palace, through streets strewn with confetti and flowers and streamers in yet another parade.[34]

The next day Zapata and Madero talked over lunch. Probably accustomed to eating his food with tortillas, Zapata may have found the silver knives and the several forks of a citified luncheon a trial in themselves. It was the kind of fanciness that made him hate the capital. On the other hand, he would finally get a chance to look Madero in the eye. To this meeting he brought certain fears: fears bred of the death of Tepepa and the selection of Carreón; fears bred too of the orders of Madero's officials, in May, to leave certain haciendas alone because their owners had belatedly joined the revolution.[35] As Madero spoke it became clear that he had different priorities than Zapata. He was most concerned with reestablishing order: he wanted Zapata's forces discharged, and he wanted the quarrel with Figueroa stopped.

Zapata listened to Madero for a while, making a few objections, and then clarified his own stance. "What interests us," he said, "is that the lands be returned to the pueblos at once, and that the promises of the Revolution be fulfilled." When Madero responded that this would take study and legislation, Zapata supposedly stood to illustrate his position on land and on the disarming of troops with an analogy. Rifle in hand, he asked Madero whether, if he used that rifle to take Madero's watch, Madero would later have the right to demand its return when he was armed as well. Naturally, Madero responded that he would. This, Zapata declared, was exactly what had happened with land in his state. He reiterated that his followers wanted their land, and he invited Madero to visit Morelos to see for himself the needs of the people. Madero agreed to come, but made the mistake of adding that Zapata deserved "a good ranch" for his services, a bribe that Zapata dismissed with disgust. He had not, he roared, entered the revolution to become an hacendado. A few minutes later, and not without mutual professions of good will, the conversation ended with nothing resolved.[36]

Shortly after noon on June 12 Madero arrived in Cuernavaca with an entourage of eighty people. Among them were various Morelian merchants, led by a Jojutla area farmer and businessman named Tomás Ruiz de Velasco, who had once employed Figueroa and was now serving as spokesman for the state's hacendados. After the usual reception and some speech-making, Governor Carreón threw a banquet in Madero's honor at the elegant Borda Gardens, which had been frequented by the Emperor Maximilian. All the local worthies were there. Because this was neither his crowd nor his setting, Zapata refused to attend. Instead, he arrived, armed, near the end of the feast to invite Madero to review his troops. To do so Madero ascended to the balcony of the Bank of Morelos, where he watched Zapata's peasant followers march around and around the block in front of him in an effort to exaggerate their numbers. "Tell Zapata," he supposedly said, when he had lost his patience, "that it's time to stop the circle!" Later Madero and Zapata did briefly confer, but this was hardly the kind of trip Zapata had imagined when he made the invitation. When he left the next morning for Guerrero, Madero knew little more about the needs of the campesinos than when he arrived.[37]

He continued, however, to hear the stories of Ruiz de Velasco and other respectables: the planters, the businessmen, the well-to-do townsmen of the state. These people believed themselves "the class that thinks, feels, and loves," and the source of the nation's vitality and hope. They felt threatened and bullied by the "unconscious masses" with their "unruly appetites" that the revolution had awakened, and they let Madero know it. As a result, when he passed through Tlaquiltenango, Morelos on his way back to Mexico City, he informed a crowd that complained of Tepepa's execution that Figueroa had been correct in ordering it. The banditry had to stop. From there he proceeded to Cuautla, where he faced a controversy about the battle that took place there in May. In an orgy of violence after the fighting was over, he was told, Zapata's troops had destroyed homes, stores, factories, and hotels, and burned nineteen wounded federal soldiers alive. Zapata himself stood accused of avenging past grievances by shooting the ex-secretary of the jefe político point blank, and then dumping him into a well to drown. It was certainly true that Cuautla was in shambles—probably due, in reality, to both the desperate battle that took place there and a limited amount of sacking. And though he avoided openly blaming Zapata for the destruction, Madero, the apostle of an orderly revolution, was shaken.[38]

Meanwhile, fresh charges were also being levelled against Zapata. We have already seen that Carreón accused Zapata's followers with misbehavior at the end of May, and the weeks before Madero's trip to Morelos were filled with similar complaints. On June 5, for instance, Felipe Ruiz de Velasco, a relative of Tomás, echoed Carreón when he informed Robles Domínguez that the citizens of Jojutla were terrified of what Zapata might do if Figueroa left the town unprotected. Two days later an employee of a paper company that logged in the shadow of Popocatepetl complained that a "horde of savages," equipped with Zapata's permission to request arms, money, and pasturage in return for a receipt, had beaten him and stolen his liquor. Other representatives of the company added that Zapata had done nothing to resolve such matters.[39]

Unlike Torres Burgos, Zapata had been able to accept a certain amount of looting and brutality in his rebellion. In fact, he could not have led that rebellion without doing so. Still, his failure to somehow produce an antiseptic revolt was now a problem, especially since the violence did not magically end when the Treaty of Ciudad Juárez was signed. On the way to exile Porfirio Díaz supposedly remarked, "Madero has unleashed a tiger. Now let's see if he can control it." Zapata, too, had a tiger on his hands. He continued to be plagued by subordinates he could not completely control, who hurt him politically as they worked out their revenge. This was not surprising or unusual. Zapata's adherents were far from the only perpetrators of disorder in the area during the spring and summer of 1911—every leader operating in or around Morelos had a share of undisciplined followers, and there were bandits at work who had never really been under anyone's command. Zapata's troops, in other words, were not *especially* violent; the problem was that Zapata had made some powerful enemies, who were intent on making political capital of the brutality that did occur.[40]

The death of Tepepa, the choice of Carreón, the growing evidence that Mexico City's Maderistas mistrusted Zapata—all were part of a coordinated political offensive against Zapata that had begun by late April and would continue throughout the summer. The main issue was not really violence against people: too many refugees from Morelos lived to tell harrowing tales of their escapes in the capital for those tales to be completely credible. In fact, stories of injury and outrage almost inevitably boiled down to the theft of a horse, the destruction of a home, the seizure of land. The controversy, in other words, was largely about property, and about a system of production that made that property pay. Land was indeed being taken, as the campesinos of many villages, presumably with Zapata's at least tacit approval, occupied territory they claimed, just as Zapata had done before the rebellion. Moreover, the planters wailed, the lower classes, imbued with revolutionary ideas and encouraged by Zapata's insistence that he needed them under arms, imperiled the sugar industry by refusing to do its work.[41]

Headquartered in Guerrero and with mostly political goals, Ambrosio Figueroa did not seem a threat to the hacendados. Already during the peace talks of late April at Jojutla they were feeling him out and finding him malleable. Zapata, on the other hand, refused to make deals, and had displayed a disturbing penchant for occupying hacienda lands. If they were not already trying to use Figueroa to kill

Zapata at Jojutla in April, they concluded soon thereafter that they would need his forces to counter Zapata's insistence on social justice.

Then with the Treaty of Ciudad Juárez the cause of the planters received a considerable boost, because its terms hardly spelled the demise of the Porfirian system. The federal army—another tool that might be used against Zapata—remained intact, and the conservative Porfirian politician Francisco León de la Barra assumed the interim presidency. Compromise was in the air, and it even seemed that Madero himself—head of the revolution and heavily favored to become president in fall elections—was the kind of man they might talk around to their point of view. At any rate they were able, with Asúnsolo's help, to secure in Carreón their *own* conservative executive, and they quickly convinced Robles Domínguez that Figueroa's troops were needed to keep order in places like Jojutla and Cuernavaca.[42]

Still, Tomás Ruiz de Velasco's trip south with Madero was far from a complete success. In fact, it appeared that Madero had committed the unpardonable sin of appointing Zapata chief of arms—head of the federal police—in Morelos. As a result, two days after returning with Madero to Mexico City, Ruiz de Velasco called a meeting of the planters that would crank their campaign into high gear.[43]

For this they could depend on the help of much of the Mexico City press. Owned by wealthy conservatives who shared the outlook of the hacendados, and written by men with no understanding of events in the Morelian countryside, newspapers like *El Imparcial* revealed the charges made at this and subsequent meetings to the public. On June 19 the citizens of Mexico read that a previously upstanding Tepepa had become a bandit at Zapata's instigation, and that the young girls of Cuernavaca had fled in terror from Zapata's hordes, Zapata himself having ravaged at least three of them before they did so. Not even Madero's presence, the paper continued, had been sufficient to control the savage campesinos. On the night Madero spent in Cuernavaca, Eufemio Zapata had taken target practice on the streetlights outside the revolutionary leader's hotel. In conciliating Zapata, Ruiz de Velasco argued and the reporters wrote, Madero was ignoring threats to the interests and lives of the best citizens of Morelos.[44]

With the headline, "Zapata is the Modern Attila," *El Imparcial* introduced a whole new set of accusations on the next day. It charged that some of Zapata's men had been caught plotting Figueroa's assassination outside his Mexico City headquarters, and that other such agents wandered the city on similar missions. Equally frightening were the signs of open rebellion in Morelos. With the words, "the only government I recognize is my pistols," Zapata had supposedly raided Cuernavaca's temporary armory despite Carreón's protests, claiming the right as Madero's new chief of arms in the state to the weapons and dynamite that were stored there. Once he had armed his troops, the paper asserted, he phoned Mexico City to demand a train to move them.[45]

Though these allegations were either exaggerations or complete fabrications, for Zapata they signified a crisis. His spokesman, an ex-law student from Puebla named Abrahám Martínez, did his best to explain the most serious of them away, bending the truth in his favor when he informed the *Diario del Hogar* that the alleged raid on the arms cache was actually an arms swap done with Carreón's approval. But by the time the charges of June 20 hit the newsstands, Zapata was on his way to the capital, summoned by Madero to answer the attacks in person.[46]

It was no wonder that Zapata called reporters *guacamayos*— macaws—in memory of that bird's disagreeable screeches. But much as he had on his earlier trip to the city, he tried to win their favor now by making himself accessible, even granting an interview to *El Imparcial*. To defuse the controversy about his rumored appointment as chief of arms, as well as any fears that he might run for governor, Zapata announced that he intended to return to private life once his troops were discharged. He was sick at the moment, anyway, and needed a chance to rest. He also tried to dismiss the capital's growing impression that he was a bandit who merely sought personal gain, an impression that would come to hurt him

2. *Trying to make a good impression in Mexico City, June 21, 1911.*
Zapata is seated in the center, with his brother Eufemio on his right.
Standing at his right shoulder is Abrahám Martínez; Gildardo Magaña is
the second figure on the left. (Archivo General de la Nación, Mexico
City, Archivo Fotográfico Díaz, Delgado y García)

deeply. By dint of hard work, he noted, he had all the land and money he needed. Motivated only by patriotism, he had rebelled "to overthrow the dictatorial regime, and that has been accomplished."[47]

This was a conciliatory description of Zapata's cause, and perhaps of his aspirations too. In truth he might have enjoyed being governor, or at least chief of arms, but he sounded tired as he defended himself, and it may be that Madero had already admonished him for whatever his true contribution to the Cuernavaca arms scandal was. If there was tension between the two men, however, it did not show in public. It was said that they laughed together about the philosophy on guns and government that *El Imparcial* had attributed to Zapata; and Madero spoke to de la Barra on Zapata's behalf. But in private, Zapata took the opportunity to make his case again. He reminded Madero that the people of Morelos were still waiting for their land, and argued that Figueroa and Carreón were both lackeys of the hacendados. Madero agreed that there should be a new governor, and promised to convoke elections soon for a state legislature that would begin to address the land problem. Again they parted on good terms. But in response to a warning that he was about to be arrested by the de la Barra government, Zapata completed his trip to Mexico City in flight.[48]

Ironically, in making it necessary for Zapata to come to Mexico City, the hacendados disrupted a process that was of utmost importance to them—the discharging of his troops that had begun about a week earlier near Cuernavaca. Overseeing this operation at Madero's behest was Gabriel Robles Domínguez, Alfredo's brother, who like Alfredo himself had some credibility with Zapata because of the pro-Leyva speeches he had made in Morelos in 1909. On the outskirts of Cuernavaca three small tables had been set up. There Zapata, Robles Domínguez, and Abrahám Martínez had rewarded each retiring rebel with a document of discharge praising his contribution to the fight for "democratic ideals." Each also received between ten and twenty pesos, depending on how far he had travelled to be discharged and how many weapons he surrendered. In a matter of days almost 3,500 guns were collected; only about 400 troops remained to be disarmed, and they were already waiting around Cuautla.[49]

As he made clear to Madero during their first exchange of opinions, Zapata was nervous about disarming, and that nervousness would lead him to resist complete disarmament in the following months. Despite his natural mistrust of the still-intact forces of reaction, however, he was again demonstrating a remarkable willingness to cooperate. But even the discharging of 3,500 men was not enough for the planters, who accused the rebels of turning in their worst guns and keeping their best. Though there was undoubtedly some truth to this claim, Zapata's adherents were lucky to have one firearm, let alone two. In many cases, despite the hacendados' disbelief, the rusty antiques being collected had in fact helped bring down the old regime. Whatever the degree of the actual disarmament, charges like these made the situation increasingly tense. Moreover, there were rumors that de la Barra's Minister of the Interior, Emilio Vázquez Gómez, was reinforcing his increasingly precarious political position by rearming the rebels of Morelos. The possibility of sending federal troops to the state began to be discussed, and it came to Zapata's attention that several haciendas were receiving arms and ammunition.[50]

Beyond Morelos, too, it began to seem that conspiracy was everywhere in the summer of 1911. In mid-July Abrahám Martínez, who had been placed in charge of revolutionary troops in Puebla, heard rumors of an ostensible reactionary plot to kill Madero during a visit he planned to that city. In a complicated series of events that displayed the many contradictions and cross-purposes embodied in de la Barra's interim government, Martínez arrested the alleged conspirators, and Martínez himself was arrested for usurping authority he supposedly lacked. This led to escalating tension in Puebla between federal forces and revolutionary troops, and eventually to a bloodbath that claimed between fifty and a hundred Maderista lives. For this violence much of the press blamed Zapata, because Martínez was his secretary, of course, and because a circular that promised revenge for the revolutionaries who were killed appeared on the streets of Puebla in Zapata's name. There is no evidence that Zapata was giving Martínez orders, and it is unclear if he actually produced the circular, but he was ready to march to Puebla, in part again to help protect Madero. Madero, however, ordered Zapata to stay put and, to his dismay, seemed to take the side of the federals.[51]

Perhaps it was these events, along with Madero's early July dissolution of the Anti-Reelectionist party he had used to run against Díaz, that inspired a group of troubled Maderistas to meet with President de la Barra on July 18. Among those present was a representative of Zapata, who joined the others to demand strict compliance with the dictates of the Plan of San Luis Potosí, the expulsion of Don Porfirio's científicos from public life, and the naming of a revolutionary general to serve as inspector of revolutionary forces. They also asked that Emilio Vázquez Gómez, one of the few men in the cabinet with revolutionary credentials, continue in his position despite recent friction between him and both de la Barra and Madero. Power, they saw, was somehow slipping away; it had to be placed more firmly in revolutionary hands.[52]

If Zapata was involved at all in this effort to influence de la Barra, it is worth noting that he chose not to make the trip to the capital himself. When he was invited later in the month to join Madero at the spa of Tehuacán, Puebla, his refusal reflected his state of mind: he feared that their enemies might seize the opportunity to kill them both. Zapata may have been paranoid in seeing conspiracies everywhere, but he was not far wrong. The planters had even been so bold as to try to coopt *him* by making a weak offer on the land issue, and proposing to support him as candidate for governor if he ran on their terms. Above all, he had discovered that this was an hacendado's revolution, and even if Madero was a well-intentioned hacendado he still had an affinity for order and for property—and for the champions of order and property—that threatened all prospects for change. Given time Madero might have set things right in Morelos, but there was no time, and Zapata seems to have sensed it. It was no longer really a question of protecting Madero or swaying national policy: Zapata was withdrawing into Morelos to protect himself by preparing for a siege that he knew was on the way.[53]

3 The Birth of Zapatismo

DESPITE THE WARNING ISSUED TO DE LA BARRA IN July, Emilio Vázquez Gómez, whose ambition and outspokenness annoyed both de la Barra and Madero, was forced from the government on August 2. Though he apparently did not authorize the signing of his name to a document that protested this incident, Zapata was undoubtedly disturbed, especially when Vázquez Gómez was replaced in the Ministry of the Interior by the Porfirian Alberto García Granados. It seemed that there were no guardians of the revolution left in de la Barra's government. Still Zapata insisted on his loyalty to Madero, "the only man in whom," he asserted, "all the hopes and aspirations of the Mexican people have been placed."[1]

Meanwhile, the hacendados continued to plead their case. Land they considered theirs remained occupied by unruly peasants, and Zapata still had men under arms, giving him a great deal of political leverage on the local scene. On the ninth of August the government responded to planter complaints by announcing that a vicious old Indian fighter, General Victoriano Huerta, was going to Morelos with instructions to finish the disarming of Zapata's men—by force if necessary. On the same day Madero and de la Barra also acceded to the demand of the hacendados that Governor Carreón, who could not restore the kind of order they craved, be replaced. To the planters' favorite strong-man, Ambrosio Figueroa, Madero offered both the governorship and the post of state military commander. It was obvious to almost everyone that giving Figueroa these posts would only increase tensions, but Madero's frustration with Zapata was apparent. "I hope that your patriotism," he wrote Figueroa, "will convince you to accept the invitation, and that you will put Zapata in his place for us, because we can no longer bear him."[2]

As Huerta moved south from Mexico City, all the key players of a dramatic August were in place. In the field was Huerta himself— arrogant, brutal, ambitious, and spoiling for a fight. Figueroa too had been alerted, and though he rejected Madero's political offerings for the time being—leaving Carreón in the governorship—he too would send his forces after Zapata before the month was out. Presiding over policy in Mexico City were de la Barra and García Granados, who, with their nostalgia for Porfirian order and their dignity of office, had no sympathy with or understanding of Zapata's position. Down around Cuautla, Zapata waited for promises of land and protection that would make disarming feel safe, and wondered how it was possible that Porfirian politicians were sending federal troops after him so soon after the triumph of the revolution. Finally, in the midst of the sharks swam Francisco Madero. Sometimes blind and always vacillating, he would try to hold his grab-bag revolution together, and he would fail.

When Huerta crossed into Morelos on August 9 the shock waves rippled across the state. From their mountain hideouts at the border with the Federal District the volunteers of Genovevo de la O shot at the invaders, and some of Almazán's men greeted them in Cuernavaca with a similar warning. At Villa de Ayala Gabriel Robles Domínguez, still trying to discharge Zapata's troops, found himself in a precarious situation. The village, he wrote on the eleventh, was "very excited due to the presence of federal forces in Cuernavaca," and telegraph lines were already being cut. To get out of the line of fire until he knew what was happening, he beat a hasty retreat to Mexico City.[3]

Zapata was also worried. At his headquarters in Cuautla he and such educated advisors as Otilio Montaño and Enrique Villa hoped to surmount the crisis. On August 12 they were still seeking an explanation for Huerta's intrusion. Zapata informed Gabriel Robles Domínguez, now in the capital, that the situation was rapidly deteriorating, and asked to be told immediately what to expect. In another telegram he charged Carreón with creating the present disorder with his calumny, and added, "I am a traitor neither to my country, nor to the supreme government, nor to Mr. Madero." Finally, he asked García Granados if Huerta's troops had been sent against him, and warned that if blood was spilled it would be the government's doing. Fearing the responsibility of leading more people to their deaths, Zapata obviously wanted peace. But his forces were hurriedly preparing for war—establishing their defenses, digging up whatever hidden arms were available, and taking control of Yautepec and Jojutla. This was just as well, because de la Barra was also at work on the twelfth, seizing upon the skirmish with de la O to justify new orders for Huerta, who was now to proceed against Zapata until he secured an unconditional surrender. There were no formal ties as yet between de la O and Zapata, but from the perspective of Mexico City the agrarian rebels of Morelos looked pretty much alike.[4]

Meanwhile, Zapata's agents in Mexico City had convinced Madero to try to resolve the situation without bloodshed. Since Zapata had already drawn his conclusions about the safety of the capital, and refused an invitation to visit Madero there, on August 13 Madero demonstrated that he had not yet given up on Zapata by travelling to Cuernavaca. During the next two days the two men discussed their problems over the phone. On Zapata's end of the line, Otilio Montaño did most of the talking, while Zapata listened with his assistants and confidants over beer and cigars. Again and again Montaño insisted that Zapata thought it best that the federal forces depart. Then Zapata got on the phone to repeat Montaño's arguments once more. When someone on Madero's end asked if he was afraid of Huerta, Zapata bristled: he had left his fear behind in an old pair of pants, he answered, when he joined the revolution. Madero counselled patience, even with the federal troops, but patience was an increasingly rare commodity.

Still, it was agreed that they would talk again at Cuautla, and in anticipation of this Zapata sent Madero a list of demands. Since the people—and not Zapata alone—found their presence unacceptable, Zapata asked once more that the federal forces be retired. In exchange he promised to discharge his men, but suggested that some be retained as rural police, so that *they* could keep order in Huerta's absence. He wanted Carreón removed as governor and rejected Ramón Oliveros—another candidate of the hacendados—as a possible replacement. The new provisional governor, he insisted, should be one that the people could trust. He also asked that a state legislature be elected as soon as possible. It could then address the agrarian issue, and he would accept what it decided. Finally, he indicated, as he had in June, that he himself was "disposed to retire to private life."[5]

Indeed, Zapata would clearly have been more than happy to leave the strife behind. Earlier in the summer he and twenty-two year old Josefa Espejo of Villa de Ayala were married in a late night, civil ceremony, Zapata having prevailed, in the course of a year or so, over the objections of her relatively prominent family. About the time that news of Huerta's entry into the state arrived, they were celebrating a church wedding. At the age of thirty-two Zapata was ready to settle down with a legitimate family.[6]

But de la Barra was in no mood to allow Zapata repose. He believed that Zapata was stalling for time, and it was against his principles to deal with "bandits." Thus he alerted Madero on the fifteenth that Huerta had orders to proceed unless he was convinced that the disarming of Zapata's men was immanent. Madero agreed to this course of action, but he did not know Huerta well. To leave things to Huerta's discretion was to leave them in the hands of a man predisposed to violent solutions. In his mind the failure of talks was a foregone conclusion, and so an hour after Madero left Cuernavaca for Mexico City on the sixteenth, Huerta began to march toward Cuautla. He intended, he wrote, to "be in contact with Za-

3. *Zapata and Josefa Espejo: hoping for a quiet life. (Archivo General de la Nación, Mexico City, Archivo Fotográfico Díaz, Delgado y García)*

pata to impose on him the supreme reason of the government" when Madero's efforts at peace proved fruitless. Later that day, after speaking with Madero, de la Barra ordered Huerta to suspend his movements. Huerta, however, was not an easy man to stop. He continued his advance until the morning of the eighteenth, and again sent a shudder of fear across the state. Though he assured Zapata that Huerta had misinterpreted de la Barra's orders, even Madero was beginning to resign himself to war.[7]

Zapata now warned de la Barra that people were becoming increasingly upset, and announced patriotically to Madero that "the eyes of the entire nation are upon us." Despite fears that his life would be in danger if he travelled south again, Madero left Mexico City to continue his shuttle diplomacy on the seventeenth. When he stopped that night at the village of Ozumba in Mexico state, Zapata's partisans welcomed him with cries of "death to Madero." They did, however, let him pass, and he arrived safely in Cuautla just before noon on the following day. There he greeted Zapata, with a touch of the politician's hypocrisy, as his "most honorable General." He then met with representatives of various villages who had been summoned by Zapata to "hear from the Jefe of the Revolution what they could expect from him" and, of course, to back Zapata's claims about the nature of local demands. It was now agreed that Madero's former aide, Eduardo Hay, might serve as the next governor of Morelos, and that Zapata would again start to disarm on the following day. To de la Barra, however, Madero wrote that it would be best if federal forces returned to Cuernavaca. With them so near, Zapata was understandably hesitant to give up his weapons.[8]

In fact, Zapata had to be extremely careful, for he was now as close to losing control of his following as he would ever be. The troops were "so angry," claimed one of his jefes, "that I'm afraid they'll cut our throats." The stopping and starting of federal forces, the veiled and coded messages, the conspiracy theories, and the unclear agenda of national authorities were guaranteed to heighten the turmoil to fever pitch. Finally, on August 17 allies of Zapata cut loose in the Jojutla area, and three days of sacking ensued. Smelling blood, the planters barraged the capital with their versions of these events, and insisted that Zapata himself had ordered the pillage. With this kind of justification, de la Barra naturally held fast: the federals would not retreat until Zapata was disarmed. In private he disclosed that he would bring Zapata to account for his "crimes" whether he discharged his troops or not.[9]

Still Zapata and Madero tried. Though he was not really in a position to know the details, Madero repeatedly informed de la Barra that complaints about Zapata's forces sacking Jojutla were either exaggerated or simply untrue. Perhaps less willing to vouch for events beyond his ken, Zapata merely told the press that, "at least close to me," there was order. Although it seems certain that by now his men were hiding their best arms, he also went through the motions of discharging them once again. But if there was still a chance at peace, Huerta ended it abruptly on the nineteenth by ignoring Madero's frantic telegrams that everything was settled, and resuming his march toward Yautepec and Cuautla at de la Barra's orders. He and the president may even have hoped that such a move would cause an angry Zapata to execute Madero for what looked like betrayal. In fact, some claim that brother Eufemio did suggest that measure during one difficult moment.[10]

As the federals approached Yautepec on the following day gunfire was exchanged in the nearby hills. Madero hurried to that town, with Zapata close behind him, to try to resolve this latest crisis. Huerta eventually offered to detain his march for forty-eight hours, in order to prepare the road ahead for his artillery, and Zapata was given these two days to disarm. If he did so, revolutionaries from other states would move in to replace federal troops; if he did not, Huerta would proceed. In what seemed yet another supreme gesture of good will, Zapata agreed to withdraw from Yautepec. Whether he was stalling for time or was really still hopeful, he had little trust left: that night at Cuautla he made the rounds himself to make sure his sentries were awake.[11]

Over the next few days the drama of stretching nerves and temporary, nominal concessions continued along similar lines. Formally, at least, the discharging of Zapata's forces began, then stopped, then began again. De la Barra and Huerta advocated the occupation of Yautepec, while Madero patiently explained to them what they must already have known, that such an action would make any real disarmament impossible. Carreón shrilled that Eufemio Zapata was preparing an attack on Cuernavaca; Madero responded that Eufemio was with him, "submissive and obedient." Madero and Zapata agreed on a governor to replace Carreón, but de la Barra raised new objections. Huerta chafed at his collar, and on the twenty-third entered Yautepec on the pretense that his troops were running short on water. To de la Barra he argued that the process of disarmament was indeed illusory, and that Madero was in on the farce. It was time to move on Zapata, he wrote, "until we either hang him or throw him from the country."[12]

Finally giving up on peace, Madero left for Mexico City on the twenty-fourth, where he accused de la Barra of seeking a violent outcome. De la Barra, meanwhile, fantasized to Huerta that a bloodless strike at Cuautla would be enough to solve the problem of Zapata. Huerta soon snuck out of Yautepec to Cocoyoc, where he noted that "bandits" roaming in the area could only be controlled by attacking Cuautla. On August 29 he got the order he wanted: in conjunction with Generals Arnaldo Casso López and Ambrosio Figueroa, he was to pacify Morelos.[13]

The hunt was on. As Huerta and Casso López came for him at Cuautla, an outmanned and surrounded Zapata retrieved whatever arms he could and moved south to safer terrain. For his fighting that spring and his loyalty that summer, Zapata had only Madero's assurance that he would be rewarded when Madero reached the presidency. On August 27 he had aired his grievances about that in his first manifesto, in which he blasted the científicos who still conspired against the revolution, spelled out agreements he had made with Madero, and complained of being called a bandit. Four days later he wrote de la Barra to refute rumors in the press that he was in open rebellion. Clearly he was not. Rather, he was fleeing from an attack that he had tried to stave off with negotiations. If the government had sought a workable compromise by offering him and his people a measure of security and meeting their most basic demands, Zapata would gladly have come to terms.[14]

Instead, on September first he was finally forced to fight. At the hacienda of Chinameca he was nearly captured by Figueroa's hitman, Federico Morales, before fleeing through a field of sugarcane. On the same day Huerta took Villa de Ayala after a brief skirmish. Superior firepower, it seemed, would soon triumph, much as Huerta and de la Barra expected.[15] On September 11 four federal columns converged on Zapata's ultimate Morelos redoubt at Huautla, and Huerta began to claim that garrisons at Axochiapan, Chinameca, Jojutla, and Puente de Ixtla could now guarantee the security of Morelos's southern border. He had, he bragged with a villain's sarcasm, "travelled the entire state sowing confidence, if the word fits . . . preaching harmony, peace, and fraternity with the word, and with the guns and the cannons of the Federal Government." By the end of the month he believed that victory was his.[16]

But Zapata generally knew when fighting was pointless. He had kept enough men in arms to protect himself, but hardly enough to oppose the onslaught of well-armed federal troops. And so when he faded quietly into the mountains at the southern border of Morelos, it was not in defeat but in preparation. With sore feet from his flight and only fifty men around him, he began to ready a new "rebellion." At a ranch near the Puebla-Guerrero border he ran into Almazán, whose own problems with the government had him on the run too. Together they rounded up forces dispersed in the area, and on September 13 and 14 announced their defiance by taking Huamuxtitlán, Guerrero. Simultaneously, at the head of other small groups that had fanned out into the mountainous parts of Puebla, Guerrero, and Oaxaca, other jefes, Zapata's jefes, were also cautiously testing their strength in a revolution that was suddenly all their own.[17]

Perhaps Zapata was intimidated by the responsibility of being under arms without the legitimacy that Madero's national revolt conferred. With a crude list of demands addressed to the president, he was again seeking peace by late September. But this was not a document that reflected desperation. Offering only the promise of recognition and respect for de la Barra, it asked that new provisional governors and commanders be chosen by the will of the people, that the upcoming election for president be postponed, and that the office of jefe político be abolished. In addition, Zapata and his cohort again requested the withdrawal of federal forces from the area, and the return of village lands. Since the government was also getting a taste of how difficult the fighting would be, Zapata's overture received some attention. On the twenty-eighth, two of his representatives travelled to Mexico City with Almazán to meet with de la Barra. With Huerta's support Almazán soon came to terms, but there was no reasonable offer for Zapata. In fact, Huerta did all he could to make sure that the "ridiculous pretensions of these bandits" were not recognized, and de la Barra was of similar mind. If he surrendered, Zapata would be pardoned for rebellion, but he would be tried for the "crimes" the rebellion had occasioned. Almazán's desire for personal gain could be accommodated in the capital; Zapata's demand for justice could not.[18]

Zapata now decided to put the lie to Huerta's claim that he had pacified the state. True, Zapata's forces had been dispersed, but they had not been routed, and the bond of trust that tied them to him had made it through the difficult summer largely intact. It was merely a matter of gathering them together again, and giving them their orders. And so in October the campesinos went on the offensive. Sneaking around government troops that were trying in vain to track them through the mountains of Puebla, they poured back into Morelos in the first week of October. On the seventh they took Axochiapan; on the tenth they skirmished at Tenextepango; on the twentieth they threatened Cuautla. Then, perhaps in an attempt to improve his bargaining position, Zapata marched three thousand men on the capital. On the twenty-fourth Milpa Alta fell, only fifteen miles from the center of Mexico City. There, it is said, Zapata fulfilled a recent vow to his chieftains that he would soon dine in the Federal District by sitting down to celebrate while the public buildings and the homes of the principal citizens burned. Though it was not long before they were driven back, this incursion had the kind of results that Zapata must have hoped for. The sophisticated urbanites of the capital shuddered at the approach of the peasant "hordes," impassioned speeches were made in Congress, Huerta was recalled from the field, and a shake-up in de la Barra's cabinet claimed several jobs, including that of García Granados.[19]

Elected to the presidency in October, Madero took office on November 6, and it seemed that Zapata might have a real chance at peace on his own terms. In writing to congratulate Madero, he expressed the hope that the new president would be able to carry out his "noble goals in favor of peace and prosperity." A cease-fire was easily arranged. But Zapata was not willing simply to trust Madero after all that had happened. "We'll see," he supposedly said in August as Madero departed, "how you fulfill [your promises] when you ascend to power." Now to Madero's agent, Gabriel Robles Domínguez, who had already come to Morelos in late October to begin talks, he issued his usual set of demands. Among them were a state government responsive to the will of the people, action on the agrarian question, and steps to protect himself and his men that included the withdrawal of federal troops from Morelos within forty-five days.[20]

To Robles Domínguez these seemed excellent conditions—the kind of conditions that Madero himself, as an emissary of peace, had found reasonable in August. On November 12, however, Madero informed him that Zapata's forces would be offered only a pardon for rebelling, and that Zapata would be expected to leave Morelos for a time. A scene eerily reminiscent of Huerta's August advance on Cuautla now began to unfold around Villa de Ayala, but with Madero assuming a very different role. Now it was he who had the government's dignity to defend, and he had to protect his own credibility as well: he had to look strong before those who ridiculed his stature and his idealism; he had to discredit rumors that he had been in cahoots with Zapata from the beginning as a means of keeping de la Barra and the federal troops honest. He also apparently felt that his demonstrations of good faith in the past should have been enough to earn Zapata's unconditional support and was upset that they were not.

On the following day, from Cuautla, Robles Domínguez sent Madero's curt and meager offer to Zapata, along with the plea that he accept it as more than it appeared to be. He even promised, on his own initiative, that the land issue would be settled within three months. Robles Domínguez could not, however, journey to Villa de Ayala to make his case in person, because a thousand federal troops under General Casso López had already begun to circle Zapata's five hundred men. Zapata never got a chance to respond to the proposal. Claiming that superior orders justified his actions, Casso López had hindered Robles Domínguez's mission of peace from the start. Now he was dealing it a death blow.[21]

At least this time there was less hesitation. Apparently on Madero's orders, the federals quickly attacked. Zapata also got straight to the point. "Tell Robles Domínguez to tell Madero," he instructed a messenger, "that if he doesn't fulfill his promises to the people, I won't stop hoping to see him hang from the highest tree in Chapultepec. . . . Also tell Robles Domínguez," he continued with typical bravado, "that I'm waiting for him and his federals at the hill of Aguacate." Backpedaling and scattering through the lines of government troops, Zapata's men escaped under cover of darkness. Yet another defeated man of peace, Robles Domínguez could only return to Mexico City, where he complained that Madero had sabotaged the peace process and sent Zapata assurances of worthless good will.[22]

Suddenly Zapata had the responsibility, which he had probably not completely foreseen, of leading his own revolution. In Mexico City, where public opinion was formed, he was generally considered a bandit. This charge cut him deeply, and it reminded him of the Plateados, with whom he had been compared and with whom he compared himself. Lacking an explicit program, they had failed to capture broad support among the people, and had eventually been hunted down and killed. With Madero, the leader of the national revolution, finally in power, a similar thing might happen to him.

Some of his partisans, confused about the nature of their struggle and perhaps questioning its legitimacy, were already making separate peaces with Madero, and more such temptations were to come. Zapata had to explain to the campesinos of south/central Mexico, to the nation, and to the world what his movement was all about. He needed a recruiting pitch, a justification, an ideology, a definition.[23]

Like most peasant leaders, Zapata was unprepared to do this explaining by himself. He was, however, lucky enough to have Otilio Montaño at hand. Son of peasants from Villa de Ayala, Montaño grew up with Zapata, and by serving as godfather to his son Nicolás became Zapata's compadre prior to the revolution. Not enthusiastic about spending his life working the land, he acquired a better education than most locals and served as school teacher in various villages around the state, including both Anenecuilco and Villa de Ayala. Though his formal education was limited by urban standards, his occupation was enough to earn him the title of professor in the rural milieu, and with the title the admiration of many of the villagers.[24]

The man the villagers so admired often cut a ridiculous figure. Surely among the shortest and stoutest of revolutionaries, Montaño nevertheless took himself with intense seriousness. His pride and posturing were visible between the curly-cues of his baroque signature, and in the "bandanna he tied around his head like [the independence leader] Morelos." Still he had already served the revolution well. Montaño, it was said, often with a mixture of wonderment and mirth, could talk from morning until sundown in a town square, and when he was done the people of the town would sign up with Zapata.[25]

And so it made sense that Montaño should disappear with Zapata into the mountains of Puebla in an effort, essentially, to hammer his recruiting pitch into a shape in which it could be directed to the nation at large. The result was the Plan of Ayala. Legend has it that Zapata provided the contents and Montaño the form of this document, but of course contents and form are not so easily separated. It is enough to say that the plan was the product of a close

4. Otilio Montaño (Centro de Estudios Sobre la Universidad, Mexico City, Archivo de Gildardo Magaña)

collaboration between the leader of the movement and its top intellectual, two men who knew and understood each other well.[26]

The Plan of Ayala presented Zapata's demands for land, liberty, and justice in a fairly straightforward way. Conceived as a series of reforms of Madero's Plan of San Luis Potosí, it looked to that plan for legitimacy within the revolutionary community even as it proclaimed Madero just another tyrant who had betrayed the Mexican people in pursuit of personal power. The result of this betrayal was "the most horrible anarchy in recent history." In phrases such as this one, Zapata's rage over Madero's failure to fulfill his promises—and over the renewed shedding of blood—was written large. Though it was of secondary importance and did not appear in the plan itself, Zapata also had a more personal complaint against Madero. "Since I am no politician," read a letter he sent one adherent, "I don't understand these half-triumphs, these half-triumphs in which the defeated win, these half-triumphs in which, as in my case, they offer me, they demand . . . that I leave not only my State, but also my Fatherland." Zapata did not demand rewards, but the notion that he might be punished by temporary exile for his service to the revolution—a measure suggested by his hacendado enemies—was more than he could bear.[27]

Naturally, then, the Plan of Ayala announced Zapata's repudiation of Madero both as president and as head of the revolution. But though he was trying to establish his own legitimacy with this plan, Zapata was not yet prepared to strike out alone. The people of Morelos distrusted politicians, and perhaps Zapata distrusted himself. It would not do to make it seem as if he sought personal power by appointing himself to lead the revolution. Moreover, Zapata continued to understand his rebellion as a regional movement that needed national ties.[28] Without such ties he could not hope to affect change by winning a revolution; without such ties he was perhaps a bandit after all. Thus, in an attempt to forge an alliance that might make his campesinos members of a new national movement, he offered the job of head of the revolution to Pascual Orozco, the mule skinner from Chihuahua who had been Madero's most able lieutenant in the north during the spring. Only if Orozco chose not to serve—he had after all not yet decided to rebel against Madero—would the position devolve upon Zapata.

Zapata had good reasons for picking Orozco. It was Orozco who—with Pancho Villa's help—had forced the Díaz regime to its knees in May by attacking Ciudad Juárez against Madero's orders. In doing so he had gained enormous prestige. He had also created a tension between himself and Madero that had only grown during the summer and fall as the nature of Madero's revolution, and of Orozco's rewards, became clear. There was every indication that he might rebel again, and if he did it would be no minor revolt. Above all, he might supply Zapata with the armaments that a revolutionary in the north could secure from the United States. Still, Zapata's choice of Orozco was more than just a way to get guns. Though Orozco's northern Mexico environment was foreign to Zapata, Orozco shared Zapata's limited education and his roughly middle class, rural background. He was a man of the people in a way the wealthy Madero could never be, and it seemed likely that he had a program for social change, even if he had not yet spelled it out. Zapata, in other words, had no trouble finding common ground with Orozco, and he was serious about the alliance that the Plan of Ayala proclaimed. Zapata and Orozco would communicate with one another occasionally in 1912—after the northerner made the decision to rebel—and when one of Orozco's manifestos arrived in Morelos, Zapata took the time to correct it on such topics as labor legislation and how to construct a new government. Orozco may even have formally signed on in support of the Plan of Ayala.[29]

If the Plan of Ayala recognized the legitimacy of the Plan of San Luis Potosí, it also looked further back, to the Constitution of 1857 and Reform-era statesman Benito Juárez, who presided over the creation of that document. Since the legal bases for the Porfiriato's push against village lands were to be found in this constitution, there was more than a little irony in the allegiance. Juárez, however, was a national hero, and it was well known that don Porfirio had cynically betrayed the promises of civil rights and democracy that the constitution contained. Furthermore, there was precedent in Morelos for uniting liberalism with the protection of village lands— caudillo Juan Alvarez, for instance, had stood for both in the region during the 1850s. To Zapata and Montaño, then, recapturing the spirit of the Reform era was a worthy goal, and if there were minor problems in the constitution they could be corrected.[30]

Thus the Plan of Ayala ended with the slogan "Liberty, Justice, and Law"—a perfect summary of nineteenth-century liberal goals— and in the course of 1912 this was amended to "Reform, Liberty, Justice, and Law" to make the allusion more explicit. Zapata sought justice so the campesinos could have their land. He demanded liberty so they could protect themselves from future outrages by choosing their own leaders and running their own affairs. For him this local self-rule was democracy, and though the word democracy was not used in the Plan of Ayala, the document was full of democratic feeling. It complained that Madero had betrayed his own principle of effective suffrage; and it made provisions for the selection of both interim and constitutionally elected officials who enjoyed popular support.[31]

In articles six, seven, and eight the Plan of Ayala dealt with the crucial question of land reform. Article six expressed an old demand: land and water taken by the haciendas were to be returned to the pueblos or citizens who held title to them. If the planters—or "usurpers" as this clause called them—believed they had a right to lands in question, the burden was on *them* to prove it in court. But Zapata was now ready to go beyond this demand for restitution with which his movement had begun. By calling for the expropriation of one third of estate "monopolies" in order to provide *ejidos* for peasants without claims, and so to "improve thoroughly and for everyone Mexico's lack of prosperity and well-being," article seven added a demand for basic social justice. Not out to destroy the hacienda system, however, and not wanting to alienate any potential allies, Zapata and Montaño called for indemnification of the planters for this expropriated land. Only under the provisions of article eight would estates be completely dismantled, without indemnification.

"The property of hacendados, científicos, or caciques who directly or indirectly oppose the present plan," it read, "will be nationalized." The two-thirds of their holdings that they would otherwise have kept would serve as pensions for the widows and orphans of the revolution.[32]

A careful reading of these clauses demonstrates that there was also a certain liberalism in the economic provisions of the Plan of Ayala, in that they were not devoid of the spirit of progress. True, the campesinos of Morelos were not entrepreneurs who fully embraced the capitalist world. Most just wanted to get by, and to see that their village culture survived. Morelos was, however, one of Mexico's most economically advanced states. Capitalism had begun to penetrate the area in the sixteenth century, and that circumstance inevitably helped shape the views of even those who rebelled against some of the local manifestations of progress. Thus while the Plan of Ayala was the program of a community-based movement, there was no insistence that ejido land be worked by villages as a whole. Rather, influenced by a strong tradition of individual agricultural initiative, it was apparently Zapata's intention from the beginning that each village decide whether to work its ejido communally or to assign plots to individual families. Moreover, Zapata did not conceive of his rebellion as an attack on property rights, but as a defense of those rights against the voracious hacendados. He was not rebelling against capitalism in general, then, but against a change in the nature and degree of the intrusion of capital that threatened the survival of village life in Morelos in a way that it had never been threatened before. Zapata and Montaño explicitly rejected monopoly, not private enterprise. They merely believed that if there was to be progress it should be managed in such a way that everyone could benefit.[33]

Finally, in article nine the Plan of Ayala took a liberal position against the power of the church by praising Juárez's attack on clerical wealth. This is not to say that Zapata shared the rabid anticlericalism of many northern rebels. The Plan of Ayala noted "the support of God" for the revolution, and with icons of saints and the

Virgin of Guadalupe hanging around necks and perched in sombreros, Zapata's rank and file displayed a deep peasant religiosity. Though apparently not especially religious himself, Zapata had friendships with some of the many parish priests who cooperated with him. One curate even helped type the Plan of Ayala. Clearly it was the historical role of the church hierarchy that Zapata rejected, not the Catholic religion itself.[34]

The ideology that infused the Plan of Ayala, in other words, was a popular liberalism. It was not far removed, perhaps, from the doctrine of the *puros*—the radical liberals on the national scene during the nineteenth century—but it was fundamentally the home-grown product of Morelian history. As such, it demonstrated an abiding desire to conserve whatever seemed best in that history, not just the liberal tradition of the nineteenth century but, beneath that, the religion and the relative economic balance between hacienda and village of the colonial years.[35] Innocent of the allusions to the European-born ideologies of anarchism and communism that citified intellectuals might include in such a document, it was hardly a radical program. It seemed to contradict itself at times, especially in its attitude toward the Constitution of 1857. It was awkwardly written, showing its country origins in every word.

Zapata was thrilled with the results. After all, he had proclaimed himself in *counter*revolution as recently as September, and a list of goals in one letter of that month tailed off into etceteras—as if he could not yet be bothered to think his rebellion out. Compared to these utterances the Plan of Ayala was a work of art, superbly reflecting the nature and origins of the insurrection. And so in late November Zapata called his adherents together at Ayoxustla, Puebla, to hear the plan read. Then he invited, "those who aren't afraid, come up and sign!" Though many were afraid, they lined up to sign anyway, while someone waved a flag overhead. Later—with music and fireworks and church bells—they celebrated.[36]

It was a tremendous moment of self-definition, of accomplishment, and of relief. It was a moment that Zapata himself may have feared was not forthcoming, for he seems to have wondered if he was capable of making himself heard and refuting the charges of banditry that had been levelled against him. Indeed, few peasant movements achieve this level of sophistication. But because Morelos was so close to Mexico City, and because the sugar-based economy of the state was so advanced, Zapata and his partisans hardly lived in the same kind of isolation as the Indians of Oaxaca or Chiapas. Zapata was familiar with the publications of the Partido Liberal Mexicano (PLM), and had consulted with lawyers in Mexico City about land tenure cases. Moreover, city-bred rebels who would serve Zapata as intellectuals had been trickling into his camp from the beginning of the revolution. Abrahám Martínez, as we have seen, was already around in the spring, and Gildardo Magaña and his brothers had strayed into Morelos after the exposure of their conspiracy against Díaz. Such other urban types as Dolores Jiménez y Muro, Enrique Villa, Manuel Palafox, and Genaro Amezcua were followers of Zapata by 1912. And so while the Plan of Ayala was the product of a peasant movement acting largely on its own, its authors were not wholly ignorant of other plans or uninfluenced by outside forces.[37]

Zapata began to circulate his new program almost immediately—to representatives of foreign nations, and in Mexico City, where Gildardo Magaña had it published on December 15 in the newspaper *Diario del Hogar*. The Plan of Ayala would serve as the movement's main statement of goals until 1917 or 1918, and in a sense still after that. Often it was treated as though it were law: campesinos learned to justify their land claims by specific reference to one of its clauses and, in response to desires of urban intellectuals to tighten it up, Zapata would claim that the only way to change it was to convoke a convention. For him it would be gospel until the day he died.[38]

Already as they evaporated before the murderous attack of Huerta in September, the campesino adherents of Zapata began to be called Zapatistas. Among those who now abandoned Madero's revolution to join Zapata's was brother Eufemio. Tall and strong and still afraid of nothing, he had returned from Veracruz state to fight in the spring and then stayed on. When the Zapatistas took up arms again in the fall, he later bragged, it took him only a few days to round up two thousand men, while Emiliano himself could gather only three hundred. Their nephew, Maurilio Mejía, from Villa de Ayala and not yet twenty years of age, was also among the Zapatistas, as were a couple of brothers-in-law. Cousin Amador Salazar, about the same age as Emiliano and the same kind of country dandy, returned to the hills in rebellion as well. Prior to the revolution Salazar had worked on an estate near Yautepec, and was drafted like Zapata into the Porfirian army for some behavioral lapse. His military experience, it was said, made his troops among the best disciplined of Zapata's men. Another prominent rebel was Felipe Neri, who worked at Chinameca hacienda as a kiln operator before the rebellion, and had originally joined Zapata in March. In May, during the battle of Cuautla, a home-made bomb he threw bounced back toward him before exploding. Though it left him stone-deaf he answered the call of rebellion again. Up in the northwest corner of the state Genovevo de la O now decided to join Zapata too, bringing to the movement the geographical knowledge he had acquired making charcoal in the strategically positioned mountain forests that grew between Cuernavaca and Mexico City. From across the state border at Tochimilco, Puebla, came Fortino Ayaquica. "Hard and lasting as nails," in the words of one foreigner who met him, Ayaquica was a textile worker and farmer who was affiliated with the PLM prior to 1910, and had been driven into armed rebellion by persecution and imprisonment. Then there was rancher Francisco Mendoza, from near Chietla, who had been in trouble with Madero throughout the summer for having executed seven Spanish hacienda administrators in the spring. Finally, there was sometime bandit Jesús "One-Eyed" Morales. In the days before the revolution, when Emiliano and Eufemio took refuge in Puebla, Morales owned the bar at Ayutla where they spent their Sundays drinking and singing and playing cards.[39]

These were the kind of Zapatista representatives chosen by the common people of Morelos, of southwestern Puebla, and increasingly during the year of 1912, of the Federal District and the states of Mexico and Guerrero as well. Jefes like these were usually not as poor as the average campesino, and many were not campesinos at all, but they did take part in village culture. Like Zapata, they tended to have at least limited experiences and contacts beyond their immediate communities. Most were around thirty years of age, and many were still bachelors with reputations for unruliness. Each got his status within the movement based largely on the recruits he was able to bring to it, though a family relationship or one of *parentesco* with Zapata or another important chieftain was almost a guarantee of position, for personal relationships were extremely important. Few of these leaders had any military training. Each had a well-defined area of operations—Zapata, for instance, spent most of his time between Jojutla, Cuautla, and Jolalpan—though sometimes chieftains combined forces for a major attack on some important target. It was a loose organization, a pyramid built from personal and patron-client relationships with Zapata at the top, and with each jefe wielding broad powers within his zone.[40]

Behind these leaders fought the young men of the area's rural communities, ranging in age, for the most part, from their teens to their forties. Most were free villagers rather than hacienda peons, for rebellion for people who could afford to lose so little was a huge risk, a move of desperation, and as long as haciendas still functioned their full-time employees were too secure to be that desperate. It was not just these peasant warriors who now became Zapatistas, but often their communities with them—villages that were mostly mestizo in the valleys and plains and increasingly Indian in the higher elevations. Many joined Zapata not by taking up arms but by attending to their families and their fields, and by doing so, helping to feed those who formed the guerrillas. Others fought only part time, so that the size of Zapata's forces waxed and waned with the seasonal rains that determined when it was time to plant and when to harvest. And so while some older men did join the fighting, as did some women—frequently after their husbands were killed—these segments of the population largely served as *pacíficos*, civilians, who provided the food, maintained the communities as refuge, and reported on the movements of the enemy.[41]

Still Zapata hardly had a firm economic base for his rebellion. Many Zapatistas entered combat unarmed, and were called *zopilotes*—vultures—for the way they pounced on the bodies of enemies and friends to obtain firearms. Money, meanwhile, when there was any, generally came from hacendados and wealthy merchants and officials, who were forced to cooperate or suffer the consequences in terms of scorched cane-fields and sugar mills and looted shops and homes. By March 1912 this policy of intimidation was so successful that the principle citizens of Jojutla caused a scandal in the Mexico City press with a meeting to decide how best to pay Zapata to leave them alone.[42]

Without such resources to draw on Zapatismo would not have been viable, because the burden on the villages would have been too great. By the end of 1911 Zapata was already well aware of how delicate relations with the communities might become and how limited was the surplus they had to offer. Early on and repeatedly he instructed his jefes to levy loans and otherwise take from the rich so that hunger would not compel the troops to molest the pacíficos. He also outlined specific means of dealing with the pueblos—those in arms were not to take more of the tortillas and the fodder that they required than was willingly given; they were to respect civil authorities that had been chosen democratically; they were to protect civilians. "The better we behave," Zapata argued, "the more supporters and aid we will have among the people, and our triumph will come more quickly." But compliance with such dictates was never easy to enforce given the decentralization of guerrilla warfare. To control loose cannons Zapata ordered his chieftains to gather and discipline marauding bands. Still, if he needed to hold the support of the villages, he also needed the firepower of even those Zapatistas he sometimes called bandits. They were, he knew, at least in some sense his followers, and he was pragmatic in his desire to use them if the abuses they had committed were not excessive and repeated. And so while Zapata sought discipline and doled out punishment when there was no other recourse, village complaints of Zapatista brutality now began to arrive at his camp in a steady and unceasing stream, and he had to balance justice against military needs and against the problems inherent in sending one guerrilla band to rein in another.[43]

At least in part, these tensions within the movement reflected the fact that different Zapatistas had different reasons for joining up. At the center of the struggle in the Cuautla area and acutely felt in many other localities, the desire for land was certainly prominent among them. Land hunger drove the rebellion from its earliest days, was at the heart of the Plan of Ayala, and was accommodated by Zapata whenever possible—in the early years of the insurrection that often just meant that he approved land seizures after the fact. But material needs and not the ideological pronouncements of Zapata's plan brought people into the movement, and not all of Morelos—let alone the surrounding states—felt the same kind of economic squeeze that plagued Anenecuilco. While large-scale cultivation of sugar was widespread in Zapata's home state and in southwestern Puebla, hacienda expansion had not reached crisis proportions even in the eastern sector of Morelos. In some places where Zapata recruited, less dynamic cereal haciendas predominated; in others, where the terrain was rough or the land poor, communities still maintained much of their land in the virtual absence of large estates.[44]

Still, for one reason or another people were upset enough in many areas to make the revolution their own when it passed through. In some places by fall 1911, and in others at a somewhat later time, the key was simply that the fighting had disrupted the pattern of everyday life in a way that almost forced rebellion on the campesinos. Those who had fought with Zapata in the spring, for instance, were often brutalized by Huerta and his cronies in the fall. Suspected Zapatistas were lined up and shot without trial, and villages that might offer the rebels refuge were often burned to the ground, forcing their inhabitants either to move off to a strange town or to hook up with the guerrillas in the hills. In the mountains of the state of Mexico and the Federal District—natural hiding places for Zapatistas—people grew tired of troops of one kind or another passing by to take what they wanted, and often accepted Zapata's call to arms as an opportunity to protect themselves and the lands that they already held. We fought, explained one veteran, "so that they would leave us in peace, leave us our forests and all, leave us to work our lands as we please." It became increasingly necessary, in other words, for communities to support one side or the other. Finally, motives were often quite individual: one man joined because he was robbed by a Zapatista and decided that he could rob too; others were simply out for adventure; and family ties, which often connected people from one village to those of another, aided recruiting and helped give the movement coherence.[45]

For most who joined the movement, Zapata's reputation and personality were significant factors in their decision. Many followed him with a kind of childlike faith—some because they were virtually children for whom he was a father figure, and others out of a pervading fatalism. As one old woman explained, "we're poor mountain Indians who go tied to the tail of our jefe Zapata's horse." But Zapata's appeal was more than merely symbolic. "The people under my command," he once proclaimed, "obey me out of affection, not out of subordination," and he gave them reasons to admire him, reasons similar to those that had induced the people of Anenecuilco to make him village president. His charro posture struck a chord, maybe because it seemed a mark of competence—or at least of the ability and willingness to take charge. Perhaps equally important, Zapata was a likable man. He often participated loudly in a good joke. He had a way of making a soldier feel significant by remembering his name though he had met him only once before, or by pulling him aside by his shirt to entrust him with an urgent commission. At least during the first years of the revolt, when he had money or food to spare, he often gave it personally rather than sending it out through some revolutionary bureaucracy. Accompanied only by a small staff, Zapata was constantly on the move—from place to place and from one guerrilla band to another—keeping in touch with his followers and demonstrating that he shared with them the difficulties of revolutionary life.[46]

Thus as the Plan of Ayala grew out of the anger and demands of August, Zapatismo took shape around Zapata. In December, with the harvest done, it again made itself felt, threatening settlements around Morelos, and extending its influence farther and farther afield. Though their chances of taking an important city were small, by the end of 1911 Zapata's forces—or at least his nominal allies—could make trouble in Morelos, Puebla, Mexico, Guerrero, Michoacán, Tlaxcala, Oaxaca, and the Federal District.

In January more troops were sent to Morelos in support of General Casso López, who had been heading the campaign there since Zapata's October successes discredited Huerta. Like Huerta before him, Casso López now launched an attack on Zapata's mountain camp at Huautla, but he could only hope for a symbolic victory at best: this was Zapata's favorite terrain, and with minimal losses he again slipped away.[47]

With this exercise in futility completed, the federal government oversaw the first of several political reshufflings in Morelos. Ambrosio Figueroa, who had accepted the provisional governorship in September, now resigned that post in the recognition that his unpopularity in the state only helped fuel the rebellion. Chosen to replace him was Francisco Naranjo, a northerner with good revolutionary credentials who would not, at least, arouse the automatic antipathy that Figueroa inspired. Then in February Juvencio Robles entered the scene as the area's new military commander. Like others who had tried and failed against Zapata, Robles's strategy was to garrison the principal populations and then chase the rebels in the countryside. The difference was that while Figueroa had often treated the campesinos brutally, Robles was armed with martial law, which the federal government decreed in January. An old Indian fighter like Huerta, he shared that commander's callous disregard for life. If the Morelenses resist me, Robles promised, "I shall hang them like earrings to the trees." And so, despite Naranjo's apparent good will, an even harsher phase of the struggle began. On February 9 the future was foreshadowed when Genovevo de la O's village of Santa María was burned to the ground—in the fire his daughter died.

Then on the tenth, four of Zapata's female relatives were sent to Cuernavaca as hostages. Several days later fourteen peasants were executed at Yautepec, on the assumption that they were Zapatistas. In the weeks that followed many other communities around the state were burned, and their inhabitants moved to larger towns where the army could watch them.[48]

In March Robles complemented his explicit policy of terror with yet another grand advance on Huautla. Employing four columns of two hundred men each, he too succeeded in gaining his territorial objective, but again without doing Zapata much harm. Eufemio Zapata immediately demonstrated his enduring defiance by popping up on the outskirts of Puebla to demand that city's surrender, and de la O never ceased his intense, hit-and-run warfare north of Cuernavaca. Nevertheless, in early April Robles was accorded a triumph in Mexico City, where he claimed that he had finished Zapata in Morelos. On the sixth of April—Holy Saturday, his lucky day—Zapata himself answered this assertion by leading more than a thousand troops in an attack on Jojutla, where he captured most of the town and considerable arms and ammunition before being driven off by government reinforcements. As a result, more federal troops were sent into the state by the end of the month, and it seems that Robles's scorched-earth policy began to take a toll on Zapatismo. Militarily, Zapata lay low in Guerrero during May and June. He was, however, hardly ready to surrender. In fact, he took this time to inform the representatives of foreign countries that he would soon attack Mexico City, and to notify the United States that he would not recognize transactions between the Madero government and foreign powers.[49]

As the struggle against Juvencio Robles began, it looked as if events in the north might give Zapata the national revolution he sought—the kind of revolution that might make his threat concerning Mexico City less idle. In early March Pascual Orozco finally answered the hopes of the Plan of Ayala by rebelling in Chihuahua. Loosely linked for a time to Emilio Vázquez Gómez, who had earlier declared against Madero, Orozco's movement promised to help Za-

pata by dividing the attentions of government forces. Vázquez Gómez, meanwhile, was a possible political head for Zapata's
revolution. In fact, Zapata designated him his "future 'President of
Mexico'" in March, though the month before he had denied that he
was a "Vazquista" as the papers had begun to call him. Unfortunately, neither Orozco nor Vázquez Gómez proved to be a useful
ally. Orozco never sent Zapata the arms and ammunition he sought,
and by May his uprising was already waning. For his part, Vázquez
Gómez would repeatedly demonstrate that he had little but ambition to offer the revolution.[50]

Despite the ferocity of Robles's assault on Morelos, the Madero
regime never completely gave up hope that more peaceful means
might eventually subdue Zapata. Whether directed to Zapata himself, to lesser chieftains, or to the Zapatista rank-and-file, offers of
peace of one kind or another were almost always on the table. By
early 1912 land reform and better deals for sharecroppers were offered to the campesinos of Morelos if they would only lay down
their arms, and in Mexico City such Zapatista agents as Gildardo
Magaña and his brother Rodolfo had at least sporadic contact with
government officials.

Then in July 1912 new political winds began to blow in both
Morelos and Mexico City, and efforts at peace increased. In May,
voting for the Morelos state legislature had resulted in the election
of a number of moderate reformers. Taking office in mid-July, these
deputies—largely political neophytes, but full of enthusiasm and
good will—even went so far as to broach the agrarian question. More
importantly, local politicians now induced Madero to recall Juvencio Robles, who was replaced by General Felipe Angeles, a military
intellectual more inclined to find peaceful solutions to Zapatismo
than military ones. Accepting the argument that Robles's brutality
had helped swell the ranks of Zapatismo, Angeles quickly moved to
change the tenor of the campaign by reconstructing village life instead of destroying it. Meanwhile, removed from the office of governor in July in favor of a native son, Francisco Naranjo expressed
his intention to talk peace with Zapata himself.[51]

But peace was not destined to follow. On July 20 Genovevo de la O attacked a train near the station of La Cima, high in the mountains just south of the border between Morelos and the Federal District. In the ensuing battle, forty-three federal soldiers and thirty-five civilian passengers were killed. Less than a month later at Ticumán in central Morelos a similar ambush, led this time by Amador Salazar, took the lives of thirty-five soldiers and more civilians, including three journalists. There was some indication that the journalists were killed intentionally rather than by stray bullets, perhaps because of rumors that assassins were coming for Zapata in this guise. Though Zapata and his jefes had issued warnings against civilian train travel that the government chose to ignore, the furor over the "Attila of the South" again reached massive proportions in the Mexico City press.[52]

Despite the uproar, the government continued to pursue its policy of moderation, and gradually that policy bore fruit. Tired of fighting, many peasants took the opportunity Angeles provided to return to their villages and give reform a chance. Zapata, however, was in no mood to settle for such small hopes. Discouraged by the memory of past peace talks, he occasionally entertained the proposals of Madero's agents, but he expected little from the olive branch. He had once informed two of his jefes that "everything the government offers you is a lie," and he saw no reason yet to change his mind. Indeed the obstacles to peace were many: Madero could hardly see his way, for instance, to pardon the now notorious de la O and Salazar, and without such pardons there could be no deal. In September, apparently tired of the constant speculation, Zapata finally threatened to shoot any future emissaries of peace as spies. His, he insisted, was no longer a local rebellion but a national revolution—its work would not be finished until Madero fell.[53]

Still, it looked for a time as though the government's new strategy might succeed in crippling Zapata. But then in September a new, more conservative state legislature took up its duties, and proved Zapata right by nipping the reform impulse in the bud. The fighting went on, with little gained or lost by either side. Again swelling in numbers, Zapata's guerrillas now returned to the constant cycle of raids and retreats, of scattering and regrouping, with an occasional coordinated thrust at Cuernavaca or Puebla to keep the city folks alarmed. In the hope that an inebriated and momentarily inspired populace would join the fight on their side, in August Zapata and his comrades envisioned an attack on Mexico City to coincide with the Independence celebrations of September 15, but this was merely a dream. Zapata did not have the firepower for any such show of force, and even if he did his jefes lacked the discipline to launch a precisely timed attack. As 1912 ended and 1913 began Zapatismo passed the anniversary of the Plan of Ayala, and still for Zapata there was no end in sight.[54]

4 Victory, In Part

On February 9, 1913, a battle broke out in the heart of Mexico City. Zapata, Orozco, and Emilio Vázquez Gómez were far from the only critics of Francisco Madero's moderate revolution. Many conservatives still hoped that the old regime could somehow be resurrected, and two prominent generals from the federal army—Bernardo Reyes and don Porfirio's ambitious nephew, Félix Díaz—had both already rebelled against Madero and been imprisoned for their efforts. They had, however, been planning a coup for months from their respective prison cells, and on that February morning they were released from captivity by their fellow conspirators to attack the National Palace. Recklessly leading the charge on a white horse, Reyes was immediately killed, but the fighting continued without him. Though troops loyal to Madero repelled the attack on the palace, over the next ten days those nominally loyal and those in rebellion lobbed shells at one another until thousands of civilians were dead. Perhaps the high civilian body-count reflected a reluctance among soldiers of both sides to actually hit each other with their shells. At any rate, on February 18 U.S. Ambassador Henry Lane Wilson found it rather easy to bring the two sides together and arrange an end to the fighting—and to the Madero government. Félix Díaz and Victoriano Huerta—whom Madero had chosen to lead his defenses—removed Madero from the presidency. Within days Madero was dead, one logical conclusion to his dangerous vacillation between the forces of conservatism and change.[1]

Zapata had warned Madero that the federal army was dangerous, but it seems unlikely that he derived much satisfaction from being right. True, the coup did provide him with some opportunities. During the ten days of bloodshed in the capital, Madero called Felipe Angeles and many of his troops to his aid, permitting the Zapatistas to occupy Cuautla, Yautepec, and Jonacatepec. More importantly, though, there were new problems. Zapata was soon confronted by a government of which his old nemesis Huerta had taken control, and by the end of February the state of Morelos and adjacent areas were flooded with Huerta's peace commissioners. Rumblings from the north—from Sonora, Chihuahua, and Coahuila—had already served notice that not all Mexicans would accept the coup passively, that the reestablishment of Porfirian order that Huerta envisioned would be difficult to accomplish. But Huerta had a card to play. Pascual Orozco, the Chihuahuan rebel that Zapata had chosen to head his revolution, had made a deal with the new government. With Orozco's help, Huerta hoped, he could bargain with Zapata too, and then turn his full attention to the trouble in the north.[2]

This was a confusing twist to the trajectory of the revolution. Zapata had come to hate Madero, and had fought against him for well over a year, but the memory of Huerta trampling through Morelos was still fresh in his mind: small wonder that the letters of Huerta's agents suggested throwing "a veil over the past." Orozco had done this, and under some circumstances Zapata might have joined him—later in his revolutionary career, at least, he would learn or pretend to forget. But usually he chose to remember the past, and he was a master at holding a grudge. More importantly, he had always known that men like Huerta could not be trusted. Huerta had now proved himself a traitor, and to Zapata no crime was more damning. It was hardly the time to start following Madero's foolish example. Finally, the Plan of Ayala had made national demands that a local compromise of the kind Huerta would offer could not accommodate. Such a compromise might still have tempted Zapata if the offer was convincing, but it could not be convincing coming from Huerta.[3]

Even if all this was clear to Zapata from the start, Huerta's envoys still posed some problems. As a way of insisting that he would not negotiate, Zapata had often declared that the struggle would continue until Madero fell. Now that Madero was gone, there were many tired Zapatistas in the field who wondered if the revolution was over. And to many of them Huerta's messengers came directly with their offers of peace, for Huerta realized that even if he could not make arrangements with Zapata, he might hurt him by talking over a significant number of his men. Thus during February and March Zapata was forced to explain to his troops the new situation and the new set of difficulties that came with it. He assured them that he was not engaged in peace talks—no matter what the papers said—and insisted that if they stayed united they would soon triumph: like Madero before him, Huerta would inevitably fall. They were to continue fighting, he instructed, and not enter into treaties with the enemy. Still a handful did defect. Some were summarily shot when they turned in their arms to the government, and others were imprisoned—among them Zapata's compadre, "One-Eyed" Morales, who was reportedly offered fifty thousand pesos to end his rebellion. But though the defection of Morales was a personal blow to Zapata, and temporarily weakened the movement in southwest Puebla, it could have been much worse. Most Zapatistas hung firm.[4]

Among Huerta's envoys there were several who planned personal appeals to Zapata. Luis Cajigal had apparently been his friend before the revolution, but in August 1911 he was working as an hacendado's informant, and it seems the Zapatistas blamed him for inviting Zapata to dine at Chinameca as the troops of Federico Morales moved in on September first. Jacobo Ramos Martínez, meanwhile, had taken part in Francisco Naranjo's unsuccessful campaign for peace in the summer and fall of 1912, and was hoping that this more recent connection to Zapata would somehow be useful. Then there was Simón Beltrán, who had just defected from Zapatismo with one hundred men, and now came south in the belief that Zapata still held him in esteem. Finally, at the head of the initiative as it converged from the various camps of lesser jefes on Zapata's hideout in southwestern Morelos was Pascual Orozco, Sr., father of the Chihuahuan rebel. Orozco brought a letter from his son that invited Zapata to talk with him personally in Mexico City, a move that would surely have left him dead.[5]

Soon these men made the specifics of Huerta's offer clear. Their position was that "the revolution has triumphed with all of its guarantees." In exchange for acknowledging this triumph, Zapata would be free to choose the governor of Morelos. As had Madero at various times, they also offered him troops, political position, and personal security. For his followers there would be back pay, of course, since any triumphant revolution must reward its faithful. There would be pensions for widows and orphans as well, and a resolution of the land problem "as soon as possible." The proposals came liberally sprinkled with appeals to patriotism, nationalism, and manly honor; and from Orozco, Sr. came the suggestion that together his son and Zapata, the true revolutionaries, could make Huerta honor his commitments to reform.[6]

Zapata initially attempted to take advantage of the situation. Prefatory to talks he demanded that Orozco, Sr. have all federal troops removed from Morelos and nearby parts of Mexico. Then, when Orozco consented, he told his jefes to ambush the federals as they retreated, destroying communications and occupying key positions. North of Cuernavaca the increasingly important Zapatista warrior Francisco Pacheco was playing a similar game, trying to talk his way into the strategic mountain village of Huitzilac—his home. But Zapata and his jefes may not have been the only ones acting in bad faith. Based on the story of a Mexico City informant and on the movements of federal forces, which instead of retreating approached the hacienda of Temilpa where Orozco wanted to hold talks, it was rumored that the peace commissioners intended to assassinate Zapata.[7]

Something decisive clearly had to be done with these would-be peace-makers. Perhaps it was the rumors, or perhaps the real or supposed past transgressions of many of the envoys, that suggested to Zapata that they might be tried for treason. Ramos Martínez was taken captive at Tlancualpicán, Puebla on March 18, and during the next week Orozco, Beltrán, Cajigal and a host of others were captured as well. For some justice was a brief affair. On March 30, almost immediately after his arrest, Beltrán was executed as a traitor—a graphic warning to any Zapatistas still contemplating them that individual peace talks did not pay.[8]

The others had the relative pleasure of being brought before Zapata's prosecutor for the case, Manuel Palafox. Originally from Puebla, Palafox was an ex-engineering student who had gone into sales. In this capacity he had travelled extensively throughout Mexico and, in the last years of the Porfiriato, spent some time in Mexico City. In October 1911 he appeared before Zapata as an employee of the hacienda of Tenango, with a bid to buy protection. Though Zapata would soon see the benefits of similar arrangements, at that time Palafox might still have been shot for broaching such a deal. But because Zapata needed the educated, he instead forgave Palafox and put him to work.[9]

Possessed of a rapid metabolism that enabled him, though small, to eat enormous amounts of food, Palafox was certainly the nervous type. Surviving photographs reveal a face deeply marked by smallpox and radiating a look of serious self-importance. In accord with that self-importance, Palafox strove for a dignified and casual bearing in front of the camera, but he seems never to have known what to do with his arms, and his clothing often appears twisted around his limbs in betrayal of the furious motion that preceded a cool pose. Most Zapatistas found Palafox annoying, but he was consumed by an ambition that allowed him to overcome his personality traits and the disadvantageous way in which he joined Zapata. Doing all he could to worm his way into Zapata's heart, with the fall of Madero, Manuel Palafox began to make his mark. He would now become the first of several urban intellectuals to play a central role in the movement.[10]

5. *Manuel Palafox (Centro de Estudios Sobre la Universidad, Mexico City, Archivo de Gildardo Magaña)*

On March 27 Palafox began to interrogate each of the prisoners, and by the first days of April all had appeared before Zapata as well, to make their offers of peace so they could be formally rejected. In the process charges were levelled. Most were accused of trying to divide the revolution by courting individual chieftains when the only appropriate form of diplomacy, from Zapata's point of view, was to come directly to the top. Orozco and those who were with him were also charged with planning to kill Zapata. In fact, the Zapatistas pointed out, the whole initiative was devious—Orozco had lied, for instance, when he claimed to represent his son alone rather than the entire government. But for Zapata the crux of the matter was the nature of the regime that had sent them. Since to be legitimate any new government had to be constituted along lines prescribed by the Plan of Ayala, it made no sense to deal with one that was not.[11]

Initially, it seems, Zapata planned a fair and rather conventional trial. Justice was, after all, a component of the Zapatista slogan, and by now he was quite conscious of the value of propaganda and the need to be consistent. He also knew that he was making history. Ideally, the trial would provide more evidence to the press and to public opinion in the capital of the legitimacy of his movement. And so the Zapatistas invoked past decrees to justify specific actions and charges, and made real efforts to collect evidence and to discover incriminating contradictions in the testimony of the accused.[12]

The judicial process was complicated, however, by another drama—much more important for Zapatismo—that was taking place alongside this trial. As Palafox rose through the ranks of the movement it was inevitable that there would be a power struggle with Montaño, and this struggle was now coming to a head. Chosen to serve as judge in the trial in question, Montaño repeatedly criticized Palafox's work as prosecutor. He berated Palafox for such perceived shortcomings as his inability to secure proof of the charges against Orozco and, worried about public opinion, insisted that such proof was necessary for a conviction. He also made the mistake of repeatedly calling Orozco and his cohort a commission of peace, a status that Zapata did not recognize. Zapata began to grow angry, and as Palafox and Montaño did their work it became increasingly clear that viscerally it was prosecution—revolutionary justice—that Zapata preferred, not the subtle justice of the Constitution of 1857 that had always been stacked against the common people of Morelos. As Zapata, Palafox, and Montaño exchanged opinions, the judicial process dragged on into the summer. At some point it seems that Montaño, tired of waiting for Palafox to support his charges, ruled that there was insufficient evidence against the prisoners and declared them at liberty to go. His decision was apparently reversed, for in Morelos they remained, and their trial continued.[13]

Palafox was in a perfect position to benefit from Zapata's mounting frustration with Montaño. His star was already on the rise, and he had the advantage of being the prosecutor, and of being much less concerned than Montaño about judicial niceties. Nor was he loath to serve as Zapata's yes-man. Finally, he had a wonderful foil. Throughout this episode Montaño's silly self-importance, his tortured prose, and his muddled thinking were constantly on display. In contrast, the few responses Palafox made to Montaño's taunts were remarkable for their clarity. They were also invidious, probably by design. While expressing his unhappiness with Montaño's efforts to "offend and ridicule" him, Palafox made sure to note that it was the expansion of his work-load as secretary of Zapata's general quarters that made it difficult for him to complete his investigations. Farther than Palafox from Zapata's side, by May 1913 Montaño was reduced to pleading with him that Palafox had a "systematic inclination" to thwart his efforts on behalf of the revolution. There is no indication that Zapata even responded.[14]

Trying Huerta's agents was not, of course, the only way in which Zapata expressed his defiance of the new government. In March and April he sent a series of open letters to Félix Díaz, Huerta, Orozco, Jr., and Emilio Vázquez Gómez's brother Francisco. Intended as propaganda devices, the letters covered similar terrain. Each explained why the Zapatistas considered Huerta's government illegal, and then suggested that the errors of the coup-makers could be corrected and a legitimate government created by following the Plan of Ayala. The letter to Orozco included what may have been one of Zapata's most serious personal considerations: it was not fair to betray the revolution when so many had died for its principles.[15]

Meanwhile, the fighting went on. In fact, almost immediately after Huerta took office the Zapatistas were again destroying trains and making themselves felt in the sierra—the Ajusco—that separated Cuernavaca from Mexico City. Nor was Huerta relying solely on negotiations. "The best means to handle them [the Zapatistas] with," he pronounced in one private conversation, "is an eighteen cents rope wherefrom to hang them."[16] At the end of February his troops reoccupied the important towns of Morelos, occasioning skirmishes of varying intensity as Zapata's men retreated. By the beginning of April the capture of his envoys and the letters rejecting his government made it quite clear to Huerta that peace talks would not succeed. He responded by sending a thousand more men, under General Alberto Rasgado, to begin a new offensive.

Much more foreboding, however, was the return of Juvencio Robles in the middle of the month. Again Robles brought with him his scorched-earth policies of summary execution, village burning, and generalized terror. To make matters worse, Huerta soon reintroduced the levy—that old Porfirian means of securing troops—in response to the spreading rebellion against his rule. By early summer thousands of campesinos had already been sent from Morelos and surrounding areas to fight in the north. In Zapatista country the levy became a whole new reason for people to support the insurrection. "Better to die voluntarily," thought one man who now joined Zapata, "than because I was forced" by the draft. In case anyone was still in doubt about the new state of affairs, Robles quickly simplified things by deposing the civil authorities of Morelos and making himself military governor—with the obvious intent of centralizing power in order to more efficiently prosecute his campaign. There was now no legitimate state government that might undercut Zapatismo with a program of peaceful if limited reform. For the campesinos there were no choices left. Both government and press began to discuss bringing in thirty thousand Japanese to replace hacienda workers who were killed or removed or driven into the hills. The stakes had increased markedly: the government was now ready to remake the population of Morelos if that was what it took to stop Zapata.[17]

And so the coup that brought Victoriano Huerta to power began to change the situation and with it Zapatismo. The return of both Robles and the levy created considerable growth in Zapatista ranks. Zapata would now be better able to mobilize actual armies and threaten important cities—including eventually the capital. But such mobilization would demand organization of a different kind than the loose guerrilla structure, with its many centrifugal forces, that had characterized Zapatismo so far. If Zapata's troops were to take Mexico City, they needed more discipline, in order both to fight together efficiently in larger groups and to avoid incidents that would further alienate public opinion in the capital.

Naturally Zapata had a solution in mind. Early in the rebellion he allegedly told Montaño that he needed urban intellectuals to help control his followers, because "once the battle begins, there is no God that can restrain them." Accordingly, those few from the city who found themselves among the Zapatistas were quickly put to use. Now, with Huerta, came a happy coincidence: just as more campesinos entered the Zapatista fold, the atmosphere of repression that Huerta created in Mexico City caused growing numbers of urbanites to join Zapata as well. Sometimes they even came in groups, as they did after May 27, 1914, when Huerta closed the Casa del Obrero Mundial (COM), a radical worker's organization that had provided a forum for intellectuals who shared its anarchist and anarcho-syndicalist leanings. Partly because they identified with Zapata's position, and partly because he offered the closest available refuge, many of these COM ideologues fled to Morelos. Among the urban intellectuals who became Zapatistas while Huerta ruled were Antonio Díaz Soto y Gama, Angel Barrios, Paulino Martínez,

Gustavo Baz, Rafael Cal y Mayor, Luis Iñiguez, Miguel Mendoza López Schwerdtfeger, Santiago Orozco, and Enrique Bonilla.[18]

The locals had a complicated love/hate relationship with this growing contingent from the city. Many of the intellectuals seemed to enjoy almost immediate trust when they arrived in Zapatista territory. Baz, who had been a medical student in Mexico City, won his spurs by curing the daughter of Francisco Pacheco, while Alfredo Serratos would later impress Zapata by letting him know that he spoke English. Though in these two cases the welcome was tied to skills that would be particularly useful to the movement, one's skill level did not have to be especially high to win acceptance. As a general rule, if you could read and write you were needed, for not even under Huerta was there an overabundance of candidates for the secretarial pool.[19]

If much of this acceptance was based on need, there were clearly other forces at play. The Zapatistas had considerable admiration for education and for those who possessed it. In this largely illiterate society, which had guarded its colonial documents for centuries because it believed them the keys to eventual justice, the written word had been invested with an almost magical quality. And so it was not just knowledge that the villagers expected from people who read and wrote, but at times a kind of wisdom. It is said, for example, that Zapata himself could not understand why an educated man would be a drunk. Moreover, the newcomers earned appreciation and acceptance. They demonstrated remarkable bravery by merely entering this countryside afire with rebellion, and many went so far as to lead troops into battle, sometimes generating great loyalty in the process.[20]

On the other hand, it was natural that there should be an underlying lack of trust for these people who came from beyond the village structure, with its close ties of family and god-parenthood, and its peculiar material interests held more or less in common. In fact, when an unfamiliar intellectual arrived from Mexico City in his fancy city clothing, the villagers often threatened to shoot him for his dress alone. For them he was a *catrín*—a citified fop—or even worse, a científico. The latter slur demonstrated that more than just a natural mistrust of outsiders was involved. It revealed that for the campesinos anyone dressed in the city way was implicated in the Porfirian system—that it was the city and all its inhabitants that the peasants understood themselves to be fighting against. In particular, they feared that now that things were beginning to go well, these newly arrived urbanites would appropriate all that had been won in years of fighting. Thus though the educated quickly changed their clothing to try to fit into the Zapatista world, deep-seated trust between local and outsider was rarely attained.[21]

Zapata frequently revealed his own impatience with his educated help. He had never liked anything about the city, and even if the charge that he once threatened drunkenly to have Díaz Soto y Gama and Montaño shot rings false, he certainly recognized the shortcomings of his intellectuals. He apparently believed, for example, that the doctrines of anarchism and communism that they dabbled in lacked common sense. He shook his head in amazement in 1915 over the stubbornness with which his agrarian engineers sought straight lines where there were none as they marked out village lands. And he recognized that the impulsiveness of certain young intellectuals limited their usefulness. These were not the kind of people one could trust without condition. Still it seemed worthwhile to let them try to help. Unlike most peasant leaders, Zapata had not needed much direct aid from the outside to spell out his basic principles and goals and launch a viable revolution. As his insurrection evolved, however, the challenges it faced grew larger, and it was perhaps inevitable that he would accept such aid when it was offered.[22]

One good example of Zapata's use of urban intellectuals to deal with organizational problems can be found in the case of Angel Barrios. An engineer of impressive radical credentials, Barrios had been among the leaders of the Maderista rebellion in Oaxaca, and had then taken up arms against Madero—something that must have endeared him to Zapata. By the time of Madero's death, however, his insurrection was faltering badly, so in March 1913 he signed a truce with Huerta and then snuck off to Morelos.[23]

Zapata soon sent Barrios to Zapatismo's northern frontier in the state of Mexico and the Federal District to turn up the pressure on Mexico City, in part by trying to bridge the conflict that raged between the two most important chiefs in that area, Genovevo de la O and Francisco Pacheco. Going back at least to 1912, their feud had its roots in a history of disagreements between de la O's village of Santa María and Pacheco's Huitzilac. To complicate matters further, de la O and Pacheco were among the angriest and most inflexible of Zapata's men. Pacheco had a strong streak of religious fanaticism, and as God's right-hand man, Barrios soon testified, "settles everything with killing."[24] De la O, meanwhile, had begun the revolution early and independently of Zapata, and years of vicious fighting to control lines of communication between Cuernavaca and Mexico City had seen his village burned and his daughter murdered. Neither man was much inclined to follow orders he did not like; both had tempers that often terrified their own followers; and they surely hated one another as much as they hated Huerta.

In many ways the clash of Pacheco and de la O merely reflected certain general tensions within Zapatismo: disputes between neighboring villages and their leaders were common. But because this conflict took place in such a strategically important area it was crucial that it be stopped. During 1912 Zapata often entreated the two to cooperate for the common good. He also seems to have tried to avoid jealousies by keeping both at about the same rank, though he made it clear that de la O was Pacheco's immediate boss. Despite Zapata's best efforts, however, communications between the two often mentioned unity as a prospect—as if they were not both already Zapatistas. Pacheco often failed to recognize de la O's correct rank, and rarely or never accepted his orders.[25]

This is how things stood when Barrios—instantly a Zapatista general—arrived on the front in May 1913 full of enthusiasm for his assignment. In general his job was to "moralize" and orient the forces there, to make sure that they fully understood the ideological program preferred at Zapata's headquarters and that, far from damaging that program with episodes of arbitrary brutality, they would work together and follow orders to advance it. But Barrios did much more than this: he made bombs and oversaw justice, instructed the troops on how to conserve munitions, spread propaganda in countryside and capital, signed up new recruits, collected information about Zapatista forces in the area, dreamed up organizing projects for the entire army, and eventually got involved in the fighting as well. In everything he acted as an extension of Zapata's headquarters, an agent of a leader who was trying to centralize.[26]

Pacheco and de la O rejected his busy interference from the start. For weeks de la O refused even to acknowledge Barrios's efforts to present his credentials, and while Pacheco did answer his communications, petulantly, he also apparently instructed the villagers in the area to give Barrios nothing. Barrios tried flattery, and he tried pointing out that he was merely relaying Zapata's commands. Still he made little headway. Pacheco, for instance, eventually announced himself ready to accept Barrios's instructions as "advice," but he would never accept his authority—or orders—as inspector of troops in the zone.[27]

Zapata's desire to assert greater control over their operations clearly disturbed de la O and Pacheco. But this was not the only problem. They were upset too by his use of an outsider like Barrios, by "these men," as de la O put it, "who have only recently joined us, but who want to rule us merely because of their intelligence." In fact, Barrios's presence may actually have made matters worse. As the summer of 1913 progressed it was evident that he had become a third pole in the Pacheco/de la O controversy, each of the three men complaining constantly to Zapata of the other two.[28]

For most of the summer Zapata answered these complaints by insisting that Barrios's orders be followed. These directions, however, created a great deal of tension, and Zapata must have sympathized to some degree with his two jefes. Even if it seemed a logical way to improve his organization, the centralization process did after all run counter to the grass-roots democracy that had characterized the movement from the start. Furthermore, Zapata knew how bothersome the city-bred could be, and was learning about Barrios in particular. Perhaps because he felt Zapata's resolve wavering, in the middle of August Barrios threatened to abandon his assignment, "if you don't support me or help me make the authority that has been conferred on me respected." Here and in frequent complaints about his poverty, Barrios's tone was rather insolent—it was easy to see how he might have fed the angers and the fears of de la O and Pacheco. By the fall he and Zapata were in open disagreement. Though Zapata would not drop his general plan to centralize control over his movement, he gave de la O permission to operate more independently, and it was clear that Barrios's mission had largely failed.[29]

As this struggle for organizational change got underway, so did the fight against Robles. Zapata greeted him in April by besieging Jonacatepec with 2,500 men, and taking it on the nineteenth after thirty-six hours of battle. In doing so, he captured Higinio Aguilar, the ancient and corrupt federal general in charge of the town's defenses, along with a number of his troops. Hoping as always to disprove charges that he was an ignorant, brutal bandit, Zapata then pardoned his captives on the condition that they not take up arms against Zapatismo again. The opportunistic Aguilar gave him a brief propaganda coup—he snuck back to the federals in May—by dramatically pledging to fight for the Plan of Ayala.

In early May Zapatismo continued to make headlines in the capital. On the first day of the month an attack on a train at Nepantla in the state of Mexico was said to have claimed the lives of 114 civilians; on the fifth a Zapatista assault on Cuernavaca led Huerta to promise, "Zapatismo will be exterminated, cost what it may." Zapata, however, had grown used to such threats. Later in May he signed a brief document that reformed the Plan of Ayala, proclaiming Huerta worse even than Madero and stripping Orozco, now "a social zero," of his leadership of the insurrection for the crime of betrayal. As the Plan of Ayala stipulated, the responsibility of leading the national revolution now fell, from the Zapatista point of view, to Zapata himself.[30]

Slowed by the summer rains, Zapata did little of military significance in the months that followed. Robles, meanwhile, set about reliving old glories, even to the extent of again having a group of Zapata's female relatives arrested and, in August, turning up the heat with yet another pledge to root out Zapatismo with an attack on Huautla. This time the strike force consisted of 1,500 men in three converging columns. Led by General Rasgado, who burned villages as he went, on the nineteenth of August the federals again entered Huautla, and levelled it. In a search of the surrounding area, they claimed to have found Zapata's archive, as well as large stores of arms, ammunition, and foodstuffs. Less well hidden were the bodies of Orozco, Sr., Cajigal, and another of Huerta's unlucky peace commissioners, whose inconclusive trial Zapata had just ended with a furious, summary execution as he watched the destructive troops advance into the mountains. The principle of revolutionary justice had finally won. Back in Mexico City the crafty Juvencio Robles soon got a very different reward for his service to Huerta. Announcing that Zapatismo was dead, he was now promoted to divisional general.[31]

As usual the Zapatistas answered with attacks elsewhere, and Zapata himself simply moved down into Guerrero. Far from being on the run, between skirmishes he was making big plans. A national revolution had to have a strategy to match, and though he had mastered the fundamentally defensive tactics of guerrilla warfare, Zapata had no thought of letting the bloodshed continue indefinitely. More particularly, he may already have felt threatened by the competition of the Constitutionalist movement—composed of such northern revolutionaries as Venustiano Carranza and Francisco "Pancho" Villa—or by presidential elections scheduled for October that might produce a more credible conservative regime. At any rate, when the rains ended he hoped to move Zapatismo into high gear, to begin to capture the arms and munitions necessary to take larger towns and cities. By late August he was already discussing with Barrios the launching of a major assault on the Federal District, and certainly by October he was sending more troops to this front. He also had a plan for Guerrero. If the various rebels there could be united and organized, then the whole state, with poorer communications and smaller federal garrisons than Morelos, might soon fall into Zapatista hands. It might then serve as a base, in terms both of confidence and resources, for an attack on the capital.[32]

In an October manifesto that summarized the history and the goals of his movement, Zapata proclaimed that "victory was near," and exhorted the Mexican people to one final push against the dictator. At the end of that month, though Barrios was still setting his sights on Mexico City, Zapata finally removed him from his post. He was now sent on a mission to Guerrero with Montaño, a mission that would get him away from Pacheco and de la O, of course, but also one of considerable diplomatic importance. Barrios and Montaño were first to work with the rebels in Guerrero, and then to travel up the west coast to northern Mexico and the United States with communications from Zapata for the revolutionaries there. In doing so, Zapata hoped, they might help arrange that last onslaught against Huerta.[33]

From the moment he met Ambrosio Figueroa, Zapata must have understood that things were different in Guerrero. Relations between haciendas and peasants in this large, undeveloped, and isolated southern state had generally not deteriorated as far as they had in Morelos. Still there was some agrarian discontent to work with and, like Morelos, Guerrero had been in turmoil ever since the revolution began.

Zapata's cause in the state was bolstered by the execution of Figueroa by federal forces in June 1913. Perhaps more importantly, Zapata himself had taken refuge in Guerrero several times over the years, becoming increasingly more familiar with the state in the process, and making friends among the local chieftains. Jesús Salgado, who also fought against Madero, had come to Morelos as early as February 1912 to speak with Zapata. Julio Gómez, meanwhile, operating down near the Puebla/Guerrero border, had been interested in Zapatismo since he read the Plan of Ayala, and had signed several important Zapatista documents in the spring. Others had come more informally to call themselves Zapatistas.

Still others were either loosely identified with the northern, Constitutionalist rebellion or maintained a stubborn, local independence, and it was to persuade them to sign on in support of the Plan of Ayala that Zapata sent Montaño and Barrios into the area. After all, as the insurrection against Huerta began to build toward an eventual victory, it made increasing sense for local leaders to sign up with larger movements if they hoped to empower themselves or their programs. Plagued by a lack of funds and an illness that slowed Montaño, it seemed at first that the initiative was destined to fail. Indeed, it never got north of Guerrero. But by January Montaño and Barrios did manage to recruit many of the most important leaders in the state, including Julián Blanco, a power in central Guerrero, whose conversion to Zapatismo was guided by detailed instructions from headquarters.[34]

This was not the only commission now working to spread Zapatismo. While many self-proclaimed Zapatistas in other states had arisen spontaneously and had little or no communication with Zapata, Zapata was now trying to initiate, or at least control, rebellions that were pretty far afield. Again urban intellectuals were often his chosen tools. Genaro Amezcua, for instance, was sent to Oaxaca in March 1913 to collaborate with rebels already in arms there. Cándido Navarro was similarly commissioned to spark rebellion in his home state of Guanajuato, but died in the attempt. To "get more people in arms and invade new regions, in order to make revolutionary propaganda," Zapata also encouraged a stronger push into Michoacán by jefes based in Mexico state and Guerrero.[35]

In January 1914 Zapata bragged that his army of the "South and Center" of Mexico had a presence in Morelos, Guerrero, Oaxaca, Puebla, Mexico, the Federal District, Michoacán, Guanajuato, Hidalgo, Veracruz, Jalisco, San Luis Potosí, Sonora, Chihuahua, and Durango. If there was exaggeration in this, it is nevertheless true that Zapatismo was spreading. The Constitutionalists, meanwhile, were preparing their plunge south toward the capital. Huerta was on the ropes. Beginning with Juvencio Robles's departure in September 1913—when the failure of his last Huautla campaign became evident—military governors and their troops shuffled breathlessly in and out of Morelos in an effort to find a solution to Zapata. But federal forces were increasingly incapable of solving anything. Composed largely of unwilling victims of the levy and increasingly unpaid by a government in dire economic straits, they began to crumble and defect, encouraged to do so by individual negotiations with various Zapatistas and by a general pardon issued by Zapata in November.[36]

Zapata too continued to have problems of discipline. More threatening, in fact, than the de la O/Pacheco feud were Zapata's own difficulties with Felipe Neri. An explosives expert who made bombs in salmon cans, Neri fought with no holds barred. Deaf after suffering a severe wound in the battle of Cuautla in May 1911, he nevertheless took up operations again in the fall of that year in northeastern Morelos, southeastern Mexico state, and the Federal District. In June 1913 he was injured for a second time by a bomb of his own making, but still he fought on. Unfortunately, some of the fury that drove Neri was taken out on his fellow Zapatistas. In the spring of 1912, for example, his troops had a shoot-out with those of de la O, and this was not an isolated incident.[37]

Zapata promised de la O that he would keep Neri where he could watch him, "because left to himself this man is very disorderly." There was, however, never any guarantee that such a measure could control him, for Zapata himself had nearly exchanged gunfire with the troops of a drunken Neri in the early days of the revolution. Proud of his reputation as a warrior, it seems that Neri had always "wanted to be more than Zapata." Finally, in November 1913 a dispute over arms Neri had taken from the men of two other jefes earned him a scolding from Zapata—a scolding he answered with a disturbing letter. Refusing to send the arms in question to headquarters as demanded, Neri accused Zapata of personalism for favoring Camilo Duarte—one of the other officers involved in the incident—simply because he was his compadre. In fact, the letter charged, Zapata had never given Neri the credit he deserved. "Even though I find myself without the use of my ears," Neri bragged, "I serve you as no one else has." Zapata, he concluded, could have the guns, but if he sent someone to collect them Neri was done with him. He would fight Huerta on his own.[38]

In nine years of revolutionary correspondence no other Zapatista ever dared to address Zapata so bluntly. If the unruly behavior of jefes like de la O and Pacheco made centralizing the movement difficult, this kind of challenge to Zapata himself could divide it irreparably, for Neri commanded at least some loyalty from such important Zapatistas as Amador Salazar, to whom he was apparently related. Something had to be done. On January 23, 1914, Neri was gunned down in or near Tepoztlán by the troops of a Zapatista named Antonio Barona. Strong circumstantial evidence indicates that Zapata ordered him killed, the only way to stop a guerrillero out of control. Though the hit order is missing—or was never committed to paper—the coincidence that Neri should die in this way is striking, especially if one considers that Barona was the logical man for Zapata to have charged with the job. As tough a character as Neri, he too was Zapata's compadre, and could thus presumably be trusted to keep secret Zapata's role in Neri's death. Not surprisingly, Barona was never called to account for the crime.[39]

With Neri out of the way and his forces as well organized as he could get them, in March Zapata was ready to undertake the biggest enterprise yet of his insurrection: the Guerreran campaign he had begun planning in the fall. His goal was to launch an attack on the state capital of Chilpancingo, which lay at the center of Guerrero and would thus provide access to the port of Acapulco and, to the north, the important railhead of Iguala. The key, Zapata hoped, to the conquest of the entire state, the taking of Chilpancingo would serve notice to Huerta that he could not hold the near south of Mexico for much longer. It would also establish Zapata, once and for all, as the south's preeminent revolutionary leader.[40]

With perhaps a thousand fellow Morelenses Zapata now left his home state. As he passed through Jolalpan and Cohetzala, Puebla, and then down into the heat of Guerrero—Temalac, Copalillo, Tlacozotitlán, Zitlala—allied troops converged around him. Most of the federal garrison at the larger town of Chilapa chose to join him as well rather than fight against the growing odds. On March 12 he stopped at Tixtla to set up headquarters. Just east of Chilpancingo and higher in elevation, Tixtla provided a good vantage point from which to observe the state capital, already surrounded by Guerreran chieftains. From here Zapata would oversee the siege, while Jesús Salgado, who knew the area, led attacking troops that now numbered about five thousand.

The siege was in place by the fourteenth and the attack planned for the twenty-sixth, but patience and discipline were still not Zapatista strong-points. Assigned to impede the passage of any federal reinforcements that might come south from Iguala, Guerreran jefe Encarnación "Chon" Díaz was not content with his supporting role. Gambling that Iguala was too vulnerable itself to send men south, he quickly marched toward Chilpancingo. On the way he met another Guerreran general, Heliodoro Castillo, who informed him that the attack was planned for the twenty-sixth. Some say that Díaz then announced that he intended to dine that evening in Chilpancingo, and invited Castillo to join him. At any rate, when Díaz and Castillo hit the front lines the battle was on three days early. By the morning of the twenty-fourth, though too late for dinner, the plaza was theirs.

Chilpancingo was defended by some 1,300 troops under General Luis G. Cartón, who had earlier helped Juvencio Robles carry out his policy of destruction in Morelos. Realizing that he could not expect clemency, Cartón beat a hasty retreat toward Acapulco, but surrendered when his son was killed by the fire of the pursuing Zapatistas. Captured with him were more than 600 soldiers. Since most of them were draftees, Zapata gave them the same choice he had given the forces of Higinio Aguilar: "those who want to go with me, good, and those who don't . . . it's better that you go home!" Though he furnished those who preferred to leave with money for their travels and safe-conduct passes, many were impressed enough with his kindness to choose the first option.[41]

Zapata was not as generous, however, with their officers, who were quickly charged with various crimes. In many respects what resulted were show trials. The general hatred for the man who was said to carry with him a coffin and chains to represent his pledge to catch Zapata dead or alive had no bounds, and so Cartón's conviction for taking part in the burning of pueblos and the shooting of pacíficos in Morelos was a virtual certainty. Still, care was taken to make these procedures seem fair, perhaps because the Orozco episode had been bad propaganda, perhaps because Zapata was still wrestling with his definition of justice. And so while Cartón's defense that he was merely following orders did not wash, and he was sentenced to death on April 2, many other federal officers were either not convicted or subsequently pardoned. There was a show, at least, of carefully weighing the evidence, which in some cases involved months of consideration, much as it had for Huerta's ambassadors.[42]

Most of Guerrero was now in rebel hands, and what the federals retained was soon taken—Iguala on April 7, and the stronghold of Acapulco in July. Having presided over the election by the chieftains of Guerrero of Salgado as provisional governor of the state—the first such official that Zapatismo created—Zapata returned to Morelos, taking with him the sizable stores of arms and ammunition that had been captured at Chilpancingo.[43]

Zapata's return, of course, meant that the Zapatistas could bring many more troops and resources to their operations in Morelos and around Mexico City. While he was in Guerrero, the forces he left behind stepped up their activities to distract the federals. De la O and Pacheco moved on various plazas in the state of Mexico, Francisco Mendoza attacked around Jonacatepec, and Eufemio Zapata made his presence felt near the hacienda Atencingo in southwestern Puebla. Amador Salazar, meanwhile, put pressure on Yautepec, and Maurilio Mejía captured Villa de Ayala. By the middle of April, with Zapata back, government forces were losing ground everywhere and reconcentrating in larger towns. Finally, on the twenty-fifth they withdrew from Jonacatepec, Cuautla, and Yautepec, many leaving the state entirely for Puebla or the capital. Zapata now held the eastern half of Morelos, and settled his previously mobile headquarters at Yautepec.[44]

But Huerta had one last chance to turn things around. United States President Woodrow Wilson had never liked Huerta's undemocratic methods, and had never recognized his government. In fact, he had declared an arms embargo against Huerta in the hope of helping the rebels overthrow him. Apparently impatient with the results of that embargo, however, on April 21, 1913, he took even stronger measures. Seizing on a minor diplomatic incident and a report that a German ship would soon arrive with munitions for the Mexican government, Wilson sent marines to the port of Veracruz, which they occupied after inflicting hundreds of Mexican casualties. While this invasion was the immediate reason for the withdrawal of troops from eastern Morelos, it was perhaps more important in that it gave Huerta the opportunity to appeal to patriotic sentiment in a final diplomatic barrage. Already on April 22 emissaries had contacted de la O, and the same thing was happening in other Zapatista camps. Again there were former Zapatistas among the ambassadors, including Jesús "One-Eyed" Morales, who hoped to make a personal appeal to Zapata.

When emissaries arrived to speak to Zapata himself, he called a junta of his most prominent jefes to discuss the issue. His approach to the United States had generally been rather pragmatic. Despite his distance from the border, like other revolutionaries he hoped to get arms and money from Mexico's northern neighbor, and to that end he had made occasional efforts to secure U.S. recognition of his belligerency. In a letter of 1912 he scolded William Howard Taft for supporting Madero, and tried to explain his own struggle. In 1913 he thanked Wilson for not recognizing Huerta, and made Francisco Vázquez Gómez his lobbyist in Washington. His letters to Taft and Wilson expressed admiration for the democratic institutions of the United States, and there is no reason to believe that this was feigned.

On the other hand, it is worth recalling that as a child Zapata had heard the story of the 1860s French occupation and of the struggle for Independence with its important Cuautla episode. There was a strong sense of national history underpinning the Plan of Ayala, and Mexican patriotism was a force to be reckoned with in Morelos. And so though Zapata had less personal experience with the problematic power of the United States than did many northern revolutionaries, when informed of the invasion, he claimed, "I felt like my blood was boiling." But Huerta too made his blood boil, and he would not consider even a temporary accord with the dictator. He and his jefes decided instead to fight the Americans independently if they proceeded inland, and argued that since the reason for the invasion would disappear if Huerta renounced the presidency, federal soldiers should join the Zapatistas rather than the other way around.[45]

To deal with those of Huerta's envoys who had defected from Zapatismo, Palafox was quickly appointed to head court-martial proceedings, and Morales and two others were tried as traitors. For Zapata betrayal was becoming an increasingly painful issue. He had charged both Madero and Orozco with the crime of betraying the Mexican nation, and he had already executed people who had betrayed Zapatismo by leaving the movement to fight for the other side. It was the most damning charge that he could make, and in the case of Morales it had a deeply personal component, because Morales was his friend and compadre. As a result, Zapata now made himself scarce, as he would often do at emotionally difficult times. He would not have wanted to be on hand when a convicted Morales asked that he perform the execution himself. And so Zapata missed seeing Morales, who was tied to a tree so he could be shot in the back as befitted a traitor, turn his head at the last minute to face the bullets.[46]

Further beleaguered by the invasion of Veracruz and unable to use it to rally support for his government, Huerta was obviously finished. At the beginning of May Zapata led 3,600 men on Jojutla, and after eight hours of fighting and of piecemeal surrenders of federal troops, this district seat was in rebel hands. Those troops that remained loyal to Huerta sought refuge behind the walls of nearby haciendas, but they were eventually captured and some of their officers executed.[47] In Morelos Huerta now held only the city of Cuernavaca and surrounding areas, along with some territory near Jojutla. Then in late May Zapata ordered Cuernavaca besieged, while from the north such Constitutionalist generals as Pancho Villa and Alvaro Obregón marched toward the center of the country. On July 8 Huerta decided to resign, and like Díaz before him he soon set sail for Europe, leaving fellow conservative Francisco Carbajal, one of the authors of the Treaty of Ciudad Juárez, in possession of the presidency.

With the triumph of the revolution "only a question of days," Zapata decided to explain his position to the nation once again. This he did on July 19, 1914, with the "Act of Ratification of the Plan of Ayala." Signed at San Pablo Ostotepec in the southern Federal District, where Zapata had gone to oversee the ongoing attack on the capital, this act was written in part to adjust the Plan of Ayala to the new conditions. But the May 1913 "Reforms of the Plan of Ayala" had already done much of that. More importantly, the "Act of Ratification" was a notice of what the Zapatistas expected from the Constitutionalists if the two groups were to cooperate in bringing revolutionary rule to Mexico. Naturally, it insisted on the indispensability of the Plan of Ayala for the revolutionary process. Noting that the plan clearly stated that a provisional president was to be chosen by the revolutionary community, it repudiated Carbajal's claim to that position, which he had simply received at the hands of Huerta. But what it intended above all was to assert that the revolution "seeks, first of all, the improvement of economic conditions for the great majority of Mexicans." In fact, it promised that the Zapatistas would see the Plan of Ayala's principles on the agrarian question raised to constitutional precepts. Finally, it reiterated that Pascual Orozco was deposed as head of the revolution for betrayal, and that Zapata, again in accord with the Plan of Ayala, was now the leader of the revolutionary movement. Perhaps it was out of modesty that Zapata himself neglected to sign.[48]

During the approximately seventeen months that Huerta ruled in Mexico City, Zapatismo changed dramatically. More warriors and more intellectuals both required and facilitated a difficult, halting evolution of the movement in the direction of more organization and more centralized control. In many ways this evolution began prior to Huerta's coup, for the rebellion that started in the localities of Morelos had from the beginning to be consolidated if anything was to be accomplished. Indeed, we have seen that Zapata came early to the understanding that a lack of organization and discipline would hurt him both in the national press and in the villages he depended on for support. And so, for example, when he issued detailed instructions about how trains should be approached after the scandal occasioned by the incidents at La Cima and Ticumán in 1912, he was already centralizing by imposing a single set of rules on the day-to-day operations of all of his jefes.[49]

But if the center of the movement was to set and enforce such standards, it had to be strengthened. To a large degree such a strengthening of the center was the inevitable outcome of the arrival of urban intellectuals with their secretarial and organizational skills at Zapata's general headquarters, but there were also some active attempts to build formal institutions. That is what was happening when the responsibilities of the "Revolutionary Junta of the South and Center of the Republic" were drawn up on June 2, 1913. This body, of which Zapata was President, was the latest manifestation of the roughly democratic junta of chieftains that had sprung up more or less spontaneously and informally in the earliest days of the movement. Composed of such important jefes as Pacheco, Neri, de la O, Eufemio Zapata, Montaño, Salazar, and Mendoza, the junta was to approve all documentation that would see "public light," and to travel with Zapata's headquarters. In practice, of course, these chieftains were not often together at headquarters, especially as their rebellion grew and spread, and so much of the work assigned to the junta naturally fell to its secretary—Manuel Palafox.[50]

If directions from headquarters were to be followed, of course, it was also necessary to make the military structure more functional.

Hardly a soldier when his rebellion began, by 1912 Zapata had become something of a student of military matters—in at least one case he recommended books on military organization and strategy to de la O. In the same year there were rumors that he was paying federal soldiers to defect and help train his men, and Higinio Aguilar briefly provided such aid in 1913. Then, in the summer and fall of 1913, Zapata collected detailed information on his troops, and instructed his jefes to appoint corporals and sergeants so they could more efficiently mobilize their men. With decrees like that of July 1913 he also tried to encourage obedience and some minimal discipline. All jefes, he directed, were to operate in accord with orders from himself or from the head of their zone, acting on their own initiative only if distance made communications impossible. In addition, each commander was to send an account of his activities to the head of his zone or to Zapata every fifteen days.

In spite of these developments the system remained vague and flexible. Though the process of assigning military rank grew somewhat more formal over time, the making of jefes had begun as an exercise in democracy, and with Zapata's approval it maintained much of that character. The soldiers were still generally expected to elect their own chieftains, and they were frequently permitted to switch from a jefe they disliked to another. Meanwhile, the common tendency to consider a man a general if he had forty or fifty followers meant that there would always be a lot of "generals" around despite Zapata's desire to make the rank structure less top-heavy. Finally, Zapata often sent troops that answered directly to him into zones theoretically controlled by other jefes. While this may have been useful in keeping track of what was happening in a given area, it tended to scramble the chain of command and sometimes produced conflict.[51]

Obviously neither the mere presence of intellectuals like Barrios nor such measured efforts to increase organization would quickly solve the problems that beset Zapata. Forced loans levied on villagers, robberies, murders, rape, the destruction of village property—the complaints about his troops went on and on. So did the lack of military professionalism—like "Chon" Díaz at Chilpancingo many warriors ignored orders, and the results were rarely so positive. One colonel wrote that his one hundred men had simply disappeared "as if by magic"; and of one bandit general Eufemio Zapata griped, "he hasn't seen a battle in all of the time of the revolution."[52]

Zapata put considerable effort into investigating such complaints. So did the officers under him, for though Zapata frequently issued instructions that the accused were to be tried and punished at his headquarters alone, each chieftain received protests similar to those that came to Zapata and some insisted on taking their own actions, leaving Zapata to approve of them after the fact. Though in some cases justice was summary for those Zapatistas who misbehaved, Zapata counselled "prudence" and usually followed his own advice. It was, after all, dangerous to alienate people who might take their knowledge of the region's terrain over to the enemy. Often, too, justice was complicated by false charges emanating from a feud like that between Pacheco and de la O or, as in the case of Neri, by the involvement of a relative or a compadre. Indeed, Neri's charge of personalism may well have had some merit. The task of rendering impartial justice among his followers was a central part of Zapata's leadership role. Strong ties of family and godparenthood, however, almost demanded favoritism, and Zapata's pragmatism also qualified the way in which justice was dispensed. Thus while the ideal of impartial justice was always present within Zapatismo, as in the case of Huerta's messengers there was some distance between ideal and reality, and this distance was often a source of tension.[53]

Rather than punish, then, Zapata preferred to "moralize" his troops: to try to guide and educate them better as a way of preventing future atrocities. Recognizing, for instance, that alcohol was a precipitating factor in many episodes of brutality, in 1913 he ordered that his followers not appear drunk in public. In February 1914 he went further. Though a drinker himself, he now outlawed the sale of alcohol in the area he controlled, and charged local officials and military leaders with enforcing the measure. In general, orders about behavior emerged steadily from his headquarters, sometimes elaborating on similar orders issued in the past, but often just rehashing them, and thus demonstrating how persistent the problems were. Here again concessions to the jefes and the local, democratic roots of the rebellion often enervated instructions meant to impose greater order. In June 1914, for instance, a decree forbad one jefe to disarm a subordinate of another without permission from headquarters— unless, that is, he had "good reason."[54]

Even when his guidance repeatedly failed to impress a given jefe, Zapata sometimes merely moved the troublemaker closer to his side—as he originally did with Neri—instead of punishing him. He had always understood that violence and brutality were inevitable by-products of revolution. Especially with Robles and his collaborators destroying villages in the area, conflict among the Zapatistas was understandable: the fighting brutalized those who took part in it, and the broad economic destruction it occasioned left often desperate Zapatistas competing with each other for limited amounts of food and weapons.

To minimize the strife, these deeper issues had to be addressed. As Zapatismo came to dominate larger areas for extended periods of time, it was increasingly possible to create a new order out of the chaos that Robles had wrought. Provisions were made for the election of municipal authorities and the recovery of communal lands. To deal with more immediate economic problems, meanwhile, Zapata tried to maximize and rationalize the use of the available resources. He expanded his system of exacting weekly contributions from haciendas by convincing such jefes as de la O that it was honorable and sensible to participate in this money-making endeavor. When mines fell into his hands, he sold concessions to work them, and used the proceeds to buy weapons. He outlawed the trading of goods across enemy lines. He also constantly solicited corn and other staples from villages all over the area, and it may be that these foodstuffs were distributed from Huautla. Finally, he issued further orders concerning cooperation between troops and pacíficos in utilizing scarce resources—establishing guidelines for the slaughter of cattle, for instance, so the burden would fall on the haciendas and not on the poorest villagers. In a show of altruism he may have donated at least some of his own livestock to the cause.[55]

The years of revolution had changed Zapata, and it showed every time he signed his name. At first the careful and shaky product of a country education, his signature had by now evolved into the kind of scrawl that would have done any politician proud. It began with an exaggerated "E" for Emiliano, and then the letters grew smaller as they spelled out the surname, which ended with a vigorous, confident loop underneath. It was the simple, direct signature of a man who had learned how to lead. As Zapata changed, Zapatismo changed too. When Huerta left Mexico in July 1914, the movement was larger and stronger than it had ever been before. In possession of much of south/central Mexico, it had captured the Guerreran capital of Chilpancingo in a major campaign and Cuernavaca, presently under siege, would soon fall into its grasp. With the help of a growing cadre of urban intellectuals, an ongoing tendency toward greater organization and centralization had recently picked up steam. True, within the movement there were many powerful remnants of a simpler day when the common people of diverse villages heard tell of Francisco Madero and decided it was time to pick up their guns and go to war. Dozens of Neris and Pachecos and de la Os still strained against the centripetal forces that Zapata brought to bear, and sometimes threatened Zapata himself in the process. Still, Zapatismo would prove a steady enough vehicle in the months to come to carry Zapata to a triumph in Mexico City and push him to the summit of national power. There, among those struggling to define a supposedly victorious revolution, Zapata would face the most crucial and difficult tests of his revolutionary career.

5 The National Challenge

ON JUNE 24, 1914, ZAPATA SIGNED A MANIFESTO ADdressed to the inhabitants of Mexico City. "The campesino revolution," this document warned, "is already on your thresholds knocking at your doors, and the echo of horses and the war-cry of the liberators will soon shake your buildings and your streets." Less figuratively, Zapata promised to shake the city with bombs after the middle of July, and the inhabitants of the city had never had so much reason to conclude that he might carry out his threats as they did in the summer of 1914. Since the fall of Chilpancingo he had had one success after another. The southern revolution was now reaching full crest, and Zapata himself began to oversee the attack in the Federal District. On July 19, for instance, he led the taking of Topilejo, chasing off about fifty federal troops, and on the twentieth he took Milpa Alta with four thousand men. Zapatistas from as far south as Guerrero were ordered to the front, and a sustained push of ten days was to begin on July 25.[1]

Meanwhile, the attack on Cuernavaca continued. With deep ravines to its east and west and garrisoned by several thousand soldiers, Cuernavaca's defenses were substantial. Sand bags, barbed wire, and machine guns protected the bridges over the ravines, and to the north and south of the city the defenders were dug in well. They could not, however, keep supply lines open, and by July they were out of food. General Pedro Ojeda would make no deals even after Huerta resigned, but groups of soldiers increasingly surrendered, and those who did not began to pressure Ojeda to get out while he could. Finally, on August 13 the federals—joined by many civilians—broke through Zapatista lines to the south, for the way north was too well guarded. Pressing the attack much as they had when victory neared in May 1911, the Zapatistas harried the loyalist troops and their charges as they fled. Some say that six thousand of the eight thousand who evacuated became either deserters or casualties. Along the path of evacuation, south of Cuernavaca then west and north toward Toluca, the bodies of the dead could be seen for days.[2]

The siege of Cuernavaca kept many Zapatistas in Morelos. It also meant that Zapata's own attentions were divided—he moved back and forth constantly between Morelos and the Federal District. Other difficulties, too, undermined the struggle on Zapatismo's northern front. Efforts to secure supplies were not sufficient to solve the chronic shortage of munitions. Moreover, many of the Guerrerans Zapata ordered north simply never showed up to fight. As a result, the taking of Mexico City was postponed again and again. Zapatismo stumbled in the southern reaches of the Federal District, where loyalist troops burned the villages they grudgingly surrendered to the ground, as if they meant to leave nothing worth having behind.[3]

Still it was clear that the capital would soon fall. The main issue—with potentially enormous political ramifications—was to whom. The Constitutionalist faction, which started its struggle far to the north in Sonora, Chihuahua, and Coahuila, had fought its way into the center of the country by midsummer of 1914. With its origins so near to the United States border, Constitutionalism had always had access to arms and money, which allowed it to become a professional fighting force more quickly and more thoroughly than Zapatismo could. Furthermore, in general terms the northerners lacked the intense love of land and locality that moved so many of Zapata's guerrilleros to fight and held them firmly where they were. The product of New Spain's northward surge, the frontier's military tradition, and perhaps even a stint of migrant labor in the United States, the average Constitutionalist soldier was more mobile than the average Zapatista. He could be induced in a way that a Zapatista perhaps could not to march even a thousand miles in search of something as chimerical as a revolutionary triumph. For all these reasons Zapata, whose forces had looked down from the Ajusco at the capital for years without being able to touch it, had to worry that the Constitutionalists, now also on the threshold of the city, would get there first.

Whichever group occupied Mexico City, of course, would have to deal in some way with the other. Dealing with Constitutionalism, or at least with the movement's leader, Venustiano Carranza, was something that Zapata had put off until now. As early as the spring of 1913 Carranza had asked Zapata to join his coalition, and Zapata had sent ambassadors north, but their reports on Carranza were hardly encouraging, and Zapata refused the invitation. A large-landholder from Coahuila, in terms both of class and geography Carranza came from a very different part of the Mexican experience than did Zapata. From Zapata's point of view this loyal Maderista was merely another hacendado who had little concern for social reform and hoped to use the revolution to fulfill his own ambitions. About this he was not far wrong. While Carranza would eventually pay lip-service to land reform for political purposes, he was hardly an ardent proponent of this project so near to Zapatista hearts. In fact, after securing a full presidential term in 1917, he would start to overturn even the limited land distribution that had been carried out, more or less independently, by certain of his generals. His allegiance—sketched out in the purely political Plan of Guadalupe—was to legalism, order, and power. There was little in this to interest Zapata.[4]

The Zapatista rank and file, however, was not dead set against the Constitutionalists. Most of the Zapatistas were tired of fighting and they had, after all, been fighting to topple Huerta. Now that Huerta was gone the notion that the warfare might continue seemed somehow unfair, especially since—despite the lesson provided by

Madero—it seemed only logical to many that all revolutionary factions were more or less the same. Francisco Pacheco even went so far as to refer to the Zapatistas as the "Constitutionalists of the South." In other words, the distrust of the villagers for outsiders, while significant, should not be overstated. There was no innate aversion to the Constitutionalist troops of Lucio Blanco when, in August 1914, the Zapatistas met them in the Federal District. Rather, the soldiers fraternized across factional lines as often as they shot across them. Though a northerner, the typical Constitutionalist soldier was, after all, something of a campesino too.[5]

However they felt about the Carrancistas, neither Zapata's jefes nor his soldiers were encouraged to take part in the diplomatic process. As we have seen, Zapata met the problems of growth in his files with efforts to centralize his movement. Though he still sometimes convoked juntas of generals for group decision-making, this was becoming more and more impractical due to military exigencies. Democracy and consensus, the means of decision-making with which Zapatismo began on the village level, were no match for the complexities of revolution in 1914, and this was especially true with regard to interfactional diplomacy.[6] Allowing individual chieftains to think of themselves as diplomats would only serve to test the still rather fragile unity of Zapatismo.

And so as he had when Huerta sent his envoys in 1913 Zapata, with Palafox's encouragement, now moved to make diplomacy the province of his headquarters, or at least of its intellectual agents. On July 31, for instance, he ordered that of those camped near Mexico City only Angel Barrios, who had recently returned to the area, was empowered to answer communications addressed to Zapata. Even he was to do so only if the matter was not delicate. While some of the movement's most important generals still presumed to send their own representatives to Carranza, few understood the complexities of national politics. Indeed, as revolutionaries surrounded the capital the situation on the front lines was extremely confusing—full of rumors and disinformation, spies and con-men. From all appearances even the most opinionated and stubborn of Zapata's warriors at most simply helped to collect information, and then they waited for a sign from headquarters of where the struggle would lead.[7]

The two general strategies from which Zapata had to choose—rapprochement with the northerners or intransigence—reflected tendencies at work within early Zapatismo. The specific diplomatic function of many of the intellectuals, both before and after Huerta came to power, was to help foster what the Zapatistas called "revolutionary unity." In the effort to unify the revolution, first against Madero and then against Huerta, Zapata sent the Magaña brothers, Abrahám Martínez, and even Palafox to the north of Mexico and into the United States between 1912 and early 1914. There they made contact with revolutionaries like Orozco, Carranza, and Pancho Villa. Zapata also had agents seeking revolutionary unity in Mexico City, as well as the loans and equipment that all of his envoys were to try to secure. On the other hand, Zapata had been disillusioned by what he considered his betrayal at the hands of Madero and Orozco. He had always been a cautious man at the head of a cautious people, and these disappointments had made him even less trusting of the leaders of other revolutionary factions. And so as the summer of 1914 approached, there was a rough balance between the old perception that Zapatismo needed alliances on the national level, and the growing feeling that perhaps there were no allies worth having.[8]

Under these circumstances it is hardly surprising that Zapata's intellectuals, as a group, were undecided about which path to take. We have already seen—in the case of Orozco, Sr.—that Montaño and Palafox may have had fundamental differences over how best to deal with other factions. A more compelling example of such differences can be found in an exchange of opinions involving Palafox, Zapata, and Barrios. Already in 1913 Barrios had concluded that "the Revolution is one everywhere in the Republic," though he recognized that Carranza's Plan of Guadalupe did not satisfy the aspirations of all revolutionaries. Again positioned on the outskirts of Mexico City in July and early August 1914, and thus in a position to act on such an assumption, he became involved in several diplomatic ventures that fully demonstrated his faith in negotiations.[9]

First there was the rather murky Carbajal affair that began in late July. Apparently hoping to hold onto the presidency—or at least to salvage part of the conservative agenda—Francisco Carbajal allowed some tired offers of agrarian compromise to be made to Zapata. Having just announced, in ratifying the Plan of Ayala, that he would make no deals until the government handed over national power, Zapata naturally found these terms unacceptable. But Barrios pursued the matter, sending messengers to Carbajal in the hope of convincing him to surrender the capital to the Zapatistas. This Carbajal surprisingly offered to do, once he had heard from Zapata's own lips the usual promises that lives and property would be protected. This may, of course, have been nothing more than a way of buying time, but it soon resulted in the arrival of an alleged envoy of Carbajal's in Barrios's camp, an unsuccessful search for Zapata, and a trip to the Federal District by Palafox. According to one account, the subsequent conversation between Barrios and Palafox—Carbajal's ostensible ambassador had already left—led to the mutual drawing of pistols before cooler heads prevailed. Complaining that Barrios should have arrested the would-be peace-maker, Palafox informed Zapata on August 6 that there was nothing to the offer he had been sent to investigate, and Zapata dismissed the issue to attend to the siege of Cuernavaca. On August 7 Palafox wrote Barrios for Zapata to suggest, "if you don't find yourself capable of carrying out the matters that have been assigned to you in the way that I've indicated, it would be better if you returned to these General Quarters." On August 12 Carbajal ran out of options and left for exile. The next day, in the Treaty of Teoloyucán, the governor of the Federal District surrendered the capital to the Constitutionalists without condition. Venustiano Carranza had won the race.[10]

Perhaps more promising were the initiatives of those who sought to bring Zapata and Carranza together. By July representatives of Carranza as well as more independent agents were approaching Zapata in growing numbers in an attempt to broker a peace.

Many blundered immediately, having no more idea than had Huerta's ambassadors about the realities of Zapatismo. Carranza's secretary Alfredo Breceda, for instance, foolishly contacted Jacobo Ramos Martínez, one of Huerta's old envoys who had been lucky enough to survive that experience but still had the gall—while keeping his distance—to pose as Zapata's spokesman.[11]

Better informed were independents Manuel N. Robles and Antenor Sala, who in mid-July made their way into Zapatista territory in the Federal District. Apprised of their presence there, Palafox wrote Zapata suggesting they be arrested and tried, for he claimed to have incriminating evidence against them. Indeed, no one among the Zapatistas had anything good to say about Sala—a Tabascan hacendado pushing a program of compromise land reform—and he would not prove himself a friend to the movement. Robles, however, was a different story. It was he who warned Zapata to flee Mexico City in late June 1911, and he considered himself the originator of the idea, in May 1913, that Carranza and Zapata should unite. Perhaps it was due to his past services that he was able to join Zapatismo and escape Palafox's grasp, surviving to serve as one of Zapata's commissioners to the Convention of Aguascalientes in October and to write, much later, that Zapata had protected him from the conspiracies of Zapatista headquarters.

About a week after speaking against Robles and Sala, Palafox had the opportunity to make a similar recommendation with regard to Guillermo García Aragón. García Aragón had flirted with the Zapatistas in years past while leading troops in Guerrero and Michoacán. He had also, however, helped arrange the short-lived and suspect accord between Zapata and Figueroa at Jolalpan in April 1911, and had fought against Zapata later that year under Figueroa's command. Now, Palafox claimed, he was doing Carrancista propaganda among them, and so should be shot as a traitor.[12]

Finally, Gerardo Murillo (the painter Dr. Atl) met Zapata and Barrios in the church at San Francisco in the Ajusco on July 28. Atl had friends among Zapata's intellectuals—Antonio Díaz Soto y Gama, for example, had helped him found the Casa del Obrero Mundial—and he joined them in espousing radical social reform. Now he was on a fact-finding mission from Carranza, there to ask Zapata's conditions for making the transition to a revolutionary regime. These he received in no uncertain terms: the only way to achieve peace, Zapata answered, was if all revolutionaries signed on with the Plan of Ayala. Pledging himself in favor of the plan, Atl assured Zapata that an accord with Carranza could be reached, and quickly wrote to explain the situation to his chief. While the description of Zapatismo that this letter contained was not completely flattering, it did not demonstrate bad will either. It seems that Atl was legitimate in his efforts to make peace.

But though Zapata himself was present at this encounter, Barrios soon received a letter, surely authored by Palafox, that accused him of misconducting the interview. No one, the letter noted, had demanded Atl's credentials as Carranza's representative. Moreover, his acceptance of the Plan of Ayala had been too conditional and too personal. If Atl was truly Carranza's representative he should have been forced to accept the plan for Carranza as well, as Zapata had apparently suggested during the course of the interview. "To my way of thinking," Palafox concluded, "it looks like this 'Atl' has been toying with us." Barrios was to be more careful in the future.[13]

It soon became clear that Carranza was in no hurry to answer Atl's query about Zapata's demands. Atl explained to Zapata that communications with Carranza were poor and, to buy time, promised on August 5 to join Zapatismo if Carranza did not accept the Plan of Ayala. This was not a promise he would fulfill. It may even be that he was now working to make sure that Zapata reached no agreement with Carbajal before Carranza could, for he bad-mouthed the chief of state in several of his letters to Zapata. In addition, his bold request on August 7 that Zapata make him his official representative in the capital was suspicious. Zapata ignored his letters for a while and then, back at headquarters with Palafox in the middle of August, let him know rather bluntly that he had no representative in the city because he chose to work out of Yautepec. Plagued now by the provisions of the Treaty of Teoloyucán, which infuriated

Zapata by allowing Carranza's troops to take over federal positions facing the Zapatistas in the southern part of the Federal District, Atl nevertheless continued to try to appease Zapata, sending foodstuffs south and promising munitions. He also helped facilitate the trip to Morelos of Carmen Serdán, of the Puebla family famous for starting Madero's revolution too early in November 1910. But Serdán and the letters she brought from important Carrancistas were poorly received by Zapata, and though he testified at the end of August that "General Zapata, tenacious and invincible, is a symbol of the just aspirations of the people," Atl's moment in interfactional diplomacy was over. In September he heard that Palafox wanted him dead.[14]

With the Carrancistas in control of Mexico City and Atl's venture scuttled, Angel Barrios began to crack under the pressure of the scoldings he had received for not being sufficiently suspicious of strangers. Discredited by his failure with Pacheco and de la O, he was in no position to maintain an independent stance, and was visibly backing away from his pro-unity posture by the middle of August. On the sixteenth of that month he allowed that it was dangerous even to talk to the Carrancistas, and that renewed warfare seemed inevitable, but still he insisted that there were honorable members of the northern faction who might join the Zapatistas should the fight continue. The letter to Zapata that offered this insight included a postscript in which Barrios indicated, with some resignation, that he knew his suggestions would not be heard. In another communication of the same day, in an angrier mood, he explained himself more thoroughly. As had Montaño, he accused Palafox of jealously undermining his work, adding that if Palafox continued to behave in this way, "it will occasion grave evils for the Revolution, and in this case I predict a noisy failure for both the Revolution and for you [Zapata] yourself." Having made this prophetic statement, Barrios concluded by threatening to leave the movement.[15]

Though Barrios tried to place the blame solely on Palafox, Zapata had clearly started down the path of intransigence himself. He was not, however, completely decided. Indeed, communications continued even with Carranza. But when Zapata's fact-finders made their way to Carranza's camp outside Mexico City for informal talks, they found a stubborn man. If Zapata had come to disdain Carranza, Carranza returned the bad feeling full force. Zapata, he believed, was nothing more than a local bandit, with little right to make demands. Carranza tried to appear conciliatory—even offering once to meet Zapata wherever he chose—but when his will was challenged he bristled and fell back on threats of force. The Plan of Guadalupe, he argued, was what the Constitutionalists had fought for. Its provisions put him in power, at least temporarily, and on this he would brook no debate: on August 20 he entered the capital and proclaimed himself Mexico's newest chief executive. But Zapata too had accounts to render, and the mandate he perceived was quite different. It was probably Díaz Soto y Gama who now authored a new explanation of the reasoning behind the Plan of Ayala in a manifesto entitled "To the Mexican People." Land reform was necessary, this document explained, because it was just, but also because power was more than a matter of who became President. It was a matter of economic control as well, and in Morelos as in much of the rest of Mexico that meant control of land. Without land reform power could not really change hands, and Zapata had no reason to believe that Carranza meant to take the necessary steps.[16]

But even as he wrote Carranza off, Zapata still hoped, like Barrios, that other Constitutionalists might prove more tractable, and in pursuit of their sympathies he posted a series of letters between the twenty-first and the twenty-fifth of August. Indeed the list of potential allies within the loose bag of ambitions and factions and ideologies that was Constitutionalism was endless. Among those whom Zapata now contacted was the Chihuahuan revolutionary Pancho Villa. Through the efforts of people like Gildardo Magaña who, in 1912, taught Villa to read in a Mexico City penitentiary, Zapata and Villa had been in touch for some time. By the fall of 1913, in fact, Zapata had named Villa the head of his revolution in Chihuahua. Now, on August 20, 1914, Magaña wrote Zapata from

Cuernavaca that he had new word from Villa and other "principled" jefes of the north. The next day Zapata wrote Villa even before hearing what that word was, and he wrote him again a few days later.

Despite the past communications, these new letters were somewhat cautious. Zapata was feeling Villa out—flattering a little, complaining of Carranza, and making it clear that the Plan of Ayala was sacred. His hope, of course, was that Villa might join him to remove Carranza from Mexico City, one way or another. This was a reasonable expectation, because though nominally still a Constitutionalist, Villa was the prime example of the shakiness of Carranza's coalition. A volatile ex-bandit, he had never liked or trusted the hacendado, and the feeling was mutual. In fact, their relationship was deteriorating rapidly. At the head of his wild cavalry charges, Villa had done much of the fighting and winning in the north while Carranza, a virtual non-combatant, watched and plotted. In June 1914, after Villa won the pivotal battle of Zacatecas, Carranza rewarded him by depriving him of the transportation he needed to go farther south, so that a general he trusted more might reach Mexico City first. Now both men were preparing for open rupture. Zapata and Villa, on the other hand, had much in common despite the geography that separated them. Country born and bred and largely uneducated, it was they who best represented the rough, populist thrust of the revolution, which contrasted markedly with Carranza's legalistic pose as the rightful heir to Madero. True, Villa had not been clear on the issue of land reform, but he seemed to mean well, and had at least taken the haciendas away from their owners in the area he controlled.[17]

Another recipient of a letter from Zapata was Lucio Blanco, the general from Coahuila whose troops now faced the Zapatistas in the Federal District. Hardly an unconditional adherent of Carranza, Blanco had presided over agrarian reform around Matamoros, Tamaulipas, and Carranza had punished him for it. Moreover, he had recently sent word, through Dr. Atl, that he wanted to speak to Zapata to find out how he could help him bring his program to fruition. In terms similar to those used in the letters to Villa, Zapata now answered that he had always considered Blanco a patriot, and invited him to visit Yautepec. If Blanco could not do this, Zapata continued, he would come to Blanco when time permitted. Though hardly sanguine about the prospects for peace—"I will tell you frankly," he wrote, "that this Mr. Carranza does not inspire much confidence in me"—he also promised to suspend his attacks on Mexico City as a gesture of good will.[18]

In other words, Zapatismo's official posture toward potentially sympathetic Carrancistas was clear in late August when Zapata invited two such men to Cuernavaca through yet another Constitutionalist envoy named Juan Sarabia. Carranza appeared to be too conservative and power hungry to deal with, but it was possible that his ability to maintain power in Mexico City could be undermined by stripping him of the support of those who had helped him win it. Thus when Antonio I. Villarreal and Luis Cabrera accepted Zapata's invitation and joined Sarabia to form a Carrancista peace commission, it was one of the most important diplomatic opportunities of the revolution. Zapata had invited Villarreal and Cabrera south because they, like Sarabia himself, had the kind of revolutionary credentials he admired. In one way or another all three had been involved in land reform projects during the revolution's early years, and Villarreal and Sarabia had been active members of the PLM. In fact, Zapata had just solicited Villarreal's support for the Plan of Ayala in a letter full of praise for its recipient.[19]

If there was hope that these commissioners might be drawn to Zapatismo, it lay partly in the fact that they, like Dr. Atl, had friends among Zapata's urban intellectuals. Díaz Soto y Gama had also been a member of the PLM, and Sarabia knew Genaro Amezcua as well. But though Sarabia initially believed that these and other Zapatista intellectuals would work in favor of peace, neither Díaz Soto y Gama nor Amezcua was in any better position to do so than Montaño or Barrios. Sarabia later wrote that the atmosphere in the Zapatista camp was so tense that the normally opinionated Díaz Soto y Gama, "hardly dares to speak in front of his jefe." Nor would

Zapata bring to the conference any of his hopes for diplomacy. Instead he claimed he was ill, and perhaps he was—ill with the weight of such momentous events. At any rate, when Villarreal and Cabrera arrived on August 27, Zapata disappeared.[20]

It was thus left to Palafox to run the show with the help of a newcomer named Alfredo Serratos, who had come to Morelos earlier in the month playing some revolutionary angle and had managed—using flattery, his command of English, and friends among the Zapatistas—to slip by Palafox's guard and get in good with Zapata. Palafox had been absent when Zapata made his invitation to Villarreal and Cabrera, and he apparently considered that invitation a mistake. While the other intellectuals looked on in relative silence and Serratos chimed in with opportune support, Palafox immediately took the offensive. "Despotic, domineering, and presumptuous," he demanded that the Carrancistas "submit" to the Plan of Ayala and, waving the recent letter from Villa in the air, argued with a fool's confidence that if it came to war the Constitutionalists alone would suffer.[21]

Disappointed by Zapata's absence and offended by Palafox's harangues, when allowed to speak Carranza's agents nevertheless expressed their willingness to recognize the principles of the Zapatista plan. Palafox responded that this was not enough: they would have to accept the Plan of Ayala "without changing a word or a comma." But there were good reasons for the Carrancistas to be reticent about this. The Plan of Ayala did not fully appreciate northern realities, and so it was understandable that northerners might want to add certain clauses on their own behalf. Moreover, its amendments recognized Zapata as head of the revolution, a status they were understandably wary of trusting him with. Since this was no sticking point for Zapata—who never gave any indication that he was fighting for personal power on the national level—Palafox might well have made a concession here. In fact, there was no need to ask more of these Carrancistas than the recognition of the plan's principles, for no more than that was ever demanded of Pancho Villa.[22]

In the opinion of Carranza's messengers, when Zapata finally arrived on the third day of talks he was simply manipulated by Palafox and Serratos, who were visibly feeding his anger. Somewhat distant, as he often was when he was mad, Zapata may also have been plagued by the feeling that probably made him avoid the conference in the first place, the feeling that he was out of his depth and might make a crucial mistake. He was no mere lump of clay; the decision on this peace initiative was ultimately his to make, and he intended to make it; but in situations like this he had to rely on his advisors.[23]

And so by appealing to the ache in the pit of Zapata's stomach that recalled the bitter fruits of other such conferences, Palafox seems to have taken advantage of his confusion and his fear. In any event, Zapata allowed Palafox to continue the process of alienating Carranza's spokesmen, really becoming involved himself only when a military issue was raised. When Cabrera suggested that Zapata and Carranza would eventually come to understand one other, Zapata responded, "that he could understand anyone, if not on friendly terms, then by blows." After more delays and more threats, the Zapatista conditions for peace were finally presented in a formal manner: Carranza, they demanded, should submit to the Plan of Ayala; Xochimilco was to be handed over to the Zapatistas; and any future talks were to be held in Zapata's headquarters.[24]

Only one Zapatista condition showed the spirit of compromise. Carranza, it was allowed, might refuse to relinquish national power—as a strict reading of the Plan of Ayala would have required—if he was willing to accept a representative of Zapata at his side. There can be little doubt who Palafox envisioned in this position in the unlikely event that Carranza should agree. He was beginning to eye power on the national level, perhaps even the presidency itself. And if Carranza did not accept Zapatista demands, the second best way for Palafox to gain such power was to destroy the diplomatic initiative altogether. Men like Villarreal, Cabrera, and Sarabia already had national reputations. To them the upstart Palafox was a "mediocrity of the people in every sense." If they joined the emerging Zapatista/Villista coalition, with or without

Carranza, Palafox's political prospects would be greatly diminished. The intransigent posture of Manuel Palafox was not, in other words, completely at the service of some radical Zapatista agenda. He was also, quite significantly, looking out for himself.[25]

After some delay, apparently due to a discussion over whether they should be held captive, Carranza's commissioners were allowed to return to Mexico City. There Carranza quickly rejected Zapata's demands, and his representatives informed Zapata that they would not come back to Morelos as long as Palafox was around. They did, however, reiterate that they agreed with the agrarian precepts of the Plan of Ayala.[26]

Any attempt to distinguish the positions of Zapata and Palafox during this period of critical diplomatic activity raises thorny questions about the nature of Zapata's relationship with his intellectuals. Since the documents available for the study of Zapatismo were nearly all composed by an intellectual of one kind or another, uncovering Zapata's true perspective on the subject is problematic. It is necessary, nevertheless, to risk some general conclusions about how Zapata interacted with his advisors. The contention of some that he made his decisions without counsel is surely a twisting of fact. He had learned a lot from experience, and with little outside help had taken his cause to the nation in the Plan of Ayala. This was a remarkable achievement, which reflected the fact that Zapata and the other villagers of Morelos were not completely isolated from and ignorant of the rest of the world. But Zapata's education and background still did not prepare him for national politics. Some kind of outside leadership is generally necessary for peasant rebels to operate effectively in the national arena, and that was certainly true in this case. That Zapata recognized this need can be seen in the presence of at least one intellectual medium at all critical diplomatic meetings.[27]

Zapata was too strong and too cautious, however, to give his advisors full sway over interfactional relations. In fact, he would later tell Villa that he could trust his intellectuals only because he had been carefully nurturing them for some time, and joke that he often warned them of fatal consequences if they did not prove worthy of his trust. He obviously wanted to maintain control, to lead his intellectuals rather than letting them lead him. And so though he delegated a fair amount of authority to various intellectuals at various times, he was always in on the making of big decisions, collecting the advice of others and then deciding himself on the best course of action.[28]

Still the task of bringing regionalist Zapatismo to the nation was extremely complicated. Zapata needed the educated as mediators, to give him the national perspective he lacked. But if he needed them to intercede between himself and the politicians and intellectuals of other movements, then who was to intercede between him and them—to make sure he fully understood what they were doing in his name, to enable him to control them as he wished to? There is evidence in his dealings with such emissaries as Atl, Serratos, Robles, and Sarabia that Zapata was inclined to be a somewhat flexible diplomat. He was, after all, a personalist in many ways. If he hated hacendados and jefes políticos in general, he had still gotten along with such individuals as Ignacio de la Torre y Mier. In the country one judged a man by sitting down, looking him in the eye, and finding out where he stood.

Urbanites like Palafox, meanwhile, strove to be more consistent. They thought in terms of systems—feudalism, capitalism, anarchism, communism—and saw people more rigidly as members of groups or classes. This way of measuring people was often accurate, and perhaps none of the envoys of the summer of 1914 were completely clean from a radical agrarian point of view. Palafox may have been right that most deserved arrest, and trial, and execution. It seems nevertheless that Palafox's preference that Zapatismo be intractable with all but Pancho Villa served his own agenda. And in pursuit of that agenda it seems that he did what he could to limit the effectiveness of Zapata's system of gathering advice by intimidating such competitors for Zapata's ear as Montaño and Barrios.

This is not to say that none of the blame for this failed conference can be put at the feet of Carranza's men. Sarabia's initial report was as much that of a spy as of a peace commissioner, and in it he proved as callous as Palafox about the prospect of renewed fighting. He was also full of condescension for Zapata, an attitude he may not have been able to hide, and an attitude that his fellow delegates apparently shared. Villarreal, meanwhile, seemed to be alienating the Zapatistas intentionally when he claimed to know nothing of the Plan of Ayala, though Zapata had mentioned it to him in his recent letter. Finally, the commission lacked the broad authorization to represent Carranza that Zapata and Palafox had expected.[29]

Still the evidence of Zapatista bad faith is compelling, and as a result the enmity between Zapata and Carranza now came to include the ambassadors of the latter. But the stakes were much higher than this. What was happening was more than just the alienation of a handful of individuals—some of whom were not really amenable to Zapatismo in the first place. Rather, each episode rippled through the revolutionary community, engendering reports of Zapatista hostility that cannot have encouraged the many other powerful Carrancistas who might have been idealistic enough to dump Carranza in the name of peace and social reform, or ambitious enough to try to take his place.

Meanwhile, Zapata communicated his official position to his forces in the Federal District and Mexico state, where Constitutionalists and Zapatistas scrambled for positions along their common front. Having spent much time there in recent weeks, Zapata knew how confusing and dangerous the situation was. There had even been cases of rogue federals masquerading as Carrancistas to ambush overly-trusting Zapatistas. And so Zapata answered Constitutionalist advances with threats, and ordered that all armed troops be met in combat. Tensions rose. When Fortino Ayaquica received instructions from a Carrancista officer to vacate his positions around Atlixco, Puebla, in accord with an imaginary cease-fire, his answer admirably reflected Zapata's attitude. "Obeying the desire manifest in your memo in question," Ayaquica retorted, "our forces already have orders to abandon their positions in order to advance on yours." A number of Carrancistas were now taken captive.[30]

In the middle of September Palafox served notice of growing hysteria at headquarters by bruiting that the Carrancistas planned to invade Morelos by commandeering automobiles and racing down to Cuernavaca. It might be necessary, he suggested, to destroy the road so that only horses could pass. Still, it is questionable whether most Zapatistas were ready for war. Though skirmishes between the two armies continued to take place, many of Zapata's forces were not too worried about holding the line. After a visit to Pacheco's camp a frustrated Serratos reported that "everyone, including the troops, is completely drunk, and in that condition they're no good for anything." De la O, meanwhile, warned Palafox to stop arresting people on the mere suspicion that they were spies.[31]

Despite past failures, some Constitutionalists continued their diplomatic efforts. Primary among them was Lucio Blanco, who was in touch with Zapata frequently in September, pushing the idea of a convention of military chieftains. Carranza had agreed to such a convention, but he wanted one composed of people he could control. Blanco, on the other hand, hoped to broaden participation by including Zapatistas and Villistas, so that Carranza might be voted out of power. And so he primed the pump by giving Zapata a saddle, and even turned over some positions in the Federal District to him, despite clashes around Xochimilco that he blamed on the Zapatistas. Zapata, however, was hesitant. He was ready, he said, to convene a convention that would elect an interim president. He was not, however, in favor of the kind of meeting Carranza and Blanco had in mind, for it was intended to deal with reforms, a task Zapata now believed should await a duly constituted revolutionary government. Perhaps when it came to reform Zapata wanted a convention that *he* could control, and it seemed unlikely that he would get it under these circumstances.[32]

As a result, when the Convention finally convened on October 1 in Mexico City it was attended only by adherents of Carranza. Zapata did not receive a formal invitation to participate, and Villa, who had never come down to the capital, refused to send delegates onto Carranza's turf. But even under these optimum conditions Carranza could not control the Convention. As a Zapatista agent looked on, Carranza's own jefes soon voted to move the proceedings north to Aguascalientes, where the Villistas were willing to join them. There the Convention declared itself sovereign on October 14, and then voted to send a commission south to invite Zapata to take part.

The commission that arrived in Cuernavaca on the nineteenth of October was led by Felipe Angeles, the federal general who left Morelos with the fall of Madero and was now Villa's right-hand man. Its reception in the villages along the way had been a warm one, and in Cuernavaca too Angeles and his travelling companions—Rafael Buelna, Calixto Contreras, and Guillermo Castillo Tapia—were well received. De la O was particularly enthusiastic about their arrival, and had a portrait of himself and young Buelna painted as a souvenir. For his part, Zapata praised Angeles for fighting fairly when he was last in Morelos, and presented him with two magnificent horses.

But in general "there was, around Zapata, expectation, uncertainty, and reserve." Zapata again displayed his dislike of national politics by not meeting with his visitors until the morning of the twentieth. When they did meet he looked tired and rumpled as he posed, cigar in hand, for a photograph that celebrated the occasion. Still, in occupying the photo's center—his guests ranged carefully around him—he sent a message, and he was equally forceful in tabling his concerns. Most importantly, he asked whether the Convention would accept the Plan of Ayala and depose Carranza. Angeles assured him on both accounts: Carranza, he thought, would soon be asked to step down, and the principles of the Zapatista plan would be accepted. This time principles were enough for Zapata, and he began to assemble a brigade of twenty-six intellectuals to represent him in Aguascalientes. They would go as commissioners, to present the Zapatista point of view, not as delegates. If the Convention met Zapata's expectations, delegates would be selected later by the individual chieftains. On October 23 the intellectuals started north, while Zapata, along with the other villagers who believed national politics the province of the educated, stayed home and waited.[33]

The Convention of Aguascalientes was yet another opportunity to court individual Constitutionalists before the fighting—almost inevitable now—started up again. It was also a chance to make a good first impression on the representatives of Villa. Heading the Zapatista commission was a Mexico City journalist named Paulino Martínez, but its most important member was Antonio Díaz Soto y Gama. In his early thirties and a lawyer by training, self-proclaimed anarchist Díaz Soto y Gama already had a considerable career of radical opposition politics behind him, having participated not only in the PLM but in the founding of the Casa del Obrero Mundial as well. After joining Zapata in the spring he had become his new word man, taking over this facet of Montaño's early role as Palafox had assumed the post of main advisor. It was thus up to him to make the Zapatista case heard.[34]

Díaz Soto y Gama's big moment came when he was asked to make a speech on October 27, the first day of Zapatista attendance at Aguascalientes. Even if it is true that in August he would secretly have preferred that Zapatismo be more conciliatory to his friends from the city, he was not exactly a diplomatic man. In fact, he had always specialized in arousing strong passions. Now, hanging beside the podium as he prepared to speak, was the Mexican flag that the Villista and Carrancista delegates had solemnly signed as a pledge of loyalty to the Convention. This provided him with the vehicle he needed to discuss Mexico's failed promises to the disinherited. The flag, he proclaimed, reaching out to touch it, symbolized Agustín de Iturbide's reactionary movement for Independence, not independence for Mexico's indigenous masses. He himself would never sign it.[35]

This was a nice conceit, which expressed Díaz Soto y Gama's own radicalism wonderfully. It also reflected a fair amount of bravery, since he might have been shot during the pandemonium that ensued. But what was it designed to accomplish? Coming face to face with the Constitutionalists who were straddling the growing abyss between Carranza and the emerging Villista/Zapatista coalition, Díaz Soto y Gama seized the moment to reinforce the confrontational course already outlined by Palafox, to make sure the negative signals sent earlier were fully understood. Like Palafox he was now prepared to milk the anti-diplomatic stance of Zapatismo for all it was worth, for by this time intransigence toward the followers of Carranza had indeed hardened into policy. But in doing so he seemed to have lost track, like Zapata himself perhaps, of the general goals of the movement. In doing so, he continued and deepened the failure of Zapata's intellectuals to serve him in his time of greatest need. The Zapatistas would never have the power to win the revolution alone; they needed allies who were sympathetic to their goals; and if it was the job of the intellectuals to understand and explain national politics, then it was time for them to argue for a mature diplomacy, a bargaining from a position of strength for the biggest piece of the revolution that Zapatismo could get. Instead, this speech did more than merely anger the wavering followers of Carranza, it also drove the first stake into the heart of the alliance with Villa. Villista Roque González Garza, soon to become acting president of the government that would emanate from the Convention, described it as a "hysterical critique of the origins of the flag." Though he formally accepted the principles of the Plan of Ayala only moments later, he did so with a bad taste in his mouth. In the courting of Villa there was still a flicker of the pro-alliance tendency that had always been present within Zapatismo. But with this address the stage was already set for future confrontations that would rock the Convention government.[36]

Though Díaz Soto y Gama adopted charro dress for its delivery, this speech cannot be justified as an indispensable expression of Zapatista principle. The product of momentary inspiration, it did not have Zapata's stamp of approval. It did, however, reflect certain broader trends in Zapatista discourse. Since 1913 Zapatista pronouncements had taken on new tone and meaning, with the craftsmanship of urban intellectuals ever more apparent. For a brief moment in 1913 Zapata even experimented with the slogan "Land

and Liberty," which he borrowed from the PLM. More lasting was
the new vocabulary of Zapatista manifestos—bourgeoisie, proletariat, feudalism and capitalism—and the articulations of class conflict
and the workings of economic imperialism that came with such a
lexicon. At the same time many of the goals of the Constitution of
1857—freedom of the press, democracy, the proper administration
of justice—were now rejected as meaningless for campesinos who
had more fundamental problems to confront. In fact, most of the
urban intellectuals disparaged the Constitution of 1857.[37]

Rhetorically, in other words, Zapata's constituency had gone
from being the suffering campesinos of concrete, discrete villages to
a faceless, downtrodden national proletariat. It is doubtful, however,
that Zapata and his followers recognized themselves in this new
portrait. Zapata's reputed attitude toward the creeds of anarchism
and communism with which his intellectuals toyed ranged from the
belief that they were simply too ambitious, to the threat that he
would shoot anyone who tried to take the product of *his* labor to
share it with others. From all appearances he and the other villagers
continued to honor the Constitution of 1857, and if it contradicted
their goal of land reform, they could address that problem with some
kind of amendment. They were not being radicalized by the new
rhetoric; rather, it was another layer of discourse that their complex
movement could support, but which was hardly reflective of its
core.[38]

In sum, the fundamental goals and allegiances of Zapata and his
followers probably remained the same as they had always been.
Given that assumption, it also seems fair to assume that if this
speech were delivered to a meeting of Zapatistas, they too would
have waved their guns threateningly in the air, recalling the day
they held the flag overhead as they signed the Plan of Ayala. The
preening radicalism of Díaz Soto y Gama was quite different from
the radicalism—if one can call it that—of the peasants of Morelos.
Though in shaping Zapata's demands for the consumption of the
nation such intellectuals as Díaz Soto y Gama were bound to distort
them to some extent, the gap between what the Zapatistas were and

how they were represented was widened by the proclivities and eccentricities of the urbanites. Even when the ideas he communicated were of vital importance to his movement, the way that Díaz Soto y Gama presented himself was more upsetting to delegates of both Carranza and Villa than it needed to be. In fact, many of his fellow Convention delegates would eventually vote to have him examined by a doctor to determine whether he was insane or just a habitual drunk. Díaz Soto y Gama himself admitted, later in life, that he had been too provocative.[39]

Opportunity, however, continued to exist even after Díaz Soto y Gama's flag speech, for with the arrival of the Zapatistas, the jockeying for power began in earnest. Keeping in touch with Paulino Martínez, and receiving a visit from intrepid traveller Gildardo Magaña as well, Zapata soon learned that the Convention had voted to accept the principles of articles 4, 6, 7, 8, 9, and 12 of the Plan of Ayala and to ask that Carranza resign. In the process there was conflict over whether the informal Zapatista commission could vote, and more than one shouting match between Díaz Soto y Gama and Alvaro Obregón, the ambitious Carrancista general from Sonora who was among those testing the political waters. When the Zapatistas blocked the candidacy of the popular Villarreal, the Convention made Eulalio Gutiérrez its provisional president, on November first, for a period of twenty days. Meanwhile, the crafty Carranza maneuvered, threatened, and imposed conditions. Uneasy in Mexico City where Blanco's suspect troops surrounded him, he finally used the excuse of a sight-seeing trip to the pyramids of Teotihuacán to flee east toward Veracruz with a small following. Carranza would permit no bloodless coup—it was now only a question of which of his men would stick with the Convention and which with him. When Villa began to descend menacingly toward Aguascalientes with six thousand men in early November, it was time for choices, and in the end Carranza maintained a crucial part of his support, including such vacillators as Villarreal and Obregón.[40]

Even without the aggressive behavior on the part of Zapata's commissioners there were many obstacles to forging a broad alliance within the Convention. Because the Villistas shared Palafox's assumption that they would win a war against the Constitutionalists, they too made poor diplomats, and their role in estranging the Carrancistas was probably more important than was that of the Zapatistas. Palafox was certainly not alone in believing that the revolution—and with it power—could be won, and in feeling that power won was better than power negotiated and shared. Furthermore, as a group the leaders of Carrancismo were quite different from their Zapatista counterparts. Most came from the North, where social and economic conditions did not lead them to place a clear priority on land reform, but rather to see it as one of a number of political and social issues that needed to be addressed. Many were not driven to address these issues by a sense of outraged justice, but because they represented obstacles to progress and development— the preeminent goals in this more mobile, more urban, more commercial part of Mexico that bordered on that wonderland of progress, the United States. Many held private property to be sacred—certainly an obstacle to thoroughgoing land reform. Many hated the Catholicism that the Zapatistas held dear. Many hoped to create a more efficient and centralized state that would inevitably intrude on the village liberties for which Zapata was fighting. And many held racist notions about the brown-skinned villagers from the South who followed Zapata.[41]

Still the mere fact that an alliance with Villa was evolving proved that some headway could be made with northerners: there was nothing in this fluid situation that predetermined the factional split exactly as it happened. As we have seen, many prominent Constitutionalists supported land reform. We have also seen that Zapatismo was neither fundamentally anticapitalist nor antiprogress. Finally, a perfect ideological match was never a prerequisite for an alliance in the Mexican Revolution. Rather, a "logic of the revolution" brought many practical revolutionaries—and counterrevolutionaries—together in response to particular circumstances, and Zapata was not above such liaisons.[42]

By the middle of November battle was joined between fifty-five to seventy thousand Carrancistas and perhaps as many as ninety thousand troops loyal to the Convention—including about twenty-five thousand Zapatistas. Zapata again set his sights on the capital, which Carranza now decided he could not hold. While Obregón withdrew his forces at Carranza's orders and the still uncertain Blanco wavered, the Zapatistas occupied San Angel on the twenty-third, and the next day advanced north as far as Mixcoac. On the night of the twenty-fourth the forces of Antonio Barona arrived at the National Palace at the city's center.[43]

After years of accounts of the barbarous hordes that followed Mexico's Attila, the alarm was great in Mexico City when the Zapatistas finally made their visit. But Zapata's efforts to impress on his forces the need for discipline as they approached the capital paid off. All over the city people were soon commenting about how much better behaved the Zapatistas were than their Carrancista counterparts—rather than simply taking food, they politely begged it. The Zapatistas had much to learn. They became acquainted with the Mexican institution known as Sanborn's, a restaurant where they paid their tabs, at least at first. Less happily, they were introduced to a fire engine in action, which they attacked in the assumption that it was a machine of war. For Zapata, of course, the experience was not so novel. Knowing what he knew of Mexico City, when he came up late on the twenty-sixth he lay low at a hotel near the San Lázaro train station, a place from which he could make a quick escape. He answered the press in monosyllables and avoided the grand reception planned for him at the National Palace, where his brother Eufemio and his troops had occupied the poorest, most isolated rooms. Attending quickly to his business, on the twenty-ninth Zapata returned to Morelos.[44]

Meanwhile, Pancho Villa was travelling south, and in early December he sent Serratos and Roque González Garza to arrange a meeting with a still-cautious Zapata. On Friday, December 4, the revolution's two most celebrated caudillos finally came face to face on Zapata's turf at Xochimilco. Wearing a black jacket and trousers, a light blue silk tie, and a lavender shirt, Zapata arrived first. At about noon Villa trotted into town on horseback, and was greeted with a speech by Montaño before being led to Zapata. Taller and heavier than his counterpart from the south, Villa came in khaki, as the general who intended to win the revolution.[45]

While music played in the corridor Zapata and Villa sat down to talk at a lunch table in a schoolhouse on the outskirts of town. With Zapata were Eufemio, his sister María de Jesús, and his oldest son, Nicolás, now eight, who slept throughout the meeting. For about half an hour the conversation was labored—"like two country sweethearts," someone wrote—as Zapata scrutinized Villa, perhaps searching for a clue to his future. Then Villa mentioned Carranza, and the hatred that they held in common for the First Chief of Constitutionalism got the conversation rolling. "That Carranza," pronounced Zapata, "is riffraff." Palafox and Serratos egged them on. Zapata soon showed that he had kept up on Villa's campaigns, and they discussed military matters as well as the problem—about which Zapata was more optimistic than Villa—of having to trust the educated to govern. Then they came to the subject of land reform. So far Villa had done most of the talking, but now Zapata made a short speech: "They [the people] have a great deal of love for the land. They still don't believe it when you tell them: 'This land is yours.' They think it's a dream."

As they shared their expectations for their new relationship, Zapata and Villa seemed to grow closer. They spoke of hat styles—of Zapata's sombrero and Villa's pith helmet—and then about Pascual Orozco: "as soon as I killed his father," Zapata bragged, "I called to him too, to do the same thing." At Zapata's insistence they celebrated their union with a glass of cognac, the teetotaller Villa choking on the toast. At about two o'clock Zapata, Villa, and Palafox retired to another room to speak privately, which they did for over an hour. There they agreed on a formal military alliance in which Villa would supply Zapata with armaments. Villa accepted the agrarian contents of the Plan of Ayala, but specifically rejected its commentary on Madero, to whom he had always remained loyal. Finally, they pledged that when the fighting was over they would elevate a civilian to the presidency. Then they finished their meeting with a small banquet. A handful of speeches were made—Villa spoke, Zapata did not—and they embraced to seal their pact.[46]

On December 6, riding side by side, the two men made their official entry into Mexico City at the head of about fifty thousand troops. Everywhere Zapata went now the crowds rejoiced. It was impossible to tell anymore whether they meant it, and especially here it was hard to believe in the enthusiasm of those who lined the streets, hung from the windows, and colored the air with confetti and streamers. Zapata was already schooled in partial, ambiguous victories, and this one, celebrated in a city he hated, with the weight of national politics upon him and civil war again underway, was the most partial and ambiguous of them all. When they arrived at the National Palace they posed for photographs: Villa sitting in the president's chair, overwhelmed by a broad, irrepressible grin; Zapata beside him, pensive, his sombrero on his knee; behind them a pyramid of expectant faces. Displaying what had by now apparently become a deep-seated fear that corruption automatically came with national politics, Zapata refused to take his turn in the seat of power. Some say he suggested it be burned, "to put an end to ambitions."[47]

Finally, there was yet another banquet. Flanking Eulalio Gutiérrez, whose twenty-day presidency had been extended, Zapata and Villa sat at a long table set with china and loaded with food, their hangers-on standing in rows behind them. Still animated, Villa ate with abandon, as if he could actually enjoy the food in such a setting, and as he ate he talked excitedly with Gutiérrez. Both seemed oblivious to the movie camera that recorded the proceedings. Zapata, however, was not. Slumped uncomfortably over his plate, and displaying little interest in the food, he rubbed his nose nervously when he realized the camera was on him. He then cocked his head toward Gutiérrez and Villa, as if suddenly intent on their words, or as if he hoped to be included in their conversation. As the camera swung past him, he jerked back abruptly in his seat, left alone again to think. In those remarkable days he certainly had a lot on his mind. Whatever he saw in Villa's eyes when they met at Xochimilco, he must have realized that he and Villa were far too different ever to be true companions. Could he trust him? Perhaps Zapata had not yet decided about that, but he had made his choice nevertheless. As it turned out, it would not much matter if the two were personally compatible or not, for after Zapata left Mexico City on the ninth to oversee the battle for Puebla, he would spend very little time with Pancho Villa.[48]

6 A Political Whirlwind

NEVER BEFORE HAD ZAPATA FACED AS COMPLICATED a situation as that which began to develop in the summer of 1914. He was now charged with governing his region, with participating in a national regime, and with prosecuting a civil war. Antenor Sala, in one of his many letters to Zapata in the fall, called it a "political whirlwind," and expressed his surprise that a man like Zapata should allow himself to become swept up in it at all. But Zapata had little choice. Though he had always insisted that he was no politician, revolution was a profoundly political matter, and his rebellion had brought him power whether he wanted it or not.[1]

Throughout the fall of 1914 Zapata sought recruits. He sent a propaganda expedition to Zacatecas, and signed up allies as far south as the Isthmus of Tehuantepec. More importantly, he continued to seek the help of federal soldiers even after Huerta fell. In early August he announced a general amnesty that gave even federal officers the chance to enter revolutionary ranks, as long as they were not guilty of any specific crimes. Now in the position of having to settle their individual fates as best they could, and unable to turn to Carranza, who was rigid in his rejection of ex-federals, such one-time Huertistas as Benjamín Argumedo, José Trinidad Ruiz, Higinio Aguilar, and Juan Andrew Almazán soon tried to take advantage of Zapata's flexibility on this issue. These men had done more than just fight for Huerta. Aguilar, Ruiz, and Almazán had left Zapata to do so, betraying the Plan of Ayala they had pledged to uphold. Almazán had gone so far as to tell the journalists of the capital that Zapata was a bandit. Argumedo, meanwhile, had joined Huerta with Orozco. But they had serviceable artillery pieces, which were still rare among the Zapatistas, and trained troops—"civilized men" in the words of one veteran. Zapata needed the firepower they could provide for the next stage of the revolution, and in the military sphere, at least, he was willing to be practical about his liaisons.[2]

Thus in mid-September, when Argumedo and Aguilar wrote to praise the Plan of Ayala and to ask that Zapata join them in attacking the Yankees at Veracruz, Zapata managed to pardon their betrayal. He responded that they should sign the Plan of Ayala and follow his orders, and asked them to fight in Puebla and to destroy communications between Veracruz and Oaxaca. In the meantime, Almazán had written Zapata a long letter of explanation and flattery, promising that he could round up four thousand men in the Iguala, Guerrero, area within two months if Zapata would forgive him as he had forgiven others. Soon all of these men were indeed operating at Zapata's orders in Puebla. When Villa, who also had personal scores to settle with them, asked in December that Aguilar, Almazán, and Argumedo be turned over to him for punishment, Zapata refused.[3]

The immediate task for which Zapata hoped to use the ex-federals was the taking of the city of Puebla itself, one of Mexico's largest and most important population centers. Though this job had only been officially allotted to him in a discussion with Villa on December 7, by the middle of November the Zapatistas, led by Eufemio Zapata, had already had important successes against the Constitutionalists at Izúcar de Matamoros and Atlixco. Now in mid-December, at the head of perhaps twenty thousand men, Zapata won one of his biggest victories of all: after four days of hard fighting in the area, his forces occupied Puebla early in the morning of December 16. To Villa, who had gone north, Zapata wrote that he had driven the Carrancistas completely from the state, taking two thousand prisoners in the process, as well as a considerable cache of arms and ammunition.[4] With the fall of Puebla the Constitutionalists were on the ropes. Villa's forces held much of the north, and it seemed as if there was nothing to stop the Conventionists from moving east to attack Carranza at his refuge in the city of Veracruz, which United States troops had turned over to him in November.[5]

There were, however, some problems—significant enough problems, in fact, that the victory at Puebla would prove to be the military high-water mark of the Conventionist effort. Villa and Zapata had decided that Veracruz and the rest of the south were to be Zapata's sphere of action, but Zapata was not prepared to act. Theoretically, such an operation would not have been impossible for him. True, the Zapatistas preferred to fight on their home turf, but they had undertaken short campaigns before—to Chilpancingo, for instance—and Veracruz was less than a hundred and fifty miles from Puebla. Moreover, the ex-federals were used to travelling, and Zapata had other allies in Puebla and Tlaxcala and in the state of Veracruz itself.[6]

More important than Zapatismo's geographical predilections was the fact that the seeds of conflict within the Convention had already begun to sprout. During the combat at Puebla, Zapata had been hindered by a lack of arms—and especially of artillery pieces—that Villa had promised to deliver. In part this seems to have been due to the plotting of certain Convention officials, who apparently refused Zapata the munitions he needed in compliance with an evolving plan of President Eulalio Gutiérrez's to limit the power of both Zapata and Villa. Zapata could not have known exactly what was happening, but he knew that there was trouble. On December 16 he informed Villa that their enemies were intriguing to divide them, and proclaimed that only men whose behavior did not provoke mistrust should occupy public posts. He may even have begun to suspect the motives of Villa himself.[7]

Meanwhile, old scores were being settled in Mexico City. On December 13 Villa's bloodiest general, Rodolfo Fierro, gunned down Paulino Martínez. While no one was willing to pin the blame di-

6. *At the center of the whirlwind. (Archivo General de la Nación, Mexico City, Archivo Fotográfico, Díaz, Delgado y García)*

rectly on Villa, it may well be that he ordered the execution in revenge for a newspaper attack Martínez had once made on Madero, whose memory Villa continued to revere. Though this was perhaps the episode that most disgusted Zapata, it was far from the only brutality of the day. In fact, once accustomed to life in the city, even his own forces did not prove as meek as they appeared when they first entered the capital in late November. During December both accusations and gunshots flew with great frequency: perhaps as many as a hundred and fifty people of sundry affiliations were killed for alleged political crimes by the middle of the month. Palafox was rumored to have threatened the life of Lucio Blanco, and one of his summer wishes was fulfilled when the Zapatistas executed Convention delegate Guillermo García Aragón. Juan Banderas, a Sinaloan who had recently joined Zapata after escaping from a Mexico City jail, ran amuck in the Hotel Cosmos, killing Villista general Rafael Garay. Though Villa tried late in the month to dismiss Zapata's fear of intrigue, their relationship was strained. At the end of December an American diplomat even predicted that Villa would soon break with Zapata. When the break came, he added, "Señor Palafox will be one of the first Villa will attend to." Though the prediction was incorrect, it was evident that personal conflict had already reached the highest levels of the alliance. Zapata had reason to be distrustful and disillusioned; he had no reason to believe that he would get the support necessary for a move into Veracruz.[8]

Perhaps an equally important obstacle to Zapata's war effort was that there were already signs of the decay that would now beset his movement despite its recent successes. Some Zapatistas were undoubtedly less than willing warriors because they were frustrated that the fighting had continued at all. Others simply preferred the attractions of Mexico City to life in camp, for though Zapata himself had no desire to live high on the hog in the capital—he continued to fear that the city and its politics would contaminate him—this was not true of all of his chieftains. Already during the battle for Puebla he had difficulty getting some jefes to leave the capital for the front.[9]

Though it did not bubble to the surface until the end of the month, some Zapatistas were also demoralized by the presence of so many ex-federal soldiers in their ranks. Naturally the exclusivist Palafox was worried: in one letter to Zapata he pointed out that Villa and the Convention government were opposed to the employment. of these soldiers and suggested that Zapata follow suit. For Zapata, however, this was a military decision, not a political one, and so Palafox's opinion counted little. "On the issue of the ex-federals," he responded, "there's a certain bad faith on the part of our enemies." But Palafox was not the only one who complained. In late December Francisco Mendoza wrote from Puebla that Aguilar and Argumedo refused to fight. Though he still trusted them enough at that time to suggest that they be left to garrison the city of Puebla while he went out to do the fighting, he would later express the feelings of more than one jefe when he informed Zapata that he would not admit old enemies into his own ranks.[10]

Zapata reacted to these problems by returning to Morelos for Christmas, leaving Palafox to try to impose some order in Mexico City from the headquarters he ran there. This is not to say that Zapata was necessarily shirking his duties or rejecting national power. The prevailing conditions made any immediate move into Veracruz too risky, and he had never been one to stay at the front indefinitely unless a major push was on. In the political sphere there is little indication that he believed that there was much for him to do in the capital. Apparently still largely loyal to the notion of the state embodied in the Constitution of 1857, his central demands were that land reform become state policy, and that power be decentralized enough that municipalities might wield a greater share. The task of enacting these adjustments to the present constitution he would largely leave to his intellectual advisors, and this was as it should be: members of a formal government, it was their job to represent him and his generals, with whom they would naturally confer.

Furthermore, Zapata was not one to lose his soul in the fight. His fame now reached across the nation and beyond. Poems had been written for and about him, and in their rush to flatter him people sometimes compared him with Independence caudillo Vicente Guerrero. There were so many requests for photographs of him that he ran out—even the Minister of Japan was said to have two such pictures on his desk. In August cinematographer José Alencaster filmed his entrance into Cuernavaca, and Zapata's compadre Antonio Barona, who knew him well enough that he might have thought such a fuss ridiculous, concluded that the event "is of much interest for history." Zapata had even become accustomed to riding in automobiles. But when he was offered one as a gift he was quick to turn it down. "I like my horse better," he said, "I feel more secure on it, and I've got to tell you that the horse is the salvation of a man."[11]

Morelos also represented salvation for Zapata. Back home, he knew, there was something he wanted from all this for himself. As he came down from the mountains into his home state, then made his way south through the dry hills of winter and the glowing green of the irrigated valleys, he could see and smell and hear again what that was. Here was the peaceful life he had sought to recapture in the summer of 1911 when he married Josefa Espejo. As he had then, he made it clear now that he wanted nothing more than to return to private life, that he would accept no official public post. But he was doing more than returning to private life, he was returning to a daily life that he had revolutionized. The haciendas and jefes políticos of the old regime were gone, of course, but so was the oppression of the cleansing years of warfare. The years of hiding in the mountains with no food or water. The years of wandering at night due to insomnia and fear, of sneaking out of his own camp to sleep so no one could find him defenseless, of sleeping "on an oilcloth poncho and a horse blanket, under a tree," with a saddle for a pillow. Of sleeping alone, because bringing a woman at times like these was too much trouble and danger. The warfare had finally destroyed this kind of daily life, at least for now. True, hacienda and village, city and countryside, had been looted and burned, but in the destruction lay the chance to start again. That was what it was time for now.[12]

His destination was Tlaltizapán, in the heat of southern Mo-

relos, near Jojutla. A town of almost two thousand people, Tlaltizapán was famous for its soursop and bananas. It overflowed with
bougainvillea, and birds chattered loudly in the tall trees of its shady
square. Here Zapata had established his headquarters, in an old mill
on the tracks of the Interoceanic railroad, because from the towers
of the church one could see the enemy approaching—across the
plain to the northwest or coming down the valley of the Yautepec
river—and get into the nearby mountains on time. For that reason
the Plateados had settled here too, and because the rich life of low-
land Morelos ran in their blood as it did in Zapata's.

A row of small rooms, Zapata's office and living quarters faced
the street, with a large patio behind them. He had a dining room
here, and a bedroom equipped with a single bed and a phonograph.
In the rooms flanking the patio the soldiers of his escort were
housed, as well as his personal secretaries, and a man nicknamed
"Polilla"—odd job—who attended to various errands. From here Zapata undertook to run the revolution in its local and regional manifestations, greeting the stream of friends, politicians, warriors, and
spies who came to his door with their reports and petitions.[13]

Though he often said that anyone could attest that he had better
horses, saddles, and clothing before the revolution than during it, in
Morelos Zapata's prerogatives and opportunities as leader of a temporarily triumphant revolution were many. He was virtually wor-
shipped by most of the populace, and there was nothing he enjoyed
doing that was not readily available to him now. He was constantly
receiving presents—a sombrero, a machete, a good serape—and invitations to various festivities, many in his honor. In August 1915,
for instance, Tlaltizapán itself threw him a birthday fiesta in the
school building, complete with songs, speeches, poems, and skits;
and he was often asked, by one village or another, to preside over the
anniversary of the birth of the caudillo Morelos or over Independence celebrations, or to come help celebrate a saint's day or the
completion of a new church. Then there were the cock-fights. Having already placed his bet, one general asked the loan of three of
Zapata's own roosters so that he might win it, and suggested that

Zapata make a "little escape" to participate in the event. Zapata also took an active part in various jaripeos, and even when he could not attend he sometimes helped pay for them. Another of his favorite forms of entertainment was music. While in the capital he purchased a piano, a trombone, and several clarinets, presumably for the band that served his headquarters, which he often loaned out for special occasions. When Anenecuilco wanted to form its own such group, "to enhance our village," he helped with that as well.[14]

In returning to Morelos, in other words, Zapata could again enjoy the fireworks and bullfights, the drinking and smoking and singing, the card games, the corridos, the reading aloud of newspapers, and the reciting of heroic poems that characterized his life in the country during peacetime. By now, too, that life included several children: Nicolás, already eight; María Elena, five years old; and two newborn girls, María Luisa and Ana María, one of whom had nearly died in July. None of them were legitimate—the two children he had with Josefa Espejo had not survived the hard years of wartime—but their number is not surprising, for Zapata always had many women. Up in the mountains near Huautla, for example, at a place called Quilamula where he had often hidden in years past, lived Gregoria Zúñiga, the nineteen year old mother of María Luisa. "Don Eufemio and Emiliano Zapata," she recalled, "became curious and showed up and said, this old man has nice girls, they said, my mother there waiting on them . . . and us in the kitchen making tortillas and grinding. That's how we began, later he took me away." That was in 1912, in Tepalcingo. Since then she had spent most of her time helping raise Nicolás and grinding corn for tortillas for the visitors that came to see Zapata when he was in Quilamula. Zapata called her "china," and was now at pains to establish telephone and telegraph service between Tlaltizapán and Quilamula in part because of her presence there. Though her beauty was renowned, however, he did not want her with him in Tlaltizapán, where she might have interfered with other such relationships.[15]

But Zapata did not come home merely for his own pleasure—his responsibilities also beckoned him. In the words of balladeer Marciano Silva, who travelled among the Zapatistas after 1912, Huerta's generals had left:

> Our pueblos only plains
> White ashes, pictures of horror
> Sad deserts, isolated places
> Where only sorrow stirs;
> Ill-fated remains we venerate
> Like relics of our love,
> Where we were born, where we were raised
> And happily saw the sunlight.

As a result of this destruction, Zapata's headquarters in Tlaltiza-pán were flooded with solicitations of favors, loans, intercession, mediation, and justice from an exhausted and desperate people. Many of these requests came from friends and family, but many too were of impersonal tone, echoing the petitions that the campesinos of Anenecuilco had addressed to Porfirian authorities prior to the revolution. In either case they placed powerful demands on Zapata, for they were what the fighting had all been about. Addressing the small, individual needs of the villagers around him, Zapata took babies to the baptismal font and supplied clothing, money, and food—at least in a piecemeal, personal fashion—to the aged and the widowed. But he did not merely wait for these requests to come to him. To conduct this kind of business he moved from town to town—from Yautepec to Cuautla to Cuernavaca and Jojutla—and he tried to make sure that he had enough money on hand that he would not have to turn anyone down.[16]

It was also time, at last, to try to fully implement agrarian reform. In those parts of Morelos, Puebla, Mexico, Guerrero, and the Federal District where land was an issue, land tenure had been changing hands informally from almost the moment that Zapata first took up arms, as villages simply occupied hacienda holdings. There had also been more formal revindication—Zapata signed a land reform decree at Ixcamilpa, Puebla, in 1912 for instance—but while warfare raged in the region such formalities were generally difficult or pointless, because there was little guarantee that federal troops would not soon return to any given area. Furthermore, the money the hacendados paid for protection was crucial to the war effort. As Zapata gained military control of his region in 1914, however, it was increasingly possible to apply the dictates of the Plan of Ayala. In February 1914 he ordered that the land of the enemies of the revolution be divided. Presumably this was to be done by Zapata's military leaders, who were first to return those lands that the campesinos already had title to, and then divide up the rest in equal parts, assigning each part by lot. They were then to send a map reflecting their work to headquarters for inspection. If it was determined that the arrangements were fair, title would be given, later to be legalized by a government emanating from the revolution. Once all this was done, village landholdings were to be inalienable as a means of protecting them from future hacendado greed.[17]

As late as June 1914, however, many jefes were collecting protection money from haciendas, but in July Zapata began to demand that only his headquarters was to collect such funds, obviously as a prelude to further efforts to organize land reform. Then when talks with the Carrancistas failed in August, there was no longer any reason to delay radical measures. On September 8 Zapata again ordered that his officers move to nationalize the property of the enemies of the revolution. The decree in which he did this served as a virtual declaration of war against the conservative Carranza, as well as a means of firming up Zapata's support at the village level by demonstrating that he meant to keep his promises. The fullest expression yet of Zapatista intent with regard to agrarian reform, this document contained a number of new considerations. It outlined the respective roles of military and civilian authorities in the process of confiscating and redistributing land. It allowed for the confiscation of urban properties, which would be used to create banking institutions to support agriculture and to aid the widows and orphans of the revolution. And it stated directly that each community could chose whether to hold its lands communally or individually. Again the authorities involved were to make a full report to headquarters, including a description of the properties confiscated.[18]

The Plan of Ayala clearly meant to do nothing more than reestablish a balance between hacienda and village, but things had changed dramatically since that plan had been written. Three more years of brutal fighting had won total control in the state of Morelos for Zapata, and he now set his sights on a more thorough overhaul of landholding patterns than he had originally envisioned. In one letter he bragged that all the haciendas in Morelos had been confiscated, and added that this should be done everywhere in Mexico because "all of the hacendados have aided past governments."[19]

It seems unlikely, though, that this represented a fundamental radicalization of Zapata's thought on the agrarian question. The confiscation of the property of the enemies of the revolution was, after all, already provided for in article eight of the Plan of Ayala— the only difference now was that three more years of fighting had made it clearer how many enemies there were. Moreover, Zapata never actually gave a blanket order that all large property holdings were to be confiscated. There was at least some effort to appear fair in judging even the wealthy who might merely have been neutral in the revolutionary struggle. True, it only took a charge brought by a local colonel or Zapatista official or group of villagers—those people presumed to be in the best position to know who the enemies of the cause in a given locality were—for land and other property to be confiscated immediately. But it was also recognized that such charges could be used by the unscrupulous to settle personal scores or satisfy their own greed, and so there was a process of appeal to various judicial authorities, to Zapatista headquarters, or to Zapata himself. Eventually commissions were established to deal with the issue.[20]

Finally, it is worth noting that when it came to justice for the enemies of the revolution—as with most other things—there was often an element of personalism involved. Zapata's various jefes were sometimes not interested in the procedures dreamed up at headquarters. In September 1914, for example, the local perspective of de la O clashed with Palafox's broader view of such a case; and in November Pacheco judged and shot three alleged caciques in Huitzilac in his own, summary fashion. In fact, even Zapata bent the rules in specific instances. The most interesting case in this regard was that of Ignacio de la Torre y Mier, the former hacendado of Tenextepango who had employed Zapata before the revolution and then had the bad luck to fall into Zapatista hands in 1914. Many Zapatistas clamored for the exemplary punishment of the planter, and Zapata himself insisted that he meant to try de la Torre for his crimes against the revolution. However, no trial ever took place. Instead, after spending a month in jail in Mexico City, de la Torre was brought down to Cuautla, where Zapata repaid him for past favors by giving him the city for his prison. There the planter led a quiet life until 1916, and then managed to escape—some say with Zapata's help.[21]

Of course, dispensing justice was not the only challenge Zapata faced in trying to implement his land reform program. In general it seems that the response to the decree of September 8 was quick and enthusiastic: already by the nineteenth of that month Eufemio Zapata could report that land reform was well underway in his zone around Cuautla. But as the villagers rushed to claim their share of the land, it became obvious that neither oral tradition nor the maps and titles that now came out from their hiding places provided the kind of precise data that was needed. Indeed, based on these sources the claims of one village often overlapped those of another, and dangerous disputes between armed villagers were often the result. There were also problems with jefes who tried to keep haciendas for themselves, or to continue to collect payments from hacendados in their zones. Some of his subordinates, Zapata knew, could simply not be trusted.[22]

In a May 1915 letter to Zapata Fortino Ayaquica expressed what many of his fellow Zapatistas had come to recognize months before. "I beg you . . . ," he wrote, "to send an agrarian commission for this work [of distributing land], because you well know we cannot do more than what is within our capacity, because if we set about recognizing what the maps or documents from viceregal times claim for each village, we would have to eliminate various modern pueblos that now exist." To Zapata, as to Ayaquica, it seemed apparent that the campesinos needed help to carry out their land reform. To begin to deal with the difficulties they faced he made a bid to get the kind of attention from Mexico City, finally, that he had sought from the Madero government in 1911. In fact, he now demanded more than he had then, for he had learned not to trust anyone but a confirmed Zapatista to manage the land reform process. Zapata now saw to it that on January 1, 1915, Manuel Palafox was sworn in as head of a new Ministry of Agriculture. Naturally Palafox had grandiose goals, including, for Morelos alone, a Rural Loan Bank, a regional school of Agriculture, and a factory to make agricultural implements. And he intended to waste no time. When asked after his appointment if he would now begin to study the agrarian situation, Palafox replied: "I've already amply studied the agrarian question. I will dedicate myself to carrying it into the field of practice."[23]

Palafox quickly made plans to send agrarian commissions— composed of engineers and engineering students from the National School of Agriculture—to Morelos, Puebla, Guerrero, Mexico, Hidalgo, and the Federal District. These commissions were to survey the terrain in order to help make permanent decisions on land tenure, and in the process, of course, resolve intervillage conflicts. In late January, however, when they began to fan out into the countryside of Morelos to take up residence in their respective district seats, it became clear that they would provide no magic solution. Despite their skills and their youthful enthusiasm, they remained untrustworthy representatives of the city in the eyes of the campesinos, and land distribution was a touchy subject. When the locals got drunk, testified one commissioner, "there was no lack of machos who wanted to test those still-catrines—though dressed in country clothing—who were our companions." Many of the engineers gained some respect as time passed, and apparently none of them were killed in this encounter of urban and rural worlds. Still, friendships between them and the villagers were rare, and when it came to ancient intervillage feuds they simply lacked the authority to make their decisions stick. Like Barrios in the case of Pacheco and de la O, in fact, they often just provided another pole in a given controversy. Some locals charged that the engineers slowed things down when they came to make their measurements, others complained that they were self-serving, and at least one village hoped to avoid feeding them while they visited. At Coatetelco, Morelos the campesinos opened fire on a group of surveyors. Meanwhile, intervillage disputes continued. In May 1915, for instance, the people of Xoxocotla, Morelos, refused to attend meetings called by their commission, and occupied the lands of their neighbors by force of arms.[24]

Many of these quarrels were deep enough, in other words, that only Zapata, as ultimate mediator, could hope to settle them. Furthermore, his input was needed in the many cases that the commissions could not get to, for there were many more solicitations of land than the engineers could immediately address. Finally, only a local like Zapata could fully appreciate and honor the feelings of the villagers on certain issues. In participating in the division of lands between Yautepec and Anenecuilco Zapata instructed, "The pueblos say that this stone wall is their boundary. . . . You engineers are often quite fond of your straight lines, but this stone wall is going to be the boundary, even if you have to work six months measuring all its ins and outs."[25]

Naturally the job of reviving the economy in a region emerging from years of warfare entailed more than simply distributing land. As the fighting wound down villages like Milpa Alta, D.F.; Huehuetlán, Puebla; Miacatlán, Morelos; and Tixtla, Guerrero, were ready to stop making sacrifices. They were running out of food, they claimed, and needed help from the Zapatistas instead of their repeated exactions. At least at Miacatlán the claim was apparently true, for the local guerrilleros reported in September 1914 that the villagers were starving.[26]

To lighten the burden on the villages Zapata continued to stress that his forces were not to demand aid, but merely to take what was offered. He also reiterated past instructions on the slaughter of cattle, which were now quite scarce. And by the fall of 1914 he was trying to run those sugar mills in Morelos that remained relatively functional for the benefit of the troops and the needy, appointing various of his generals to oversee them. The mills at Zacatepec, Santa Inés, Miacatlán, and San José were soon at work, and Atlaco-mulco, Chiconcuac, Hospital, Temixco, Atlihuayán, Cuautlixco, and others would eventually follow. The remains of the great estates now served as centers of industry for Morelos, producing not only sugar but alcohol and in some cases ammunition as well, and serv-ing at times as marketplaces for other goods. Zapata's role in all this was considerable. He—or at least his headquarters—offered advice ranging from the price of alcohol to how to obtain more mules, and he labored to sell his vision of a rebuilt, revolutionary Morelos. In starting up hacienda Hospital again, for instance, Zapata spent days around Cuautla trying to convince people to grow sugar, arguing that this was a better way to emerge from poverty than taking up subsistence agriculture.[27]

Not everyone, however, was willing to cooperate. From Hospital, Emigdio Marmolejo complained that his laborers worked only spo-radically because they had their own land to plant, and because they found the hacienda's mules too unruly and its cane in poor condition for cutting. Moreover, few campesinos apparently trusted Zapata enough to grow sugar when, by planting foodstuffs, it seemed they could guarantee themselves a better year ahead. Finally, the mills suffered from war damage, from a lack of markets and capital, from competing military demands for scarce resources, and from the loss to the villages of much of the land and water upon which the haci-endas used to depend. The plantation complex had been destroyed, and it would take time to create something new in its place.[28]

In the further pursuit of economic justice and efficiency, Zapata set up commercial enterprises in towns like Cuautla to market the products of the plantations at low prices, and in general tried to make sure that taxes and business practices were fair. The Zapa-tistas worked to get the railroads, telegraph, and telephone services running full-strength again. They took over the mines around Huau-tla and, beneath Popocatepetl's towering cone, the San Rafael paper company, which generated revenue by supplying Mexico City with much of its paper. Using some of that paper themselves, they began several newspapers in Morelos and the capital.[29]

Yet another task in which Zapata was now involved was the rebuilding of communities. He encouraged irrigation works at Anenecuilco, where some citizens asked that he order municipal authorities to motivate the less industrious villagers to help, "to begin to bring water to this pueblo and see it alive and flowering." He assisted in the reestablishment of schools, at least in a piecemeal fashion. He even offered to support the reconstruction of the church at Tejalpa, Morelos, though to other petitioners he often pointed out that religious concerns were not his business.[30]

With regard to local government, already established policies continued. It had long been Zapatista practice to hold elections when a given plaza was taken, and direct elections of village officials continued into this period, at least in some places. On the state level, however, popular democracy was never achieved. In Morelos Zapatista officers came together to elect de la O provisional governor—though Zapata backed Pacheco—after Cuernavaca fell in August 1914. The following March, after periodic calls for another junta, the jefes gathered again and chose Lorenzo Vázquez to replace de la O. Though Zapata claimed immediately thereafter to be preparing for popular elections for governor, other more pressing issues evidently got in the way, for such elections were never held. This failure to hold a popular vote for governor probably mattered little, however, in terms of how Morelos was run, for neither de la O nor Vázquez got much power from their provisional positions. Soon after his selection, in fact, Vázquez protested that his fellow jefes suffered from the "erroneous belief that officials must be under the foot of any revolutionary that has no more authority than the power of his arms." Under the prevailing conditions of revolutionary ferment, only Zapata's prestige was worth much in terms of imposing order on the state level.[31]

Among the more pressing issues with which Zapata was concerned, of course, were events on the national stage. Even if he did hope to run from national politics when he returned to Morelos in December 1914, it could not have been done, for they constantly called to him, and they were often so intimately connected to local and regional pursuits that they could not simply be ignored. This is not to say that he always handled them well. In Mexico City the misbehavior of Zapatista forces continued, and Antonio Barona was a key player. Refusing to go to Puebla to fight, by the first part of January Barona was on a prodigious drunken spree that eventually came to include a shoot-out with the Inspector General of Police. In addition, charged Palafox, who was often the bearer of such bad tidings, he was not paying the salaries of his soldiers with the money he was given to do so.

In mid-January Zapata was forced to call Barona south for a talk. As we have seen, Zapata had a considerable temper, and he seems always to have hated and tried to avoid the kind of personal conflict that might bring that temper out—his absences during the trial of "One-Eyed" Morales and the visit of Villarreal, Cabrera, and Sarabia are cases in point. Surely Zapata knew that Barona, the man who had killed Felipe Neri, would not sit quietly and listen to his admonitions: if Zapata chose to punish Barona, there would be a confrontation. Furthermore, as Felipe Neri pointed out, Zapata's personalism ran strong when it came to the indiscretions of a compadre. He would much rather share a beer, a cigar, and a few commonplaces than sit down to discipline an old and loyal friend. Finally, since his own anger often boiled close to the surface, perhaps Zapata could understand Barona's behavior as a release of the kind of rage that made revolutionaries, and that he himself felt again whenever he set foot in the capital. At any rate, he operated with his characteristic prudence in the exercise of justice in this case. Instead of punishing Barona he accepted his explanation of the shoot-out— that he was "in immanent risk of being harmed"—and suggested to Palafox that he and Barona iron things out, and that Barona again be given the money for his troops. Apparently nothing was done to discourage such behavior in the future.[32]

As Zapata addressed the Barona incident, news of a governmental crisis not unconnected to it permeated the relative peacefulness of Tlaltizapán. As early as the end of December Palafox reported that President Gutiérrez had planned to flee the capital, and that Villa held him there as a virtual prisoner. Then in mid-January Gutiérrez again tried to run and succeeded. By the time Zapata heard of his flight, the man who still claimed the presidency and much of his government were well on their way to Gutiérrez's home turf around San Luis Potosí, with a furious Villa on their trail. As he left, Gutiérrez issued a manifesto blasting Villa and Zapata, and deposing them as heads of their respective armed forces. He accused Zapata of ordering the death of García Aragón and of intending to execute other officials. Along with Villa, the manifesto continued, he had used the power his army gave him to impede government operations, especially in the region that he controlled, where no reform or elections had taken place and Zapata ruled as a dictator. There was certainly a grain of truth to the charges. Jealous of the prerogatives they had become accustomed to earlier in the revolution, Zapata and Villa had not really allowed the Convention to govern. Now, with Gutiérrez's departure, its credibility was seriously undermined.[33]

Furthermore, the flight of Gutiérrez with a not inconsiderable number of troops only added to a military crisis that was brewing. Seizing the initiative that Zapata had not taken, on the last day of December Alvaro Obregón had begun to make his way west from Veracruz with a reorganized army, and around Puebla the situation began to deteriorate rapidly. Zapata may have gone to the front briefly at the beginning of January, but there was little he could do. Still undisciplined and in desperate need of ammunition and artillery pieces, his army was no match for the man who would soon prove the revolution's most successful general. After a full day of fighting, Puebla fell to Obregón on January 5.[34]

But Obregón did not stop there. Even before Gutiérrez departed, Palafox informed Zapata that he lacked sufficient forces to protect the capital, and Obregón was preparing to take advantage of the situation. On January 9 Zapata sent reinforcements toward both

Puebla and Mexico City, but cooperation from the Villistas and from his own men was still hard to come by, and he did not return to the front himself—perhaps a sign that he was now totally disillusioned with the war effort. On the twenty-eighth of January Obregón occupied the capital as the Zapatistas retreated in disarray. The Convention government set up quarters in Cuernavaca, while Villa demonstrated his lack of confidence in it by forming his own cabinet in Chihuahua on January 31.[35]

With the Convention in Morelos, national affairs were suddenly uncomfortably close to Zapata's Tlaltizapán doorstep, and young, educated Roque González Garza, Villa's personal representative to the Convention and the new executive officer of that government, did not hesitate to knock. Though he assumed his new position with more limited powers than those of Gutiérrez, he clearly intended to make his mark. On the second of February, with the injunction, "today more than ever we must consolidate our union," he asked Zapata to come to Cuernavaca to discuss with him the governing of both republic and state, as well as the prosecution of the military campaign. In a second communication of the same day he repeated the invitation, and rather condescendingly suggested that Zapata help Villa militarily by carefully selecting people to fight in the Federal District, Puebla, Mexico, Michoacán, and Guerrero. In fact, he had already recommended to Palafox that troops misbehaving in Cuernavaca be sent to the front in the Federal District.[36]

On the following day González Garza made his predicament clear when he again requested that Zapata come to Cuernavaca, "so that you will be the one who personally gives the orders in order that they be duly obeyed." Though he would obviously have preferred to avoid González Garza, Zapata now agreed to go to Cuernavaca on February 5. Together he and González Garza tried to solve one of the many problems that was undermining the new executive's authority with Zapata's men. Having captured Mexico City—at least temporarily—and created a national government, Zapata and his followers had increasingly come to expect that regular pay would replace aid from their village supporters. This was, after all, how mobile, professional forces like the Villistas were run, and by paying salaries the government could help alleviate the hard times that the fighting had occasioned. Given the bad faith of the Gutiérrez government, however, no mutually satisfactory system for making such payments had yet been established, and that was creating a great deal of misunderstanding. Now Zapata and González Garza decided on the assignment of paymasters and on the regular payment of salaries to Zapatista forces.[37]

Though they managed this accord, however, the two men were miles apart on other issues. Plagued by the blatant disobedience of his orders that negated the presidential powers he was supposed to hold, González Garza had reason to be frustrated. From his point of view the government was simply not functioning as a government should. But González Garza was a pushy and somewhat patronizing man, and there was already veiled anger in his letters to Zapata. His eagerness to interfere with the command of Zapatista troops as well as with the government of Morelos cannot have failed to offend Zapata, who had grown used to running things his own way. Moreover, Zapata had fought for goals he must have known González Garza did not completely share. He had fought so that the people of Morelos could govern themselves, not to enable this Coahuilan to descend on them in a fit of orderliness. Finally, having just suffered the charges of the outgoing Gutiérrez that he had, among other things, interfered too much with the workings of the Convention government, Zapata may well have found González Garza's repeated demands that he participate more actively in that government somewhat ironic.

For some time Zapata had been receiving the disconcerting news from Guerrero that the Carrancistas were making considerable conquests there of both territory and public opinion. In an attempt to firm up his support in this crucial state, of course, but also undoubtedly to put a little distance between himself and González Garza, he now decided to take his project for rebuilding local life on the road. Ignoring González Garza's generous offer to join him in such a trip, Zapata was in Iguala, breathing somewhat more freely, by February 8.[38]

Here as in Morelos local concerns kept Zapata busy. His presence occasioned a ripple of activity as villages swore their allegiance to the Plan of Ayala and drew up acts concerning the division of lands. One man who tried to see him at Iguala reported his inability to do so because of "the agglomeration of people who bring their business for your consideration." Here, too, intervillage conflicts festered. Claiming that circumstances in Guerrero required quick action—perhaps because the loyalties of the campesinos hung in the balance—Zapata sent word to Morelos that agrarian engineers should be rounded up for work in the state.[39]

Zapata also took steps to better organize his movement. In accord with ongoing efforts to professionalize his forces that had gained some momentum from contact with the more classic military structure of the Villistas, he now decreed a new provisional organization for both infantry and cavalry that regulated numbers for and relationships between the various tactical units—squadrons, companies, battalions, brigades—that were to compose his army. Two days later another decree exacted good behavior and cooperation from the jefes of Michoacán and Guerrero, as well as action on land reform and the election of local officials.[40]

Another concern was monetary. Though Zapata was no economist, it took no more than a little common sense and a brief glance at some of the competing brands of paper money—backed only by military power—that the revolution had engendered, to recognize that Mexico's monetary system was on shaky ground. As a result, he had come to believe that currency should have intrinsic value to protect the interests of the people that used it. With the important silver mines of Guerrero at hand he had the means to give it such value, so he now made efforts to expedite and regulate the working of the mines. The money question, however, was of *immediate* significance in this state, because the bills issued by the state bank inspired no confidence. González Garza had just sent currency to Guerrero to replace the money presently in circulation, but accord-

ing to Zapata the bills that had arrived, invalidated by the Convention government, were worse than those they were meant to replace,
"making me appear ridiculous in front of the people of Guerrero,
who have fixed their hopes on me as an intermediary to improve in
part their financial situation." While González Garza apologized for
a mix-up he blamed on the treasury, an angry Zapata rushed a commission back to Morelos to get the notes he wanted.[41]

As he came home from Guerrero in mid-February it was obvious
that Zapata would not be able to avoid dealing with González Garza,
and equally obvious that their personal relationship would be a
rocky one. But Zapata had plenty of help in keeping things stirred
up. Intellectual Santiago Orozco quickly reopened the controversy
about pay for the troops, and this conflict raged through February
and March as the Zapatistas insisted that they needed more money
than they had agreed to, and González Garza pleaded poverty. There
were also complaints about Zapatista chieftains interfering with
train traffic for their own ends—many of them coming from Zapata's own intellectuals, who hoped to rationalize the system. Zapata
ordered that this interference be stopped, but apparently with little
success.[42]

Not surprisingly, with the loss of Mexico City the deterioration
of Zapatista morale continued. Many chieftains blamed Palafox,
who had overseen the defense of the capital, for their defeat, and by
implication accused Zapata of giving his intellectuals too much
power. To Santiago Orozco Pacheco wrote that the way to retake
Mexico City was to form a circle and have everyone attack at once.
Calling Palafox's orders "preposterous," he added the hope that
Orozco might "revindicate the ridicule in which his [Palafox's] bad
tactics have left us." To Zapata Pacheco complained that "Palafox
treats everyone with vituperation" and blamed him for the lack of
pay for the forces on the front. If they were not fed, he threatened in
a second communication, they might commit acts "that disgrace
us."[43]

There was certainly plenty of disgrace as the Zapatistas fought
to retake the capital in February. "In the midst of battle," Pacheco

wrote of one harrowing incident, "General Banderas turned his cannons on General Cotero, occasioning the complete demoralization of my forces and allowing the enemy to triumph." Both Banderas and Cotero, of course, were Zapatistas. Then, in an apparently unrelated incident, Banderas got a close look at how dangerous such antics could be. Drunk again, his long-time enemy Antonio Barona led a late-night artillery attack on Banderas's headquarters at Tepepan in the Federal District. Banderas miraculously escaped with only a bullet-hole in his hat, but some of his men were not so lucky. González Garza suggested that Zapata's presence on the front might quiet things, and Zapata quickly promised to go. He also warned Banderas to stay in his own zone and had another talk with Barona.[44]

Despite the infighting and the continuing shortage of ammunition, Zapata's forces managed to keep up the pressure on Mexico City, destroying the pumps for its water supply at Xochimilco and cutting off shipments of food. On the twentieth Zapata again wrote Villa to ask for munitions, holding out the promise, rather hollow by now, of an eventual move on Veracruz. Then, perhaps with the hope of getting González Garza and his constant demands out of Morelos, he went north to oversee the battle for Mexico City. On the twenty-fifth he was in the Federal District, ordering all his troops there to attack the capital between five and six on the morning of February 27. Those who did not, the directive read, "will be subjected to a court-martial." A second effort at a mass attack on March 8 may have helped reinforce Obregón's growing conviction that the capital was a military liability. At any rate, he began to withdraw his troops, and on the eleventh the Zapatistas made their reentry.[45]

Back in Mexico City, the Convention—dominated now by Zapatista delegates whose numbers had swelled in Cuernavaca—again took up its highly charged discussions, full of controversy and backbiting between Villistas and Zapatistas. On March 23 González Garza asked the legislators for more time to submit his nominations for a new cabinet he was charged with forming, arguing that poor communications had made it impossible to consult Villa in the north. When his request was denied he sent a messenger to Zapata, then operating east of the city. Angry and drunk, according to González Garza's account of the incident, Zapata supposedly greeted this new intrusion of the bickering on the national scene with abusive words for both Villa and some of his own intellectuals. González Garza reacted to his messenger's report by threatening to resign, as he had already done once in February.

Again the ploy worked. González Garza's resignation would have made the Convention look even weaker and more divided. To avoid that eventuality, Zapata was forced to agree to another uncomfortable face-to-face encounter with the Convention's chief officer. González Garza rode east of the city to the village of Los Reyes, just across the line into Mexico state. There Zapata waited in a railroad car, not now feigning illness as he did in other, similar situations, but drinking instead. After a rather angry greeting that may even have involved the drawing of revolvers, the two men took a walk while González Garza scolded Zapata for not fighting hard enough, for his movement's insatiable demands for money, and for listening to intriguers who hoped to divide them. Whether because he knew that some of these charges were well-founded or simply because he preferred to avoid more shouting, Zapata listened quietly. He then accepted González Garza's invitation to return with him to Mexico City, and they departed quickly by car. In the capital they agreed on the cabinet appointments, but Zapata predictably refused to stay for dinner. Still a little drunk, he commandeered a horse and headed south.[46]

One of the subjects that Zapata and González Garza probably discussed was Villa's recent suggestion that the Convention move north to Chihuahua, where his forces could protect it. This proposition was touchy for a number of reasons. It embodied the feeling, common among the Villistas, that the Zapatistas were an undisciplined and ineffective fighting force that could not hold Mexico City if any concerted effort was made to take it. Furthermore, in November 1914 Zapata had insisted that the Convention come south from Aguascalientes to the capital: he can hardly have been enthusiastic now about letting it move so far from his control. On the other hand, by permitting such a relocation he could send Villa a gesture of good faith in difficult times, and the temptation to put another thousand miles between himself and the fractious national government must have been great. Eliciting the promise that the government's resources, such as they were, would not be lost to him, Zapata eventually acceded to Villa's request.[47]

For Palafox, however, the idea was extremely inconvenient. Sick in bed on March 28, he wrote Zapata to complain of the plan, apparently unaware that Zapata had already at least tacitly approved it. If forced to go north with the rest of the Convention government, Palafox might have lost a great deal of power, for his power depended on his ability to communicate with Zapata and to carry out agrarian reform in Morelos and surrounding states. Arguing that his many duties kept him, at least temporarily, where he was and that in Chihuahua he would not be able to implement the Plan of Ayala, he wrote that he had demanded an indefinite leave from his cabinet post. Clearly he meant to delay his own departure and let the rest of the government go. Perhaps his reservations reinforced Zapata's own doubts, however, for the Convention did not leave as scheduled on March 29. Conflicting orders from various Zapatista authorities made it impossible for the would-be travellers to secure train transportation. When González Garza protested, Zapata promised on April first that his men would not obstruct him, "if there is no reason for it." But by this time it was too late. During the first days of April the way north was cut off as Obregón marched into the center of the country in preparation for the biggest and most decisive battles of the revolution.[48]

If Zapata sometimes frustrated González Garza, Zapata's intellectual aids were beginning to drive him to distraction. In part the problem was ideological: the two groups of intellectuals that composed the Convention had different priorities and different notions about what a national government should do and how it should be run. To some extent these differences sprang from fundamental disparities between Zapatismo and Villismo. Villa's delegates were mostly liberals, while many of Zapata's professed anarchism. The Zapatistas as a group were certainly more committed to land reform and to challenging liberal notions of private property than were their northern allies. They were probably also more committed to the decentralization of state power, and to the rights of labor. But the conflict that naturally existed within the Convention government was increased by the strong personalities of people like González Garza, Palafox, and Díaz Soto y Gama.[49]

Infuriated by the long dispute over military equipment and money for Zapatista troops, Palafox, for instance, was far from seeking compromise with the more cautious Villistas. On April 6 he informed Zapata that his delegates in Mexico City were not being radical enough; the next day he walked into González Garza's office and vented his rage. González Garza responded by demanding Palafox's resignation. Though he backed down two days later after obtaining promises from Díaz Soto y Gama and another Zapatista fence-mender that Palafox would make no more trouble, the gauntlet had been thrown. Through the rest of the month tensions heightened until González Garza decided again that he could not work with Palafox. On April 30 he went before a secret session of the legislature to present his charges and ask permission to remove Palafox from his cabinet. This he got despite the Zapatista majority, a sure sign that many who knew him well agreed that Palafox was impossible.[50]

Zapata, however, was not of that opinion. In the first months of 1915 Palafox's driving ambition and boundless energy made him as essential as ever to his chief. By tackling several jobs at once—overseeing troop movements, for example, while running the Ministry of Agriculture—he did much to shield Zapata from the day to day politics of Mexico City, and that was precisely what Zapata seems to have wanted from his intellectuals. And so on May 2 Zapata warned González Garza to postpone all action on Palafox's ouster; and on May 4 he wrote ominously that he was coming to the city, with troops, to resolve the situation. Whether he did meet again with González Garza is uncertain, but several days later he issued his opinion: if Palafox was forced to resign, then González Garza must do so as well; if González Garza stayed, then so must Palafox. "I'm prepared," he concluded, "to see that these propositions are respected."[51]

Even as he outlined his position on this controversy, Zapata began receiving news of another that was perhaps related. On May 7 Antonio Barona shot General Francisco Estrada of González Garza's staff dead at a dance hall, then attacked the Hotel Lascuraín, supposedly in search of Juan Banderas, who was staying there. In fact, this hotel was also the lodging of González Garza, and though both Villistas and Zapatistas were quick to call it a coincidence, the atmosphere was poisoned enough that it seems possible González Garza was one of Barona's targets. Barona then took refuge in the San Angel Inn, installing machine guns to defend it. After dragging his feet for a couple of days Zapata ordered Barona's withdrawal from the Federal District, but again apparently failed to impose any appreciable punishment.[52]

The struggle between Palafox and González Garza soon came to paralyze the Convention. In the middle of May Díaz Soto y Gama informed Zapata that a movement was underway to remove González Garza from his position, and asked that he and other prominent Zapatistas in Morelos formally request the chief executive's resignation. On May 19, seeking a different solution, a commission of Villa's Conventionists—Luis Zubiría y Campa, Mauricio Contreras, and Alberto Piña—came to speak with Zapata at Tlaltizapán. Resorting to the usual claim that he was ill, Zapata put the meeting off until the twentieth, when he met the commissioners with ex-Mexico City journalist Enrique Bonilla at his side. A member of Zapata's Convention faction and a close friend of Palafox, Bonilla took part in the conversation "principally when it concerned the personality of General Palafox." He may have been there, in other words, to try to keep Zapata from undermining the position that his representatives were taking in the capital. In any event, though Zapata was friendly enough—regaling his visitors over dinner with stories of his struggle—he stuck to his guns. He insisted that Palafox remain at his post, and when apprised that this meant González Garza would abandon his, he replied in a tone of indifference, "if he wants to then he should resign."[53]

On May 20 González Garza took the offensive, airing long-standing grievances against the Zapatistas on the floor of the Convention and insisting that he would not give Palafox his job back. He was, he made clear about a week later, simply incompatible with Palafox, who had "a marked tendency to interfere with and impose his will on all branches of the government." He would be glad to resign, he informed Zapata, but the only legal way to replace him was to choose a provisional president, a status that González Garza—who was merely acting executive—had not been accorded. As he had from Cuernavaca in February, González Garza again asked Zapata, repeatedly, to come quickly to his side to help resolve the crisis. That was the last thing Zapata wanted to do. Despite the fact that he had so recently given the Convention an ultimatum concerning Palafox's ouster, he now fell back on the argument that it was up to the Convention to decide such matters.[54]

In early June the struggle came to an end when Woodrow Wilson hinted that the United States might soon intervene if Mexico could not solve its own problems. Despite the fact that no provisional president had been agreed upon, the Villistas decided to give in, in the hope of achieving a semblance of Convention unity to face the foreign challenge. Though Palafox, Montaño, and Díaz Soto y Gama came to Morelos to confer with Zapata, he now had little direct input into the proceedings, having already traced their general outline. On June 9, after further limiting the powers of the office of the executive, the Convention passed it on to Francisco Lagos Cházaro, a Villista of limited importance who had served as González Garza's private secretary. The next day Zapata received a telegram from Lagos Cházaro asking for his support. Ignorant of the most recent developments in the capital, Villa wrote Zapata two days later to defend González Garza's right to remove Palafox, whom he called an "obstructionist" and an "intriguer." Another crisis was over, but there was little reason to believe that the change would do any lasting good.[55]

Indeed, as we shall see, storm clouds were already moving south toward Zapatista turf, but Zapata had always been able to live for the moment. As the González Garza affair wound down, he took the time to join Amador Salazar and the promising young matador Juan Silveti in a bullfight at Yautepec. More significantly, he continued to push local reforms with a tenacity that suggested he believed they would stand. The need for Zapata to intercede in the reform process continued to be great, for its increasing bureaucratization sometimes seemed only to mean that anyone in an official position could slow it down. By the end of March, for example, Palafox had personnel for twenty agrarian commissions, but charged that González Garza would not release the money to fund them. Even when the commissions were in the field, Zapata found, they did not always obey his directives to distribute the land quickly. In general, land reform, though moving along, was almost as difficult of solution as national politics.[56]

A month before the nationalization decree of September 1914, for instance, the citizens of Ocuituco, Morelos, wrote to question Zapata's award of a particular expanse of land to nearby Metepec. This land, they claimed, was closer to them than to Metepec, and they had used it for years. Two weeks later Zapata's headquarters arranged a temporary solution, arguing that since Metepec had nowhere else to plant they would farm the lands in question that year, though it was understood that they belonged to Ocuituco. What was fair for the long-term would be decided at a later date. About a year later, however, when an agrarian commission arrived in the area to do that deciding and tried to give Metepec lands on a more permanent basis, the people of Ocuituco refused to heed the commission and took up arms to evict their neighbors.[57]

Other agrarian conflicts also festered on, forcing Zapata to improvise and to try to simplify the land reform process. He did what he could to budge officials who were blocking reform, and in early March 1915 he declared that the villages of Morelos had their lands, and that their holdings would be considered definitive unless there were interpueblo spats. Only then would the Ministry of Agriculture get involved. There were, however, plenty of disputes, and in many cases Zapata could do little more than exhort the parties to work things out, or simply decree an equal division of the lands in question between them. Despite his best efforts campesinos still sometimes died in the strife, fighting for their land as Zapata told them they would always have to do.[58]

From the summer of 1914 to the summer of 1915 Zapatismo was triumphant. Zapata's national power had reached its peak, and he was able to enact his program of social reform—at least in his own region. Due in part to his fortitude and guidance, many of the villagers of Morelos, southwestern Puebla, Guerrero, Mexico state, the Federal District, and even farther afield were working the land for themselves. Miraculously, the hacendados of Morelos, such powerful symbols of Mexican progress just five years before, had completely disappeared from the scene. For Zapata it was in many ways a time of great prosperity. But prosperity can be troublesome as people clarify and expand their expectations and their demands, and that was certainly the case here. During this year, in fact, conflict tugged at prosperity from all sides. On the local and regional scenes Zapata's peace of mind—as well as the peace of the countryside—was threatened by conflict within the movement and within and between the villages it represented. The old problem of finding a balance between discipline and the village democracy that Zapata would not betray continued to resist any comfortable solution.

The precarious balance that was Zapatismo also had an impact on the national scene. Zapata had disciplined his forces enough to attempt, at least, to participate in a national government, but in the capital antics like those of Antonio Barona outraged not only the Villistas but often Zapata's own followers as well. Still his personalism, and perhaps his understanding that even mindless violence was inevitable in a revolution, led him to take little or no action against Barona, and cases of Zapatista misconduct in Mexico City were many.[59]

There were, of course, other reasons that Zapata's failure in interfactional diplomacy continued into 1915. His posture with regard to the national government angered both Gutiérrez and González Garza. Zapata seems to have wanted the Convention government to operate independently, partly because he knew that was proper and partly because he wanted little to do with the day to day workings of national politics. His priorities and his heart were in Morelos. The attractions and the responsibilities of power, however, combined with the importunities of various members of the government, constantly brought him into the fray and put him in a difficult and inconsistent position. Thus it was not a case, exactly, of shunning a national role or of refusing national power. The problem was that his participation was piecemeal and unpredictable, especially to people like González Garza, who never fully understood the emphasis he placed on concrete, local reform—on doing reform from the bottom up.[60]

Finally, Zapata's intellectuals did not help the situation. Most crucial to the movement as interpreters of the national scene, they did little or nothing to impress upon Zapata that if the Convention coalition did not succeed he had no hope of playing the national role that would help consolidate regional reforms. Instead they seemed to do all they could to destroy the alliance, and Palafox precipitated the final González Garza crisis almost single-handedly, for reasons that were probably at least as much personal as they were ideological. The resulting failure of cooperation between Villista and Zapatista began almost as soon as the government was formed and only worsened as time went by.

7 Decline and Betrayal

EARLY IN 1915 ZAPATA EXPRESSED HIS CONTENTMENT with the village he had chosen as home during the revolution's most fulfilling months by ordering the construction of a memorial to his movement in Tlaltizapán. What eventually took shape was a peculiarly Mexican monument: a small step-pyramid with neo-classical elements, painted mustard-yellow, which was to serve as a tomb for those who had fought most steadfastly for the Plan of Ayala. Built in a dusty church-yard at the top of a hill, its shape echoed the nearby mountains, with their memories of years on the run from the troops that Porfirio Díaz, Francisco Madero, and Victoriano Huerta had sent after Zapata.[1]

If there were memories in those mountains, however, there was also a future there, for as the tomb was built military matters grew more and more grim. Far from Zapata's realm, on the broad plain north of Mexico City, the fate of the Convention government—and of the Zapatistas—was being decided in a series of massive battles between Pancho Villa and Alvaro Obregón. In April at the city of Celaya, Obregón's barbed wire and machine guns shredded Villa's cavalry charges. In June at León, Obregón lost an arm, but even without him the Carrancistas sent the Villistas scurrying north toward more familiar turf.[2]

Though these were largely Villa's failures, they also reflected on Zapata. When the Constitutionalists were on the defensive in December 1914 he had either been unwilling or unable to discipline his troops sufficiently to lead them into Veracruz. In April 1915, when González Garza and Villa begged him to cut Obregón's precarious lines of supply just north of Mexico City, Zapata essentially blackmailed them by predicating his willingness to cooperate on the receipt of ammunition. Though the Zapatistas did ultimately make some efforts to cut these lines, they were limited and ineffective, and Zapata never became directly involved. Later he would claim that his forces had been occupied in protecting the capital—that González Garza should have used troops available to him to cut Obregón's lines—but his frustration with the Villistas was evident.[3]

As the Palafox/González Garza spat played itself out, the atmosphere of growing conflict within the Convention made the effective mobilization of troops rather unlikely even if Zapata had set his mind to it, for the demoralization of the Zapatistas continued. Perhaps because he lost the governorship of Morelos, de la O was in a funk during much of the spring of 1915. Refusing to heed González Garza's repeated requests that he move to the front, he instead sent his forces out to work their plots of land, insisting that they would stay there until their back wages were paid. When he did cut communications, during the critical days of early April, it was the train traffic between Mexico City and Cuernavaca that he stopped— hardly what González Garza had in mind. Rumors flew that de la O intended to return to the capital to "shoot the multitude of persons who in his opinion are hostile to him." This group certainly included Palafox—with whom he had been fighting since at least September 1914—and it may have included González Garza as well. Zapata ordered that de la O be coddled, but the opportunity now existed to play one superior off against another, and it seems that González Garza had temporarily talked de la O around to his side of the Convention squabble by mid-May.[4]

If this was so then de la O was competing for the executive's attentions with his old enemy Pacheco, who joined González Garza's cabinet as Minister of War in late May. Long exasperated by Palafox and recently angered by Díaz Soto y Gama, Pacheco was looking for allies wherever he could find them. By the end of March Palafox understood the problem. "Frankly I'm very displeased with the conduct of González Garza," he wrote Zapata, "not because he predisposes all of the jefes of the south against me, so that they constantly tell you I'm not suitable for the revolution, but because he's trying to divide the army of the south." Indeed, the loyalties of many Zapatista chieftains were wavering. They were increasingly questioning their leadership—or at least its intellectual component—and there would soon be some doubt whether Zapata could control them at all.[5]

Adding to the complexity of the situation Zapata faced was the fact that relations with the United States were now entering a critical period. U.S. policy had never favored Zapata. Persuaded by newspaper accounts of Zapatista barbarism, the administration of President Woodrow Wilson had sought to keep the Zapatistas out of Mexico City during the summer and fall of 1914. It had also tried to encourage talks between the revolutionary factions as a way of re-establishing order. Above all it wanted to keep peace in the capital. Unfortunately, its agents often blundered. For a time they were taken in by Jacobo Ramos Martínez, the would-be peace-maker for both Madero and Huerta who now claimed to be Zapata's spokesman in what was apparently an effort—complete with code names—to swindle funds from the U.S. government for his personal use. By demanding money to keep Zapata out of the capital, Ramos Martínez naturally made Zapata look bad.[6]

Whether Zapata was aware of Ramos Martínez's activities is unclear, but when two members of the American Red Cross and two American journalists travelled to Yautepec to meet him in August 1914, Zapata was anxious to court their approval. Fully understanding the value of U.S. recognition, which would bring with it arms and money, he had a long conversation with the Americans and then gave them a letter for Wilson that had been authored by Díaz Soto y Gama. Crediting Wilson with an understanding of the social and economic nature of the revolution, this letter explained the causes and motives of Zapatismo. It announced that there could be no peace until the social and political demands of the Plan of Ayala were met. It also promised guarantees for the lives and the legitimate interests of Mexican citizens and foreigners alike. In concluding, Zapata praised Wilson's foreign policy, and indicated that he would be among the American president's many admirers as long as the United States respected Mexico's sovereignty.[7]

In reality, Zapata's attitude toward Wilson and the United States was more complicated than this letter suggested. The invasion of Veracruz continued to rankle, and even before the Americans handed that port over to Carranza in November 1914 Zapata had apparently concluded that they sided with the Constitutionalists. Still, efforts to conciliate them continued. Once in power in Mexico City, Zapata and Palafox often tip-toed around foreign interests to avoid outraging the American sense of property. No action was to be taken against foreign property, in fact, without the explicit instructions of Zapatista headquarters, and some effort was made to assure the U.S. that any confiscated holdings of its citizens would be paid for. It would be difficult, however, for Zapata to pursue his goals without offending the United States. It was rumored, for example, that some enemies of the revolution were selling their holdings to foreigners to avoid confiscation. Moreover, the lack of strict discipline among the Zapatistas inevitably led to unhappy incidents. From Puebla, consular agent William O. Jenkins reported Zapatista atrocities that, while not as bad as Carrancista behavior, left a very poor impression. Finally, Palafox's rhetoric on the issue of foreign relations was much more inflammatory than was actual Zapatista policy—one American agent quickly concluded that he was a fool with "rabid socialistic ideas." The halting, careful rejection in late 1914 of the offices of informal American envoy Hubert L. Hall—a long-time resident of Cuernavaca who was entangled in the Ramos Martínez scheme—demonstrated both Zapata's distrust of Mexico's northern neighbor and his desire not to displease it.[8]

When Palafox charged Wilson with aiding the Constitutionalists and called him a hypocrite in March 1915, it was evident that Zapata's relations with the United States were growing increasingly tense. Still the U.S. continued to press for a solution to Mexico's civil war, and so in April 1915 a Texas judge named Duval West, one of a number of special agents that Wilson sent south, arrived in Mexico. On behalf of the Convention government, Palafox was the first high-ranking Zapatista to meet him. To Zapata he reported that West did not favor their cause, and that he had ties to científico exiles in San Antonio.[9]

But West's arrival was important to the Conventionists. If they made a good impression, many hoped, it might lead to U.S. recognition. Thus, despite Palafox's appraisal of West and a certain amount of nationalistic anger among the Zapatistas, Zapata received the American agent in Tlaltizapán on the evening of April 16. The two men spoke for a couple of hours. West had already discovered that Zapata was resentful that his August 1914 letter to Wilson had never been answered, and had secured something of an apology from the president, which he passed along. Later someone, probably Zapata, suggested that the Convention send representatives to Wilson with the idea of securing recognition if possible, and West expressed his belief that Wilson would accept such a commission.[10]

Another subject that Zapata and West considered was the choice of a preconstitutional president, who would replace acting-executive González Garza and prepare the way for elections. This was an issue that Zapata and Villa were already discussing in their occasional letters. Villa had proposed Felipe Angeles, but Zapata would not entrust the position to an ex-federal soldier. He preferred Calixto Contreras, the Ocuila Indian caudillo from the Laguna region of north-central Mexico. In any event, he would have none of West's suggested candidates because, he told Villa, that would be "like accepting the tutelage" of the United States. While Zapata made considerable efforts to please his American visitor, in other words, he was not willing to give in completely. Perhaps that independence of mind helps explain why West formed a poor opinion of him, concluding that he was too provincial and did not understand Mexico's problems or national politics. Several days later U.S. Secretary of State William Jennings Bryan notified West that Wilson would not meet with a commission from the Convention, for he had accepted no such delegation from any other revolutionary faction.[11]

This is how things stood on June 2, when Wilson sent his note to the various revolutionary factions suggesting that they quickly find a way to unite, and hinting that the U.S. would soon take action if they did not. To this veiled threat Zapata responded with bravado. More concerned with the Palafox/González Garza struggle that was nearing its resolution than with Wilson's ultimatum, he informed González Garza that he would deal with the Americans if and when they invaded. Then on June 5, Díaz Soto y Gama capped the Zapatista show of disdain for Wilson's note by accusing West and other U.S. agents of corruption, and expressing the wish that they be hanged in Mexico City's Chapultepec park.[12]

As Díaz Soto y Gama indulged in more of his accustomed rhetoric, Villa was fleeing the decisive battle of León in defeat. By August, when the United States and the ministers of six Latin American countries offered their services as mediators of Mexico's conflict, it must have been clear to Zapata that Convention forces had lost the war, and that the Constitutionalists would soon be in a position to impose themselves on the towns and the valleys of Morelos. Though he refused to see the Americans who came to Tlaltizapán with this latest proposal for peace, Zapata again tried to cooperate with the Wilson administration in a measured way, eventually replying that "we effusively accept your fraternal mediation." Still he demonstrated little willingness to compromise with Carranza, for whom he had by now developed a passionate hatred. What Zapata was willing to do, however, mattered little, because for Carranza there was nothing to gain from mediation. The Constitutionalist chief spurned the invitation from Washington, but nevertheless received *de facto* recognition in October from a frustrated Wilson, who could do little to affect the situation short of invading again. Looking increasingly desperate, Zapata still took the time in November to outline instructions—albeit rather uncompromising ones—for his delegates to the peace conference that the would-be mediators proposed.[13]

Zapata's growing recognition that the revolution was slipping out of his hands was also evident in new efforts to motivate his forces. In a circular of June 20, for example, he charged that many chieftains were not spending their time at the front, but were instead occupying themselves "in theaters, cantinas, and brothels" in Mexico City. They were now to join the fighting immediately, and those who did not were to be sent to him. Despite this injunction, Constitutionalist troops under the command of General Pablo González continued to slog slowly toward Mexico City from the east. Bread riots broke out in the besieged city, and in late June the looting began as the Zapatistas prepared to evacuate. On July 9 they pulled out, the Convention government moving west to Toluca, in Mexico state. On the following day the Carrancistas moved in.[14]

About a week later the situation improved when Villista general Rodolfo Fierro drove south and forced González to evacuate Mexico City. The Zapatistas reoccupied the capital, and Zapata himself led an offensive in Puebla. On July 22, after three hours of battle, he took San Martín Texmelucan, and made plans to attack nearby Puebla and Atlixco to isolate the Constitutionalists that remained in the Federal District. But neither Atlixco nor Puebla fell, and Fierro proved only a momentary threat to Carrancista designs. González was soon able to return his attentions to Mexico City. Not trusting Zapata to defend the capital, the Convention remained in Toluca, while Mexico City—without effective government—was evacuated and reoccupied three times between the twenty-fifth and the thirtieth of July by the nervous Zapatistas. People were beginning to starve as basic foodstuffs grew more and more scarce. Finally, after skirmishing in the streets with some of Amador Salazar's forces, on August 2 the Constitutionalists entered the city for good.[15] Perhaps slightly wounded in this round of warfare, Zapata now returned to Morelos, where he continued to exhort his troops to fight. In mid-September he again briefly joined the fray east of the capital, but by early October he was back in his home state. After October 10, when the Constitutionalist advance on Toluca forced the Convention to disband—most Villistas fleeing north and most Zapatistas going south—Zapatismo was again merely a regional phenomenon.[16]

Even at the regional level the difficulties Zapata faced were now enormous. Never really resolved even when the Convention was at its most powerful, shortages of currency and munitions became acute with the loss of Mexico City. The cartridge factory that Zapata had established at Atlihuayán hacienda continued to function, but the bullets it produced—made largely of copper—were only effective at close range. Nor was the money press the Zapatistas brought south to Morelos sufficient to meet their needs. Unable to print bills fast enough to pay his troops or the railroad and telegraph employees who served them, Zapata now usurped González Garza's place as the bearer of bad tidings in this regard. "Complete wages cannot be paid due to insufficiency of funds," read his marginal response to a March 1916 plea for help, "all of the troops are in the same circumstances." Increasingly after August 1915, in fact, Zapatista forces went unpaid, and in April 1916 the payment of wages was suspended altogether.[17]

Though shortages of funds and weapons were no more critical than they had been during the first years of the revolution, expectations were quite different after the Convention experiment. Tired of fighting by 1914 and having become accustomed to receiving at least occasional pay, the Zapatistas were reluctant to return to the difficult period in which they depended on the villages for aid. Many villagers felt the same way. As the Constitutionalists neared a given settlement, the campesinos there often stopped accepting the Convention's currency in their commercial transactions, for they found it untrustworthy and knew it would incriminate them should the Carrancistas arrive. As early as March 1915 Francisco Mendoza told Zapata, "the district of Jonacatepec no longer has any desire to give its services to the Revolution." The system of close cooperation between guerrilla and community that had worked so well from 1911 to 1914 was starting to break down.[18]

Part of the problem was that the villages of the Zapatista heartland were apparently not in a position to feed as many troops as were now in the field. Due partly to poor distribution, partly to bad harvests in some areas, and partly to the hoarding of speculators and of those who feared future shortages as the military effort went sour, Zapatista documents began to reflect a lack of food in Morelos and surrounding states as early as the middle of 1915. In June Zapata informed González Garza that the poor were streaming into Tlaltizapán for corn, and Eufemio had already explained that the food situation in Puebla "is of more urgency than free love." Though there may have been some exaggeration of such difficulties as the Zapatistas sought support from the national government, there was surely some truth to these claims.[19]

Moreover, as the Constitutionalists nibbled away at Zapatismo's periphery and then finally invaded Morelos in early 1916, Zapatista troops often took out their frustrations on the pacíficos. Though Zapata himself kept his mind fixed on the people he meant to serve, many of his jefes demonstrated their understanding that coercion and terror were useful tools in obtaining village support when good will did not suffice. Judging from the complaints that flowed into Zapata's headquarters, by the end of 1915 crimes committed by Zapatista troops probably increased, and in many areas villagers learned to flee as quickly to the mountains from Zapatistas as from Constitutionalists. The result was what Fortino Ayaquica would call "the sad situation of civilians and soldiers." It was a situation that would deteriorate over the years to come, until some Zapatistas allegedly notched the ears of villagers accused of supporting the Carrancistas, as a way of promising greater punishment should their allegiance to Zapata waver again.[20]

Zapata naturally took steps to deal with these difficulties. In mid-1915 he began to recommend the formation of armed patrols to individual villages that complained of crimes, and in a circular of May 1916 he *ordered* municipal authorities to establish such police forces. Zapatista troops were now required to justify their presence in a given community, and those that had a reason to be stationed in a village were to work with civilian authorities to extract the needed aid. But though they may have helped in specific instances, such instructions had never been enough to stop abuses altogether. By early 1915 several of Zapata's generals were indicating a need for stricter justice to help them resolve their sundry disputes. Francisco Pacheco gave his usual ultimatums, and Emigdio Marmolejo threatened that if Zapata did not do something about a certain Jesús Mendoza, "we're going to quarrel, he and I." Perhaps Zapata also felt the need for a harsher justice to hold his men in line. Apprised that the often unruly Modesto Rangel had killed a soldier in self-defense, Zapata demanded witnesses, "because the life of a soldier is not the life of a dog." And after a number of protests about a Colonel Miguel Capistrán, he finally answered one with finality: "we proceeded to execute him in my recent trip there [to Tepalcingo], and in doing so carried out proper justice." Still justice continued to be limited by practical considerations, and most complaints resulted only in warnings for the accused.[21]

Like the individual chieftains in the field, Zapata's headquarters now returned to the practice of scrounging weapons and ammunition, money and food, medicine and clothing from wherever they could get them. Zapata distributed the scarce resources in a piecemeal fashion, using munitions and wages to appease his angriest jefes—whatever their specific complaints—in the effort to hold his movement together. Though by early 1916 there was no longer money for such luxuries as musical instruments, Zapata continued to try to aid individual villagers as well: it was necessary, he said, to help the poor while he could, for it was impossible to know what suffering they would have to endure should the Constitutionalists invade Morelos. "When this happens," he added with a touch of guilt, "it won't be my fault, but that of events that have to come." As economic difficulties grew he recommended that town councils fix the price of corn in their localities, and outlawed commerce with the enemy as well as the holding of Carrancista currency. He also insisted that goods circulate, ordering various chieftains to distribute the corn he heard they were hoarding, and sending a civilian friend to Cuernavaca to sniff out clothing reportedly stashed there by speculators.[22]

As part of his economic program—and to help firm up his wavering support—Zapata continued to pursue the land reform project that lay at the heart of his movement with a great deal of energy. In an effort to centralize control over the sugar mills, he and Palafox first appointed inspectors for them, and then, in early 1916, asked the jefes who were running them to turn them over to agents of the Rural Loan Bank. Part of the reason for this new policy was that a number of the chieftains, including Zapata's nephew Maurilio Mejía, stood accused by some of making personal profits on the mills they ran. Meanwhile, to broaden the land reform process Zapata ordered chieftains as far afield as Jalisco and Guanajuato to help their people occupy the land, while Palafox worked frantically to create new agrarian commissions for the states of Puebla, Guerrero, Mexico, and Tlaxcala. Finally, despite Zapata's March 1915 claim that the land reform process in Morelos was nearly over, even in his home state there was still much work to do. Throughout the period tension between the villages and those who managed the remnants of the estates remained high, as did conflict among the pueblos. As a result, definitive resolution of many land claims had not been achieved.[23]

In sum, the difficulties Zapata faced as he tried to keep his movement united were substantial, and it often seemed as though his efforts were doomed to failure. From communities near the front lines came protests against his decree forbidding trade with the Carrancistas. Claiming that they were nearly naked, for instance, about twenty citizens of Cuaxitlan asked permission to buy clothes in the nearby city of Puebla. Such contact across enemy lines might naturally undermine loyalty to Zapatismo, but when he refused to grant their request, Zapata ran the risk that they would desert him altogether. Another problem was the conflict that continued to embroil the agrarian engineers, to the extent that Trinidad Paniagua, the man charged with dispensing funds, refused to give Palafox money for his Ministry. The "banqueting engineers," Paniagua said, could wait like everyone else for their pay, and perhaps Zapata found some logic in this reasoning, for Palafox soon took him to task for not acting quickly enough to solve the issue. Tired of local suspiciousness and the lack of wages, the agrarian commissioners began to abandon Zapatismo, until Palafox was unable to staff even two commissions to Guerrero.[24]

Near the end of 1915 Antonio Barona's violent revolutionary career finally reached its logical conclusion. Over the years Barona and de la O had developed a relationship similar to that of de la O and Pacheco, especially after Zapata ordered Barona into de la O's zone to get him away from the followers of the deceased Felipe Neri. Subsequently, de la O had threatened at least once to "exterminate" Barona, and in October 1914 Zapata called a Colonel Silva of de la O's forces to order, "for the outrages he committed in the house of the mother of General Barona." Finally, on November 29, 1915, Barona got drunk in Cuernavaca and killed Antonio Silva—probably the same man who had violated his mother's home. De la O's forces responded by shooting Barona and mutilating his body. When Barona's mother asked Zapata to punish her son's murderers, she got no reply for over a month, and even then received only Zapata's regrets at her son's death. Though Zapata had always been unwilling to discipline Barona himself, he could hardly blame de la O for taking things into his own hands in this case, and he would have had great difficulty punishing him even if he chose to.[25]

Despite its failure in both military and political terms, Zapata did not part easily with the Convention. From Toluca the Zapatista Conventionists fled to Cuernavaca, where Zapata presided over the government's "reconstitution" on October 19, 1915. Hoping to show that the Zapatistas were prepared to rule the nation, Zapata asked his intellectuals to continue to produce legislation as if they still constituted a national government. This was a dream. Even if they proved themselves perfectly capable of governing alone in Morelos, Zapata and his intellectuals had demonstrated resoundingly that they could not govern the nation when they failed in the coalition building and the compromise that that task required. Lacking its Villista component, the Convention now became a national government only in theory. As such it was a striking illustration of the tensions within Zapatismo, embodying both Zapata's residual desire to maintain a national presence and the inability of his movement as presently oriented to do so.[26]

Recalling the difficulties they had had with Gutiérrez, González Garza, and Lagos Cházaro, the Conventionists decided, apparently at Zapata's suggestion, that there should at present be no new chief executive. They instead created an executive council composed of Palafox, Montaño, Luis Zubiría y Campa, Genaro Amezcua, and Miguel Mendoza López Schwerdtfeger. Since the body of the Convention was not immediately reconvened, it was this executive council that now began the impressive flurry of legislation that lasted from October 1915 to April 1916.

In late October 1915 the council promulgated an agrarian law that outlined specific means for applying the Plan of Ayala on the national level. Clearly inspired by the practical experience in land reform that the Zapatistas had acquired over the past year, this law again dealt with the categories of restitution, expropriation, and confiscation that concerned earlier Zapatista documents. New, however, was the recognition that conditions were not everywhere the same as they were in Morelos, but that the climate, the quality of the soil, and the availability of water in a given locality should affect the maximum permissible landholding there. New too were detailed criteria for proclaiming someone an enemy of the revolution and thus subject to outright confiscation. There was also an article regulating the cooperatives that the recipients of land might establish. Finally, the document was notable for its efforts to concentrate power in the hands of Palafox's agricultural ministry, a measure it claimed was necessary to expedite the land reform process. Cutting against Zapata's usual preference for decentralized government, this law gave the states no input into the reform and made the technicians, the agrarian banks and schools, and the agricultural colonies for which it provided dependent solely on the Ministry of Agriculture. Though certainly the product of Palafox's ambition, the powers given the ministry in this law also reflected Zapata's constantly expanding understanding of the political obstacles that confronted his program. In general, this was the kind of legislation into which Zapata surely had some personal input, and it seems fair to see it as the logical outcome of the ideas expressed in the Plan of Ayala as they interacted with subsequent experience.[27]

Other parts of the legislative program also addressed matters of great importance to Zapata. He had always been interested, for instance, in fomenting grass-roots, municipal democracy, and several laws in the reform package worked toward this goal by allowing for plebiscites, putting an end to jefes políticos, establishing political and economic independence for municipalities, and ordering the creation of "Boards of Revolutionary Reform" on the local level to oversee reform efforts. New laws called for direct elections and tried to adjust electoral regulations to avoid falsification of the votes of the illiterate. In other realms, too, the program was in tune with traditional Zapatista goals. Zapata's Conventionists now sought to end monopolies, to encourage colonization—first domestic and then foreign—and to provide fairer, quicker, more independent, and more effective justice. They also insisted that liberty of religion be respected—especially the liberty to practice Catholicism, which the often anti-clerical Constitutionalists threatened. [28]

While often less closely identified with the central thrust of Zapatismo, most of the other issues that the legislation addressed were true to the spirit of the movement and might be seen as a reflection of Zapata's growth in understanding as well as of the concerns of his intellectual aides. No doubt motivated by Zapata's experience with the levy and by Zapatista identification with the anti-military liberalism of the nineteenth century, the executive council decreed that the standing army be replaced by the people in arms in the form of a national guard. Other laws dealt with the tax structure in such a way that the lower sectors of society—artisans, small businessmen, and of course campesinos—would benefit. There was legislation on education as well, which made practical and popular instruction a priority.[29]

A considerable amount of attention was also given to labor leg-

islation, an area of increasing concern to Zapata as he tried to coun-
teract the Casa del Obrero Mundial's support of the Constitutionalists—pledged in early 1915—and reinforce the allegiance of followers in parts of Puebla and Tlaxcala where such industrial concerns as textile factories were of more importance than they were in
Morelos. Shortly after the executive council was formed it elevated
the Department of Labor to a Ministry, and it had soon addressed
many of the labor movement's key issues—disability compensation,
the eight hour day, pensions, working conditions, the right to organize and to strike, child labor, and the minimum wage.[30]

Finally, there were several respects in which the reform agenda
of 1915 and 1916 clearly went beyond what Zapata and other locals
had previously envisioned, dealing instead with concerns that the
intellectuals had brought from the city. It seems unlikely that Zapata was much interested in the liberation of women discussed in a
law permitting divorce—or in the emancipation of the National
University. He seems equally unlikely to have been especially forceful in advocating the abolition of the death penalty on the premise
that it was ultimately society that was guilty of all crimes. Nor was
he probably too worried about the liberty of the press that had devoted so much ink to abusing him.

Indeed, it seems clear that Zapata was not much involved in the
day to day work of his legislators—for him the mere fact that the
process of legislating continued was perhaps the most important
consideration. Still by the time the Convention finished its work in
the humble environs of Jojutla, Morelos, in May 1916 it had developed a program of which Zapata must have been proud, and one
might argue that there was some logical continuity between the
Plan of Ayala's cry for land, liberty, and social justice and even those
issues farthest removed from the daily concerns of the Morelian
peasantry. Though the "General Labor Law" did mention socializ-
ing the means of production, the program in general was not a strong
statement in favor of any of the forms of radicalism that the urban
intellectuals espoused. In fact, progress and capitalism appeared
more openly here than they had in previous Zapatista documents.

The law on colonization, for instance, was infused with the rhetoric and spirit of progress, and another document announced that the goals of the revolution were simple: "war to the death against the hacendado, ample guarantees for all other classes of society." Here was a taste of the moderate, conciliatory discourse of the years to come, years in which Zapatismo could not afford to exaggerate its radicalism rhetorically as it often had during Palafox's ascendancy in 1914 and 1915. Somewhere between socialism and liberalism, then, the program that Zapatismo now produced embodied a vision of community that frequently put society as a whole ahead of individuals and their property. It demanded that resources be redistributed by an activist state, with the ultimate goal of creating, "in a word, a nation of dignified men," of making an "hombre libre"—a free man—of the oppressed campesino. Though he would not have expressed it in exactly this way, giving the peasants of Mexico a chance at freedom and dignity had been Zapata's goal from the start of the revolution.[31]

Though impressive, this legislative onslaught was not enough to convince any sane observer that the Zapatistas were ready to rule Mexico. Frustrated by the lack of wages and the military failure of the Convention, less than fully loyal chieftains and intellectuals began to look elsewhere for the winners of the revolution, and words like intrigue and betrayal were now on everyone's lips. Rumors of spies, assassination attempts, and illicit peace talks helped spawn a growing climate of fear. And when troops did defect they further undercut Zapata's war effort by taking with them not only scarce munitions but their knowledge of the countryside as well. Naturally, these defections fed Zapata's loathing for traitors, whom he still generally punished with death when they fell into his hands. Neither this punishment, however, nor a late 1915 circular that demonstrated how serious the problem of desertion had become by ordering officers to watch their troops more closely, produced any evident results.[32]

Initially those who defected were mostly recent and sometimes more or less nominal adherents to the cause, whose positions on the fringes of the Zapatista world brought them under Carrancista pressure first. In Guerrero, for instance, many jefes had joined Zapata largely for practical reasons, and in the latter half of 1915, when the Constitutionalists began to make inroads into the southern and western parts of the state, an alliance with Zapata became increasingly impractical. There was, moreover, considerable tension among Guerreran leaders, and between them and the jefes from Morelos with whom they competed for resources. It is hardly surprising, then, that some Guerrerans now drifted into the Constitutionalist camp, and others struck a pose of local independence. In response to these unsettling trends, Zapata sought to reduce conflict in the state by assigning Lorenzo Vázquez and Montaño the task of arbitrating among Zapatista jefes there. In cases where such mediation did not work he demonstrated a willingness to go further, ordering that even such an officially loyal chieftain as Pedro Saavedra be killed for repeated misbehavior.[33]

With the defection of Francisco Pacheco in early 1916 came proof that even long-standing, high-ranking members of Zapatismo were capable of considering Constitutionalist offers. If anything, Pacheco's complaints about wages, the chain of command, and the lack of respect he received grew worse in the latter half of 1915. An ongoing land dispute of some violence between his village of Huitzilac and de la O's Santa María naturally irritated him, especially when Palafox seemed to take de la O's side. Military failure upset him too. Finally, the Convention experience had made him perhaps even more critical of Zapata's leadership. Using the position of Minister of War as a soapbox, in August 1915 he informed Zapata, "my face burns with the memory of how many times the enemy has driven us from the City [of Mexico], everyone running for Cuernavaca, committing intolerable abuses due to lack of discipline. Who if not you, compañero," he added, "is in a position to prevent this and to admonish the Jefes who allow it?"[34]

When Pacheco began to insist on his loyalty to the cause in the fall of 1915, Zapata must have known there was serious trouble. As usual, he did his best to calm and reassure the volatile chieftain. He rejected Pacheco's angry attempt, in November, to resign as Minister of War, arguing that until the military situation improved he would simply have to accept conditions that were less than perfect. He asked for his patience until the conflict between Huitzilac and Santa María could be settled. Still it must have seemed increasingly possible that Pacheco would soon spin out of control. Perhaps Zapata permitted Pacheco to engage in talks with the enemy, then, not only due to his increasingly poor military position but also to his effort to convince Pacheco that he was trusted and appreciated. In any event, it was a considerable gamble. Positioned as he was on the northern frontier of Zapatismo, Pacheco had undertaken discussions with enemy officers before, whether in the effort to trick them into giving up some advantage or to talk them over to the Zapatista side. But this was a touchy business, and as we have seen Zapata had long understood the risks of letting his jefes conduct their own diplomacy, for as they made their offers to the enemy, the enemy invariably made offers to them as well.[35]

There is no reason to assume that Pacheco had the firm intention of betraying Zapata when he began a dialogue with Pablo González in December 1915. He surely recognized that such talks could be used to exact concessions from headquarters, and he may well have planned to carry out Zapata's agenda—presumably either to talk González into joining Zapatismo or to try to kill him in an ambush. Indeed, Pacheco did get more attention: in early March 1916 Zapata promised to settle the land dispute between Huitzilac and Santa María personally. By this time the chess game was getting tense, however, and so he also instructed de la O to keep his eyes open. As the pressure increased Pacheco's behavior grew increasingly erratic. On March 13 he abandoned his stronghold at Huitzilac and moved south, leaving Cuernavaca open to attack from the north. There were also reports that he had ordered his forces not to shoot at the advancing enemy, and that he had counselled the citizens of Cuentepec, Morelos, to give the Carrancistas a warm reception when they arrived—with music if possible. Though these measures might still have been part of a strategy to fool González, they had become increasingly drastic. Unsettled by Pacheco's conduct and seeing his worst nightmares realized with Constitutionalist incursions into Morelos, Zapata rode to the front north of Tepoztlán in the hope of slowing the enemy advance.[36]

Though de la O announced on March 19 that Pacheco had declared against Zapatismo, four days later Zapata was still cautious, assuring Pacheco, "you don't have to have any fear that I harbor distrust toward you." On the same day he warned de la O that he needed to get proof for his accusations. But then on the twenty-seventh Zapata received a strange letter. In a somber tone Pacheco now unveiled a plan to circle a strong column behind the advancing enemy—a move that would place him and most of his men outside Zapata's increasingly limited reach—and asked Zapata to protect the forces he left behind from de la O and other rival chieftains. Surely Zapata was now convinced of Pacheco's betrayal, and it may be that it was he who laid plans to snare him. In any event, near the end of the month a general of de la O's named Rafael Castillo surprised Pacheco at Miacatlán—some say he found him hiding under a bed—and immediately put him to death. After receiving a commission from de la O, Zapata gave the execution his approval, and he soon rewarded de la O with food and money for his men.[37]

In terms of troops and territory Pacheco was one of Zapata's most powerful jefes, and his loss was a crippling blow. The Zapatistas had largely held the Constitutionalists out of Morelos in late 1915 and early 1916—de la O had even swept them well back in Guerrero—but with the strategic mountain barrier north of Cuernavaca now largely in Constitutionalist hands, there was little Zapata could do to stop an invasion. Thirty thousand enemy troops now poured into the state. A year earlier, during the heyday of Zapatista intransigence, Manuel Palafox had counselled that "it was better to return to the hills" than to compromise, and return to the hills they now would. By the first week in April the troops of Pablo González were on the outskirts of Cuernavaca, and before the month was over the major population centers of the state began to fall. Cuernavaca was captured on May 2, despite Zapata's own attempts to defend it. Of course, more than territory was lost. On April 16 a stray bullet struck Zapata's cousin, Amador Salazar, in the neck. Though the veteran warrior remained upright on his horse, he died almost instantaneously, and was buried in the Tlaltizapán mausoleum. Zapata's forces still raided well beyond the borders of Morelos—on May 25, for instance, two hundred Zapatistas entered the city of Puebla for a brief skirmish—but to do so they had to return to guerrilla warfare. From the mountains and the smaller, more isolated communities they again struck out at a force far superior in numbers and in arms.[38]

In the middle of June Zapata lost Tlaltizapán, and was nearly captured in the process. Safe in the familiar mountains around Huautla after a hurried retreat, his frustration was evident. "They pursue me," he supposedly growled, "for the crime of wanting those who have always been hungry to have enough to eat." Meanwhile, 286 men, women, and children of Tlaltizapán who were not lucky enough to escape the Carrancista attack were being massacred as presumed supporters of Zapata. Scarcely three months later Carrancista Colonel Jesús Guajardo would repeat the offense in the same village. Though the Constitutionalists would always count the victims of such incidents among those killed in battle, Pablo González's manifesto of July 19, 1916, made it clear that such cruelty was policy. After asking for the cooperation of the people of the state, he echoed Huerta in the promise that he would pacify Morelos by whatever means necessary. Like Huerta and Díaz before him, González began to ship prisoners out of state, bound for forced labor camps in Yucatán. Even those who survived often considered the new wave of enemy brutality worse than anything that had come before.[39]

With the advent of the Carrancistas, of course, the pressure on Zapata's movement became even greater and the appreciation of all that had been lost grew deeper. Pacíficos and soldiers alike moved their families to Guerrero to escape the invasion, giving Zapata fewer troops and fewer farmers to depend on. Indeed, due to the exactions of troops on both sides of the conflict who demanded food from campesinos or simply plundered it from their fields, the scarcity now became so great that whole villages feared they might have to hit the road begging. Even as Morelenses fled to Guerrero, migrants from Mexico state—where things were worse—streamed down like locusts into Morelos, consuming "even the grass."[40]

To Zapata it must have seemed as though the fall-out from the failure of the Convention and from Pacheco's subsequent defection would soon bring Zapatismo to its knees. He became increasingly bitter and, angrier than usual at the lack of cooperation and discipline that plagued his ranks, he took vigorous action to try to stem the tide of decay and betrayal. On August 10, 1916, he decreed that those who had fled from the enemy since May first—and who had, in the process, held scarce weapons without using them, given unmerited promotions, and mistreated the pacíficos—would be discharged from the Zapatista army. Five days later Lorenzo Vázquez, Zapata's friend since before the revolution, was the first to suffer this indignity, "because he is unfit to form part of the revolutionary forces, in virtue of his notorious cowardice." Vázquez had avoided combat as the Carrancistas invaded and moved toward Tlaltizapán, and he was suspected of sympathy with Pacheco. He had also been foolish enough to proclaim his unhappiness with Palafox—and thus indirectly with Zapata as well—too loudly during late 1915 and early 1916.[41]

As usual, though, Zapata was careful to use the carrot with the stick. In the same decree that dismissed Vázquez he rewarded Everardo González, who operated around Juchitepec in eastern Mexico state, for his military prowess by making him a Brigadier General. Two months later he again praised González publicly—along with fellow general Valentín Reyes—this time for an exemplary campaign in the environs of Mexico City.

In general, Zapata's propaganda now sought to hearten his followers by exaggerating the movement's rather isolated military successes. Another means of unifying Zapatismo was to demonize Carranza. A manifesto of May 29, 1916, for instance, called the leader of Constitutionalism an "old courtesan" who represented the hacendados in their fight against the campesinos. Zapata also displayed his anger at United States support for Constitutionalism in a number of documents, attacking Carranza for permitting the United States to send troops into northern Mexico in pursuit of Villa after his March 1916 raid on Columbus, New Mexico. Carranza, he declared, was discredited: it was simply a matter of the people joining arms to bring him down.[42]

There was, of course, no magical uprising of the people, and no real stopping the rash of betrayals. In fact, things just got harder in September, when Pablo González imitated Juvencio Robles in initiating a policy of concentrating villagers in the larger towns and cities. Still the hope embodied in Zapata's propaganda and legislative programs, combined with his thorough understanding of the men he led, enabled him to salvage his movement in part. Not all of those who seem to have flirted with the idea of betrayal ended up leaving Zapatismo. By early 1916, for example, Francisco Mendoza's ongoing conflicts with such jefes of neighboring zones as Fortino Ayaquica and Maurilio Mejía led him, like Pacheco, to complain of intrigues and of Zapata's neglect, and to refute rumors that he would defect. Later that year he even suspected that Zapata had ordered him killed, and it is certainly possible that he had, but that no one was able to carry out the command. At any rate, Zapata was clearly furious with Mendoza in November when he instructed him to collect his troops, "in order to control them and make them gather at the front, where they never present themselves, preferring instead to do as they please, spreading sorrow with their abuses against the pueblos." In a meeting at Tepalcingo in January 1917, he went so far as to direct the forces of Mejía and Mendoza to form a single column under the leadership of a third general. When the opportunity arose, however, Zapata combined this hard-line approach to Mendoza's misconduct with efforts to reassure and appease him, insisting that he remained a valued member of the movement and promising to control Ayaquica and Mejía. Perhaps helped in part by the example made of Pacheco and others, Zapata's flexible leadership was ultimately successful in keeping Mendoza loyal.[43]

Surely it did not hurt Zapata's relations with Mendoza and other recalcitrant jefes that as the end of 1916 approached it became clear that the war was not yet completely lost. Pacheco's defection had given the Constitutionalists a great advantage, but Pablo González was a poor general, and he now began to discover, as others had before him, that terrorizing the pueblos would not be enough to put an end to Zapatismo. González's troops suffered from malaria and dysentery in the semi-tropical climate to which most were unaccustomed, and the Carrancistas had other rebels to chase, so that resources for the fight in Morelos were limited. They were so limited, in fact, that González began to accuse Obregón—his main political rival and, in late 1916, Carranza's Secretary of War—of deliberately undermining his campaign.

As Carrancismo displayed its own military shortcomings and internal divisions, Zapata and those of his followers who still felt the cause smoldering in their hearts demonstrated a remarkable tenacity. With only about five thousand men in the field they started, almost miraculously, to fight back. Much as they had done in October 1911 to discredit Huerta's attempt to wipe them out, in the fall of 1916 Zapata's forces got Mexico City's attention with several disruptive raids in the Federal District. In early October one band penetrated as far north as San Angel to make its announcement of Zapatista persistence; and on November 8 four hundred passengers—some of them Carrancista soldiers and others civilians—died when their train was attacked in the mountains just south of the capital. Three days later Pablo González promised immediate execution for anyone in Morelos suspected of aiding Zapata, directly or indirectly. But it was too late for González to make his campaign a success. On November 22 he began to prepare a retreat, having learned like so many before him how difficult it was to control Morelos with the Zapatistas in arms. His thirty thousand troops, the Constitutionalists had decided, might be used more effectively elsewhere. As González began to withdraw, Zapata pressed the offensive. Already back in Tlaltizapán, at the beginning of December he had launched simultaneous attacks along the line from Cuernavaca to Jojutla, around Jonacatepec, and on several important towns in

Puebla. Jojutla quickly fell, and in late December the Carrancistas began to depart in earnest. The Zapatistas occupied Jonacatepec, Yautepec, and Cuautla in early January 1917. In the middle of the month they rode into Cuernavaca.[44]

Zapata found devastation in the state capital of a kind that he had not seen in earlier stages of the fighting. "They've left Cuernavaca unrecognizable," one of his letters informed an absent secretary,

> the houses are without doors, the streets and the plazas
> converted into dungheaps, the churches broken open, and
> the holy images destroyed and stripped of their
> vestments. The city is abandoned, because they took the
> pacíficos by force, to the extent that when we took
> possession of the plaza we met only three families who
> escaped the removal of pacíficos by hiding.

The rest of the state was in similar shambles. Zapata's letter blamed the Carrancistas for the damage, and during their stay in Morelos the troops of Pablo González had indeed done their part to add a new verb to the Mexican lexicon: *carrancear*—to loot. But Zapata knew that his own forces were not completely innocent of the destruction that blanketed Morelos. Even before González arrived and despite Zapata's pleas for order, the Zapatistas themselves had begun to dismantle the haciendas as they scavenged for the resources needed to continue the war. The destruction of war was deeply rooted. It had become a way of life, and it would be an ongoing process: the looting and burning and killing were only temporarily postponed; meanwhile, the copper of the hacienda machinery would continue to be reworked into inferior ammunition in makeshift Zapatista factories or smuggled across Constitutionalist lines in exchange for munitions, money, and food. The state of Morelos was falling to pieces, and the prosperity that Zapata sought for his campesino followers had never seemed so distant. Thus for Zapata feelings of triumph must have been muted by worry and guilt over what his rebellion had wrought, and the misery of the past eighteen months remained alongside the hope that came with the new year.[45]

8 The Road to Chinameca

MIXED EMOTIONS OR NOT, THE TASK AT HAND WAS plain: there was nothing to do but rebuild. Tlaltiza-pán—"the Mecca of Zapatismo"—where Zapata again set up his headquarters, had also been ravaged by the Constitutionalists. The bodies of the latest massacre victims still lay in the streets when Zapata arrived, and the occupying force had dragged Amador Sala-zar's corpse from the mausoleum, depriving it, some say, of its gold fillings and its charro suit. Some of the village's citizens, however, had managed to survive, and they now straggled down from the hills, ready to help "inject new life into that dead pueblo."[1]

Zapata responded to the challenge of rebuilding Tlaltizapán and the rest of Morelos with a flurry of activity. By November 1916 he had commissioned his secretaries to create what would be called the Consultation Center for Revolutionary Propaganda and Unification, an organization that actually took shape at headquarters during the first days of 1917. Lead by Díaz Soto y Gama, it was initially com-posed of fifteen of Zapata's intellectual advisors, and its job was to propagandize, to deal with conflicts among jefes and between jefes and pueblos, and to help decide difficult matters of policy. It was also to direct a set of new juntas—called Associations for the De-fense of Revolutionary Principles—that were being chosen in vil-lages throughout the Zapatista world. These associations were to foment the revolution on the local level—by holding meetings every

Sunday to publicize Zapata's laws and manifestos, by overseeing public education and the electoral machinery, and by explaining to the villagers that the armed struggle was undertaken on their behalf. More than merely an effort to rebuild, of course, this system was another attempt to temper military/civilian conflict and thus to strengthen ties to the villagers upon whom Zapatismo depended for support. It went further in this regard—at least on paper—than anything Zapata had devised before, and with it he sought to keep his followers loyal. True to his principles, however, he would not coerce that loyalty at the expense of municipal democracy; instead he hoped that the local associations could secure it through persuasion, and thus enhance his control in the region.[2]

Complimenting this new organizational thrust were efforts to address some of the movement's key issues more directly. In what was largely a gathering together of the previous dispositions of his headquarters on the subject, Zapata signed a law in March 1917 that outlined the rights and the obligations of villages and troops. "It is urgent that we demonstrate with deeds," this decree read, "that the era of abuses has ended." Another piece of legislation reinforced this insistence by seeking to stop Zapatista leaders from taking over nationalized properties for their own use, a practice that "would give arms to the enemy so they could attack us, saying that before there were the hacendados and now there are the jefes." As he had so many times in the past Zapata did what he could to reinforce the prerogatives of civil authorities. In fact, by asserting that only civilians were to deal with land and water questions on the local level, he wrote his jefes out of this difficult process more completely than ever before.[3]

Zapata also ordered the selection in each village of officials who would speak for local land and water rights. Such representatives had long existed rather informally in Morelos—indeed, Anenecuilco had chosen Zapata to perform this task in 1909. Investing these representatives with more official status was certainly meant to give them greater authority within the village structure. It was probably also meant in part to simplify the resolution of agrarian conflict by identifying more clearly who spoke for a given village in a given dispute. Zapata and his advisors had learned much from intervillage strife, as was evident in several new pieces of legislation that sought to clarify and resolve issues that they had not foreseen in the early years of the revolution. In July 1917 they even drafted a reformed agrarian law that departed from that of October 1915 most markedly in giving the goal of a rough equity among villages clear priority over any particular village's titles to land. Still though Zapata announced on March 18, 1917, that the pueblos of Morelos possessed their permanent ejidos, conflict over land and its products was ongoing.[4]

In addition, Zapata worked to maintain a governmental structure. He decreed that the administrative departments he had kept in place when the Convention ended in May of 1916 would remain in operation within his headquarters, alongside the Consultation Center. He named a commission to create a new state government for Morelos. He saw that judiciary officials were appointed, and their responsibilities carefully outlined. And in April he signed a law that gave detailed instructions to the many inexperienced new members of town councils on how municipal governments should be structured and run.[5]

Perhaps encouraged by his urban advisors, Zapata now displayed a commitment to the social mission of education. Insisting repeatedly that village officials establish schools so the revolution would not be responsible for a generation of children missing their chance to learn, he sought an educational system suited to the needs of rural Mexico. "The mind of the supreme jefe himself," one document read, "is to make a powerful initiative on behalf of children, who will have to replace us in life. This is an initiative that past governments never wanted to make because it was convenient for them that the people remained eternally ignorant, so they could always be exploited."[6]

Finally, in January Zapata also began new efforts to clarify his military organization. With the help of his intellectuals he now tried to formalize, in considerable detail, the roles and responsibilities of

7. *Looking tired but still defiant. (Archivo General de la Nación, Mexico City, Archivo Fotográfico Hermanos Mayo)*

active and reserve militias, and to regularize his army's hierarchy as well as the numerical relationships between its squadrons, sections, companies, and battalions. The guiding philosophy behind this labor—that the army should be as centralized as possible—was demonstrated in Zapata's reaction, in April, to Jesús Salgado's request that Guerrero be divided into separate military zones as a means of avoiding conflicts between different groups of Zapatistas. In a meeting with the Consultation Center, Zapata concluded that Salgado's plan "suffers from the defect of regionalizing the Army," and that "it is self-evident . . . that most of our failures have their origins in the plurality of military commands, the absence of organization." Despite the official optimism that had Zapatista policy-makers discussing what they would do when they returned to Mexico City, under the present conditions decentralization might well have meant disintegration. Zapata's organizational measures for the military represented more a struggle to hang on to some control than they did a new stage of development.[7]

As he had during 1916, Zapata often took forceful action against those who misbehaved. In one case he advised that a bandit be executed, and added "that the execution be public to satisfy all of the pueblos in which he [the criminal] committed his villainies." He also demanded that each community establish a watch that could guarantee the safety of nearby roads as well as of villages themselves. Combined with the optimism occasioned by the recapture of Morelos, these efforts apparently worked for a time—at least during the spring of 1917 reports of atrocities within the Zapatista world seem to have declined.[8]

Down on the border between Morelos and Guerrero, however, the kind of strife that Jesús Salgado hoped to avoid suddenly got out of hand. Here the infighting over resources and allegiance continued unabated, and the villagers of the area, often defenseless, naturally bore the brunt of the violence. On the last day of April 1917, the pacíficos of Buenavista de Cuéllar, Guerrero, just south of the state line, decided to fight back. Various jefes in the area had been wavering between Carrancismo and Zapatismo for months, and the

locals apparently saw in the uncertainty an opportunity to rid themselves of the Zapatistas by attacking their small garrison. Whether
they meant to support Carranza or simply wanted to be left alone is
unclear, but in either case such an uprising posed a sizable threat to
Zapata. He quickly ordered more troops—some of questionable loyalty—into Buenavista, and in the confused scuffle that followed the
unfortunate Lorenzo Vázquez lost his life. Zapata soon discovered
that documents implicating Vázquez in the rebellion were found in
the clothing he wore when he died.[9]

These documents also apparently suggested that Otilio Montaño was involved, and those who investigated the uprising soon
found more evidence to this effect. Apparently convinced of his old
friend's probable guilt, Zapata ordered him apprehended and then
fled Tlaltizapán on the pretense of urgent business elsewhere—
without seeing Montaño first. He left only the instructions, "with
regard to any crime other than *treason*, this Authority will concede
the favor of a pardon, but for the mentioned crime of *treason*, today
as always I am disposed to deny such a favor." Though practical
considerations had sometimes induced him to bend this rule in the
past, it must have seemed now that the defections would never end
unless he was firm, even with Montaño, on this point. A court
martial composed of Palafox, Díaz Soto y Gama, Angel Barrios, and
several other urban intellectuals was formed, and on Friday, May 18,
the co-author of the Plan of Ayala went before a firing squad in the
plaza at Tlaltizapán. Montaño's body was then hanged from a tree
beside that of Vázquez on the road west of town. Beneath it a sign
read, "This is the fate of those who betray their country, the tomb
that they receive in the state of Morelos."[10]

Though the nature of Montaño's participation in this insurrection remains uncertain and he vehemently denied involvement, he
was obviously unhappy, and much of this unhappiness had to do
with his displacement by the better-educated intellectuals from the
city. He had never regained the status he lost to Palafox in 1913. In
fact, he had increasingly become an object of ridicule, and in this his
fellow intellectuals led the way, for they were most conscious of

what a ludicrous figure he cut, basing his many pretensions on an education that came to nothing on their scale of achievement. Thus by 1917 he saw them not as comrades-in-arms, but as enemies. Moreover, he surely felt that these enemies had led Zapatismo astray in 1914 and 1915. He had recently hinted to Zapata that the war was getting long and—though never especially consistent—he was a confirmed liberal who tended toward flexibility and compromise in his dealings with other factions. If Montaño conspired against Zapata with Pacheco and Vázquez as the Zapatistas would soon claim, it was a remarkably clumsy conspiracy, for the conspirators allowed themselves to be picked off one by one. There may, however, have been ties of sympathy between these men. Though he was not on the scene at Buenavista de Cuéllar, in other words, Montaño probably did rebel in some sense, or at least express his frustration and alienation in a way that inspired others to do so.[11]

There could have been no more alarming sign that Zapatismo had lost its way than this fatal clash between the two authors of its constitutional document. As Zapata sought solace in a box of good cigars that Eufemio sent to cheer him, perhaps he recognized the irony. In the shambles of the Convention, the recriminations, the lack of discipline, the brutal Carrancista invasion, and of course in the wave of betrayal, the moral crisis of Zapatismo was easily read. Though he tried at times to dismiss the many defections as part of a purification process his movement was undergoing, to Zapata it must all have seemed a nightmare that even the recent Constitutionalist withdrawal could not dispel. Now with the death of Montaño came the symbolic sundering of Zapatismo's fundamental definition, as well as the triumph of Zapata's growing fixation with betrayal over such positive aspects of his character as generosity and personal loyalty. Zapata felt guilty about the invasion, and he was as angry and disappointed as anyone with the results of the intransigence that his movement had adopted in 1914 and 1915. It can hardly be surprising that as he rebuilt Morelos he had already begun to look for another path.[12]

Ironically, the new path that Zapata was in the process of choosing was one that Montaño might have advocated. As the movement's military capacity deteriorated it had become increasingly obvious to Zapata that he could not beat Carranza alone. As a result, he now decided to shift the movement's emphasis away from the peasant distrust that Manuel Palafox had made his own, toward an acceptance of the need for allies on the national scene that had always been part of Zapatismo as well. To lead the effort to find such allies Zapata chose twenty-six year-old Gildardo Magaña. Raised in Zamora, Michoacán, by a father who actively opposed the Díaz regime, and educated in Mexico City and Philadelphia, Magaña had joined Zapata in June 1911 after taking part in a failed plot against Díaz in the capital. Ever since he had been a force for diplomacy. During the summer of 1911 he struggled to resolve Zapata's difficulties with Madero. Later, in 1913, he helped bridge the thousand mile gap between Zapata and Pancho Villa, even braving Zapata's ire by suggesting that northerners might reasonably be allowed to add their own special concerns to the Plan of Ayala. He did, however, counsel that Carranza could not be trusted. In 1915 Magaña served as governor of the Federal District, and apparently managed to please Zapata with his work in that capacity without becoming entangled in the personal and political battles that capsized the Convention. Indeed, his attempt to resign his post just as González Garza was forced from power was probably an indication that he rejected all the squabbling. "Conservative and prudent" in the words of one American observer, to Zapata Magaña must have seemed as different from Palafox as a fellow urbanite could be.[13]

Perhaps to avoid the intrigue that swirled around Zapata, Magaña chose in December 1916 to set up shop at some distance from Tlaltizapán, in the isolated town of Tochimilco, Puebla, which hung in the folds of Popocatepetl at an altitude between six and seven thousand feet. From there, in close communication with Zapata, he began a diplomatic campaign that would soon send ambassadors scouring Mexico in search of other regional caudillos, semi-retired revolutionary politicos, and disgruntled Constitutionalists who might be willing to join in a unified revolt to drive Carranza from the presidency.[14]

As the Zapatista cause declined after the middle of 1915 there had already been a noticeable—though not especially systematic—drift toward a more diplomatic stance within the movement. As we have seen, there was some attempt to be conciliatory in the legislative program of the purely Zapatista Convention. Furthermore, as an extension of his mid-1915 hopes that the United States might broker talks between the factions—and as a measure of his desperation for funds and arms—in 1916 Zapata sent various agents toward the United States to pursue international diplomacy. Genaro Amezcua ran out of money in Havana, and so set up his headquarters there, but Octavio Paz Solórzano did arrive in San Antonio, Texas, in October 1916. There he tried to read revolutionary trends within the exile community and to do what he could to sway U.S. opinion to Zapata's side. Miguel Mendoza López Schwerdtfeger, meanwhile, eventually made it to San Francisco. By early 1917, though, nothing had come of these initiatives. Steady in its *de facto* recognition of Carranza, the United States was not receptive to Zapatista propaganda, and Paz had done little to move the exiles.[15]

Zapata had also begun to try to build ties with others in the south who opposed Carranza. In late 1914, when he hooked up with ex-federals like Higinio Aguilar and Benjamín Argumedo, Zapata served notice that military needs might sometimes take precedence over ideology in his diplomatic endeavors. At about the same time he came into indirect contact with Oaxacan leaders José Inés Dávila and Guillermo Meixueiro. Though the Oaxacans were commonly considered reactionaries, they indicated that they would uphold the Plan of Ayala as a first step in a rejection of Carranza that would ultimately cause them to proclaim their state sovereign in 1915.[16]

Zapata knew he could not depend on such allies. Aguilar, for instance, only cooperated when it suited his purposes, and when he challenged the authority of his old friend Argumedo in early 1915 Zapata ordered more trustworthy troops to chase him down. They were not successful in doing so, however, and by the end of the year

Aguilar was back in Zapata's good graces, operating mostly in southern Puebla and Oaxaca. Naturally such twists of allegiance were often confusing to the rank and file. On the subject of Aguilar and Argumedo, one Zapatista colonel displayed considerable frustration. "Because if they were enemies first," he asked Zapata, "and then compañeros and then enemies again, how can they be trusted?"[17]

Still Zapata's rough alliances with other, often problematic southern rebels made sense in light of his waning struggle against a regime that these forces were fighting as well. There had always been a certain ideological laxity among the rebels in the region. More than once in 1912, for instance, people took up arms against Madero with vivas both to Zapata and to Felix Díaz, don Porfirio's reactionary nephew who was then leading an uprising in Veracruz. Moreover, the Zapatistas did have some common ground with Dávila and Meixueiro in that they were all fighting against the intrusion of the rather foreign Carrancistas—mostly northerners—upon their local and regional prerogatives. And so Zapata asked the Oaxacans to prove their good will not with social reforms but with attacks into southern Puebla, and in late 1915 and early 1916 he occasionally treated them as the official Zapatista government of their state.[18]

In February 1916, when Felix Díaz landed at Veracruz to undertake another rebellion, Zapata's relationships with the conservatives of the south became considerably more complex. Since he could not go as far as to forge an accord with someone of Díaz's unquestionable reactionary credentials, on June 7, 1916, Zapata made his position clear, proclaiming Díaz his enemy and forbidding Zapatista jefes to communicate with him or with anyone in his faction. Taking advantage of the new situation, however, and seeking to maintain a certain latitude of action, many rebels—among them Aguilar and Juan Andrew Almazán—pledged to support Díaz even as they tried to maintain ties to Zapata. As a result, Zapata himself would keep certain lines of communication open in order to compete with Díaz for support he could not afford to lose in Oaxaca—Díaz's native state—in Puebla, and also in Veracruz.[19]

This is how things stood with regard to interfactional diplomacy when Zapata and Magaña really set to work at the beginning of 1917. On January 20 Zapata shared his optimism with the nation in a manifesto that invited those who had previously been neutral to work for the reconstruction of Mexico. Because people were beginning to realize that Carranza was driving the country to ruin, this document asserted, "the nightmare of Carrancismo, overflowing with horror and with blood, is almost over." As he had already in 1915, Zapata tried to conciliate with a promise to respect the rights of all but hacendados. And he again courted labor—which Carranza had begun to persecute in 1916—this time with the rather unrealistic suggestion that a plot of land would allow them to "exchange the slavery of the factory for the glorious liberty of the fields."[20]

For Zapata Carranza had now become the "the sole obstacle" to peace and reconstruction. Such a position meant, of course, that everyone else was fair game for diplomacy, and on March first Zapata appealed directly to the Constitutionalists with an offer of amnesty. Several weeks later he authorized Magaña and another urban intellectual, Enrique Bonilla, to "treat and resolve all manner of business relating to those among the enemy trying to retrace their footsteps" by leaving Carranza for Zapata. What ensued were talks with two Carrancista officers—Guillermo Castillo Tapia and Eduardo Reyes—who were both garrisoned at Atlixco, Puebla, and who soon suggested that the Zapatistas talk to Pablo González himself.[21]

González was an ambitious man. It was already evident that he hoped to ascend to the Mexican presidency when Carranza left it, and that aspiration now prompted Zapata and Magaña to dream of a struggle between González and Obregón over Carranza's political remains that would eventually induce one of the two Constitutionalist generals to join the Zapatistas. The prospect of negotiating with González can hardly have been pleasant with memories of Pacheco's betrayal and the subsequent invasion still fresh, and the new twist in the diplomatic process was probably merely an indication that Castillo Tapia and Reyes hoped to convince Magaña and his companions to join Carranza. Still, Zapata pushed fearlessly ahead, demonstrating such trust in his new chief advisor that he refused to send the detailed instructions for formal talks that Magaña repeatedly requested. Eventually, in May, Enrique Bonilla left for Mexico City to discuss with González, "revolutionary unification, on the precise and unnegotiable condition of the elimination of Venustiano Carranza." The metropolitan newspapers got wind of the visit, and some saw it as a preface to Zapata's surrender, but all hopes were soon disappointed, and Bonilla was briefly arrested at the beginning of June.[22]

Meanwhile, Zapata was faced with a new problem. In January 1917 the Constitutional Convention that Carranza had convened the previous fall at Querétaro finished its work. Despite Carranza's efforts to control them and to blunt their proposals for social reform, the body's more radical delegates again demonstrated Constitutionalism's pluralism by passing a program of thoroughgoing change. Most importantly for Zapata, in article 27 the new Constitution called for sweeping land reform on the premise that property was not an absolute right of individuals, but had to serve the public interest. Also significant were the elections that followed quickly on the heels of the Constitution's completion. Carranza—who had until now been merely the acting executive as First Chief of Constitutionalism—ran unopposed for the presidency, and was sworn in on May first.[23]

Both the reformist Constitution and the election naturally threatened to give Carranza a new aura of legitimacy. Indeed, it is possible that part of Otilio Montaño's discontent in the spring of 1917 was that he came to accept this legitimacy, reasoning that there was nothing left to fight for once agrarian reform was written into the Constitution. The agrarian provisions of the Constitution of 1917, however, did not meet Zapata's standards. They put all the power to redistribute land into the hands of the state, which was bad enough under the best circumstances and intolerable when Carranza was in power, for Zapata knew he was untrustworthy when it came to social change. And so Zapata promulgated his "Protest to the Mexican People" on the day that Carranza took office. In it he charged that what had taken place was a reelection—the sin that had sparked the revolution against Díaz back in 1910—since Carranza had previously served as chief executive. More generally, Zapata argued that the election was not democratic. Rather, it was a "cynical and brutal imposition," with no opposing candidate and no voice for anyone who dissented. Finally, the manifesto listed the many promises that Carranza had already betrayed.[24]

In June came more evidence that the crisis of confidence that pulsed beneath the surface of Zapatismo could strike at its heart at any moment. Eufemio Zapata was never as steady as Emiliano, and he was always cruder. While Emiliano worked to solve disputes subtly, his brother usually came straight to the point. In mid-1915, for instance, he demonstrated his leadership style in a letter to one of two feuding jefes. "Don't assume that the revolution will suffer setbacks because two sons-of-bitches disappear," he threatened. "I think it will serve as an example for others." Eufemio's use of alcohol undoubtedly had something to do with his volatility. He had been a hard drinker since his youth, but by 1914 he had become a habitual drunk, and his drinking grew worse in the difficult years that followed. Luckily, he developed a twitch in his right eye when he was especially intoxicated, a twitch that warned those who knew him to keep away. On June 18, however, the father of a fellow Zapatista jefe named Sidronio "Loco" Camacho apparently missed this warning, and a drunk and dispirited Eufemio beat and insulted the old man for some minor or supposed infraction. "Loco" Camacho came immediately for his revenge. He shot Eufemio down in the streets of Cuautla, and threw him, still alive, on an anthill on the outskirts of town. Later that day Eufemio died.[25]

To Zapata his brother's death was yet another emotional blow. It was a blow, too, to his own prestige in a movement where family ties were so important. But there was little he could do about it. Camacho wasted no time in fleeing to the Carrancistas, and anyway Zapata knew, like everyone else, that Eufemio "had it coming." Still, Eufemio Zapata's death was a significant loss. At least in Zapatismo's early years he had been a marvelous recruiter, and for many his relationship to Emiliano made him "our second hero," and thus a significant source of leadership and morale.[26]

Though despair claimed Eufemio, Zapata maintained his own hope, and the diplomacy went on. Throughout the spring and into the summer he and Magaña sent letters and envoys to Michoacán, San Luis Potosí, Guanajuato, Colima, and Jalisco. The mere whisper that someone of any revolutionary standing was either sympathetic with Zapatista goals or fed up with Carranza inspired an invitation to join the Zapatista drive for unification, and in their studied vagueness the letters that bore these invitations sometimes failed even to mention the Plan of Ayala, the sticking-point of negotiations in 1914. Even after Enrique Bonilla's failure with Pablo González in June, talks with the Carrancistas around Atlixco continued, and Eduardo Reyes hinted that González and Obregón might both soon move against Carranza. Meanwhile, aided by Marcelo Caraveo, an ex-Orozquista who had recently escaped prison in the capital and who was acquainted with many of the jefes of Veracruz, Zapata and Magaña remained in competition with Felix Díaz for support in that state and elsewhere. Despite his dislike of Díaz, it was increasingly in Zapata's best interests that the informal sharing of jefes between the two movements continue, for during 1917 the Felicistas were gradually replacing Zapatismo as the south's most potent military opposition. Zapata also sent two letters to Pancho Villa, with whom he had never completely lost touch. In fact, there was lasting good feeling between them, though Zapata still complained about González Garza and Lagos Cházaro. Finally, Zapata continued to ponder the international scene, now in the new light of the United States' entry into World War I. In May he sent an agent to the German minister in Mexico City in the hope that Carranza's ties to the U.S. might be used to persuade the Germans to arm the Zapatistas. On the recommendation of Paz Solórzano, he was in touch with exiles in San Antonio, Texas as well, among them his old friend Emilio Vázquez Gómez.[27]

In late August one lengthy and intricate set of negotiations went awry. Domingo Arenas was a Tlaxcalan revolutionary of notable agrarian credentials who had joined Zapata in 1914. In early 1916 Arenas had begun to complain about the lack of discipline and bravery of his fellow chiefs, and to engage in a series of often violent confrontations with the troops of other Zapatistas. There were even reports that he planned "to finish off all the old Jefes." Though Zapata and Arenas initially met the tension with mutual professions of loyalty, Arenas soon tested Zapata's patience. First he tried to expand his zone at the expense of fellow Zapatistas in the states of Hidalgo and Puebla; then in late summer of 1916 Zapata began to receive documents indicating that Arenas was in secret communication with the Carrancistas.[28]

Eventually Arenas started to question Zapata's leadership. In September, for instance, he suggested that "we try to sanitize the Revolutionary Army, that is, to destroy the new dictators who have interpreted our principles very badly. Like in the days of feudalism," he continued, "they have made themselves lords over life and death, who have in their hands the lives and the dignities of the defenseless campesinos. Made vain by the rank that your headquarters has conferred on them, they consider themselves owners of the land." A few months later he added to this critique, writing that he had seen proclamations from Felix Díaz and Higinio Aguilar, "who say they're in accord [with the Zapatistas] to work for their principles and political goals. If this is true, we are disposed to remain firm in our posts and to separate from you, now that our companions offer neither guarantees [against abuses] nor military organization."[29]

Like Pacheco and others before him, Arenas was no longer able to accept the practical considerations, the inequities, and the brutality that came with Zapata's revolution, and on December 1, 1916, he signed an accord with the Carrancistas. Zapata responded by ordering that he be hunted "after today as an enemy, until he is annihilated for his shameless treason." But that was not the end of the story. Arenas apparently hoped to use his agreement with Carranza to carve out a niche for himself between the Zapatistas and the Constitutionalists. To do that he had to avoid alienating either side completely, and so he told Zapata that he had joined Carranza only to get weapons. Zapata, however, fully understood the game Arenas was playing. He and Magaña pretended to consider Arenas's explanations, but as they did so they passed to their Constitutionalist contacts information—and misinformation—designed to pressure the Tlaxcalan to return to Zapatismo by ruining his credibility with Carranza.[30]

The maneuvering went on for months, and Arenas was getting the best of it. In the words of Fortino Ayaquica, he was "undermining our ranks with money, with clothing and with promises," so that Zapatismo was losing ground daily with no shots fired. He had become a major threat to Zapata's power, and in the summer of 1917 Zapata decided that the issue had to be settled. Talks between Magaña and Arenas began in June; at the end of August came the news that Arenas had been killed during a conference with Magaña and Ayaquica near Tochimilco. How this happened is uncertain. In various accounts over the years Ayaquica alternately claimed that Arenas provoked the scuffle that led to his death by trying to ambush them, by asking them to join Carranza, or by demanding recognition as the head of the revolution. Given that Zapatista reinforcements were immediately at hand and that the Zapatistas won the day, it is at least marginally more likely that Zapata, Magaña, and Ayaquica had planned to kill the dangerous Arenas at this meeting if he did not finally make good on his many promises to rejoin them. At any rate, they professed no unhappiness about the outcome of the parley. Arenas's body was sent to Zapata, who had it hung with those of Vázquez and Montaño on the road outside Tlaltizapán. In Tlaxcala Arenas became a martyr and Zapata and Magaña assassins, but the cross-purposes, the deceit, and the death were all just part of the practical politics of revolution.[31]

In an attempt to end the "contagious leprosy of treason," on September 20 Zapata brought forth a decree that reflected an obsession with the subject that was understandable in light of recent events. The preamble of this document began with a history of betrayal in Mexico, and then spoke of Pacheco, Vázquez, Montaño, and Arenas—"the traitor of all traitors." "The propaganda against

traitors must start," it exhorted, "in the bosom of every family."
Then came the decree itself, which merely outlined existing practice by defining those behaviors that were considered betrayal, and
prescribing the death penalty for them.[32]

In manifesto after manifesto Zapata kept his head high and his
eye on his goals—the destruction of the haciendas and the liberation
of the campesino and the worker. Again and again he insisted opti-
mistically that those whom Carranza had once fooled were now
beginning to see the light. Reality, however, had little to do with
these goals and these hopes: it was still Zapata more than Carranza
who was being betrayed and, deeper than the dramatic cases of treason, there was an ongoing erosion of Zapata's support at the village
level because fewer and fewer people could still share his optimism
and his vision.

Arenas was a problem, then, because he was able to compete
with Zapata for whole villages of supporters. He was able to compete because if the abuses committed by Zapatistas seem to have
slowed in early 1917, by the end of the year they were as bad or
worse than ever. A good example of the problem was what was
taking place around Huaquechula, Puebla. "In the plaza of Huaquechula," Magaña had written in July, "the most scandalous disorder
possible continues to reign, and the shooting between our own
forces grows every day." In Huaquechula and Tlapanalá, Ayaquica
elaborated, "they say that they no longer want even a fistful of the
land that the Plan of Ayala has given them, because the ambition
that they have at the moment is just to obtain a guarantee that
they'll live." Meanwhile, the Carrancistas were turning up the pressure, plotting another major attack on Morelos and then moving
into the eastern part of the state in November. Zapata began to fear
the loss of the prime agricultural lands at the Morelos/Guerrero
border, and villagers were already looking for ways to avoid being
incriminated in Zapatismo when the Carrancistas arrived.[33]

Despite these many strains and the demands of Magaña and
Ayaquica that Zapata take action, Zapata's mind was set on the
national scene, and in a somewhat desperate gamble he devoted his

shrinking intellectual entourage to interfactional diplomacy rather than to the resolution of local conflicts. In December he signed letters to José H. Castro, Adolfo Bonilla, Amado Azuara, Hesequio Barbosa, Magdaleno and Saturnino Cedillo, José Inés Chávez García, Samuel Espinosa de los Monteros, and Manuel N. Robles. Some were generals, some were educated civilians, some had a measure of power and some did not, some were already in rebellion, and others remained loyal to Carranza. On the twenty-seventh of the month these efforts were complimented with two manifestos repeating the usual charges against "Carranza, man of antechambers, genuine creature of the past, imbued with the lessons of the Porfirian court." Addressing the Mexican people and the revolutionary family, the manifestos again generalized the invitation to unite against a faltering regime.[34]

Though by early 1918 the Zapatistas recognized that Pablo González was an unconditional supporter of Carranza, other erstwhile Carrancistas were indeed rebelling. In December, for instance, Luis Gutiérrez and Francisco Coss had taken up arms in Carranza's home state of Coahuila over electoral improprieties. In January they heard from Zapata. Zapata and Magaña were also watching Alvaro Obregón—who had left Carranza's government in early 1917—and the new Partido Liberal Constitucionalista (PLC) that supported his political ambitions. A new batch of letters went out: to Andrés Pérez, Inés Salazar, Jesús Cíntora, Trinidad Regalado, Benjamín Hill, Eutimio Figueroa, José Siurob, Pedro Morales, and "jefes Moris and Matus who command the Yaqui Indians." Envoys left in all directions, and Zapata claimed to be in constant communication with most of the country's revolutionaries. He even allowed Magaña to approach Carranza himself in February, in search of a cease-fire that would take some pressure off the villages. Once the shooting stopped, the Zapatistas proposed, they could move on to negotiations. A cease-fire would at least buy time, and perhaps Zapata was worried enough now that he would have accepted a peace that gave him control in Morelos. Carranza apparently never answered the overture, however, and the various rebellions around the country fizzled. Beyond recent hints that some Arenistas might forget the past and rejoin him, Zapata still had little to show for his diplomatic labors.[35]

Nor was there much to show for the foreign expeditions of Paz and Amezcua, but in early February a new opportunity for Zapata to explain himself to the American public arrived at Tochimilco in the person of William Gates. Magaña informed Zapata that Gates had friends in the U.S. government, was a "professor in some University and a person of considerable culture," and wanted to write something on the agrarian question. Those qualifications were enough for Zapata, who had spent much of January fighting off the enemy at the Guerrero/Morelos border, but now came up to meet the American at Tlaltizapán. Gates already disliked Carranza, and soon promised to speak for Zapata in Washington. Then, perhaps for the first time, Zapata heard the warning that once the war in Europe was over, the United States would turn its attention to Mexico if the conflict there still raged.[36]

Though past American invasions had never been of primary concern for him, Zapata apparently took this threat seriously. He also recognized that it might serve as yet another argument in his drive to unify the rebels and bring Carranza down. In a March decree of amnesty, in fact, the Zapatistas were already asserting that the continuation of the fighting would provide an opportunity for foreign capitalists to get their governments involved in Mexico. To keep this from happening, the decree recommended "the mutual and reciprocal forgetting of all the differences that have divided revolutionaries in the past."[37] In doing so it demonstrated how dramatically Zapata's diplomacy had changed since 1914.

Two manifestos of March 15 displayed the same willingness to break down barriers that had kept rebel factions apart. One, addressed to the Revolutionaries of the Republic, demonstrated the growing Zapatista appreciation that different regions had different needs, needs that a proposed junta of the country's revolutionary leaders would naturally take into account as it deliberated on Mexico's future. The second manifesto again reached out to urban workers, arguing that they and the campesinos shared a common struggle, and expressing the desire "that the calloused hands of the fields and the calloused hands of the factory grasp one another in a fraternal greeting of concord."[38]

In April 1918 the Arenistas displayed their growing displeasure with Carranza by rebelling against him, and Zapata signed appeals in both Spanish and Nahuatl in the effort to win them back to his side. At about the same time another new rebellion, roughly Felicista, broke out on the strategically important Guerreran coast near Acapulco. Zapata quickly ordered Marcelo Caraveo into the area, and at first even hoped to send Díaz Soto y Gama along, "because it is urgent to make intense propaganda in that place by means of the spoken word." By now Zapata had obviously abandoned his mistrust and committed himself to putting unification first and saving the ideological sorting-out for later. In fact, he soon proved an even more daring diplomat than Magaña. When an agent in Mexico City went beyond the powers of representation he had been accorded and started making promises to the Felicistas, Magaña worried about the impression such a dialogue with the conservative rebels would make on revolutionaries like Villa. "If some initiatives of this nature bring good results," Zapata reassured him, "they'll be accepted, and if not we'll reject them." He underlined the irony of such a policy, after the rigidity of 1914, by soliciting the support of Antonio I. Villarreal in May.[39]

By the middle of May Zapata had arranged a tactical accord with the Arenistas. After several weeks of foot-dragging from Caraveo, he also got that ambassador off on his mission, and Zapatista propaganda proclaimed great revolutionary victories in Guerrero. Magaña's report that Gates was already in Washington, where he "has made our tendencies and our conduct known," added to the climate of hope around Zapata. Contending that the "immense majority" of revolutionary chieftains had already done so, Zapata began to ask the recipients of his letters to pledge themselves to revolutionary unity by signing a new manifesto of April 25, 1918, which described

Zapata's goals in general terms and again called for a junta to resolve on specifics once the rebels had taken the capital.[40]

Zapata also tried, in early 1918, to take some of the local problem solving upon himself. In February he went east to Zacualpan, Morelos, to smooth tensions that had risen over a land dispute. In March he travelled to the Huaquechula area, where he concluded that the villagers were not Carrancistas, and simply needed to be convinced of their errors. To Francisco Mendoza he recommended that the pacíficos there be treated well—especially since they were armed. A month later, however, when Huaquechula requested permission to propitiate the Carrancistas who operated in the area, Zapata was inclined to draw the line. "To let Huaquechula take the step it asks," he counselled Magaña, "would be to set a precedent that other pueblos would not be slow to follow, something that, you will recognize, is not convenient for the Cause."[41]

There was no way, in other words, to put the movement back together. Smuggling across enemy lines, by both troops and pacíficos, continued. So did intrigue and betrayal, among intellectuals and jefes alike. Troop numbers declined to the extent that when General Severo Várgas got sick he could only present his subordinate with seventeen men. Everardo González, pointedly honored for his fighting ability in 1916, became so violent that Zapata was forced to remove him as jefe of his zone; it was even rumored that he had plotted to assassinate Zapata. As the roads became more dangerous, many campesinos grew less enthusiastic about keeping watch as Zapata had ordered, especially outside village environs. More and more pueblos, including Tlaltizapán and Tochimilco, asserted that they were unable to feed the troops any longer. Still the demands continued. In late April at Amecac, Puebla, not far from Huaquechula, one conflict between troops and pueblos reached its natural conclusion. When a group of Caraveo's soldiers arrived for corn the pacíficos refused to give it. When they tried to take it anyway, shots were fired, and the soldiers got the worst of the encounter. One later claimed he heard a villager say, right before the fighting started, "here come just a few, it's time to wipe them out." Because this confrontation was not an isolated incident, there was pressure on Zapata to deprive the pueblos of their guns. In a circular of July 10, 1918, he compromised, ordering that firearms be licensed both by municipal and military authorities. Those pacíficos who used their arms against the Zapatista cause, he was compelled to add, would be considered traitors. There were, of course, few real military successes under such conditions, and even isolated Tochimilco was often threatened by the Carrancistas. Still the official optimism remained strong, and there were frequent plans for attacks on Puebla and other important cities, usually in league with jefes who had Felicista ties.[42]

Frustrated by the inability of Paz Solórzano to significantly influence U.S. opinion, in August Zapata tried to give his diplomatic offensive greater impetus by appointing Francisco Vázquez Gómez to represent him in the United States—something Vázquez Gómez had already done once in 1913. In discussing the matter with Magaña, Zapata again displayed his flexibility. "It is my opinion," he argued, "that to look for men of perfectly correct ideals and clean pasts . . . for the performance of a commission of the kind that is being considered is almost in vain." Two days later he added of Vázquez Gómez, "although he is bad, now what's important to my way of thinking is to let various people do what they can, and then we will decide what slant to give the matter." "Doctor Vázquez Gómez," he concluded, "is very clever at politics and he would do something."[43]

Closer to home, Zapata was busy collecting signatures on the manifesto of April 25, and again he found reason for optimism. The task of promoting revolutionary unity in Veracruz and northern Puebla was assigned to a secretary, Reynaldo Lecona, who first set out for the area early in the summer. In northern Veracruz he met Manuel Peláez. Peláez had taken up arms against Constitutionalist intrusions in 1914 and had subsequently come to control the lucrative oil fields of the region. By accepting protection money from the foreign companies that owned those fields he had made himself one of Carranza's most powerful opponents. Though his foreign connections limited his ideological appeal, Zapata and Magaña were thrilled when Lecona reported that Peláez intended to send Zapata a commission, for they knew he had money and thus presumably access to arms. To Zapata Magaña wrote: "you will understand better than anyone the transcendence of this matter."[44]

The matter was transcendent enough, in fact, that Lecona was again off to Veracruz in August, where he met a reasonably friendly Félix Díaz before returning with letters for Zapata from Peláez and a host of others. Zapata and Magaña continued to hope that Peláez would sign their unifying manifesto. "His signature," Magaña wrote, "stamped on the Manifesto of April 25, would give us immense moral force, for you are aware of the preponderance that this Jefe has in the eyes of the allied nations, for his commercial relations with the English and the Americans." So important did this initiative seem that they now laid plans to set Lecona up with a propaganda office near Peláez's territory.[45]

Still in August 1918, Zapata signed a letter to the exiled Felipe Angeles. He also contacted Villa's representative in Washington, Miguel Díaz Lombardo, whom he assured that Gates would secure U.S. recognition of the belligerency against Carranza if the rebels would only unite. Much more importantly, Zapata approached Obregón directly for the first time, sending him two letters in the space of a week. Arguing that the middle and working class radicals of the city—represented by Obregón and the PLC—were natural allies of his own campesinos, he urged Obregón to use his power and popularity to free the nation from Carranza. Zapata's hopes in Obregón were not unfounded. Obregón's dislike of Carranza was becoming increasingly clear, and members of the PLC apparently now took the time to speak with Zapata's agents. Acting on the rumor that the PLC was planning a coup in the capital, Zapata tried to arrange a diversionary raid in Puebla in September.[46]

In December the troops of Pablo González made their definitive move back into Morelos. Indeed, only the fear that they would be decimated by the brutal Spanish flu epidemic that had recently arrived among the Zapatistas had kept them from conquering the major settlements in November. As they rolled into Tlaltizapán, fell back for a few days, and then returned, there was nothing Zapata could do. Nothing, that is, but maintain an eery optimism. As his overwhelmed forces retreated, he informed Magaña that, "The Carrancista enemy is making desperate efforts to establish itself in our zone."[47]

Even as this new invasion took place, discussions with the Carrancistas stationed at Atlixco, Puebla, continued. Again these talks soon led to González, who offered to accept a commission from Zapata, and suggested that the Zapatistas congregate at a single spot in Morelos during the negotiations. González knew that he had to finish with the Zapatistas completely this time if he meant to salvage his political career, and he was hoping that they would help him. But Zapata had learned too much from Huerta and Madero to fall into this trap. He continued to try to fight, now more as a way of appearing strong for purposes of diplomacy—to which virtually all his energies were devoted—than with any hope that he might win a significant military victory. Even this was unrealistic. The opportunity to negotiate from a position of strength had passed him by years ago. Even if he could somehow arrange a victorious coalition of rebels, his power to affect its decisions would be small.[48]

However unrealistic his hopes, as 1918 came to an end Zapata was quite aware of what had been lost in 1914 and 1915. Recently Manuel Palafox had left the movement. With the rise of Magaña and the search for diplomatic solutions, Palafox had lost influence, and he had stepped on so many people as he climbed through Zapatista ranks that there were many who were eager to bring him down. By the middle of 1917 he was reduced to an errand boy, and the faithless little man responded by trying to cut a deal with the enemy. If Carranza would set him up in South American exile, he promised to bring into the Constitutionalist camp a host of intellectuals and jefes, "who on seeing that I, who fought so long for the fulfillment of the Plan of Ayala—which as I told you is impractical—seeing that the intellectual director of Zapatismo has surrendered, I am sure that they will do the same thing, and Zapatismo will be totally extinguished in this state." Zapata, however, discovered his plans, and again as in 1911 Palafox was lucky not to be executed. He became a virtual prisoner among the Zapatistas instead. *"Algo loco"*—somewhat crazy—he had little to do but brag of past accomplishments, and at one point he tried unsuccessfully to escape. In the spring of 1918 Zapata sent Palafox and his friend Enrique Bonilla to Tochimilco to get them out of his sight, but in October his need for the educated was so great that he entrusted Palafox and Bonilla with a diplomatic commission, and they used the opportunity to flee. Considering them a security risk, Magaña plotted to trick them into returning, but Zapata did not want them back.[49]

Zapata must soon have repented his decision to let Palafox go, for Palafox began almost immediately to circulate charges that Zapata was corrupt and that he had ordered the assassination of several important jefes. These charges were either exaggerations or outright fabrications—there is no evidence and little likelihood that Zapata had profited significantly from the revolution—but when combined with invitations to important Zapatistas to defect from the movement, they constituted a new threat of division. In response, by early January, Zapata produced a remarkable account of Palafox's career. Written at times in an almost confessional tone, this document began by declaring that it was hard to evaluate the motives of such newcomers to the movement as Palafox had been in 1911. At first, it noted, he received only Zapata's "indifference and suspicion," but he went to great lengths to ingratiate himself. "I began to realize," Zapata continued, "that . . . he was trying to totally displace General Otilio Montaño from my side, something he did not manage, given the importance of that warrior, and because I did not give him [Palafox] tasks beyond his capacity and knowledge." As a result, Zapata maintained, when Carranza's delegation of would-be peacemakers arrived in August 1914, Palafox did not possess any great power within the movement. Nevertheless, "among the group of persons I commissioned to deal with the gentlemen cited above [Cabrera, Villarreal, and Sarabia] was Palafox, who always distin-

guished himself in the talks by his aggressive and unyielding attitude, which naturally made a terrible impression on those who, in a
given moment, could have been our allies." The document added
that Palafox had been equally belligerent with his fellow Zapatistas,
thwarting both their ideological and their military labors, and
gravely hurting the cause in the process. Luckily, Zapata had finally
discovered the magnitude of the damage that Palafox had done, and
removed him from his position at headquarters in order to start
"curing the evil, though it was late."⁵⁰

Composed just months before Zapata's death, this rewriting of
history might serve as his final testament, at least on the subjects of
Palafox and interfactional relations. Casting his mind back over the
years, he saw failure in the intransigence of the period that encom-
passed August 1914. But whose failure was it? About that Zapata
was disingenuous. The events of late 1914 now seemed so momentous to him that he skirted his own support for Palafox, and was
only willing to plead guilty, indirectly, to the less serious crime of
having failed to control his intellectuals. Nor would he now condemn Montaño, whose sins perhaps seemed small in retrospect,
especially when compared to his contributions. With his movement
in its death throes, Zapata could not accept his own mistakes and
distorted past events to hide them.

There was also a certain lack of realism at work when Zapata
decided, in his last big diplomatic enterprise, that Francisco Vázquez
Gómez should not merely represent him in Washington, but should
serve as the head of the united revolution, "to bring to a happy
ending and leave totally consummated the work of unification."
The manifesto that announced the choice of Vázquez Gómez on
February 10 justified his selection by proposing that, with his
knowledge of international affairs, he was the man to confront the
foreign threat that hung over Mexico as World War I ended. It also
recommended him as a long-time partisan of agrarian reform. In
truth, Zapata knew that Vázquez Gomez's program for social change
was too general to be meaningful. In supporting him, in fact, he
tacitly admitted his inability to guarantee the kind of land reform

for which he had fought. As he had done with Madero, he would have to help bring Vázquez Gómez to power first and then see what happened. An even bigger problem was that bringing Vázquez Gómez to power was a long-shot. Zapata had always claimed that he was not in the revolution to further his own ambitions, and here was yet another eloquent proof that he, more than any other caudillo of the period, meant what he said. But in the end this admirable gesture of abnegation was an empty one, for it would do nothing to settle the question of who would rule Mexico. In allowing themselves to believe that a parlor revolutionary like Vázquez Gómez might somehow win the revolution, Zapata and Magaña showed how pathetic their movement had become: between the lines of the manifesto that proclaimed their public hope in Vázquez Gómez, one could read their private desperation.[51]

They had every reason to be desperate. By November 1918 the Spanish flu of which Pablo González had been so wary had joined the usual typhus, malaria, and dysentery to prey on the underfed inhabitants of Zapata's region. According to official statistics, the population of Morelos dropped twenty-five percent in 1918 alone, and Zapata was probably left with no more than two thousand soldiers, who often set out on their raids with only three or four cartridges of ammunition each. When, in early February of 1919, Magaña cited pressing business in asking Zapata to come to his zone, he apparently meant to suggest that Zapata give up military maneuvers altogether. Perhaps sensing this intention, Zapata claimed that the rigors of the campaign against Carranza made it impossible for him to come, and in truth he did seem to take a renewed interest in the fighting. Even the smallest operation, however, was a lot to ask of his forces. A Carrancista onslaught in de la O's territory in early March met no resistance because the troops were hiding with their families in the mountains. Driven yet again from their homes, the people there were starving and, since de la O could not feed them, some angrily demanded the right to reconcentrate in Cuernavaca as Pablo González had ordered. Eventually de la O got a few men together to fight, but "the demoralization had entered even into the spirits most accustomed to battle."[52]

Still Zapata maintained some hope that a diplomatic break-through would come before his movement collapsed completely. In March he received a copy of an article that William Gates had just published, and wrote to thank him for presenting Zapatismo to the American people in "full justice, simple justice," which was all he had ever asked. He also continued to work on Peláez, though Peláez wanted to become chief of the revolution himself, and soon made it clear that he would not recognize Vázquez Gómez. On March 17 Zapata directed an open letter to Carranza. "I am not speaking to the President of the Republic," read this document, "whom I don't recognize, nor to the politician, in whom I have no faith; I am speaking to the Mexican, to the man endowed with feelings and reason, who must at some time be moved (if only for an instant) by the anguish of the mothers, the suffering of the orphans, the uneasiness and the grief of the Nation." In a familiar but forceful rush all the old charges of despotism, monetary irresponsibility, and bad faith on land reform followed, and Zapata finished by demanding that Carranza "return to the people their liberty."[53]

At about the time he signed this letter Zapata began to hear rumors that a young Constitutionalist Colonel named Jesús Guajardo had recently fallen out with Pablo González. Though Guajardo had overseen a massacre at Tlaltizapán in the fall of 1916, in light of the five hundred men he commanded Zapata's willingness to forget the past ran deep. In a letter of March 21 he made Guajardo a "formal and frank invitation" to join Zapatismo. Though he had no military prospects left, Zapata remained a political thorn in Carranza's side on the strength of his propaganda efforts, and Carranza had contemplated his assassination before. Thus when González got wind of Zapata's letter he saw his chance to finish his frustrating work in Morelos, please his boss, and help set himself up for the presidency that was to come open in 1920. At his bidding Guajardo quickly accepted Zapata's offer, "in view of the great difficulties that exist between Pablo González and me."[54]

Excited by Guajardo's promise of munitions, on April first Zapata asked him to make his initial move against Carranza in two days. For a test of Guajardo's sincerity he already had a task in mind. Among the traitors who had plagued Zapata most was a jefe named Victoriano Bárcenas, who defected from the movement in 1918 and had chased Zapata into Puebla as recently as February. Bárcenas had also indulged in a number of brutalities in recent months, including the capture and mistreatment of Zapata's girlfriend, Gregoria Zúñiga, and their daughter María Luisa. Zapata now asked Guajardo to apprehend Bárcenas and his forces. Guajardo stalled. Bárcenas, he said, was presently in Cuautla with Pablo González. Moreover, the money and equipment Guajardo planned to bring with him when he defected would not be available until at least April 6.[55]

Though Zapata grew impatient, events unfolded at Guajardo's pace. Finally, on the morning of April 9 he attacked the Carrancista garrison at Jonacatepec, feigning the battle so well that several people died. The same day he arrested fifty-nine of Bárcenas's men—Bárcenas was not among them—and either turned them over to Zapata for execution or killed them himself. Combined with testimony in Guajardo's favor from Zapata's aide, Feliciano Palacios, who had spent some time with the colonel, and from a Zapatista captive in Cuautla named Eusebio Jáuregui, these actions were proof enough for Zapata of Guajardo's good will. "Maybe Zapata," wrote one eye-witness, "trusted him out of the need to believe in something or in someone." At about four o'clock that afternoon Zapata and Guajardo met at a train station south of Jonacatepec, Guajardo with several hundred men and Zapata with about thirty. Zapata congratulated Guajardo for the choice he had made; Guajardo walked his horses past Zapata to let him choose the one that pleased him most. Together they rode to nearby Tepalcingo where Guajardo, apparently fearing poison, evaded a dinner invitation on the pretense of illness and then refused the cure Zapata offered.[56]

Late that night they departed for Chinameca, Guajardo going all the way to the hacienda, and Zapata stopping on the road to sleep. At about eight the next morning, a Thursday, Zapata went down to

Chinameca with perhaps 150 men. While his troops distributed themselves in the shade beneath the trees, waiting and playing cards, Zapata and Guajardo moved away with a handful of jefes to discuss their immediate military plans. Rumors that the enemy was approaching soon interrupted them, however, and Zapata took thirty men into the nearby hills to have a look. Finding nothing, they arrived back at the hacienda shortly after noon. Guajardo was now inside somewhere, and soon he invited Zapata to join him. But Zapata was in no hurry now. He remained where he was for another half hour, talking under the trees, before acceding to Guajardo's request. Ordering ten men to follow, he mounted the horse Guajardo had given him and headed toward the hacienda gate.

He did this despite warnings from spies and seers that Guajardo had something planned, because what Guajardo offered to his moribund movement was too good to pass up, and Zapata had, after all, heard assassination rumors before. And so he brushed off those who cautioned him, and got angry when they persisted. He knew, of course, that they could be right, for such ambushes were common revolutionary practice and he himself had almost certainly arranged more than one. Entering the hacienda was a gamble, but like embarking upon the revolution itself it was a gamble he was willing to take. His desperation and his hope had brought him here, because he knew in the end that he could not count on Vázquez Gómez or Peláez, and he could not wait forever for Obregón.

Zapata had never forgotten what he was gambling for: land and liberty and the chance at basic human dignity for the poor people he lived with; the fulfillment of the promises of justice and law that generations of politicians had often polished but never honored. Of course, before the revolution he himself was doing better than most, and better than he was doing now. The hacendados had angered him by taking his land, but for himself, he had always insisted, he wanted nothing. Except maybe the chance to sit in the shade in the afternoon and smoke a cigar and drink a beer without worrying about anything bigger than the horses or the crops. The chance to settle down in peace—that was what he had been raised to expect.

After all he was almost forty. His son Mateo was now a year old and Diego about the same age; María Luisa and Paulina and Ana María were all four or five, María Elena about ten, Nicolás perhaps thirteen. He could not be sure about their ages; he had really not been around. Of course, the attention and the acclaim were nice, and he felt the love of the people, especially in the early years, but were they worth this life on the run, the burden of watching his world burn and crumble around him, the burden of being the one who had to ride his horse through that open gate into the dusty courtyard beyond where they were waiting? But Zapata had always lived life on his own terms. As he approached the gate

> "the guard appeared ready to do him the honors. The bugle sounded three times, the call of honor, and when the last note fell silent, as the General arrived at the threshold, in a manner most treacherous, most cowardly, most villainous, at point-blank range, without giving him time even to clutch his pistols, the soldiers who were presenting arms fired their rifles twice, and our general Zapata fell never to rise again."[57]

Epilogue and Conclusion

TERRIFIED BY THE UNEXPECTED GUNFIRE, THE ZAPA-
tistas fled Chinameca in disarray, many unsure for
the moment of what had happened. Zapata's body was thrown over
the back of a horse, and Guajardo began his victorious ride north
from Chinameca—through San Rafael, Moyotepec, Villa de Ayala
. . . Anenecuilco. The news spread like wildfire. Sometime after nine
that night they arrived in Cuautla, where Pablo González was waiting. González immediately telegraphed Carranza. Zapata, he
claimed, had been killed in battle with Guajardo's men. With his
death, he added hopefully, the zone in which he operated was pacified. Zapata was put on display in Cuautla to convince the populace
that he was really gone. Thousands came to look. It was then suggested that the body be taken to Mexico City too, to calm metropolitan fears of the southern Attila, but apparently it seemed too
morbid, for González sent photographs to the press instead. In one,
excited young soldiers propped up the bloated head of the corpse so
the camera might leave no doubt.[1]

It did look like Zapata, thought many people in Cuautla, but it
was not him. The finger, the mole, the birthmark—something was
not quite right. They could only conclude that he was still alive.
Others, however, accepted the truth. *"Se nos cayeron las alas del
corazón"*—the wings of our hearts fell—recalled one Zapatista, and
many of the young men who followed Zapata felt as though their

227

8. Showing off the corpse (Archivo General de la Nación, Mexico City, Archivo Fotográfico Díaz, Delgado y García)

father had died. To those who had remained loyal through all the trials and who still hoped that the revolution might allow them to fulfill their goals it was a heavy blow. Many assumed that the death of Zapata meant the end of the struggle; a few chose to fight on. On April 15 some of the remaining chiefs issued a manifesto to the Mexican people, full of praise for their dead hero. "Those wretches have assassinated the man," they announced, "but they have not been able to kill the idea."[2] Little more than the idea remained, however. González now began reconstituting the haciendas of Morelos, and many campesinos were ready for the change. From 1911 to 1914, one summarized, "everyone was more or less in agreement with the jefe." But from 1915 on "the government would arrive and burn the pueblos, the Zapatistas would arrive and commit outrages, so that when Zapata died the people desired peace more than anything, even if the Plan of Ayala was not fulfilled."[3]

Throughout the summer Magaña tried to call a junta to elect a successor to Zapata, and thus put an end to the new uncertainty about who led the movement. Meanwhile, jefes received appeals for their support from all directions, including some from Palafox, who wrote of returning to occupy his proper place in the movement, as if he thought no one would remember how he left. Finally, a junta met on September 4, 1919, at Huautla, and chose Magaña himself the new head of the army despite the explicit recognition that he hardly measured up to the old chief. Even given this admission, not everyone was happy with the choice. De la O had refused to answer Magaña's communications for months after Zapata's death, and he did not attend the junta that elected him. Both he and Francisco Mendoza had apparently hoped to lead Zapatismo themselves.[4]

When de la O softened enough to congratulate Magaña for his election in mid-November, it looked like Magaña might truly succeed Zapata in leading a relatively united movement. But later in the month he made a crucial mistake. Through with the war in Europe, the government of the United States was now wrangling with Carranza over his arrest of the U.S. consular agent in Puebla— William O. Jenkins—who was charged with trying to discredit Carranza internationally by feigning his own kidnapping in October. Regardless of Jenkins's guilt or innocence, it seemed possible for a moment that another U.S. invasion was on the way. Perhaps tired and losing hope for a diplomatic breakthrough, Magaña informed his fellow Zapatistas that he had decided to surrender in light of the grave international situation. He suggested that they all show their patriotism by doing the same. Though some jefes followed his lead, he soon discovered how little moral authority he wielded over many of his nominal subordinates. Many chiefs simply hid in the mountains, and in December de la O even attempted a military offensive. "Let's demonstrate," he told another general, "that the betrayals and capitulations of the cowards, instead of frightening us, impel us to resume the fight."[5]

Whether because he discovered that he would not get a good deal from Carranza or because the international situation quickly improved, Magaña soon began sending letters to jefes in their mountain hide-outs, telling them to remain in rebellion. Then in January 1920 he fled the capital to rejoin the conflict himself, claiming he had never truly surrendered. Still de la O was indignant. In March he charged Magaña with leaving the Zapatista army in confusion, "which led some to surrender and return to their homes, for which reason I recognize you now as a companion in the struggle, a brother in ideas, but never as Jefe of that Army." For de la O, who had never displayed much liking or trust for Zapatismo's intellectual brood, Magaña's selection to head the movement must have been a nightmare, and that probably explains his lasting anger over the abortive surrender. In any event, his rejection of Magaña's leadership had nothing to do with the general strategy of courting other factions, to which there was no serious alternative. In fact, de la O began to conduct his own diplomacy with Peláez, Obregón, and others.[6]

Meanwhile, the political maneuvering within Constitutionalism was finally coming to a head. Elections were scheduled for 1920, and Carranza was angling to keep control of Mexico by placing a puppet in the presidency. But Carranza's support had been eroding for years. He had not been able to end the violence or solve the considerable economic difficulties the revolution had created, and he had done virtually nothing to fulfill the promises of the Constitution of 1917. Obregón would no longer put his presidential ambitions on hold. As the revolution's most successful general he had the popularity to win a fair election, and when it became evident, in mid-April 1920, that Carranza would not allow such an election to take place, Obregón had little recourse but to rebel.[7] Both de la O and Magaña immediately signed on with his Plan of Agua Prieta. The Zapatistas helped Obregón flee immanent arrest in the capital and then assisted him in capturing it by force of arms. The fighting ended in a matter of weeks: on May 9 Obregón and de la O entered Mexico City together while Carranza fled toward Veracruz. Later in the month Carranza's career ended much as Zapata's had, when he was killed in the mountains of Puebla by troops loyal to Obregón.

With Obregón's lightning strike against Carranza, the Zapatistas suddenly had their piece of a triumphant revolution. Zapata had had his eye on Obregón by 1917 because he recognized that he stood the best chance of toppling Carranza should he ever attempt it. Moreover, whether because he was closer to Zapata than to Carranza in class standing or simply because he was a better politician than Carranza, Obregón had long sounded amenable to social reform in a way that Carranza was not. Now in the spring of 1920 Magaña, de la O, and the other Zapatistas heard him promise that the national government would preside over land reform.

A revolution is about power, however, and in 1920 the Zapatistas had little of that. Their piece of the revolution was small; they would have to trust Obregón to give them the reforms they sought. But Obregón was a northerner, and he had his own ideas. He did preside over the beginnings of a land reform project, but it was one that would generally be more directly concerned with economic progress and the exigencies of national politics than with the welfare of the campesinos. Perhaps that was why Obregón and his successors never took a holistic approach to the subject, so that even when land was offered the water, credit, education, and political say that might have helped the campesinos work it were often lacking.

Though the land made it possible for some of the people of Morelos to continue to struggle on as campesinos, it soon became clear that the mere ownership of land was no guarantee of a livelihood. In the countryside of Morelos the expanding central government replaced the hacendados as the arbiter of campesino destinies, and the land reform process became riddled with corruption. Around Anenecuilco, Zapata's own son, Nicolás, used his name to grab what he could and called his father a fool.

What the villagers of Morelos had always feared gradually came to pass: the city expropriated the revolution. It was there, in the city, that the increasingly powerful revolutionary state was centered and, in the name of progress, it was the city that this state favored when it distributed resources, for to the new ruling class progress meant industrialization and urbanization. As the revolution became institutionalized, its leaders set their sights on making Mexico part of the modern world, and the only modern world they could ultimately envision had no room for the village agriculturalists of central and southern Mexico, who were simply left behind. Knowingly or not, many of Zapatismo's urban intellectuals contributed to the process by which the campesinos were manipulated and defrauded. By taking jobs in the various administrations of the institutionalizing revolution, they lent them the legitimacy they needed in the countryside. And they helped create—in exchange for the scraps of power and influence they were thrown—a myth of Zapata that would make him an innocuous member of the evolving revolutionary pantheon, a symbolic pillar of the new state. As he became the center of a cult used to mollify and demobilize the people of the Mexican countryside, Zapata was betrayed yet again.[8]

In many ways Emiliano Zapata has been taken for granted. Perhaps due to our abiding vision of Zapatismo as a fundamentally homogeneous and communal rebellion, scholars have simply assumed that Zapata fit into the picture in a rather automatic and symbolic way. As a result, no one has previously gone inside the movement to evaluate his role there. But Zapatismo was far from homogeneous and not perfectly communal. Informed by varying socioeconomic conditions, campesinos from different parts of the Zapatista world sometimes disagreed on ideals and strategies; neighboring villages had long-standing feuds; and even within a given community of Zapata's supporters there were simple, human differences of opinion. There was no consensus on many issues and nothing automatic about how the movement took shape. Zapata's leadership was crucial in bringing and keeping it together.

One means that Zapata used to unite his rebellion, of course, was ideology. With the Plan of Ayala he and Otilio Montaño sought to give the campesinos of south/central Mexico a single voice loud enough to be heard in Mexico City. The Plan of Ayala was built from the concrete experiences of Zapata and many of the villagers around him, but its particular ideological constructions were not innate in the peasantry of the region. Indeed, not all of Zapata's adherents were primarily motivated by the struggle for land. That Zapata was molding opinion rather than merely following it became especially clear during the last years of the fighting, in the creation of such organizations as the Consultation Center for Revolutionary Propaganda and Unification. Though the gap that separated Zapata from his following was much smaller, his task in this regard resembled in kind that of the city-bred guerrilla leaders of more recent Latin American history, who have gone into the countryside to spread their revolutionary ideologies.

Zapata's lasting allegiance to the core demands of the Plan of Ayala earned him a reputation as the revolution's great intransigent. But his intransigence extended only to fundamental goals. He often willingly compromised and negotiated on lesser issues, and he changed strategy and top advisors on several occasions. In fact, he was a practical revolutionary in many respects. As Zapatismo grew and became increasingly complicated, Zapata struggled to centralize and discipline his following in order to build an army that could threaten Mexico City. That goal, however, often demanded toughness more than ideological clarity. When Felipe Neri challenged his authority, for instance, Zapata apparently ordered the popular jefe gunned down, and Neri's assassination was not a unique event. At other times practicality meant accepting strange bed-fellows—like the ex-federals who strayed into Zapata's world in late 1914 and then never completely left it. Zapata's willingness to deal with the unclean, and to behave brutally himself when that was what it took to maintain a modicum of discipline, brought Zapatismo the degree of coherence and military success that it achieved. Especially in the years between 1911 and 1914, Zapata's leadership succeeded on the regional level, providing a crucial centripetal force within a complex movement.

As a reward for his achievements on the regional scene, by mid-1914 Zapata was where he knew he had to be—at the center of national politics. Here he failed. Like most peasant revolutionaries he needed allies if he hoped to wield national power. But the task of securing such allies was complicated, and Zapata was probably right in believing that his education and experiences had not prepared him for it. In any event, he came to depend on his urban intellectuals to act as mediators, to help him carry out his interfactional diplomacy, to give him the national perspective he lacked.

Though Zapata never fully trusted his aides and advisors from the city, he depended on their advice too much to control them completely. And unfortunately for Zapata the unscrupulous Manuel Palafox had clawed his way to the top of the movement. When Carranza's envoys arrived in Morelos in August 1914 Palafox reinforced Zapatismo's country isolationism at the expense of other, more conciliatory, tendencies. In the months that followed, with Zapata's at least tacit approval, Palafox and other urban intellectuals used the Convention platform to continue to sabotage the diplomatic process, first with the Constitutionalists and then with the Villistas. They failed to give Zapata the insight he sought from them; they did not counsel diplomacy at a time when Zapata might have secured a large piece of the revolution by negotiating from a position of strength.

Diplomatic failure was not inevitable.[9] It seems unlikely that Zapata could have dealt profitably with Carranza himself, but an alliance with Carranza was not the only possibility rejected in 1914:

the Zapatistas might have appealed to individual Constitutionalists who were not especially loyal to their chief. Since Zapata and Magaña later tried to undermine Carranza in precisely this fashion, one can hardly claim the movement was too isolated and naturally intransigent to pursue such a strategy. There was no magical peasant consensus that supported policy exactly as it was made. Zapata and his intellectuals were constantly confronted by choices about which their constituency had no definite notions—choices that were theirs to make.

Zapata's posture was certainly not the only variable in the interfactional morass of 1914. The likelihood of diplomatic failure might have been tested, however, if Palafox had not gathered so much power and thrown his weight against diplomacy. By creating the feeling that Zapata could be a trustworthy ally, a little diplomacy *might* have won over more Constitutionalists. A broader coalition within the Convention of those who favored social reform *might* have succeeded in forcing Carranza to step down, or at least made his position militarily untenable. In that case provisions for social reform like those found in the 1917 Constitution *might* have been enacted sooner, with less bloodshed and, of crucial importance, with Zapata in a position to help see that they were enforced.[10]

Though Zapata left the daily workings of national politics in the hands of his urban advisors in the crucial months of late 1914 and early 1915, it would be wrong to simply conclude that he was too parochial and backward-looking to understand their significance. It was, instead, a matter of establishing priorities: there was also important work to be done in Morelos. There the process of allotting land and other resources, combined with the trials of having a national political presence, was causing tensions long at work within the movement to rise to the surface. Conflict was everywhere: between neighboring villages and neighboring jefes, between pacíficos and guerrilleros, between generals and intellectuals. Only Zapata could hope to mediate between these competing demands, and thus maintain the unity needed to bring Zapatista power to bear at the national level. His vision may have been limited when he deferred so much to personal ties and local loyalties that he allowed Antonio Barona and others like him to run wild, but his efforts on the local and regional scenes were not divorced from national goals.

After the summer of 1915, when Villa lost to Obregón and the Carrancistas came for the Zapatistas in Mexico City, Zapata's problems multiplied. The uneasy balance between centralization and discipline on the one hand and the movement's origins in decentralized, democratic action on the other began to break down. A wave of death and betrayal swept through Zapatismo. To try to avert disaster, Zapata relied mostly on methods that had worked in the past. He asked his intellectuals to elaborate on the program of reform that was the basis of his movement's unity, and he issued orders meant to instill discipline in his ranks. But there was little he could do. The big decisions had already been made; fate now took over. Zapata's instructions and threats, repeated over and over again, demonstrated his impotence. His diplomacy increasingly seemed a desperate race to make a deal before Zapatismo totally collapsed, but the possibility that the Zapatista program might deeply influence national politics was gone. By the time of Zapata's death his movement lay in utter decay.

There are naturally implications in the story of Zapata's life for our understanding of his movement and of how it fits into the Mexican Revolution. Zapata and Zapatismo have always been central to explanations of the larger insurrection. Those who first wrote about the revolution tended to describe it as a popular, agrarian uprising, and when they sought examples to support their generalizations they quickly turned to Zapatismo.[11] In recent decades, however, this traditional view of the revolution has come under great scrutiny. Especially in the wake of the 1968 massacre of protesters at the plaza of Tlatelolco in Mexico City—an event that discredited the still ostensibly revolutionary government—historians began to reexamine their assumptions. In careful, empirical studies of region after region, they downplayed the extent of popular mobilization during the revolutionary decade, and found that there was no monumental social reform in the 1920s. Stressing continuities between the regime of Porfirio Díaz and the years after 1920, many argued that the revolution had merely produced a more efficient and centralized state, and a reinvigorated bourgeoisie that employed this state to better control and exploit the working classes. The Mexican Revolution, they found, was not what it claimed to be; some even concluded that there had been no revolution at all. But these revisionists never subjected Zapatismo to their critique.[12] No longer an example of what the revolution was, Zapata's movement had become the shining, though unexamined, exception: what the revolution should have been and was not. Still at the center of interpretation, Zapatismo was now an island of social revolutionary sentiment in a sea of middle class rebellion, political machination, and even outright reaction.[13]

Then, in 1986, Alan Knight published a brilliant two volume study entitled *The Mexican Revolution*, which began to put Zapatismo back into the context of the larger uprising. Insisting that there had been a broadly popular, agrarian revolution in Mexico, on the surface this work was a frontal attack on the revisionist argument. Despite his rejection of many of the revisionists' conclusions, however, Knight did depend on their empirical spade-work. He was also influenced by their skepticism, examining claims of revolutionary change more carefully than did the practitioners of the traditional, "pro-revolution" school. Instead of simply representing a return to the original interpretation, in other words, *The Mexican Revolution* perhaps pointed the way toward a synthesis of traditional and revisionist positions.

In any event, my research might be seen to support such a middle position. It is true that the revolution had its limitations and imperfections. The Zapatismo that appears on these pages was not glorious and immaculate, but violent and often divided. Here as elsewhere in the Mexican Revolution it is difficult to draw a line between revolutionaries and bandits. Here as elsewhere ideology was one thing and action, often, another. Here as elsewhere peasant communalism was not the whole story and land reform was problematic. Such conclusions about even Zapatismo might, I suppose, lead one to join the most extreme revisionists and damn the entire revolution as a fraud. But that would be to ignore the obvious. Zapatismo's grass-roots, village origins, and its subsequent proclamations leave no doubt about its popular character. The veterans of the movement have been frank about the brutality and the pain and the personalism, but for them these things did not detract from the validity of their revolutionary experience. Rather, they formed an integral part of revolution, without which it could not be understood. Zapatismo can, in other words, continue to serve as a model of popular, social rebellion within the Mexican Revolution. This examination of its internal workings, however, leaves it a somewhat more conflicted and heterogeneous model than it was before—a model less different from other local and regional rebellions than was the old Zapatismo within the revisionist scheme.[14]

Such a model of the peasant rebellion that lies at the base of the Mexican Revolution might ultimately help solve what remains, I think, the main question we have about that revolution: if it was a truly popular event in the beginning, how did it become the corrupt and undemocratic entity that it was in 1930 or 1968 or 1988. Why did the revolution not fulfill its promise? There is much to recommend the typical revisionist argument that the peasants (and workers) who did the fighting were manipulated by bourgeois politicians, who blunted lower class demands for social change and appropriated the revolution for themselves. But the plot is surely more complicated than that. Above all, the story of Zapatismo suggests that the revolution was a complex web of local, regional, and national politics, and that its outcome had to do not only with relationships between factions but also within them. Given this, we surely need more studies of precisely how these politics worked. More specifically, we need to examine in detail the sometimes evasive interaction of different, but overlapping, political cultures, as revolutionaries of various backgrounds, ideals, and world views came together to build a new state.[15]

The image of Emiliano Zapata is deeply impressed upon the Mexican psyche. Even for those who do not still see his white horse roaming the mountains of Morelos, the myth of Zapata lives on. For the government this myth seems merely useful—a rubber stamp for whatever agrarian policy it chooses. When President Carlos Salinas de Gortari announced reforms of the Constitution of 1917 that will again fully expose the Mexican countryside to capitalist investment, he spoke in front of a mural of Zapata. Others have nurtured a more profound memory of the man. In January 1994, for example, a rebellion broke out in the state of Chiapas, and the guerrillas called themselves the Zapatista Army of National Liberation. These latter-day Zapatistas demanded "work, land, housing, food, health care, education, independence, freedom, democracy, justice and peace." They complained of the deterioration of their environment and called the recently signed North American Free Trade Agreement a "death sentence" for the Indians of the area.[16] It was not precisely Zapata's program—times have changed—but the rebels were not misguided in using his name to make such demands. More than representing a specific program, Zapata has come to embody a particular part of the Mexican experience. Betrayed by the jefes who left him, by the intellectuals who misled him, by Carranza and González and Guajardo who ambushed him, and by those who have used his name in pursuit of ends of which he would not have approved, he certainly represents those who have lost in Mexican history. Much more importantly, though, he stands for the lasting ability and willingness of the dispossessed to maintain their dignity and to resist. In truth, he was neither the immaculate hero embraced by the myth-makers of the institutionalized revolution, nor the Christ-like man-god of the popular tradition. He was too much the product of Mexican history to be immaculate, too close to the soil, too realistic, too real. Like other mortals he saw unclearly, acted unwisely, and suffered from the limitations of his character. Indeed, if Emiliano Zapata was a hero, he was a tragic one, destroyed by very human failings as he tried to change his world. But those who have kept his memory alive most conscientiously, in the fields and villages and even the cities of Mexico and beyond, understand the value of his effort.

Notes

Introduction

1. With John Womack, Jr., *Zapata and the Mexican Revolution* (New York: Vintage Books, 1970), x, I would define a campesino simply as a person from the fields. Womack prefers this word to the word *peasant* to denote the common people of Morelos, arguing that *peasant* is too exotic to describe the Zapatistas. While his point is taken, I find *peasant* to be a useful word—especially when one is discussing Zapatismo within a broader body of theory—and I will use it interchangeably with campesino. For a more thorough definition of the term peasant, see Joel S. Migdal, *Peasants, Politics, and Revolution:Pressures toward Political and Social Change in the Third World* (Princeton:Princeton University Press, 1974), 24–25. Migdal indicates that a peasant has some involvement in a market economy, that she or he is politically subordinate, and that agriculture is his or her central concern.

2. See the interview with Manuel Sosa Pavón, conducted by Eugenia Meyer, Mexico City, March 27, April 5, May 9, and May 17, 1973, as part of the Programa de Historia Oral of the Instituto Nacional de Antropología e Historia and the Instituto de Investigaciones Dr. José María Luis Mora (hereafter cited as PHO), 1/48, pp. 150–51. Also Antonio Díaz Soto y Gama, *La revolución agraria del sur y Emiliano Zapata, su caudillo* (Mexico City:Imprenta Policromia, 1960), 256.

3. Alicia Olivera, "¿Ha muerto Emiliano Zapata? Mitos y leyendas en torno del caudillo," *Boletín INAH*, época II, 13(1975):43–52.

4. For an appreciation of how the campesino myth and the state's hero existed side by side see Salvador Rueda Smithers, "Emiliano Zapata, los signos de un caudillo, biografía de un símbolo," in *Estadistas, caciques y caudillos,* ed. Carlos Martínez Assad (Mexico City:Instituto de Investigaciones Sociales, 1988), 146–48, 150. On Obregón's agrarian policy as a political tool see Linda B. Hall, "Alvaro Obregón and the Politics of Mexican Land Reform," *Hispanic American Historical Review* 60(1980):213–38. See also Salvador Rueda Smithers, "Los dos Emilianos Zapata, concepciones clasistas en torno a una figura," *Boletín del Centro de Estudios de la Revolución Mexicana "Lázaro Cárdenas"* 3(April 1980): 44, 47–48 and María Eugenia Arías Gómez, "Algunos cuadernos históricos sobre Emiliano Zapata y el Zapatismo," in *Emiliano Zapata y el movimiento zapatista* (Mexico City:Secretaría de Educación Pública and the Instituto Nacional de Antropología e Historia, 1980), 257.

5. See Gildardo Magaña (and Carlos Pérez Guerrero), *Emiliano Zapata y el agrarismo en México,* 5 vols. (Mexico City:Editorial Ruta, 1951–1952); Díaz Soto y Gama, *La revolución agraria;* Octavio Paz Solórzano, *Zapata,* Tres revolucionarios, tres testimonios, vol. 2 (Mexico City:Editorial Offset, 1986); and Serafín M. Robles' series of articles in *El Campesino* during the early 1950s.

6. Cited in Rueda, "Los dos Emilianos Zapata," 48.

7. Jesús Sotelo Inclán, *Raíz y razón de Zapata* (Mexico City:Editorial Etnos, 1943). In 1970 Sotelo Inclán produced a second edition of his work, which incorporated new documents as well as the reflections of subsequent scholars.

8. Womack, *Zapata,* 205.

9. For a highly influential analysis of social revolution that largely dismisses leadership see Theda Skocpol, *States and Social Revolutions:A Comparative Analysis of France, Russia, and China* (Cambridge:Cambridge University Press, 1979). Among theoretical works interested only in national leadership are Crane Brinton, *The Anatomy of Revolution,* 2nd ed. (New York:Vintage Books, 1952), 97–127 and Mostafa Rejai, *The Comparative Study of Revolutionary Strategy* (New York:David McKay, 1977), 34–35. For a recent request that peasants be viewed as conscious historical actors see Gilbert M. Joseph, "On the Trail of Latin American Bandits:A Reexamination of Peasant Resistance," *Latin American Research Review* 25 (1990):19. Finally, for work that does discuss peasant

leadership in the Mexican Revolution see Dudley Ankerson, *Agrarian Warlord:Saturnino Cedillo and the Mexican Revolution in San Luis Potosí* (DeKalb, Ill.:University of Northern Illinois Press, 1984); Paul Friedrich, *Agrarian Revolt in a Mexican Village* (Englewood Cliffs, N.J.: Prentice Hall, 1970); and several of the contributors to David Brading, ed., *Caudillo and Peasant in the Mexican Revolution* (Cambridge:Cambridge University Press, 1980) and Friedrich Katz, ed., *Riot, Rebellion, and Revolution:Rural Social Conflict in Mexico* (Princeton:Princeton University Press, 1988).

10. This failure to agree, of course, has often been the result of class differences. It seems to me, however, that culture is perhaps more important than class, both in explaining differences within Zapatismo and in explaining the movement's behavior on the national level. In general, my approach is more Weberian than Marxian, not just because Weber stresses culture, but because he leaves more room for multi-causal historical explanations that include individuals. See Raymond Aron, *Main Currents in Sociological Thought*, 2 vols., trans. by Richard Howard and Helen Weaver (New York:Basic Books, 1967), 194–95.

11. See Robert Redfield, *Tepoztlán, A Mexican Village:A Study of Folk Life* (Chicago:University of Chicago Press, 1930). For the argument against studying the individual in peasant societies, see Arturo Warman *Los campesinos:hijos predilectos del régimen*, 7th ed. (Mexico City:Editorial Nuestro Tiempo, 1979), 118. Ironically, it is Warman who has revealed much of the diversity within rural Morelos even while embracing the communal emphasis. See especially his *"We Come to Object":The Peasants of Morelos and the National State*, trans. Stephen K. Ault (Baltimore:Johns Hopkins University Press, 1980). Among those who have challenged Redfield are Oscar Lewis, *Life in a Mexican Village:Tepoztlán Restudied* (Urbana:University of Illinois Press, 1951); Guillermo de la Peña, *A Legacy of Promises:Agriculture, Politics, and Ritual in the Morelos Highlands of Mexico* (Austin:University of Texas Press, 1981); Erich Fromm and Michael Maccoby, *Social Character in a Mexican Village:A Sociopsychoanalytic Study* (Englewood Cliffs, N.J.:Prentice Hall, 1970); and Horacio Crespo and Herbert Frey, "La diferenciación social del campesinado como problema de la teoría y de la historia, hipótesis generales para el caso de Morelos, México," *Revista Mexicana de Sociología* 44(1982):285–313. Finally, for the sensible suggestion that there is a dia-

lectical relationship between conflict and solidarity in peasant communities, see John M. Ingham, *Mary, Michael, and Lucifer:Folk Catholicism in Central Mexico* (Austin:University of Texas Press, 1986), 7.

12. Bruce Mazlish, *The Leader, the Led, and the Psyche:Essays in Psychohistory* (Hanover, NH:Wesleyan University Press, 1990), 137, makes the case that the practice of psychohistory is not feasible under the conditions I have described. For an enlightening discussion of some of the methodological problems one encounters in approaching peasants in general, see Eric Van Young, "To See Someone Not Seeing:Historical Studies of Peasants and Politics in Mexico," *Mexican Studies/Estudios Mexicanos* 6 (1990):133–59.

Chapter 1: The Making of a Rebel

1. For the quote see the manifesto, "A los Habitantes de la Ciudad de México," June 24, 1914, in Laura Espejel, Alicia Olivera, and Salvador Rueda, eds., *Emiliano Zapata:antología* (Mexico City:Instituto Nacional de Estudios Históricos de la Revolución Mexicana, 1988), 196–98.

2. Zapata to Manuel Palafox, San Pedro Actopan, D.F., July 21, 1914, Archivo General de la Nación, Mexico City, Archivo de Alfredo Robles Domínguez (hereafter cited as ARD) 11:31:5; Remigio Cortés to Zapata, Olinalá, July 14, 1914, Archivo General de la Nación, Mexico City, Archivo de Genovevo de la O (hereafter cited as AO) 14:8:67; Onecima Promera to Zapata, Ototonilco[?], July 15, 1914, AO 14:8:51; Zapata to Palafox, San Pablo Actopan, July 21, 1914, AO 17:3:41; and Palafox to Zapata, Yautepec, July 28, 1914, AO 15:1:137.

3. For Zapata's rejection of Carranza see "The Pact of Xochimilco," in Manuel González Ramírez, *Planes políticos y otros documentos* (Mexico City:Fondo de Cultura Económica, 1954), 113–22. See also Genovevo de la O to Zapata, Cuernavaca, August 20, 1914, AO 17:5:8. The Plan of Ayala, written in 1911, was Zapata's fundamental statement of revolutionary purpose.

4. Lucio Rios to Zapata, Cuautla, August 2, 1914, AO 16:2:43; Alberta Merino to Zapata, October 3, 1914, Archivo General de la Nación, Mexico City, Archivo de Zapata (hereafter cited as AZ) 1:21:14; Pipino Valero to Zapata, Huautla, September 22, 1914, AZ 17:6:47; Zapata to Pipino L. Valero, Quilamula, September 24, 1914, AO 18:2:47; Antonio Barona to Zapata, Cuernavaca, August 13, 1914, AO 16:1:57; Emigdio Al-

calco to Zapata, Tepalcingo, October 25, 1914, AZ 1:22:50; and Alan Knight, *The Mexican Revolution*, 2 vols. (Cambridge:Cambridge University Press, 1986), 2:170–71.

5. Leon Canova to the Secretary of State, Mexico City, December 8, 1914, U.S. Department of State, Records Relating to the Internal Affairs of Mexico, 1910–1929 (hereafter cited as USDS-IAM) 812.00/14048; Enrique Krauze, *El amor a la tierra:Emiliano Zapata, Biografía del poder*, no. 3 (Mexico City:Fondo de Cultura Económica, 1987), 81; and Womack, *Zapata*, 219.

6. Zapata to Villa, Puebla, December 16, 1914, Centro de Estudios Sobre la Universidad, Mexico City, Archivo de Gildardo Magaña (hereafter cited as AGM) 28:19:808; Martín Luis Guzmán, *The Eagle and the Serpent*, trans. Harriet de Onis (Gloucester, Mass.:Peter Smith, 1969), 338–40; Palafox to Zapata, Mexico City, December 18, 1914, AGM 28:19: 811; Palafox to Mateo Almanza, Mexico City, December 18, 1914, AZ 2:5:92; Zapata to Palafox, Amecameca, December 10, 1914, in Isidro Fabela and Josefina E. de Fabela, eds., *Documentos históricos de la revolución mexicana*, vol. 21, *Emiliano Zapata, el Plan de Ayala, y su política agraria* (Mexico City:Editorial Jus, 1970), 141; and Francisco Ramírez Plancarte, *La Ciudad de México durante la revolución constitucionalista*, 2nd ed. (Mexico City:Ediciones Botas, 1941), 302.

7. Gregoria Zúñiga was one of Zapata's many mistresses. See the interview with Gregoria Zúñiga, conducted by Carlos Barreto, Tenextepango, October 28, 1974, PHO-Z/1/82.

8. The date given here for Zapata's birth is the traditional best guess. There is, however, some evidence that his day of birth may actually have been July 20—see the birthday wishes in Francisco Vázquez and family to Zapata, Tlaltizapán, July 20, 1915, AZ 15:17:1; and similar greetings of the same date in AO 15:1:24, 15:1:25, and 15:1:7. It is at least possible that August 8, feast day of Saint Emiliano, was the day Zapata was baptized. For good wishes on this day in 1915 see AZ 19:4:14–29. Contradictions on the year of birth are also abundant—for a rundown of the evidence see Womack, *Zapata*, 56. See also Gustavo Casasola, *Historia gráfica de la revolución mexicana, 1900–1970*, 5 vols. (Mexico City:Editorial F. Trillas, 1965–1971), 2:1323; Jesús Sotelo Inclán, *Raíz y razón de Zapata*, 2nd ed. (Mexico City:Comisión Federal de Electricidad, 1970), 415–18 (all subsequent citations of this book will refer to the second edi-

tion unless otherwise indicated); Alfonso Reyes H. *Emiliano Zapata:su vida y su obra (con documentos inéditos)*, 2nd ed. (Mexico City:Libros de México, 1963), 11; and Serafín M. Robles, "Verdadera personalidad de don Emiliano Zapata," *El Campesino*, January 1951. A mestizo is a person of mixed Indian and Spanish background. For the possibility that the Zapata family also had a strain of black blood see Francois Chevalier, "Un factor decisivo de la reforma agraria de México:el levantamiento de Zapata (1911–1919)," *Cuadernos Americanos* 113(1960):176–77.

9. For the quote see Jesús Sotelo Inclán, *La escuela de Anenecuilco*, Cuadernos Zapatistas (Cuernavaca:Gobierno del Estado Libre y Soberano de Morelos, 1979), 10–14. There is some confusion about whether Zapata went to school in Anenecuilco or Villa de Ayala. See also Alicia Hernández Chávez, *Anenecuilco:memoria y vida de un pueblo* (Mexico City:El Colegio de México, 1991), 77–78, 191–92; Serafín M. Robles, "El niño va a la escuela y concluye la primaria," *El Campesino*, March 1953; Paz Solórzano, *Zapata*, 28–29; and Díaz Soto y Gama, *La revolución agraria*, 81. The most direct evidence for Zapata's ability to write can be found on a photograph he dedicated to Gildardo Magaña on December 27, 1914, located in the Archivo Histórico de la Defensa Nacional, Mexico City, (hereafter cited as ADN) X1/111/1–105, Cancelados, Gildardo Magaña, 406. The roughness of the hand, the informal context of the note, and the apparent continuity between text and signature, make it almost certain that here, for once, we have the handwriting of Zapata himself.

10. Sotelo Inclán, *Raíz y razón*, 416–17; Alicia López de Rodríguez, *Emiliano Zapata:biografía* (Cuernavaca:Talleres Gráficos de Impresores de Morelos, 1982), 3–4; Magaña, *Emiliano Zapata*, 1:104; Oscar Lewis, *Life in a Mexican Village:Tepoztlán Restudied* (Urbana:University of Illinois Press, 1951), 100; and Alfonso Corcuera Garza, "Dominio y dependencia del campesino temporalero," in *Los Campesinos de la tierra de Zapata, II:subsistencia y explotación*, Jorge Alonso, Alfonso Corcuera, and Roberto Melville (Mexico City:Instituto Nacional de Antropología e Historia, 1974), 40–55.

11. López de Rodríguez, *Emiliano Zapata*, 3; and Serafín M. Robles, "Zapata, desde niño era un gran charro," *El Campesino*, December 1950.

12. A charro is a Mexican horseman best identified by the manner of dress described here. The Reform era (1855–1876) was a crucial period in the formation of the Mexican state, in which the Liberal party created a

constitution, fought off French intrusion, and began to establish a measure of stability. For the Plateados see Paul J. Vanderwood, *Disorder and Progress:Bandits, Police, and Mexican Development* (Lincoln:University of Nebraska Press, 1981), 8–11, 53. See also Womack, *Zapata*, 7–8; Sotelo Inclán, *Raíz y razón*, 418–21; Krauze, *El amor*, 21–22; and Porfirio Palacios, *Emiliano Zapata:datos biográfico-históricos* (Mexico City:Libro Mex, 1960), 17–19. Zapata would also have been influenced by folk songs called *corridos* that often celebrated such bandit-heroes as Plasencia—see Robert A. White, S.J., "Mexico:The Zapata Movement and the Revolution," in *Latin American Peasant Movements*, ed. Henry A. Landsberger (Ithaca, N.Y.:Cornell University Press, 1969), 125.

13. Cuautla was the headtown of the district in which Ayala and Anenecuilco fell, and the most important settlement in the eastern half of Morelos. In 1900 the town had 6,269 inhabitants, according to official figures. Villa de Ayala was about a mile to Anenecuilco's south. Womack, *Zapata*, 46, gives population figures for Ayala (2,041 in 1900) and Anenecuilco (411 in the same year). Both villages shrunk during the decade that followed. See also Sotelo Inclán, *Raíz y razón*, 202–21, 418; Womack, *Zapata*, 7–9; and Cheryl English Martin, *Rural Society in Colonial Morelos* (Albuquerque:University of New Mexico Press, 1985), 193–94. Largely for reasons of style I use the term Morelos anachronistically here and in the pages that follow, to refer to the area of the present-day state, which was not created until 1869.

14. For a sense of the nation among the peasants of Morelos in the nineteenth century see Hernández Chávez, *Anenecuilco*, 53, 71, 119; and Florencia E. Mallon, "Peasants and State Formation in Nineteenth Century Mexico:Morelos, 1848–1858," *Political Power and Social Theory* 7 (1988):1–54. For thoughts on the ties between the economic grievances of the region and its participation in various political events see Brian R. Hamnett, *Roots of Insurgency:Mexican Regions, 1750–1824* (Cambridge: Cambridge University Press, 1986), 71–72, 163–64; John Tutino, *From Insurrection to Revolution in Mexico:Social Bases of Agrarian Violence, 1750–1940* (Princeton:Princeton University Press, 1986), 187–91, 256; Sotelo Inclán, *Raíz y razón*, 199–200; and Martin, *Rural Society*, 194. The other Zapata mentioned was a second José Zapata, who will be discussed in more detail shortly.

15. The fundamental source for Anenecuilco's longevity is the Codex

Mendocino, which was composed on the orders of Viceroy Antonio Mendoza. On this codex see Sotelo Inclán, *Raíz y razón*, 19–21. See Chevalier, "Un factor," 166–67, for the idea that capitalism set in almost immediately in Morelos, resulting in a special tension between hacienda and village already in the sixteenth century. See also Ward Barrett, *The Sugar Hacienda of the Marqueses del Valle* (Minneapolis:University of Minnesota Press, 1970), 39; Martin, *Rural Society*, 23–24, 112; and "Comisión a Juan de Aguilera Para Hacer la Congregación en las Amilpas," Mexico City, July 5, 1603, in Hernández Chávez, *Anenecuilco*, 125–27.

16. For the quote on resistance see Rosa E. King, *Tempest Over Mexico* (Boston:Little, Brown and Co., 1935), 295. See also Krauze, *El amor*, 16–18, 29; Warman, *"We Come to Object,"* 32–33; Martin, *Rural Society*, 71, 92–93, 109, 197–98; and Serge Gruzinski, *Man-Gods in the Mexican Highlands:Indian Power and Colonial Society, 1520–1800*, trans. Eileen Corrigan (Stanford:Stanford University Press, 1989), 105–72.

17. Martin, *Rural Society*, 195; Tutino, *From Insurrection*, 256; Sotelo Inclán, *Raíz y razón*, 335–71, 562; Womack, *Zapata*, 89; Leticia Reina, *Las rebeliones campesinas en México (1819–1906)* (Mexico City: Siglo Veintiuno, 1980), 157–77; and Hernández Chávez, *Anenecuilco*, 27. See also Brígida von Mentz, "La región morelense en la primera mitad del siglo XIX:fuentes e hipótesis de trabajo," in *Morelos:cinco siglos de historia regional*, ed. Horacio Crespo (Mexico City:Centro de Estudios Históricos del Agrarismo en México and Universidad Autónoma del Estado de Morelos, 1984), pp. 131–47 for the argument that independence only led to more arbitrary abuses of the campesinos by the authorities. A caudillo was a military man on horseback, who competed for power on the regional and national levels.

18. See Richard N. Sinkin, *The Mexican Reform, 1855–1876:A Study in Liberal Nation-Building* (Austin:Institute of Latin American Studies, University of Texas, 1979), 124–26, 170–73; and Womack, *Zapata*, 44.

19. Roberto Melville, *Crecimiento y rebelión:el desarrollo económico de las haciendas azucareras en Morelos (1880–1910)* (Mexico City:Editorial Nueva Imagen, 1979), 35, 43–44; and Womack, *Zapata*, 42–50.

20. See Melville, *Crecimiento*, 22, 34, 38 for the provocative argument that after 1880 the haciendas' usurpation of water rights was more significant than was land-grabbing, as well as for sugar production figures

of 9,912 tons in 1870 and, in 1908–1909, 52,230 tons. See also Elizabeth Holt Büttner, "Evolución de las localidades en el estado de Morelos según los censos de población (1900–1950)," *Anuario de Geografía* 2(1962):17–18; and Hernández Chávez, *Anenecuilco*, 109–10, 252–57.

21. See Krauze, *El amor*, 18–20, 31–35; Womack, *Zapata*, 42–51, 63; Sotelo Inclán, *Raíz y razón*, 425–26, 437–38; Hernández Chávez, *Anenecuilco*, 85; and Claudio Lomnitz, *Evolución de una sociedad rural* (Mexico City:Fondo de Cultura Económica, 1982), 41.

22. Miscegenation was, of course, the major reason why by Zapata's time this was no longer precisely a struggle between Spaniards and Indians. The pace of this miscegenation is a slippery issue. Womack, *Zapata*, 70–71, finds that only about 9 percent of the population of Morelos spoke Nahuatl at the time of the revolution, and therefore contends that Zapatismo was primarily a mestizo movement. For a questioning of Womack's findings see Miguel León-Portilla, *Los manifiestos en nahuatl de Emiliano Zapata* (Mexico City:Universidad Nacional Autónoma de México, 1978), 40–44. Also see Martin, *Rural Society*, 169. In general, it seems that Womack is correct for the lowlands of Morelos, but that his overly homogeneous view of Zapatismo downplays Zapata's considerable Indian—or at least Nahuatl-speaking—constituency in the highland villages of northern Morelos, Mexico state, and the Federal District, and in more distant Tlaxcala. Clearly the percentage of Nahuatl speakers increased as one approached the relatively inaccessible sierra of Ajusco that formed Morelos's northern border with the Federal District and Mexico state. For questionable figures on Nahuatl speakers in Morelos that show a precipitous drop between 1900 and 1910 see Holt Büttner, "Evolución," 56. For a strong argument against any meaningful survival of Indian culture even in highland areas see Judith Friedlander, *Being Indian in Hueyapan:A Study of Forced Identity in Contemporary Mexico* (New York:St. Martin's Press, 1975), 190–91.

23. Armando Ayala Anguiano, *Zapata y las grandes mentiras de le revolución mexicana* (Mexico City:Editorial Vid, 1985), 17–18 likens this story to a soap opera. See also Germán List Arzubide, *Zapata*, 8th ed. (Mexico City:Federación Editorial Mexicana, 1973), 14–15; Magaña, *Emiliano Zapata*, 1:104; Serafín M. Robles, "¿No crees que esto es una injusticia?," *El Campesino*, February 1953; and Womack, *Zapata*, 6.

24. Legend has it that Zapata never worked as a day laborer on a ha-

cienda in Morelos—see for example Womack, *Zapata*, 6. For a witness who refutes this, however, see Floyd Rittenhouse, "Emiliano Zapata and the Suriano Rebellion:A Phase of the Agrarian Revolution in Mexico, 1910–1920" (Ph.D. diss., Ohio State University, 1947), 59. For Zapata dating the start of his career of rebelliousness see the "Pact of Xochimilco" in González Ramírez, *Planes políticos*, 113–22. See also Palacios, *Emiliano Zapata*, 20; Magaña, *Emiliano Zapata*, 1:104–5; Sotelo Inclán, *Raíz y razón*, 417; "México:los viejos soldados de Zapata," *Cuadernos del Tercer Mundo* 11, 2(1977):106; the interview with Consuelo Bravo, conducted by Rosalind Beimler, PHO/1/211, pp. 8–10; and Lola Romanucci-Ross, *Conflict, Violence, and Morality in a Mexican Village* (Palo Alto: National Press Books, 1973), 37, 67.

25. See Serafín M. Robles, "Emiliano Zapata:ya hombre, es el paladín del campo," *El Campesino*, August 1953; Serafín M. Robles, "Emiliano Zapata:con su amigo Sánchez combate con federales," *El Campesino*, January 1954; interview with Manuel Sosa Pavón, PHO/1/48, p. 22; and Palacios, *Emiliano Zapata*, 20.

26. For the quote see Mario Gill, "Zapata:su pueblo y sus hijos," *Historia Mexicana* 2(1952):305–6. Also see Sotelo Inclán, *Raíz y razón*, 415–17, 439–40 and Warman, *"We Come to Object,"* 75.

27. Womack, *Zapata*, 50, considers it unlikely that Zapata had a part in the Yautepec case. This may be true, but see also Miguel Angel Sedano P., *Emiliano Zapata:revolucionarios surianos y memorias de Quintín González* (Mexico City:Editorial del Magisterio, 1970), 22–23, 39–44, 50–55; Díaz Soto y Gama, *La revolución agraria*, 66–67; and Sotelo Inclán, *Raíz y razón*, 445–47.

28. Sotelo Inclán, *Raíz y razón*, 448–53, 466–69. A *jefe político* was the political boss of a district.

29. See Magaña, *Emiliano Zapata*, 1:105; Sotelo Inclán, *Raíz y razón*, 454–56; and Carlos Reyes Avilés, *Cartones Zapatistas* (Mexico City:n.p., 1928), 9–10.

30. Womack, *Zapata*, 11–36, provides an excellent treatment of this campaign. See, too, Sotelo Inclán, *Raíz y razón*, 474–88; Salvador Rueda, "Administración política y utopía hacendada:la lucha por el poder en el estado de Morelos (1869–1913)," *Historias* 13(1986):95–96; and Oscar Lewis, *Pedro Martínez:A Mexican Peasant and His Family* (New York: Vintage Books, 1964), 73. It is worth noting that Alarcón had eventually

become an hacendado—see Othón Flores Vilchis, "El problema agrario en el estado de Morelos" (Thesis, Facultad Nacional de Jurisprudencia, UNAM, 1950), 78; and Mrs. Alec Tweedie, *Mexico as I Saw it,* 2nd ed. (London:Thomas Nelson and Sons, 1911[?]), 364.

31. *México Nuevo,* 5 February 1909; *Diario del Hogar,* 12 February 1909; Joaquín Páez, "Cuatro meses de vacaciones con Zapata," *El Sol de Puebla,* 26 March 1951. Francisco Cosío Robelo, "Dígale a Zapata que ya acabe el circo," *Mujeres y Deportes,* 6 February 1937 tries to refute claims of Zapata's involvement here, but merely demonstrates that he was not an important political leader. Melchor Ocampo was a prominent Liberal of Mexico's Reform era.

32. The *científicos* were the "scientists" who formed a positivist clique around Díaz, occupying various cabinet posts.

33. Some authorities—see, for instance, Reyes Avilés, *Cartones,* 10—contend that Zapata never believed in the possibility of electoral change, but merely used this campaign to mobilize his fellow villagers. It seems to me that this interpretation credits him with too much foresight. See Sotelo Inclán, *Raíz y razón,* 484–86, 492–93 for the argument that Zapata was important enough in these elections that he was again forced to flee to Puebla. For biographical material on Torres Burgos see the same book, p. 461. Finally, see Serafín M. Robles, "Emiliano Zapata: consecuencias de la conferencia Díaz–Creelman," *El Campesino,* April 1954.

34. For Zapata's election see the remarkable prologue in Womack, *Zapata,* 39. Womack maintains that Merino was an uncle of Zapata's. See too Sotelo Inclán, *Raíz y razón,* 493–99.

35. For the quote see Sotelo Inclán, *Raíz y razón,* 497; see pages 417 and 511 as well.

36. For the quote see the interview with Leonor Alfaro, conducted by Ximena Sepúlveda, Cuautla, August 31, 1973, PHO/1/100, p. 10. See also Rittenhouse, "Emiliano Zapata," 66; interview with Mateo Díaz Lozano, conducted by Carlos Barreto Mark, Villa de Ayala, April 3, 1974, PHO-Z/CRMG/1/41, p. 5; interview with Miguel Espejo, conducted by Carlos Barreto Mark, Villa de Ayala, September 21, 1974, PHO-Z/CRMG/1/65, p. 22; Serafín M. Robles, "El General Zapata, agricultor y arriero," *El Campesino,* October 1951; Robles, "Emiliano Zapata:paladín del campo"; Womack, *Zapata,* 6–7; Oscar Lewis, *Tepoztlán:Village in Mexico* (New

York:Holt, Rinehart and Winston, 1960), 12–13; Paz Solórzano, *Zapata,* 29–30; and Warman, *"We Come to Object,"* 68–74. Zapata's sister, María de Jesús, and many others prefer to ignore or reject Zapata's ties to de la Torre y Mier—see "Emiliano Zapata iba corneado cuando se fue a la revolución," *La Prensa,* 15 April 1932—but such links were not uncommon. In fact, Zapata's godparents may have managed the hacienda Hospital. Finally, note that campesino, as I have defined it (see the introduction, note 1), is a cultural term rather than one that denotes class, so it is certainly possible to say that Zapata was in some sense middle class—a *ranchero*—and also a campesino.

37. The generalizations made in this and following paragraphs about life in Anenecuilco are largely dependent upon conclusions drawn about village culture in Morelos by anthropologists and social psychologists. See Ingham, *Mary, Michael, and Lucifer,* viii, 4–7, 142–43; Warman, *"We Come to Object,"* 55–76; Esteban Krotz, "El poder político en un pueblo de Morelos," in *Los campesinos de la tierra de Zapata, III:política y conflicto,* Elena Azaola Garrido and Esteban Krotz (Mexico City:Instituto Nacional de Antropología e Historia, 1976), 238; Fromm and Maccoby, *Social Character,* 37–40, 89, 156–78; Romanucci-Ross, *Conflict,* 28–29, 36, 45–46, 87, 98, 142; Lewis, *Life in a Mexican Village,* 321–22, 334, 451; and Crespo and Frey, "La diferenciación social."

38. See Womack, *Zapata,* 6; interview with Manuel Sosa Pavón, PHO/1/48, p. 25; Serafín M. Robles, "Se incorpora Jesús Morales:toma de Chietla, Puebla," *El Campesino,* June 1952; Juan Salazar Pérez, *Otilio Montaño* (Cuernavaca:Ediciones del Gobierno del Estado Libre y Soberano de Morelos, 1982), 26; Paz Solórzano, *Zapata,* 36.

39. See Díaz Soto y Gama, *La revolución agraria,* 83, 250, and 255; the last of these pages contains the quote. See also pages 229–30 of this work for an interesting though possibly apocryphal reflection on the importance of the moustache for Zapata's self-image. Also see Paz Solórzano, *Zapata,* 33–35; Reyes H., *Emiliano Zapata,* 13 and 122; Juan Andreu Almazán, "Memorias del General Juan Andreu Almazán," bound xerox copy at the Colegio de México (taken from *El Universal,* 1957–1958), chapter 17; Krauze, *El amor,* 43; interview with Clemente Peralta, conducted by Alicia Olivera de Bonfil, Ajusco, D.F., November 12, 1973, PHO-Z/1/20, p. 13; and Fernando Alpuche y Silva, "El General Emiliano Zapata:apuntes," *El Nacional,* 20 July 1941. Max Weber, *On Charisma*

and Institution Building, ed. S.N. Eisenstadt (Chicago:University of Chicago Press, 1968), 48, defines charisma as "a certain quality of an individual personality by virtue of which he is set apart from ordinary men and treated as endowed with supernatural, superhuman, or at least specifically exceptional powers or qualities." While charisma remains a somewhat vague concept, it is clear that Zapata had such a quality.

Chapter 2: The Hacendado's Revolution

1. Hernández Chávez, *Anenecuilco,* 15, 39, 219–22.

2. This is a difficult passage in Zapata's life to reconstruct. I have tried to choose the best documented and most logical of the stories offered. On Inés Aguilar, who is sometimes called Inés Alfaro, see *La Prensa,* 18 February 1964; interview with Leonor Alfaro, PHO/1/100; interview with Miguel Espejo, PHO-Z/CRMG/1/65; Salazar Pérez, *Otilio Montaño,* 26; Ayala Anguiano, *Zapata,* 19; and Gill, "Zapata," 307. For Zapata's reputation with women see for example Salvador Calderón Ramírez, "'La Bachillera' madrina de Zapata," *Todo,* 20 June 1940. For documentation that indicates Zapata did his military service in 1910 rather than earlier see Hector F. López, "Datos para la historia de la revolución mexicana:cuando fue consignado Emiliano Zapata," *El Hombre Libre,* 5 April 1937. For the quote see Krauze, *El amor,* 47.

3. Magaña, *Emiliano Zapata,* 1:105–6; Sotelo Inclán, *Raíz y razón,* 415, 513–22; and Joaquín Piña, "Zapata y el yerno de Don Porfirio," *Ultimas Noticias,* 9 March 1960.

4. For the new tax law see the Ley de Revalúo General de la Propiedad Raíz en el Estado, ARD 7:37:2. See also "Memorándum de la situación política del Estado de Morelos," December 29, 1911, ARD 7:37: 12–18; Womack, *Zapata,* 53; and Sotelo Inclán, *Raíz y razón,* 490–91.

5. On Madero's campaign see Stanley R. Ross, *Francisco I. Madero: Apostle of Mexican Democracy* (New York:Columbia University Press, 1955), 46–112.

6. For the first quote see the citizens of Anenecuilco to the Governor of the State of Morelos, San Miguel Anenecuilco, April 25, 1910 in Hernández Chávez, *Anenecuilco,* 226–27. For the second see Sotelo Inclán, *Raíz y razón* (1943 ed.), 182. See also Sotelo Inclán, *Raíz y razón,* 483, 490, 511, 525–32; Womack, *Zapata,* 63–64; and King, *Tempest,* 35.

7. For the quote see Serafín M. Robles, "Emiliano Zapata fue siempre

fiel a su doctrina," *El Campesino,* November 1949. For the notion that
this was not the first time that Zapata occupied land see Baltasar Dromundo, *Vida de Emiliano Zapata* (Mexico City:Editorial Guaranía, 1961),
37. It seems unlikely to me, however, that he could get away with it
more than once. Also see Sotelo Inclán, *Raíz y razón,* 532–33; and King,
Tempest, 59.

8. Sotelo Inclán, *Raíz y razón,* 535–36.

9. Charles C. Cumberland, *Mexican Revolution:Genesis Under Madero* (Austin:University of Texas Press, 1952), 101–26; and Knight, *Mexican Revolution,* 1:172–75.

10. Womack, *Zapata,* 70–71.

11. Sotelo Inclán, *Raíz y razón,* 512, 537–39; "Emiliano Zapata iba
corneado," *La Prensa,* 15 April 1932; and Hernández Chávez, *Anenecuilco,* 46, 50.

12. Womack, *Zapata,* 70–72. While there has been some question
about whether Torres Burgos actually made the trip north, like Womack I
see no reason not to believe the story.

13. See Magaña, *Emiliano Zapata,* 1:108–9; Salazar Pérez, *Otilio
Montaño,* 26–27; Sotelo Inclán, *Raíz y razón,* 540; Womack, *Zapata,* 73–
75; Serafín M. Robles, "Cunde la revolución de Madero en Morelos," *El
Campesino,* February 1952; Porfirio Palacios, "Revolucionarios del sur:
Gabriel Tepepa," *El Campesino,* April 1967; and Antonio D. Melgarejo,
Los crímenes del zapatismo (apuntes de un guerrillero) (Mexico City:Edi-
tora y Distribuidora Nacional de Publicaciones, 1979), 33.

14. Magaña, *Emiliano Zapata,* 1:109; Miguel A. Sánchez Lamego,
Historia militar de la revolución mexicana en la época maderista, 3 vols.
(Mexico City:Instituto Nacional de Estudios Históricos de la Revolución
Mexicana, 1976–1977), 1:263; Serafín M. Robles, "Se levantaron al grito
de ¡Viva Madero! ¡Muera Díaz!" *El Campesino,* March and April 1952;
and *El Imparcial,* 20 March 1911.

15. In describing the strategy of the rebels, Womack, *Zapata,* 76–77,
simply works backwards from what actually happened, and in the process
probably gives them too much foresight. Unfortunately, his version of the
argument between Zapata and Torres Burgos is only one of many, so that
it is difficult to tell what Zapata or anyone else understood in March
1911 about the problems they faced. For another version see Sergio Valverde, *Apuntes para la historia de la revolución y de la política en el es-*

tado de Morelos, desde la muerte del Governador Alarcón, pronuncia-miento de los Grales. Pablo Torres Burgos y Emiliano Zapata martires, hasta la restauración de la reacción por Vicente Estrada Cajigal impostor (Mexico City:n.p., 1933), 94. See also Magaña, *Emiliano Zapata,* 1:109–11. A *guerrillero* is a member of a guerrilla band.

16. See the "Relación de los sucesos en el estado de Morelos," AGM 12:1:19, which claims that Zapata led the sacking; *El Imparcial,* 25 and 28 March 1911; Domingo Diez, *Bosquejo histórico geográfico de Morelos* (Cuernavaca:Editorial Tlahuica, 1967), 144; and Díaz Soto y Gama, *La revolución agraria,* 95. Womack, *Zapata,* 77–78, contends that this looting took place because Tepepa's men did not understand the politics of the uprising as well as did the revolutionaries from around Villa de Ayala. This is, I think, to make a false distinction—jefes like Zapata were hardly schooled politicians in March 1911. The goal of Womack's argument is apparently to dismiss the Jojutla episode as an exception to an otherwise orderly state of affairs, but while there were surely important personality differences between Tepepa and Zapata, Zapata's troops, as we shall see, would imitate behavior described here at places like Jonacatepec, Chiautla, and Cuautla.

17. For a March 25, 1911, document drawn up at Huachinantla, Puebla that records Zapata's selection to head the movement see Eduardo Adame Medina, "De Villa de Ayala a Chinameca, 1909–1919," *El Campesino,* July 1958. Also see Magaña, *Emiliano Zapata,* 1:110–11; Arturo Figueroa Uriza, "Como surgió caudillo maderista Emiliano Zapata," *El Universal,* 24 March 1956; Romanucci-Ross, *Conflict,* 142; and Almazán, "Memorias," chapter 17. For the quote see the interview of Modesto Tejeda Enríquez, conducted by Beatriz Arroyo, Malinalco, Mexico, August 30, 1978, PHO/1/218. For Zapata's own brutality see for instance the account of Juana Belén Gutiérrez de Mendoza in María de los Angeles Mendieta Alatorre, *Juana Belén Gutiérrez de Mendoza (1875–1942):extraordinaria precursora de la revolución mexicana* (Mexico City:Impresores de Morelos, 1983), 30–31.

18. Almazán, "Memorias," chapters 17 and 18; Serafín M. Robles, "El jefe suriano combate en Amayuca, Morelos," *El Campesino,* May 1952, and "Se incorpora J. Morales"; "Zapata, ¿Bandido o Apostol?," *Hoy,* 14 February 1948; Womack, *Zapata,* 79–81; and Juan Angel Andonegui, "Cuando imperaba el zapatismo," *El Universal,* 18 April 1948. In refer-

ring to Zapata's following as "troops," I do not mean to imply a degree of organization that they could not possibly yet have attained. Rather, I use the word largely for reasons of style.

19. The quote comes from Francisco Mercado, who is cited in Rosalind Rosoff and Anita Aguilar, *Así firmaron el Plan de Ayala* (Mexico City:Secretaría de Educación Pública, 1976), 77. Warman, *"We Come to Object,"* 112, 124–25 is excellent on guerrilla warfare. See also "Memorándum de la situación política del Estado de Morelos," ARD 7:37:12–18; Antonio Carriles to Juan Pagaza, Cuernavaca, May 23–24, 1911, ARD 6:28:10–11; "Relación de los sucesos en el Estado de Morelos," AGM 12: 1:19; Sánchez Lamego, *Historia militar de la revolución mexicana en la época maderista,* 1:265–67; *El Imparcial,* 21 and 22 April 1911; and Alfonso Taracena, *Zapata:fantasía y realidad,* 2nd ed. (Mexico City:B. Costa-Amic, 1974), 87. Finally, for "liebres blancas" see the interview with Andrés Avila, conducted by Laura Espejel, Atatlahucan, Morelos, May 15, 1973, PHO/1/53.

20. Diez, *Bosquejo,* 145–46; Valverde, *Apuntes,* 39–40.

21. For the Pact of Jolalpan see Espejel et al., eds., *Emiliano Zapata,* 98–99. See also Womack, *Zapata,* 82–84. Precisely when and how Zapata became a general is unclear, but he signed with that rank on this occasion—see Arturo Figueroa Uriza, *Ciudadanos en armas:antecedencia y datos para la historia de la revolución mexicana,* 2 vols. (Mexico City:B. Costa-Amic, 1960), 1:122.

22. Francisco Leyva to the Secretaría de Guerra, Cuernavaca, April 27–28, 1911, in the notes of Luis Muro (located at the Colegio de México) on the Archivo Histórico de la Defensa Nacional, 11/481.5/177; Sánchez Lamego, *Historia militar . . . época maderista,* 1:268; Magaña, *Emiliano Zapata,* 1:127–29; Ayala Anguiano, *Zapata,* 42; Ian Jacobs, *Ranchero Revolt:The Mexican Revolution in Guerrero* (Austin:University of Texas Press, 1982), 41–59, 79–85; Figueroa Uriza, *Ciudadanos en armas,* 1:127–37; and Carlos Pérez Guerrero, "Porque el General Zapata no atacó Jojutla en 1911," *El Hombre Libre,* 8 September 1937. In support of Zapata's view of events it might be noted that Madero also rejected Figueroa's Mexico City initiative.

23. While there is no hard evidence that Zapata moved on Jonacatepec and later Cuautla because of Figueroa's machinations, the suppositions along these lines in Womack, *Zapata,* 85, make good sense to me.

See also Sánchez Lamego, *Historia militar* . . . *época maderista*, 1:268–69; Alfonso Taracena, *La tragedía zapatista* (Mexico City:Editorial Bolívar, 1931), 13; Melgarejo, *Los crímenes*, 89–121; Valverde, *Apuntes*, 40–42; and Francisco Leyva's report of May 6, Muro notes, ADN 11/481.5/177.

24. Magaña, *Emiliano Zapata*, 1:128; Sedano P., *Emiliano Zapata*, 97.

25. For the quote see Magaña, *Emiliano Zapata*, 1:130. See also Zapata to Fausto Beltrán in Emiliano Zapata, *Cartas*, eds. Chantal López and Omar Cortés (Mexico City:Antorcha, 1987), 14–15; and *El Imparcial*, 21 May 1911.

26. Warman, *"We Come to Object,"* 124–25; and Serafín M. Robles, "Temararia hazaña del pundonoroso y valiente General Mucio Bravo," *El Campesino*, July 1950.

27. For general accounts of the battle see the *Diario del Hogar*, 19 May 1911; Sánchez Lamego, *Historia militar* . . . *época maderista*, 1:269–70; Magaña, *Emiliano Zapata*, 1:128–32; and Paz Solórzano, *Zapata*, 58–65. For the taking of the aqueduct see Sedano P., *Emiliano Zapata*, 98 and Cristóbal Domínguez, interviewed in Rosoff and Aguilar, *Así firmaron*, 71. Also see Edgcumb Pinchon, *Zapata the Unconquerable* (New York:Doubleday, Doran and co.:1941), 192–93 and Díaz Soto y Gama, *La revolución agraria*, 86.

28. The quote comes from King, *Tempest*, 63–64. See also Magaña, *Emiliano Zapata*, 1:132; Melgarejo, *Los crímenes*, 97–98; Casasola, *Historia gráfica*, 1:306; Pinchon, *Zapata*, 189–90; and José I. Lugo to Alfredo Robles Domínguez, Cuernavaca, May 26, 1911, ARD 4:17:31.

29. *El Imparcial*, 19 May 1911; Rafael Sánchez Escobar, *Episodios de la revolución mexicana en el sur* (Mexico City:Talleres Tipográficos de la Casa de Orientación para Varones, 1934), 29–31; Figueroa Uriza, *Ciudadanos*, 1:174–75; and Womack, *Zapata*, 89, 93–94.

30. Carriles to Pagaza, Cuernavaca, May 23–24, 1911, ARD 6:28:10–11; Manuel Asúnsolo to Alfredo Robles Domínguez, Cuernavaca, May 25, 1911, ARD 4:17:23; Abrahám Martínez to Alfredo Robles Domínguez, Cuernavaca, May 27, 1911, ARD 4:17:28; Emiliano Zapata and Manuel Asúnsolo to Alfredo Robles Domínguez, Cuernavaca, May 27, 1911, ARD 4:17:35; Manuel Asúnsolo to Alfredo Robles Domínguez, Cuernavaca, May 27, 1911, ARD 4:17:33; Paz Solórzano, *Zapata*, 48–49, 66; Almazán,

"Memorias," chapter 18; King, *Tempest,* 66; Magaña, *Emiliano Zapata,* 165; and Womack, *Zapata,* 81, 92, 94.

31. For the quotes see Juan Carreón to Alfredo Robles Domínguez, Cuernavaca, May 31, 1911, ARD 4:17:63. See also Abrahám Martínez to Alfredo Robles Domínguez, Cuernavaca, May 29, 1911, ARD 1:6:92; and Emiliano Zapata, Asúnsolo, and Alfonso Miranda to Alfredo Robles Domínguez, Cuernavaca, May 29, 1911, ARD 4:17:56. Asúnsolo's reasons for backing Carreón, like most of his motives, remain unclear.

32. For the quote see Zapata to Alfredo Robles Domínguez, June 2, 1911, ARD 4:17:94. See also Alfredo Robles Domínguez to Zapata, June 1, 1911, ARD 4:17:73; Abrahám Martínez to Alfredo Robles Domínguez, June 1, 1911, ARD 4:17:77; Asúnsolo to Alfredo Robles Domínguez, Cuernavaca, June 1, 1911, ARD 4:17:80; Abrahám Martínez to Alfredo Robles Domínguez, June 1, 1911, ARD 4:17:135; Zapata, Asúnsolo, and Juan Andrew Almazán to Alfredo Robles Domínguez, Cuernavaca, June 2, 1911, ARD 4:17:90; Zapata to Alfredo Robles Domínguez and Francisco Madero, June 3, 1911, ARD 4:17:103; *El Imparcial,* 29 May 1911 and 21 June 1911; and *Diario del Hogar,* 2 June 1911.

33. See the Chief of Staff of Alfredo Robles Domínguez to Zapata, June 2, 1911, ARD 4:17:99; and Almazán, "Memorias," chapter 18. *El Imparcial,* 3 June 1911, reports rumors that Madero was in danger.

34. Alfredo Robles Domínguez to Emiliano Zapata, June 5, 1911, ARD 4:17:117; *El Imparcial,* 8 June 1911.

35. See for instance Alfredo Robles Domínguez to Zapata, Mexico City, May 23, 1911, ARD 4:17:5; and Womack, *Zapata,* 90.

36. For the quote see Magaña, *Emiliano Zapata,* 1:158–61. This is the best source for this encounter, but Magaña was not an eyewitness, and it may be that he added his own drama to the story. Taracena, *Zapata,* 11, takes exception to Magaña's claim that Madero offered a ranch, but to me that seems the most likely part of the account. For another critique of Magaña see Ayala Anguiano, *Zapata,* 26–29.

37. For the quote see Cosío Robelo, "Dígale." Though he was apparently not one of the state's affluent hacendados, Ruiz de Velasco's considerable interests around Jojutla made him their natural ally. See Felipe Ruiz de Velasco to Francisco León de la Barra, Mexico City, August 31, 1911, AGM 1:4R:518; Magaña, *Emiliano Zapata,* 1:162–64, 180, and 191–92; Figueroa Uriza, *Ciudadanos,* 1:287–88; Womack, *Zapata,* 97; and

King, *Tempest,* 69. Almazán, "Memorias," chapter 18, says that Zapata claimed that Jesús Morales, one of his jefes from Puebla, ordered the troops that were present to circle because others failed to arrive on time.

38. Magaña, *Emiliano Zapata,* 1:165–66, 185; *El Imparcial,* 17, 19, and 20 June 1911; "Relación de los sucesos en el estado de Morelos, AGM 12:1:19; and Teofanes Jiménez to Francisco de la Barra, August 18, 1911, Mexico City, AGM 6:J3:35. For a description of the battle of Cuautla in which fire plays an important role, see Valverde, *Apuntes,* 43–44. See also pp. 93–94 of Valverde's work. For the quotes see the Representatives of the Merchants, Professionals, and Agriculturists to de la Barra, undated, AGM 12:7:140.

39. For the quote see the letter of an employee of the San Rafael Paper Company, June 7, 1911, ARD 2:7:77–78. See also Felipe Ruiz de Velasco to Alfredo Robles Domínguez, Mexico City, June 5, 1911, ARD 4:17:115; and José de la Macorra to Francisco Cosío Robelo, June 8, 1911, ARD 2:7:90.

40. For the Díaz quote see Michael C. Meyer and William L. Sherman, *The Course of Mexican History,* 2nd ed. (New York:Oxford University Press, 1983), 511. See also Alfredo Robles Domínguez to Zapata, Mexico City, May 28, 1911, ARD 4:17:41; Almazán, "Memorias," chapters 17–18; and Zapata to Alfredo Robles Domínguez, Cuernavaca, June 4, 1911, AGM 19:3:91. In general, the authorities seem to have assumed that bandits in the area were connected to Zapata—see Alfredo Robles Domínguez to Zapata, June 8, 1911, ARD 4:17:126; Agustín del Pozo to Alfredo Robles Domínguez, Atlixco, Puebla, June 8, 1911, ARD 4:19:113; and Zapata to Alfredo Robles Domínguez, Cuernavaca, June 9, 1911, ARD 4:17:132–34.

41. For complaints see the Asociación de Productores de Azúcar y Alcohol to Francisco de la Barra, July 7, 1911, Mexico City, AGM 6:V–1: 160; Alfredo Robles Domínguez to Zapata, June 5, 1911, ARD 4:17:113; Alfonso Díaz Meoqui to Alfredo Robles Domínguez, Mexico City, May 31, 1911, ARD 4:17:65–66; Juan Pagaza et al. to the Secretario de Gobernación, undated, AGM, Box 34; *El Imparcial,* 19 June 1911; and Jiménez to de la Barra, Mexico City, August 18, 1911, AGM 6:J–3:35. On pressure for land see *El Imparcial,* 8, 25, and 27 July 1911; and Magaña, *Emiliano Zapata,* 1:204–5. For a letter that demonstrates that there was some gen-

uine fear of rebel brutality on the part of the Morelian elite see María T. Galicia to Filomena G. de Mújica, Cuautla, June 8, 1911, ARD 4:17:123.

42. For the idea that the Juárez treaty represented an alarmed reaction of elites threatened by social upheaval see Knight, *Mexican Revolution*, 1:204. On the subject of Figueroa keeping order see Alfredo Robles Domínguez to Ambrosio Figueroa, June 1, 1911, ARD 4:17:74; Alfredo Robles Domínguez to Ambrosio Figueroa, June 5, 1911, ARD 3:12:18; Guillermo García Aragón for Ambrosio Figueroa to Alfredo Robles Domínguez, Iguala, June 6, 1911, ARD 3:12:23; and Ambrosio Figueroa to Alfredo Robles Domínguez, June 9, 1911, ARD 3:12:29–32. Figueroa informed federal officials on more than one occasion that the presence of his troops in Morelos only exacerbated tensions, but the hacendados continued to get their way. See also Tomás Ruiz de Velasco to Alfredo Robles Domínguez, May 26, 1911, ARD 1:6:44, and Jacobs, *Ranchero Revolt*, 87.

43. Magaña, *Emiliano Zapata*, 1:189; and Ayala Anguiano, *Zapata*, 83. It is unclear whether Madero really made Zapata chief of arms. To *El Imparcial*, 21 June 1911 he denied having done so, but this may simply reflect the fact that the appointment had not yet gone through official channels. For two telegrams that speak to the issue, see Gabriel Robles Domínguez to Emiliano Zapata, Mexico City, June 19, 1911, ARD 4:17:160 and Gabriel Robles Domínguez to Alfredo Robles Domínguez, June 16, 1911, ARD 4:17:157. Womack, *Zapata*, 98, is probably right in considering it merely a private promise from Madero that was never carried through.

44. Magaña, *Emiliano Zapata*, 1:189–97 summarizes the charges against Zapata, but gets the dates wrong. See also *El Imparcial*, 19 June 1911; and Sánchez Escobar, *Episodios*, 33.

45. For the quotes see *El Imparcial*, 20 June 1911. See Magaña, *Emiliano Zapata*, 1:188, for the contention that the men outside Figueroa's hotel were spying to see if he was hobnobbing with the hacendados.

46. Pinchon, *Zapata*, 164; *El Imparcial*, 21 June 1911; Magaña, *Emiliano Zapata*, 1:198–202; and *Diario del Hogar*, 20 and 21 June 1911.

47. For the quote see Krauze, *El amor*, 60. See also B.V., "Emiliano Zapata," *El Popular*, 11 April 1932; *Diario del Hogar*, 21 June 1911; and *El Imparcial*, 21 June and 8 July 1911.

48. Magaña, *Emiliano Zapata*, 1:200–202; *El Imparcial*, 21 June

1911; and *Diario del Hogar*, 21 June 1911. On the subject of whether Zapata would have liked some kind of official appointment at this time one can only speculate, but it is clear that he later thrived on being a local celebrity.

49. Magaña, *Emiliano Zapata*, 1:205–6; Emilio Vázquez Gómez to Francisco Madero, Mexico City, June 14, 1911, ARD 1:5:81–82; and John H. McNeely, "Origins of the Zapata Revolt in Morelos," *Hispanic American Historical Review* 46(1966):156–57. For an example of a discharge document, drawn up at Cuernavaca, June 22, 1911, see Fabela, ed., *Documentos históricos*, 21:11. For the contention that there was a desire on the part of the government to disarm Zapata's troops more quickly than others, see Almazán, chapter 18; but for similar problems all over the country, see Manuel González Ramírez, *Manifiestos políticos* (1892–1912) (Mexico City:Fondo de Cultura Económica, 1957), 285 ff.

50. Asociación de Productores de Azúcar y Alcohol to Juan Carreón, Mexico City, June 12, 1911, ARD 4:17:144–47; Carreón to Gabriel Robles Domínguez, Cuernavaca, July 14, 1911, ARD 2:8:53; Zapata to the Secretario de Gobernación, Cuautla, July 17, 1911, in Mexico, Secretaría de Gobernación, *Exposición homenaje nacional a Emiliano Zapata en el centenario de su nacimiento* (1879–1979) (Mexico City:Secretaría de Educación Pública and Instituto de Bellas Artes, 1979–1980), 18; Zapata to the Secretario de Gobernación, Cuautla, July 17, 1911, in Fabela, *Documentos históricos*, 21:11–12; and Womack, *Zapata*, 104.

51. See [Abrahám Martínez?] to Alfredo Robles Domínguez, Tehuacán, July 10, 1911, ARD 2:8:29; Madero to Francisco Vázquez Gómez, July 13, 1911, Centro de Estudios de Historia de México, Condumex, Mexico City, Archivo de Genaro Amezcua (hereafter cited as AA) VIII–2, manuscritos, 1:28; *El Imparcial*, 14 and 16 July 1911; *The Mexican Herald*, 17 July 1911; Paz Solórzano, *Zapata*, 71–72; Taracena, *La tragedia*, 17; Magaña, *Emiliano Zapata*, 1:209–18; Womack, *Zapata*, 104–5; and David G. LaFrance, *The Mexican Revolution in Puebla, 1908–1913:The Maderista Movement and the Failure of Liberal Reform* (Wilmington, Delaware:SR Books, 1989), 114–18.

52. Magaña, *Emiliano Zapata*, 1:227–28.

53. "Memorándum," ARD 7:37:12–18; and Zapata to Madero, July 28, 1911, in Almazán, "Memorias," chapter 18.

Chapter 3: The Birth of Zapatismo

1. For the quote see Zapata to Gustavo Madero, Villa de Ayala, August 8, 1911, in Gildardo Magaña, *Emiliano Zapata*, 1:244. Also see pages 247–48 of that work; and *El Imparcial*, 5 August 1911.

2. For the quote see Francisco Madero to Ambrosio Figueroa, Mexico City, August 9, 1911, in Magaña, *Emiliano Zapata*, 1:265. See also 1:248–49 of that work; Carreón to the Secretario de Gobernación, Cuernavaca, July 29, 1911, in Fabela, ed., *Documentos históricos*, 21:12–13; Secretario de Gobierno Ruperto Zuleta for Carreón to Gabriel Robles Domínguez, August 9, 1911, ARD 7:37:3–4; and Womack, *Zapata*, 101–3. Finally, for background on Huerta see George J. Rausch, Jr., "The Early Career of Victoriano Huerta," *Americas* 21 (1964):136–45.

3. For the quote see Gabriel Robles Domínguez to Alfredo Robles Domínguez, Villa de Ayala, August 11, 1911, ARD 7:37:19–20. See also King, *Tempest*, 86; and Victoriano Huerta to de la Barra, Cuernavaca, August 19, 1911, AGM 17:8:384. Such an intrusion of federal troops would have been unsettling in many areas at this point in the revolution—see Francisco Figueroa to de la Barra, September 1911, AGM 13:3:125.

4. De la Barra to Huerta, Mexico City, August 12, 1911, AGM 15:1:41; Magaña, *Emiliano Zapata*, 1:257–60; Sánchez Lamego, *Historia militar . . . época maderista*, 2:33; *El Imparcial*, 15 August 1911; interview with Carmen Aldana, conducted by Laura Espejel, Tepalcingo, Morelos, March 2 and 30, 1974, PHO-Z/1/32, 27–29; Zapata to Gabriel Robles Domínguez, Villa de Ayala, August 12, 1911, ARD 7:37:21; and Zapata to the Minister of Gobernación, Villa de Ayala, August 12, 1911, in Fabela, ed., *Documentos históricos*, 21:14–15. For the quote see Huerta to de la Barra, Cuernavaca, August 12, 1911, AGM 15:1:40.

5. Magaña, *Emiliano Zapata*, 1:249–51, 260–64, and 269–70 includes the quote. See also Madero to de la Barra, Cuernavaca, August 14, 1911, AGM 17:8:388; Madero to de la Barra, Cuernavaca, August 14, 1911, AGM 17:8:386; and Madero to de la Barra, Cuernavaca, August 15, 1911, AGM 17:8:393.

6. López de Rodríguez, *Emiliano Zapata*, 11; Gill, "Zapata," 307; *El Imparcial*, 13 August 1911; "Informe sobre los acontecimientos verificados en el sur con motivo de la visita de inspección hecha por el Licenciado G. Robles Domínguez," undated, ARD 7:37:22–25; Sedano P.,

Emiliano Zapata, 102; Herminia Aguilar, "Doña Josefa Espejo Vda. de Zapata," *El Campesino,* May 1958; Serafín M. Robles, "El caudillo se casa en la Villa de Ayala, Morelos," *El Campesino,* November 1954; and Luis Cutierrez [sic?] y González, "Hoy visita a la viuda de Zapata," *Hoy,* 28 March 1953. Some say that Madero was present at the August 9 wedding, but this seems impossible.

7. For the quote see Huerta to de la Barra, Cuernavaca, August 16, 1911. See also de la Barra to Madero, Mexico City, August 15, 1911, AGM 17:8:390; Madero to de la Barra, August 15, 1911, AGM 17:8:391; Huerta to de la Barra, Cuernavaca, August 15, 1911, AGM 16:1:26 and AGM 14:3:68; de la Barra to Huerta, Mexico City, August 15, 1911, AGM 14:3:67 and AGM 14:3:84; de la Barra to Huerta, Mexico City, August 16, 1911, ARD 17:11:524; Huerta to de la Barra, August 16, 1911, AGM 14:3: 121; Madero to Zapata, Mexico City, August 16, 1911, AGM 14:3:107; José González Salas to Huerta, Mexico City, August 17, 1911, AGM 17: 11:527; and Carreón to de la Barra, August 17, 1911, AGM 14:4:177. For Madero hedging his bet on peace, see Ross, *Madero,* 193. Reading between the lines and the doubletalk, it seems clear that Huerta avidly desired war, and that de la Barra exploited that desire. For the argument that Huerta did nothing more than follow de la Barra's orders, see Michael C. Meyer, *Huerta:A Political Portrait* (Lincoln:University of Nebraska Press, 1972), 25.

8. De la Barra to Huerta, Mexico City, August 17, 1911, AGM 14:4: 168; Madero to Zapata, Mexico City, August 17, 1911, AA VIII-2, manuscritos, 1:35; and Dearing to the Secretary of State, Mexico City, August 21, 1911, USDS-IAM 812.00/2299. See Magaña, *Emiliano Zapata,* 1:271–72 for the first quote; the second is on page 278 of the same work. See also pages 273–80. Finally, for local civilians lobbying de la Barra, undoubtedly at Zapata's instigation, see for example the Citizens of Tepoztlán to de la Barra, Cuautla, August 17, 1911, AGM 14:4:141.

9. For the quote see Jesús Morales to Enrique Bonilla in *Diario del Hogar,* 23 August 1911. For accounts of the Jojutla episode see Carreón to de la Barra, August 19, 1911, AGM 14:4:228; Felipe Ruiz de Velasco to de la Barra, Mexico City, August 20, 1911, AGM 31:B-4:316; Juan Pagaza to de la Barra, Mexico City, August 23, 1911, AGM 8:V-5:278–79; Tomás Ruiz de Velasco to de la Barra, August 26, 1911, AGM 1:3R:441; and *Diario del Hogar,* 24 August 1911.

10. For the quote see *Diario del Hogar,* 20 August 1911. Madero to de la Barra, Cuautla, August 19, 1911, AGM 17:8:400–03, 405, 407; Magaña, *Emiliano Zapata,* 1:281–84, 311–12; Zapata to de la Barra, Cuautla, August 17, 1911, AGM 14:4:162; de la Barra to Madero, Mexico City, August 19, 1911, AGM 17:8:406; and Madero to de la Barra, Cuautla, August 20, 1911, AGM 16:1:28. For a pro-Zapata source that states that the disarming was now being faked, see Serafín M. Robles, "Segunda celada para dar muerte al jefe suriano," *El Campesino,* December 1954. For Eufemio bringing up the idea of killing Madero there exists a contemporary account:see Encarnación Muñoz, "Libro histórico para la patria," AGM 31: 395, book one.

11. Madero to de la Barra, Cuautla, August 19, 1911, AA VIII-2, manuscritos, 1:41; Magaña, *Emiliano Zapata,* 1:284–86, 301–3, 306–7; de la Barra to Huerta, Mexico City, August 20, 1911, AGM 16:1:27; Huerta to de la Barra, August 20, 1911, AGM 16:1:27 and AGM 16:1:3; de la Barra to Madero, Mexico City, August 20, 1911, AA VIII-2, manuscritos, 1:46; Madero to de la Barra, Yautepec, August 20, 1911, AGM 17:8:410; "Informe sobre los acontecimientos," ARD 7:37:22–25; and *Diario del Hogar,* 22 August 1911. For two different opinions of Zapata's intentions as Huerta approached, see Arturo Langle Ramírez, *Huerta contra Zapata: una campaña desigual* (Mexico City, Universidad Nacional Autónoma de México, 1981), 23; and Almazán, "Memorias," chapter 19.

12. For the quote see Madero to de la Barra, Cuautla, August 21, 1911, AGM 17:8:418. See also Madero to de la Barra, Cuautla, August 21, 1911, AGM 17:8:415, 17:8:419, and 17:8:420; de la Barra to Madero, Mexico City, August 21, 1911, AGM 17:8:417; Magaña, *Emiliano Zapata,* 1:307 and 2:49; Madero to de la Barra, Cuautla, August 22, 1911, AGM 18:5:266; Huerta to de la Barra, August 21, 1911, AGM 18:7:506; Madero to Zapata, Cuautla, August 22, 1911, AA VIII-2, manuscritos, 1:55; *Diario del Hogar,* 23 August 1911; and Ross, *Madero,* 197. For Huerta's quote see Huerta to de la Barra, Yautepec, August 22, 1911, AGM 17:11:530.

13. De la Barra to Huerta, Mexico City, August 24, 1911, AGM 17:8: 435; Magaña, *Emiliano Zapata,* 1:313–14, 327 and, for Madero's accusations against de la Barra, 315–22; Huerta to de la Barra, Yautepec, August 26, 1911, AGM 16:2:94; Huerta to de la Barra, August 28, 1911, AGM 16: 1:9; Huerta to de la Barra, August 29, 1911, AGM 16:2:144; and de la Barra to Huerta, August 29, 1911, AGM 16:2:145.

14. Langle Ramírez, *Huerta contra Zapata,* 46; Rosendo Casillas to Huerta, August 30, 1911, AGM 12:1:25; Zapata to de la Barra, Villa de Ayala, August 31, 1911, AGM 15:5:280; Zapata, "Al Pueblo de Morelos," Villa de Ayala, August 27, 1911, in Magaña, *Emiliano Zapata,* 1:323–25; see also page 310.

15. Huerta to de la Barra, Villa de Ayala, September 1, 1911, AGM 15:5:295; Huerta to de la Barra, Huautla, September 11, 1911, AGM 13: 1:1; Magaña, *Emiliano Zapata,* 1:328; Sánchez Lamego, *Historia militar . . . época maderista,* 1:35; and Almazán, "Memorias," chapter 20.

16. For the quote see Huerta to de la Barra, Jojutla, September 13, 1911, AGM 12:1:28. See also Martín Vicario to de la Barra, September 15, 1911, AGM 13:1:3; Ambrosio Figueroa to de la Barra, September 19, 1911, AGM 20:1:85; and Huerta to de la Barra, September 26, 1911, Chiautla, AGM 12:1:29.

17. See "Datos suministrados por José Cruz, secretario que fué de Emiliano Zapata," in Diego Arenas Guzmán, *Del Maderismo a los Tratados de Teoloyucán* (Mexico City:Instituto Nacional de Estudios Históricos de la Revolución Mexicana, 1955), 20–32. As usual Almazán's motives are difficult to gauge. *Diario del Hogar,* 15 September 1911 says he was acting in accord with the politically ambitious Porfirian General Bernardo Reyes to try to win Zapata's support. For followers of Zapata in Oaxaca see the numerous reports from Governor Benito Juárez Maza in AGM 22:6.

18. Arenas Guzmán, *Del Maderismo,* 20–32; Agustín del Pozo to de la Barra, Acatlán, Puebla, September 20, 1911, AGM 20:1:118; Huerta to de la Barra, Chietla, September 20, 1911, AGM 20:1:116; Huerta to de la Barra, Chiautla, September 26, 1911, AGM 21:2:111 and 12:1:29; Huerta to Ignacio de la Barra, Chiautla, September 27, 1911, AGM 12:1:30; Huerta to de la Barra, Piaxtla, October 5, 1911, AGM 21:4:320; Zapata to de la Barra, San Juan del Rio, September 26, 1911, AGM 24:Z-2:416; Magaña, *Emiliano Zapata,* 1, 330; and Agustín del Pozo to de la Barra, Acatlán, September 28, 1911, AGM 21:2:156.

19. Ambrosio Figueroa to de la Barra, October 8, 1911, AGM 21:4: 368; Citizens of Chalco to de la Barra, Chalco, October 23, 1911, AGM 18:2:149; Magaña, *Emiliano Zapata,* 2:24–27; Paz Solórzano, *Zapata,* 81; Womack, *Zapata,* 123; Sánchez Lamego, *Historia militar . . . época maderista,* 1:37, 40–44, 61; *El País,* 17 October 1911; Rip-Rip, "Una cena

trágica iluminada por las llamas del incendio," *Gráfico,* 17 June 1930; Cumberland, *Mexican Revolution:Genesis,* 182; Valverde, *Apuntes,* 101–2; and Luz Jiménez, *Life and Death in Milpa Alta,* trans. and ed. Fernando Horcasitas (Norman:University of Oklahoma Press, 1972), 133.

20. For the first quote see Zapata to Madero, Villa de Ayala, November 6, 1911, Archivo General de la Nación, Mexico City, Colección Revolución (hereafter cited as CR) 1:229. For the second see Magaña, *Emiliano Zapata,* 1:313. See also volume two of this work, pp. 51, 87–91; and *El País,* 31 October and 1 November 1911.

21. Magaña, *Emiliano Zapata,* 2:91–101; Sánchez Lamego, *Historia militar . . . época maderista,* 2:45–47; and Womack, *Zapata,* 124. For rumors that Madero was behind Zapata's rebellion see Francisco Figueroa to Madero, Chilpancingo, November 11, 1911, CR 1:48.

22. For the quote see Magaña, *Emiliano Zapata,* 2:102. See also pages 104–6 in the same volume. Chapultepec is Mexico City's largest park. For the argument that the break with Madero was inevitable, see Knight, *Mexican Revolution,* 1:301 and Salvador Rueda, "Oposición y subversión:testimonios zapatistas," *Historias* 3(1983):15. I would argue that the break was likely—given the differences between the two men and the circumstances in which they found themselves—but certainly not inevitable. At least from Zapata's point of view it seems evident that there was more here than the loose allegiance that Knight describes.

23. For overtures to some of Zapata's adherents—and some surrenders—see Raúl Madero to José Cruz, Mexico City, November 14, 1911, ARD 7:37:41; and Casso López to the Secretary of War, November 23, 24, and 30, 1911, Muro notes, ADN 11/481.5/177. For Zapata on the Plateados see Serafín M. Robles, "Semblanza del Plan de Ayala," *El Campesino,* January 1950.

24. For biographical information on Montaño see Sedano P., *Emiliano Zapata,* 63–68 and Salazar Pérez, *Otilio Montaño,* 25–27. To the villagers of Morelos Montaño was an intellectual, and I will use this term in the same sense that they did, to describe people with more than two or three years of schooling who—whether lawyers, doctors, students, or schoolteachers—worked with their minds on a daily basis at least as much as they did with their hands.

25. For the quote see the interview with Enrique M. Zepeda, con-

ducted by Eugenia Meyer, Mexico City, March 24, April 3, and May 11, PHO/1/47, p. 99. See also Joaquín Páez, "Cuatro meses de vacaciones con Zapata," *El Sol de Puebla*, April 2, 1951; and the film "Testimonios Zapatistas," directed by Adolfo García Videla under the auspices of the Programa de Historia Oral (PHO) of the Instituto Nacional de Antropología e Historia.

26. For the contention that Montaño merely gave the document its form see, for instance, Reyes Avilés, *Cartones*, 34–35. See also Magaña, *Emiliano Zapata*, 2:111–39. There can be little serious doubt about whether Montaño helped compose the Plan of Ayala. Both Zapatista tradition and stylistic considerations point in his direction.

27. For two slightly different versions of the Plan of Ayala see Manuel González Ramírez, *Planes políticos*, 73–83. I have used the original, rather than the later, reworked version. For a good translation of the original, and a discussion of the influences at play, see Womack, *Zapata*, 393–404. For the second quote see Zapata to Magaña, December 6, 1911, in Magaña, *Emiliano Zapata*, 1:142–43.

28. There has been considerable disagreement among scholars about Zapata's national vision. For a strong argument that he already demonstrated such vision in the Plan of Ayala see Arturo Warman, "The Political Project of Zapatismo," trans. Judith Brister, in *Riot, Rebellion, and Revolution:Rural Social Conflict in Mexico*, ed. Friedrich Katz (Princeton: Princeton University Press, 1988), 321–22. Among authors who stress the movement's limitations and localism are Arnaldo Córdova, *La ideología de la revolución mexicana:la formación del nuevo régimen*, 7th ed. (Mexico City:Ediciones Era, 1979), 149–50, and 153–54 and Salvador Rueda, "La dinámica interna del zapatismo:consideración para el estudio de la cotidianeidad campesina en el area zapatista," in *Morelos:cinco siglos de historia regional*, ed. Horacio Crespo (Mexico City:Centro de Estudios Históricos del Agrarismo en México, 1984), 235. To me it seems that Zapata always knew the importance of national politics, but that he never *fully* understood the national scene.

29. Zapata to Orozco, May 5, 1912; an undated Zapata interview with *El Imparcial*; and Zapata to Orozco, May 6, 1912 can be found in ARD 8:43:1–4, 8:43:7–12, and 8:43:16–17 respectively. For contacts with Orozco also see Ireneo Albarrán Ayala's certification of Manuel Palafox's services to the revolution, August 2, 1921, ADN X/III.2, pensionados,

Palafox, 143–52; Magaña, *Emiliano Zapata,* 2:142–43; Saúl Chávez Peralta, *Emiliano Zapata:crisol de la revolución mexicana* (Mexico City:Editorial Renacimiento, 1972), 96–97; and Michael C. Meyer, *Mexican Rebel:Pascual Orozco and the Mexican Revolution, 1910–1915* (Lincoln: University of Nebraska Press, 1967), 49–50. For the belief of some Zapatistas that they were also Orozquistas see the manifesto of June 18, 1912 in Espejel et al., eds., *Emiliano Zapata,* 120; and James M. Platt to Arnold Shanklin, Zacualpan, Mexico, August 27, 1912, USDS-IAM, 812.00/ 4792. Though Zapata never met Orozco, he had also suggested him to Madero as a possible provisional governor of Morelos in August 1911.

30. Mallon, "Peasants and State Formation," 14, 21.

31. For an indication of the importance of the evolving slogan to Zapata see Zapata to his army, Iguala, February 11, 1915, Secretaría de Gobernación, *Exposición homenaje,* 36–37. Though there is some debate about the degree of democracy that existed in the Morelian past, it is clear that Zapata had strong democratic inclinations:one of his first moves, when he took a town, was usually to preside over elections of local officials—see "Zapata, ¿Bandido o apostol?" *Hoy,* 14 February 1948.

32. A cacique was a political boss on the local level. An ejido was land owned by a village as a whole, rather than by individuals within the village. A traditional form of land ownership, it had roots in the preconquest period.

33. See Womack, *Zapata,* 399 for the recognition that the Plan of Ayala never directly mentions progress. See also Antonio Díaz Soto y Gama, *La cuestión agraria en México,* 2nd ed. (Mexico City:El Caballito, 1976), 12–13; Lewis, *Life in a Mexican Village,* 80, 300; and Zapata's manifesto, "Al Pueblo Mexicano," March 1, 1912, USDS-IAM, 812.00/ 3561.

34. See Serafín M. Robles, "Emiliano Zapata no fue fanático," *La Prensa,* 26 June 1936; Pinchon, *Zapata,* 136; Magaña, *Emiliano Zapata,* 2:114; Everardo González to Zapata, Totolapan, March 12, 1916, AZ 11:8: 10; and Chevalier, "Un factor decisivo," 172–73.

35. See Córdova, *La ideología,* 151; Millon, *Zapata,* 83, 99; Hernández Chávez, *Anenecuilco,* 113–15; and Knight, *Mexican Revolution,* 1:163–64, and 309–11 for efforts to characterize the ideology of the Plan of Ayala. For debate over whether Zapata and his followers were primarily forward or backward looking, see Knight, *The Mexican Revolution,*

1:313 and Warman, "The Political Project," 321–22. Zapata's thought was deeply influenced by the past, but I know of no time in that past when the kind of Mexico he was demanding fully existed, and so to describe him as backward looking seems rather unfair.

36. For the quote see Reyes Avilés, *Cartones*, 35–36. See also Serafín M. Robles, "Como surgió el Plan de Ayala," *El Campesino*, November 1950; Almazán and Zapata to Antonio Menchaca, Acaxtlahuacán, September 20, 1911, AGM 30:5:52; and Rosoff and Aguilar, *Así firmaron*, 37–47.

37. The Partido Liberal Mexicano was a group of intellectuals that agitated against the Díaz regime in the decade prior to the revolution. On direct communications between Zapata and such PLM figures as Ricardo Flores Magón see Ricardo S. Bravo to the Secretario de Relaciones Exteriores, Phoenix, Arizona, February 15, 1912, in Fabela, ed., *Documentos históricos*, 21:61–62; W. Dirk Raat, *Revoltosos:Mexico's Rebels in the United States, 1903–1923* (College Station, Texas:Texas A&M University Press, 1981), 259; and José Muñoz Cota, "El Partido Liberal Mexicano y Zapata," *El Nacional*, 6 December 1965. There is no evidence, however, that these lines of communication were open prior to the writing of the Plan of Ayala. See also Robles, "Cunde la revolución"; Sotelo Inclán, *Raíz y razón*, 481; Womack, *Zapata*, 62, 79–80; Magaña, *Emiliano Zapata*, 1:121–24, 126, 257; Valentín López González, *Los compañeros de Zapata* (Cuernavaca:Gobierno del Estado Libre y Soberano de Morelos, 1980), 23–24, 123–27, 137, 189; Anna Macias, "Women and the Mexican Revolution, 1910–1920," *The Americas* 37(1980):54–62; and LaFrance, *Mexican Revolution in Puebla*, 202. Finally, for a measure of Zapata's achievement in the Plan of Ayala see Timothy Wickham-Crowley, *Guerrillas and Revolution in Latin America* (Princeton:Princeton University Press, 1992), 324.

38. [Zapata] to Gildardo Magaña, October 1913, AO 17:2:34. For thoughts on the Plan of Ayala as sacred text see Carlos Fuentes, *Tiempo Mexicano* (Mexico City:Editorial Joaquín Moritz, 1971), 125, 135.

39. For the quote on Ayaquica see William Gates, "The Four Governments," 654–65. See also the newspaper clipping from *La Voz de Juárez*, 22 August 1914 in ARD 11:31:27; Rittenhouse, "Emiliano Zapata," 61; interview with Leonor Alfaro, PHO/1/100; Casasola, *Historia gráfica*, 1:602; Reyes Avilés, *Cartones*, 19–20; Jesús Romero Flores, "Mil

biografías en la historia de México," *El Nacional,* 14 December 1946;
Womack, *Zapata,* 81; Magaña, *Emiliano Zapata,* 2:158–59; Porfirio Palacios, "Revolucionarios del sur:el sordo Felipe Neri," *El Campesino,* 15
May 1967; ADN XI/III/I-309, pensionados, Fortino Ayaquica, 87–94 and
562; ADN X/III.2/1–3, pensionados, Francisco Mendoza, 361, 1702–1703,
and 2221–2; *El Campesino,* February 1956; ADN X/III, Genovevo de la O,
pensionados, 13–15; interview with Serafín Plasencia Gutiérrez, conducted by Laura Espejel and Salvador Rueda, Mexico City, September 13
and 20, 1974, PHO-Z/1/59; Robles, "Se incorpora J. Morales"; López
González, *Los compañeros,* 77–83, 145–46, 159–60, 175–76, 231–32, and
279–80; Porfirio Palacios, "Revolucionarios del sur:Francisco Mendoza
Palma," *El Campesino,* 30 November 1967; and Zapata to Genovevo de
la O, October 13, 1911, AO 12:1:1.

    40. Warman, *"We Come to Object,"* 118–19, 133. Lewis, *Tepoztlán,*
39 argues for a similarity in values between peasants and nonpeasants in
one Morelos village. The growth of Zapatismo in Mexico state during
1912 is vividly demonstrated by Medina to Madero, Toluca, March 1912,
Archivo General de la Nación, Mexico City, Archivo de Francisco Madero (hereafter cited as AM) 2:28:1042; Medina to Madero, Toluca, September 17, 1912, AM 2:28:990; and Medina to Madero, Toluca, October
15, 1912, AM 2:28:966–67. See also Rodolfo Alanis Boyzo, *Historia de la
revolución en el estado de México:los zapatistas en el poder* (Toluca:Go-
bierno del Estado de México, 1987), 16; and Rueda, "Oposición y subversión," 10–11.

    41. For evidence of the participation of women in the fighting see
Coronela Rosa B. Viuda de Casas to de la O, San Lorenzo Huehuetitlan,
October 7, 1916, AO 6:10:2; "Por que existe y como se desarrolla el zapatismo en el Estado de Morelos," *La Tribuna,* 4 June 1913; and Macias,
"Women and the Mexican Revolution," 73–75. For *pacíficos* serving as
spies see Marcial Morales et al. to Genovevo de la O, Ocotepec, October
28, 1912, AO 1:3:88 and Felicitas to de la O, Cuernavaca, May 26, 1913,
AO 1:8:35. See also Warman, *"We Come to Object,"* 110–12, 114, 126;
and Rueda, "Oposición y subversión," 11.

    42. For hacendado and other real and rumored suppliers of arms and
money see Ernest Gruening, *Mexico and its Heritage* (London:Stanley
Paul, 1928), 563; Abrahám González to Madero, February 6, 1913, CR
3:411; *El Imparcial,* 12, 15, and 23 November 1912; Zapata to de la O,

November 12, 1912, AO 11:10:24; Ambrosio Figueroa to Madero, Cuernavaca, December 25, 1911 in Fabela, ed., *Documentos históricos*, 21:54–55; and *Diario del Hogar*, 17 March 1912. For the formalization of hacienda payments for protection, see Womack, *Zapata*, 157. See also Octavio Paz Solórzano, *Hoguera que fue*, ed. Felipe Gálvez (Mexico City: Universidad Autónoma Metropolitana, 1986), 156.

43. For the quote see Zapata's circular of December 20, 1911 in Octavio Magaña's "Historia documental de la revolución mexicana," AGM (unnumbered boxes), #212, pp. 3–7. For other efforts to control his troops see his circular of October 28, 1913, Archivo General de la Nación, Mexico City, Archivo del Cuartel General del Sur (hereafter cited as ACGS) 1:3:22–23; Abrahám Martínez [circular?], Ayoxustla, Puebla, April 29, 1912, AA VIII-2, manuscritos, 1:75; Zapata to de la O, August 30, 1912, AO 11:10:8–9; and Zapata to de la O, September 20, 1912, AO 11:10:15. See also Magaña, *Emiliano Zapata*, 2:205; and the citizens of Coatetelco to de la O, October 21 [or 27], 1912, AO 1:3:87. Womack, *Zapata*, 131, 152 discusses this banditry, but seems to want to separate bandits from rebels, something I think it is impossible to do.

44. A full appreciation of the heterogeneity of Zapatismo—and especially of Zapata's following in isolated, mountainous areas—makes it clear that there were elements within the movement of what Knight, *Mexican Revolution*, 1:115–27 calls *serrano* rebellion. Serrano rebellions, in Knight's scheme, were more multiclass and less well defined ideologically than agrarian rebellions, of which Knight and others consider Zapatismo the prime example. Thus while it is useful to generalize about serranos and agraristas, it is also necessary to remember, as Knight does, that the lines between them are often fuzzy. With this understanding Zapatismo becomes somewhat less unique and more flexible, and its ability to forge even unsavory strategic alliances is less surprising.

45. For the quote see the interview with Nicolás Chávez Reyes, conducted by Alicia Olivera de Bonfil, Santo Tomás Ajusco, D.F., November 7, 1973, PHO-Z/1/17. See also Warman, *"We Come to Object,"* 105–6, 127–28; de la Peña, *Legacy*, 25, 62; LaFrance, *The Mexican Revolution in Puebla*, 184; Salvador Rueda, "Las causas del movimiento zapatista en Morelos:desniveles históricos en el origen de un conflicto agrario," in *Memorias:la revolución en las regiones* (Guadalajara:Universidad de Guadalajara, 1986), 264–65; Magaña, 1:322; and Friedlander, *Being Indian*, 57.

On different motives for rebelling by region see Salvador Rueda, "La zona armada de Genovevo de la O, *Cuicuilco*, 2(January 1981):39–40; and Laura Espejel, "El movimiento campesino en el oriente del estado de Mexico:el caso de Juchitepec," *Cuicuilco*, 2(January 1981):36. Still it is worth noting that the economic influence of the sugar hacienda was felt even in many highland areas—see Sinecio López Méndez, "Hueyapan:un pueblo de la tierra fría," in *Los campesinos de la tierra de Zapata I:adaptación, cambio y rebelión*, Laura Helguera R. et al. (Mexico City:Instituto Nacional de Antropología e Historia, 1974), 67. Finally, for Zapata's early efforts to reward his followers with land see the February 5, 1913 document in AO 1:5:6; Zapata to de la O and Pedro Celestino Ruiz, March 17, 1912, AO 11:10:2–3; and Fabela, ed., *Documentos históricos*, 21:66.

46. For the first quote see Díaz Soto y Gama, *La revolución agraria*, 10; for the second see Abrahám Martínez for Zapata to Alfredo Robles Domínguez, June 4, 1911, ARD 4:17:106–9. See also Antonio Díaz Soto y Gama, "Como Era Zapata," Archivo General de la Nación, Mexico City, Archivo de Antonio Díaz Soto y Gama (hereafter cited as ASyG), microfilm roll 3, #205–7; Rosoff and Aguilar, *Así firmaron*, 51, 60; Lewis, *Pedro Martínez*, xxxv, 93; interview with J. Tereso de Jesús Padilla Tlapaya, conducted by Beatriz Arroyo, San Esteban Tizatlan, February 14, 1976, PHO/1/184, p. 8; interview with Wenceslao Romero Acevedo, conducted by Laura Espejel, Mexico City, November 16, 1973, PHO-Z/1/23, p. 20; and interview with Ramón Caballero, conducted by Laura Espejel, San Luis, Puebla, April 25, 1973, PHO/1/51, p. 19. Scholars have often emphasized the traditional sources—in Weberian terms—of Zapata's authority, and downplayed his charisma, but it seems to me that both were significant. For provocative discussions of charisma see Alan Knight, "Peasant and Caudillo in Revolutionary Mexico 1910–1917," in *Caudillo and Peasant in the Mexican Revolution*, ed. David A. Brading (Cambridge:Cambridge University Press, 1980), 44–45; Douglas Madsen and Peter G. Snow, *The Charismatic Bond:Political Behavior in Time of Crisis* (Cambridge, Massachusetts:Harvard University Press, 1991); and Mazlish, *The Leader*, 8, 253–57.

47. Ambrosio Figueroa to Madero, Cuernavaca, December 15, 1911 and December 27, 1911, in Fabela, ed., *Documentos históricos*, 21:51–52 and 56–57 respectively; Magaña, *Emiliano Zapata*, 2:147–57; the report of

Felipe Alvírez, January 19, 1912, Muro notes, ADN XI/481.5/178; and Sánchez Lamego, *Historia militar . . . época maderista,* 2:56–57.

48. For the quote see King, *Tempest,* 92–93. For Figueroa's brutality see "Memorándum," ARD 7:37:12–18; Zapata to Madero, Villa de Ayala, November 6, 1911, CR 1:229; and *Diario del Hogar* throughout the fall of 1911. See also Womack, *Zapata,* 135–39; Valverde, *Apuntes,* 103–4; *Diario del Hogar,* 19 January and 7 and 11 February 1912; Magaña, *Emiliano Zapata,* 2:169–70, 278–99; report of the Commander of the 7th Military Zone, Yautepec, February 11, 1911 [sic], Muro notes, ADN XI/481.5/178; and Sánchez Lamego, *Historia militar . . . época maderista,* 2:85 ff. While it is true that many of the methods of terror that Robles employed were already familiar in Morelos, it is clear that Robles was their most brutal practitioner.

49. Magaña, *Emiliano Zapata,* 2:193–98; Zapata to de la O, April 3, 1912, AO 11:10:5; Zapata's interview with *El Imparcial,* [May 1912?], ARD 8:43:7–12; *Diario del Hogar,* 15, 16 and 31 March, 8, 10 and 14 April and 14 May 1912; Sánchez Lamego, *Historia militar . . . época maderista,* 2:88–95; Junta Revolucionaria del Estado de Morelos to Arnold Shanklin, May 21, 1912, USDS-IAM, 812.00/4092; Montgomery Schuyler to the Secretary of State, Mexico City, June 25, 1912, USDS-IAM, 812.00/4331; and Valverde, *Apuntes,* 104. For differing opinions about the success of Robles's tactics see Díaz Soto y Gama, *La revolución agraria,* 112, 119 and Taracena, *La tragedia,* 29. One possible explanation for Zapata's inactivity in May and June, of course, is simply that it was planting season.

50. Knight, *Mexican Revolution,* 1:249, 303–4; Magaña, *Emiliano Zapata,* 1:211, 227–28; Zapata to Emilio Vázquez Gómez, March 14, 1912, AGM 35:1:7; Baraquiel M. Alatriste to Madero, Puebla, March 3, 1912, AM 6:140–1:4124–5; *Diario del Hogar,* 13 March 1912; Paz Solórzano, *Zapata,* 104; and Ambrosio Figueroa to Madero, Cuernavaca, December 25, 1911, CR 1:353. By the fall of 1912 it seems that Zapata was disillusioned with Orozco for his increasingly obvious ties with Chihuahua conservatives—see *El País,* 1 October 1912. For the idea that in seeking such alliances as these Zapata made errors of desperation see Warman, "The Political Project," 334. I disagree with this interpretation. Such alliances might have been beneficial, and Zapata lost little when they went sour.

51. Womack, *Zapata,* 144–51; Rittenhouse, "Emiliano Zapata," 200; Magaña, *Emiliano Zapata,* 2:20–46, 313–14; *Nueva Era,* 8–11 August 1912; Paz Solórzano, *Zapata,* 107; Casso López, "Al Pueblo Morelense," Cuautla, January 4, 1912, Muro notes, ADN XI/481.5/178; Eufemio Zapata to the Ministerio Público o Representante de la Revolución, March 20, 1913, AO 13:2:24; J. Ramos Martínez to Zapata, October 24, 1912, AO 11:9:20–21; and Moisés González Navarro, "Zapata y la revolución agraria mexicana," *Cahiers du monde hispanique et Luso-Brésilien* 9(1967):14.

52. *Nueva Era,* 21 June and 30 August 1912; Magaña, *Emiliano Zapata,* 2:20–68; Womack, *Zapata,* 136–37; Taracena, *La tragedia,* 28–29; and *Diario del Hogar,* 18 June 1912. For de la O's own comments about destroying trains, see Genovevo de la O, "Memorias," *Impacto,* 14 January 1950.

53. For the quote see Zapata to de la O and Pedro Celestino Ruiz, March 17, 1912, AO 11:10:23. See also Zapata's manifesto of July 26, 1912 in Fabela, ed., *Documentos históricos,* 21:66–68; Womack, *Zapata,* 146; and *El País,* 2 and 8 September and 1 October 1912. Despite Zapata's threat against potential peacemakers, talks seem to have continued—see the clipping from *El Imparcial,* [13 November 1912?], ARD 7:37:45.

54. See Zapata to de la O, November 7, 1912, AO 11:10:25 for the kind of difficulties Zapata encountered in getting his generals to cooperate. See also LaFrance, *Mexican Revolution in Puebla,* 125, 178–79, 184; Medina to Madero, September 26, 1912, AM 2:28:982; and Womack, *Zapata,* 152–58.

Chapter 4: Victory, In Part

1. See Cumberland, *Mexican Revolution:Genesis,* 229–43 and Meyer, *Huerta,* 45–63.

2. Magaña, *Emiliano Zapata,* 3:98; and Miguel A. Sánchez Lamego, *Historia militar de la revolución zapatista bajo el régimen huertista* (Mexico City:Talleres Gráficos de la Nación, 1979), 15–17.

3. For the quote see J. Ramos Martínez to Eufemio Zapata, March 20, 1913, in Magaña, *Emiliano Zapata,* 3:106–10. See the same work, 3:131 for Zapata calling Huerta a traitor in a meeting with Pascual Orozco, Sr., March 30, 1913. For various stories about Zapata's willingness to cooperate with Madero during the February crisis, see King, *Tem-*

pest, 107–12; Rittenhouse, "Emiliano Zapata," 208; and Alfonso Taracena, "Madero quiso refugiarse con Zapata," *Revista de Revistas,* 22 September 1957. Though the extent of Zapata's desire to help Madero is questionable, these accounts may well reflect his understanding that Huerta could be no improvement.

4. For offers to individual jefes see Jacobo Ramos Martínez to Francisco Mendoza, Hacienda "Colón," March 2, 1913, AO 13:2:2; Blas Sobrino and Ignacio Ocampo to de la O, undated, AO 13:2:3; Pascual Orozco, Jr. to Francisco Pacheco, Mexico City, March 25, 1913, AO 13: 2:8; and Patricio Leyva to de la O, Cuernavaca, March 25, 1913, AO 1:6: 13. See also Zapata to de la O, February 22, 1913, AO 11:10:35; Zapata to Facundo Torres, February 23, 1913, AO 17:2:3; Zapata to de la O, March 31, 1913, AO 11:10:37; Zapata to de la O, February 28, 1913, AO 11:10: 31–34; LaFrance, *Mexican Revolution in Puebla,* 232; and Rittenhouse, "Emiliano Zapata," 215.

5. Luis Cajigal to Zapata, Mexico City, March 14, 1913, AO 13:2:4–5; interview with Vicente Estrada Cajigal, conducted by Eugenia Meyer and Alicia Olivera, Cuernavaca, February-March, 1973, PHO/4/12; Antonio Carriles to Juan Pagaza, Cuernavaca, May 23–24, 1911, ARD 6:28:10–11; Antonio Barrios to de la Barra, Mexico City, August 19, 1911, AGM 18:8:554; Montaño's interrogations of Cajigal, March 31 and April 28, 1913, AGM 27:6:89; Magaña, *Emiliano Zapata,* 3:108, 122, 125–26; and the clipping from *El Imparcial,* [13 November 1912?], in ARD 7:37:45.

6. For the first quote see Orozco, Sr. and Simón Beltrán to Zapata, Cuernavaca, March 22, 1913, in Magaña, *Emiliano Zapata,* 3:119; for the second see Orozco's first interrogation in Zapata's camp, March 27, 1913, AGM 27:6:82.

7. Pacheco to Zapata, March 16, 1913, AO 1:6:34; Zapata to Orozco, Sr. and Simón Beltrán, March 23, 1913, in Magaña, *Emiliano Zapata,* 3:119; Pascual Orozco, Sr. and Simón Beltrán to Zapata, Cuernavaca, March 22, 1913, AO 13:2:9; and Zapata to de la O, March 23, 1913, AO 11:10:36. For the plot against Zapata see the testimony of Pablo Peña, March 24, 1913, AO 13:2:28; Alberto Estrada to Zapata, March 27, 1913, AGM 30:10:207; and the report of Manuel Palafox to the Juez Instructor, undated, AGM 27:6:80.

8. Zapata to de la O, March 31, 1913, AO 11:10:37; Valverde, *Apun-*

tes, 109–10; and Paz Solórzano, *Zapata,* 117. Executed with Beltrán was Federico Morales's son Ismael.

9. For Palafox's birthplace, date of birth, and arrival in Morelos see the biographical material compiled, respectively, on October 26, 1921, and April 21, 1939, in ADN XIII.2, pensionados, Manuel Palafox, 140–54 and 776. These two documents offer contradictory information on his birth date, making it either 1879 or 1885. See also Marte R. Gómez, *Las comisiones agrarias del sur* (Mexico City:Manuel Porrua, 1961), 20; Emigdio Marmolejo to Manuel Palafox, Villa de Ayala, December 3, 1918, AGM 30:19:310; and Womack, *Zapata,* 166–67. Palafox's own account of his opposition to Díaz can be found in Palafox to Flavio Maldonado, January 27, 1914, AO 3:1:30; but also see Francisco Artigas to Zapata, Mexico City, [January 1916?], AZ 11:3:39–41 for the claim that Palafox worked for Escandón's gubernatorial candidacy in 1909.

10. See Higinio Aguilar's circular, "Rectificaciones Históricas #1," January 5, 1919, AA VIII-2, impresos, 1:24 for the means by which Palafox gained Zapata's confidence. For photographs see Casasola, ed., *Historia gráfica,* 2:857 and 932, and the photograph collection in AGM.

11. See, for example, the trial records in AGM 27:6:79, 27:6:82, and 27:6:80, and in Magaña, *Emiliano Zapata,* 3:121, 135–40.

12. Womack, *Zapata,* 163–64 dismisses these as "show trials," but it seems clear that the situation was more complex than that. For appeals to the press to print various documents see AGM 27:6:66–71.

13. Womack, *Zapata,* 161, 284–85 gives one interpretation of Montaño's fall, in which a key ingredient was a flirtation with the government of Huerta. Though Montaño was obviously better disposed to Huerta's commissioners than were Zapata and Palafox, evidence for such a flirtation is thin—see *El Imparcial,* 4 and 7 March 1913. See also Paz Solórzano, *Zapata,* 126, 139–40; Montaño to Palafox, April 28, 1913 and May 28, 1913, AGM 27:6:96 and 27:6:97 respectively; [Montaño] to Zapata, May 31, 1913, AGM 30:10:213; Montaño to Zapata, April 8, 1913, AGM 27:6:91; Zapata to Montaño in Magaña, *Emiliano Zapata,* 3:172–73; and [Montaño], undated, AGM 27:6:81.

14. Palafox to Montaño, May 31, 1913, AGM 27:6:99 and [Montaño] to Zapata, May 31, 1913, AGM 30:10:213. For Juana Belén Gutiérrez de Mendoza's impression that Montaño was now reduced to the status of a

virtual prisoner, see the fragments of her autobiography in Mendieta Alatorre, *Juana Belén Gutiérrez de Mendoza*, 29.

15. These letters are all printed in Magaña, *Emiliano Zapata*, 3:101–4, 151–57, and 160–61. Montaño authored at least those to Huerta and Orozco—see Montaño to Zapata, April 12, 1913, AO 13:3:4–5. The letter to Vázquez Gómez was in response to one that he wrote, apparently under coercion, to recommend that Zapata make peace with Huerta. For Vázquez Gómez's account, and the claim that he sent Zapata a very different verbal message, see Francisco Vázquez Gómez, *Memorias políticas (1909–1913)* (Mexico City:Imprenta Mundial, 1933), 524–25, 548–51.

16. See Henry Lane Wilson's report on his interview with Huerta, Mexico City, March 27, 1913, USDS-IAM 812.00/7101.

17. For the quote see the interview with Domingo Yedra Islas, conducted by Laura Espejel, Milpa Alta, D.F., October 3 and 21, 1973, PHO-Z/1/15. Also see the interview with Nicolás Chávez Reyes, PHO-Z/1/17; Salvador Rueda, "La zona armada," 38–40; *Semanario Oficial del Gobierno del Estado de Morelos*, 24 May and 5 July 1913; Womack, *Zapata*, 162, 165–68, 172–73, 193–94; Knight, *Mexican Revolution*, 2:58, 60–61; Magaña, *Emiliano Zapata*, 3:210, 228; and *La Tribuna*, 28 June 1913. Laura Espejel, "El movimiento campesino," 36 finds that the levy caused a marked expansion of support for Zapata in eastern Mexico state. Finally, for a huge decrease in state population between 1913 and 1914 see Elizabeth Holt Büttner, "Evolución," 29. While these statistics certainly reflect a greater difficulty in counting as well as population decline, they seem a fairly good measure of the disruption that came with Robles.

18. For the quote see Alfonso Taracena, *La tragedia*, 11–12. See also Womack, *Zapata*, 193–94. For the arrival of students Cal y Mayor and Iñiguez see Barrios to Zapata, August 7, 1913, AO 13:7:103–5 and Luis Iñiguez, "Memoria y hoja de servicios," AGM 28:17:765. Díaz Soto y Gama had long been pro-Zapatista—see for instance *Diario del Hogar*, 25 January 1912. For more on his earlier career see James D. Cockcroft, *Intellectual Precursors of the Mexican Revolution, 1900–1913* (Austin:University of Texas Press, 1968). On Paulino Martínez see Rafael Sánchez Escobar, *El ocaso de los héroes:como murieron algunos connotados revolucionarios* (Mexico City:Casa de Orientación para Varones, 1934), 115. On Mendoza López Schwerdtfeger see Barry Carr, "Marxism and Anar-

chism in the Formation of the Mexican Communist Party, 1910–1929," *Hispanic American Historical Review* 63 (1983):277–305. While these arrived, other intellectuals passed from the scene, most notably Abrahám Martínez, who was executed by the Huerta regime in June 1913.

19. For the great need for the literate see the interview with Félix Vázquez Jiménez, conducted by Laura Espejel, San Juan Ixtayopan, D.F., August 10, 1973, PHO-Z/1/9. Also see the interview with Gustavo Baz Prada, conducted by Alicia Olivera and Eugenia Meyer, Mexico City, August 7, 1970, PHO/4/6; and the interview with Enrique Zepeda, PHO/1/47.

20. For Zapatista pride in having attracted a group of intellectuals see the circular from Zapata and Santiago Orozco, July 17, 1914, AGM 27:21:438; and Encarnación Muñoz, "Francisco Mendoza," AZ 5, p. 59. See also the interview with Cayetano Hidalgo Salazar, conducted by América Teresa Briseño, Mexico City, March-June, 1973, PHO/1/50; Salvador Rueda, "La dinámica interna," 242; and the act of the ex-forces of Santiago Orozco, April 19, 1916, AZ 12:2:143.

21. Luis Cajigal to Antonio Barrios, Cuautla, August 21, 1911, AGM 31:B-4:315; Joaquín Páez, "Cuatro meses de vacaciones con Zapata," *El Sol de Puebla*, 26 March and 27 April, 1951; and Gómez, *Las comisiones*, 103–4, 133.

22. See Taracena, *La tragedia*, 52; interview with Enrique M. Zepeda, PHO/1/47; Serafín M. Robles, "Lo que pensaba Zapata sobre el comunismo," *El Campesino*, October 1949; Magaña, *Emiliano Zapata*, 4:251; Zapata to Gildardo Magaña, June 9, 1917, AZ 13:16:45; and Díaz Soto y Gama, *La revolución agraria*, 219. For the commonly held idea that peasant revolutionaries almost always need help from nonpeasants, see for instance Ted Robert Gurr, *Why Men Rebel* (Princeton:Princeton University Press, 1970), 336.

23. On Barrios's career see Héctor Gerardo Martínez Medina, "Génesis y desarrollo del maderismo en Oaxaca," in *La revolución en Oaxaca*, 1900–1930, ed. Víctor Raúl Martínez Vásquez (Oaxaca:Instituto de Administración Pública de Oaxaca, 1985), 112–15, 124, 148; Ronald Waterbury, "Non-revolutionary Peasants:Oaxaca Compared to Morelos in the Mexican Revolution," *Comparative Studies in Society and History* 17 (1975):429–31; ADN, A/III/3–97, generales, Serafín M. Robles, 312; and "Siete meses de gobierno de Benito Juárez Maza," in *Oaxaca en México*

46:3 (April 1939):12. Barrios was apparently trained in Mexico City's Colegio Militar—see Magaña, *Emiliano Zapata,* 4:208, 211.

24. Barrios to Zapata, August 16, 1913, AO 13:7:90–92.

25. For a typical dispute see Pacheco to de la O, October 28, 1912 and October 29, 1912, AO 1:3:100 and AO 1:3:102 respectively. Also see Zapata to Pacheco, August 18, 1912, AO 11:9:4–5; Pacheco to de la O, September 1, 1912, September 23, 1912 and December 31, 1913, AO 1:3: 71, AO 1:3:54, and AO 2:6:40 respectively; Zapata to de la O, October 24, 1912, AO 11:10:23; Rueda, "La zona armada," 40–41; Sánchez Escobar, *El ocaso,* 129–37; and Paz Solórzano, *Hoguera que fue,* 340–41. Arguing that the common struggle tied one village to another in Morelos in a unique way, many scholars have downplayed intervillage conflicts—see for instance Womack, *Zapata,* 225. While it is true that the villages of Morelos and surrounding areas fought together in a way that those of Oaxaca, for instance, could not have, often their unity was *extremely* problematic. Thus the notion that intervillage strife largely disappeared from Morelos during the revolution needs substantial qualification. For one recognition of the prevalence of such strife, see de la Peña, *A Legacy,* 86.

26. See Barrios to Zapata, August 21, 1913, AO 13:7:95–96; Barrios to de la O, June 23, 1913, AO 2:1:9; the manifestos in AO 19:8:11–13; Barrios to Pacheco, August 16, 1913, AO 13:7:73–74; Barrios to de la O, September 12, 1913, AO 2:4:27; Barrios to Zapata, September 14, 1913, AO 13:8:25–27; Barrios to Zapata, August 11, 1913, AO 13:7:97–98; Barrios to Zapata, October 14, 1913, AO 13:9:27–28; Iñiguez, "Memoria," AGM 28: 17:765; Barrios to de la O, May 28, 1913, AO 1:8:4; and Barrios to Zapata, August [4?], 1913, AO 13:7:77–79.

27. See Barrios to Pacheco, August 23, 1913, AO 13:7:66; Barrios to de la O, June 7, 1913, AO 2:1:6; Barrios to de la O, July 4, 1913, AO 2:2: 46; Barrios to de la O, July 13, 1913, AO 2:2:51; Barrios to Zapata, August 3, 1913, AO 13:7:23–24; Barrios to Zapata, July 13, 1913, AO 13:6:10; Barrios to de la O, May 27, 1913, AO 1:8:27; Barrios to de la O, June 19, 1913, AO 2:1:8; and Pacheco to Zapata, October 3, 1913, AO 13:9:18–20.

28. For the quote see de la O to Zapata, September 21, 1913, AO 17: 5:2–3.

29. For the quote see Barrios to Zapata, August 16, 1913, AO 13:7: 90–92. For a fellow intellectual putting all the blame on Barrios, see Iñiguez, "Memoria," AGM 28:17:765. See also Genaro Bórneo Arellano to

de la O, July 19, 1913, AO 2:2:14; Zapata to Genaro Bórneo Arellano, July 30, 1913, AO 17:2:12; and Barrios to Zapata, September 14, 1913, AO 13: 8:25–27.

30. For the quote see Magaña, *Emiliano Zapata*, 3:113. See also the same work, 3:184–87, 216; Sánchez Lamego, *Historia militar . . . régimen huertista*, 27–29; Valverde, *Apuntes*, 111; *La Tribuna*, 6 March and 3, 6, and 23 May 1913; *El País*, 3, 4 and 6 April 1913; the interview with José Lora Mirasol, conducted by Laura Espejel, Mexico City, October 2 and 4, 1973, PHO-Z/1/14, p. 31; and Javier Garciadiego, "Higinio Aguilar:milicia, rebelión y corrupción como modus vivendi," *Historia Mexicano* 41 (1992):439–43. For the "Reformas al Plan de Ayala," see Fabela, ed., *Documentos históricos*, 21:72–73; and for the document of Aguilar's temporary adhesion to Zapatismo, April 21, 1913, see Héctor Ribot, *El Atila del sur* (Mexico City:Imprenta 1a de Humboldt, [1913?]), 57–59.

31. Magaña, *Emiliano Zapata*, 3:223, 273–78, 286–87; Womack, *Zapata*, 174–75; and Roger Parkinson, *Zapata* (Briarclift Manor, N.Y.:Stein and Day, 1980), 160–62. For the contention of Jacobo Ramos Martínez that Zapata personally carried out these executions, and that five more of Huerta's envoys were killed earlier in the month, see Valverde, *Apuntes*, 121. In what seems an effort to justify the timing of the executions, Paz Solórzano, *Zapata*, 125–26, 133–34 claims that Orozco, Sr. had encouraged the attack on Huautla by mail. For a couple of Huerta's agents who managed to escape, see the testimony of José Abelar, undated, in AA VIII-2, manuscritos, 4:309; and *El País*, 11 April 1913.

32. See Barrios to Pacheco, August 23, 1913, AO 13:7:66; Zapata to de la O, October 6, 1913, AO 11:10:53–54; Barrios to Zapata, August 25, 1913, AO 13:7:93–94; Zapata to Montaño, February 3, 1914, AO 17:3:4; Sánchez Lamego, *Historia militar . . . régimen huertista*, 44–47, 51–52; and Womack, *Zapata*, 179–80.

33. Barrios to Zapata, October 18, 1913, AO 13:9:26; Magaña, *Emiliano Zapata*, 3:312–17, 332–33; Iñiguez, "Memoria," AGM 28:17:765; and Valverde, *Apuntes*, 121.

34. See Magaña, *Emiliano Zapata*, 2:166 and 3:218; the act reaffirming Blanco's adhesion to the movement, January 18, 1914, AO 14:1:42; Guillermo Martínez Martínez, "El Gral. Emiliano Zapata y el movimiento zapatista en el Estado de Guerrero," in *Emiliano Zapata y el movimiento zapatista:cinco ensayos* (Mexico City:Instituto Nacional de

Antropología e Historia, 1980), 363–64; Rueda, "La zona armada," 38;
Iñiguez, "Memorias," AGM 28:17:765; Barrios to Zapata, November 6,
1913, AO 13:10:22; Zapata to Barrios, December 20, 1913, AO 17:12:39;
and Zapata's "Instrucciones a que Deberán Sujetarse los C.C. Generales
Julián Blanco y Otilio Montaño . . . ," December 26, 1913, AGM 30:1:9.
There has been some debate about how firm these Guerreran ties were.
Clearly some Guerreran leaders merely feigned alliance with Zapata, and
others joined for practical rather than ideological reasons. Still, given the
subsequent attack on Chilpancingo, it is evident that most of the alli-
ances were functional for the time being. On this question see Knight,
Mexican Revolution, 2:61 ff.; Jacobs, *Ranchero Revolt*, 97–100; Montaño
to Zapata, Dos Caminos, January 18, 1914, AO 14:1:73; and Custodio
Valverde, *Julián Blanco y la revolución en el Estado de Guerrero* (Mexico
City:Imprenta de J. Chávez y Hno., 1916), 47–48.

35. See Zapata to Genaro Amezcua, March 10, 1913, AGM 12:5:6;
Valverde, *Apuntes*, 113–16; and for the quote Zapata to E. Aguilar Frías,
June 2, 1913, AO 17:2:10. Womack, *Zapata*, 171 perhaps underplays Zapa-
ta's influence in states other than Morelos. Zapatistas in Guerrero and
Mexico, for instance, were not "out of touch," though it would often
prove difficult for Zapata to control them.

36. See Valverde, *Apuntes*, 123–27; Zapata to Julián Radilla and Sil-
vestre Mariscal, January 27, 1914, AO 17:3:1; AO 17:3:7–8; Antonio G.
Olea to the Secretary of War, Zacualpan, Guerrero, April 4, 1914, Muro
notes, ADN, XI/481.5/128–32, Box 74; Barrios to Zapata, August 7, 1913,
AO 13:7:103–5; Pacheco to Zapata, February 8, 1914, AO 14:2:4–5; and
Mucio Bravo to Zapata, December 29, 1913, AO 13:11:57. For Zapata's
November 11, 1913, decree of amnesty and its extension in January of
the following year, see Espejel et al., eds., *Emiliano Zapata*, 161–62,
177–78.

37. For some of Neri's many squabbles see AO 12:1:8 and AO 12:1:
10; Constancio Falfán to Zapata, November 22, 1913, AO 13:10:63; and
Yreneo Albarrán Ayala to Zapata, November 10, 1913, AO 13:10:58–59.
See also ADN, X/III, pensionados, de la O, 19; Zapata to de la O, June 27,
1913, AO 11:10:48; Antonio Díaz Soto y Gama, "Un gran guerrillero:Fe-
lipe Neri," in ASyG, roll 1, 249–50; and the interview with Angel Capistrán, conducted by Rosalind Beimler, PHO/1/199. For Neri's highly
touted fighting ability, see "El Exterminio de Morelos," in Carlos Barreto

Mark, ed. *Los corridos de Marciano Silva* (Cuernavaca:Gobierno del Estado de Morelos, 1983), 12.

38. For Zapata's quote on Neri see Zapata to de la O, 1912, AO 11: 10:26. For the second quote see the interview with Serafín Plasencia Gutiérrez, PHO-Z/1/59, p. 51. For the third see Neri to Zapata, Tlayacapan, November 11, 1913, AO 13:10:14–16. Almazán, "Memorias," chapter 17 describes Zapata's near shoot-out with Neri.

39. On other, less sensitive occasions Zapata did issue written hit orders—see for instance Zapata to Lorenzo Vázquez, January 31, 1916, AGM 31:2:100. For various accounts of Neri's death see Juan Solas for Antonio Barona to Zapata, January 23, 1914, AO 14:1:66; Amador Salazar to Zapata, January 23, 1914, AO 14:1:65; Sedano P., *Emiliano Zapata*, 62; and Porfirio Palacios, "Revolucionarios del sur:el sordo Felipe Neri." For one veteran's claim that he both heard Zapata's order and helped carry it out, see the interview with Carmen Aldana, PHO-Z/1/32. Others have also testified that they heard Neri's death was ordered, and Palafox would later make the accusation—see Palafox to Arturo Deloy, August 10, 1919, in Amado Cháverri Matamoros, "El Archivo de Zapata," *La Prensa*, 7 October 1935. Finally, see the letter from Zapatista chronicler Encarnación Muñoz to [Zapata?], Zacualpan de Amilpas, March 7, 1915, AZ 6:4:47. Muñoz indicates here, rather suspiciously, that he has found it best to write nothing about Neri's death.

40. For the taking of Chilpancingo see Magaña, *Emiliano Zapata*, 3:376–91; Jacobs, *Ranchero Revolt*, 97–99; Womack, *Zapata*, 180–83; and Sánchez Lamego, *Historia militar . . . régimen huertista*, 61–65.

41. For the quote see the interview with Jesús Chávez, conducted by María Alba Pastor, Cuautla, August 31, 1973, PHO/1/99, pp. 25–26, 44–45.

42. For the trials of Cartón and his companions see Magaña, *Emiliano Zapata*, 4:11–18; the various trial documents in AGM 27:19:426–27, 429–31 and AO 18:9:19, 22, 31, 75, 82; Warman, *"We Come to Object,"* 126; and Barrios to Zapata, Yautepec, July 3, 1914, AO 15:2:116. Finally, for the interesting tradition that Zapata taunted Cartón with freedom before sentencing him to death, see "Historia de la derrota y muerte del General Luis Cartón cuando cayó en Chilpancingo en manos del General Ignacio Maya," in Barreto Mark, *Los corridos*, 17.

43. Magaña, *Emiliano Zapata*, 4:18–23.

44. See Magaña, *Emiliano Zapata*, 4:170–77, 214–17; Paz Solórzano, *Zapata*, 137–38; Parkinson, *Zapata*, 176; and Serafín Robles's autobiographical information in ADN A/III/3–97, generales, Robles, 31.

45. For the quote see Magaña, *Emiliano Zapata*, 4:194. See also pages 188–96 of the same work; Valverde, *Apuntes*, 109; Leovigildo C. Alvarez to de la O, Tenancingo, April 24, 1914, AO 3:4:54; Agustín Bretón to the Secretary of War, Cuernavaca, April 27, 1914, Muro notes, ADN XI/481.5/185; Agustín Bretón to José R. Reyes, Cuernavaca, April 26, 1914, AO 3:4:61; Zapata to Francisco Vázquez Gómez, October 24, 1913, AGM 27:6:74; Francisco Vázquez Gómez to Zapata, Washington, December 20, 1913, AO 13:11:16; Zapata to the United States Ambassador in Mexico City, September 15, 1912, USDS-IAM 812.00/5628; and Nelson O'Shaughnessy to the Secretary of State, Mexico City, July 26, 1913, USDS-IAM 812.00/8313.

46. See Magaña, *Emiliano Zapata*, 4:195–96; the interview with Serafín Plasencia Gutiérrez, PHO-Z/1/59, p. 68; Paz Solórzano, *Zapata*, 140; Encarnación Muñoz, "Francisco Mendoza," in AZ, box 5; and Morales's execution-day letter to his son, Alfonso Morales, Tlaltizapán, May 12, 1914, AO 3:5:22. For the suggestion that the upbringing of many Morelenses may have helped make betrayal a very personal issue, see Ingham, *Mary, Michael, and Lucifer*, 71; on the role of trust and betrayal in Mexican politics see Roderic A. Camp, *Mexico's Leaders:Their Education and Recruitment* (Tucson:University of Arizona Press, 1980), 15–17.

47. Among the officers executed after the battle around Jojutla was General Flavio Maldonado, an old pal of Palafox's whom Palafox had recently invited to defect—see Palafox to Flavio Maldonado, January 27, 1914, AO 3:1:30.

48. For the quotes see the Act of Ratification of the Plan of Ayala, July 19, 1914, AGM 27:21:439. This document is wrongly dated June 19 by Magaña and by many who have used his work.

49. Zapata to de la O and Celestino Ruiz, March 17, 1912, AO 11:10:4; Zapata to Pacheco, August 18, 1912, AO 11:9:4–5; and Zapata to de la O, October 2, 1912, AO 11:10:17–18. In Weberian terms one might argue that what was underway was an incomplete transition from the charismatic authority embodied in Zapata and the traditional authority that emanated from each locality, to a more institutional form of authority that might more firmly tie localities and their various jefes together.

50. See the Reglamento de la Junta Revolucionaria del Sur y Centro de la República, June 2, 1913, Centro de Estudios Históricos del Agrarismo en México (CEHAM), *El ejército campesino del sur (ideología, organización y programa)* (Mexico City:Federación Editorial Mexicana, 1982), 43–45. See also Magaña, *Emiliano Zapata,* 3:214–15.

51. See Instrucciones a que Deberán Sugetarse los Jefes y Oficiales del Ejército Libertador del Sur y Centro, July 28, 1913, CEHAM, *El ejército campesino,* 46–47; Zapata's circular, Tlacozoltitlán, Guerrero, October 4, 1913, in Magaña, *Emiliano Zapata,* 3:329–32; Parkinson, *Zapata,* 162; Salvador Rueda, "La dinámica interna," 239; *Diario del Hogar,* 23 May 1912; Zapata to de la O, August 20, 1912, AO 11:10:10; Zapata to de la O, July 22, 1913, AO 11:10:50; Ayaquica to Zapata, July 19, 1914, AO 14:8:35; Rosoff and Aguilar, *Así firmaron,* 19, 28; Barrios to Zapata, August 16, 1913, AO 13:7:90–92; the interview with Angel Capistrán, PHO/1/199; Adán Soriano to Zapata, Tlahuapan, Puebla, November 18, 1914, AZ 2:2:49; and Garciadiego, "Higinio Aguilar," 450.

52. For Eufemio's quote see Eufemio Zapata to Zapata, July 5, 1914, AO 15:2:51; for the second quotation see Manuel Román to Zapata, July 27, 1914, AO 15:3:111. For some examples of the *many* complaints, see the citizens of San Andrés de la Cal to Zapata, October 14, 1913, AO 13:9:33–34; Timoteo Sánchez to Zapata, Tepoztlán, March 30, 1914, AO 14:4:28; Francisco Mendoza to Zapata, September 15, 1913, AO 13:8:5; and Fortino Ayaquica to Zapata, September 29, 1913, AO 13:8:15 and February 18, 1914, AO 14:3:15. See also Timoteo Sánchez to Zapata, Tepoztlán, October 24, 1913, AO 13:9:10 and the testimony of Agustín Ortiz in Rosoff and Aguilar, *Así firmaron,* 63.

53. On the complicated question of Zapatista justice see Salvador Rueda, "La dinámica interna," 237, 244–46. For another case in which Zapata was accused of favoritism see Palafox to a Juez Instructor, [May 27, 1913?], AO 13:4:4–6. Zapata did sometimes permit compadres like Jesús Morales to be executed, but usually this was for the crime of betrayal, not mere brutality.

54. See CEHAM, *El ejército campesino,* 46–47; the circulars of February 10 and 11, 1914, in Espejel et al., eds., *Emiliano Zapata,* 179–80; Lorenzo Vázquez to Zapata, Jojutla, July 20, 1914, AO 14:8:137; Zapata to de la O, February 28, 1913, AO 11:10:31–34; Zapata's decree of June 18, 1914, ARD 11:31:3; and Zapata to de la O, April 3, 1913, AO 11:10:44.

55. See Zapata's circular of October 28, 1913, in Magaña, *Emiliano Zapata*, 3:319–20; CEHAM, *El ejército campesino*, 46–47; Instrucciones a que Deberán Sujetarse los C.C. Generales Julián Blanco y Otilio Montaño . . . , AGM 30:1:9; Barrios to de la O, July 13, 1913, AO 2:2:52; Zapata to Antonio Galván, October 31, 1913, AO 18:1:2; Zapata to de la O, November 12, 1912, AO 11:10:24; the act of May 27, 1913, AO 13:4:2–3; Jesús Capistrán to Zapata, December 26, 1913, AO 13:11:101; Zapata to the Municipal President of Huautla, April 9, 1914, AO 18:2:25; AO 18:1–2 generally; Zapata to de la O, February 28, 1913, AO 11:10:31–34; Zapata to Mendoza, June 28, 1913, ADN X/III.2/1–3m, pensionados, Mendoza, 19; and Mendoza to Zapata, December 31, 1913, AO 13:11:45. For jefes competing for the right to exact money from a specific hacienda—an indication that Zapata's system for doing this was not perfected—see Luis Iñiguez, "Memoria," AGM 28:17:765 and Mendoza to Zapata, Jonacatepec, July 10, 1914, AO 15:1:64. Competition for scarce munitions was also fierce, and often seems to have been the primary reason that one group of Zapatistas disarmed another. Interestingly, Felipe Neri requested munitions from Zapata shortly before blowing up over the disarming incident—see Neri to Zapata, October 15, 1913, AO 13:9:32.

Chapter 5: The National Challenge

1. For the quote see the manifesto, "A los Habitantes de la Ciudad de México," June 24, 1914, in Espejel et al., eds., *Emiliano Zapata*, 196–98. See also Zapata to de la O, July 12, 1914, AO 11:10:74; Abrahám García to Zapata, July 13, 1914, AO 14:8:134; Lorenzo Vázquez to Zapata, Jojutla, July 22, 1914, AO 15:3:110; Zapata to Palafox, San Pedro Actopan, D.F., July 21, 1914, ARD 11:31:5; and Muñoz, "Francisco Mendoza," AZ, box 5, 59–69.

2. See Antonio Barona to Zapata, Cuernavaca, August 13, 1914, AO 16:1:57; Paz Solórzano, *Zapata*, 141–44; Magaña, *Emiliano Zapata*, 4:217–33 and 5:105; King, *Tempest*, 158–246; Sánchez Lamego, *Historia militar . . . régimen huertista*, 74–80, 83–86; and Muñoz, "Francisco Mendoza," AZ, box 5, 24–48.

3. See Palafox's circular, Yautepec, July 17, 1914, AO 19:6:22 in Espejel et al., eds., *Emiliano Zapata*, 212–13; Vicente Rojas to Zapata, Ozumba, July 28, 1914, AO 15:1:104; Banderas to Zapata, Milpa Alta,

July 22, 1914, AO 15:3:55; and Barrios to Zapata, Milpa Alta, August 16, 1914, AO 16:3:49.

4. For the Plan of Guadalupe see González Ramírez, *Planes políticos,* 137–40. On Zapata's lasting dislike for Maderistas see the report of Juan Sarabia, August 25, 1914, ARD 11:31:64–66. For Carranza's attitude toward land reform see Magaña, *Emiliano Zapata,* 4:268–69. See also Díaz Soto y Gama, *La revolución agraria,* 167–71; Douglas Richmond, *Venustiano Carranza's Nationalist Struggle, 1893–1920* (Lincoln:University of Nebraska Press, 1983), 223; Zapata to Francisco Vázquez Gómez, October 24, 1913, in Zapata, *Cartas,* 42–44; Carranza to Zapata, Piedras Negras, May 16, 1913, in Fabela ed., *Documentos históricos,* 21:70–71; Guillermo García Aragón to Alfredo Robles Domínguez, Mexico City, August 5, 1914, in Arenas Guzmán, *Del maderismo,* 176–79; and Paulino Martínez, "Causas de la revolución en México y cómo efectuar la paz," in *La cuestión de la tierra,* 1913–1914, vol. 3, Jesús Silva Herzog, ed. (Mexico City: Instituto Mexicana de Investigaciones Económicas, 1961), 224.

5. See Zapata's circular, Milpa Alta, D.F., August 14, 1914, AO 17:3: 105; Francisco Pacheco's circular, Contreras, D.F., July 22, 1914, in Espejel et al., eds., *Emiliano Zapata,* 217; *The Mexican Herald,* 23 August 1914; and José de la Luz Valdés, *El mito de Zapata* (Saltillo:Editorial Espigas, 1974), 120. Womack, *Zapata,* 194, 206, 210 hints that there was some compatibility among the soldiers of the two sides and notes that the Zapatistas were tired of fighting. Still he assumes that the eventual decision to reject Carranza and the Constitutionalists was rather unanimous. However, if one accepts the argument of Knight, *Mexican Revolution,* 1:78 that this was fundamentally a rural revolution, it is natural to question how much aversion there was between Zapatistas and Constitutionalists on the grass roots level—despite important differences between north and south—especially since not all Zapatistas were thoroughgoing agrarians.

6. For a strong—and I think exaggerated—argument about Zapata's use of consensus, see Arturo Warman, "The Political Project," 325–26. Womack, *Zapata,* 161 also displays the assumption that democracy or consensus was the usual means of deciding such questions.

7. See de la O to Zapata, August 22, 1914, AO 17:5:12; José Vides Barona to de la O, Miacatlan, August 22, 1914, AO 4:2:97; Magaña, *Emiliano Zapata,* 3:215, 4:267–71, and 5:13; the interview with Serafín

Plasencia Gutiérrez, PHO-Z/1/59, p. 68; Trinidad S. Tenorio to Zapata, Atlautla, Mexico, July 18, 1914, AO 14:8:77; the Interim President of Ocuilán to de la O, August 24, 1914, AO 4:2:144; and Sánchez Escobar, *Episodios*, 173–78. For some efforts to centralize diplomacy see Zapata to de la O, July 1, 1914; Zapata's circular, Yautepec, August 22, 1914; and Zapata's instructions for his agent in Mexico City, August 20, 1913, all in Espejel et al., eds., *Emiliano Zapata*, 211, 225, and 144–45 respectively; as well as the clipping from *La Voz de Juárez*, 22 August 1914, in ARD 11:31:27; Zapata to Barrios, Yautepec, July 31, 1914, AO 17:3:58; and Fortino Ayaquica to Zapata, July 28, 1914, AO 15:3:57. For a diplomatic event from which Zapata rather symbolically shut his jefes out see Juan Sarabia to John Kenneth Turner, January 26, 1915, in Carlos Basave del Castillo Negrete, *Notas para la historia de la Convención Revolucionaria, 1914–1915* (Mexico City:Editorial Stylo, 1947), 76–93.

8. For some of the diplomacy of these years and the philosophy behind it see Zapata to Luis Iñigas [sic], October 28, 1913, AGM 28:17:764; Zapata to Magaña, 1913, AO 17:2:34; the circulars from Zapata to various revolutionaries of September 12, 1913, AO 13:8:9–12; Magaña, *Emiliano Zapata*, 2:218–21 and 233–36; Palafox's service record, October 26, 1921, ADN X/III.2, pensionados, Palafox, 140–54; Zapata to the northern revolutionaries, September 12, 1913, AO 13:8:12; Zapata to Villa, October 29, 1913, AO 17:2:18; Amado Azuara to Zapata, Matamoros, February 26, 1914, AGM 27:10:171; Mendieta Alatorre, *Juana Belén Gutiérrez*, 28–36; and Espejel et al., eds., *Emiliano Zapata*, 144–45. Womack, *Zapata*, 186–88 stresses the distrust at work in the summer of 1914, and tends to discount the tradition of diplomacy.

9. For the quote see Barrios to Zapata, September 14, 1913, AO 13:8: 25–27. See also Barrios to Zapata, August 3, 1913, AO 13:7:16–19.

10. For the quote see Palafox for Zapata to Barrios, Yautepec, August 7, 1914, AO 16:1:12. See also the Comité Civil de la Defensa Nacional to Zapata and other jefes of the South, Mexico City, July 25, 1914, ARD 12: 34a:2; Magaña, *Emiliano Zapata*, 4:210–13; Enrique Bonilla to Zapata, Mexico City, August 7, 1914, AO 16:2:23; Zapata to Enrique Bonilla, August 14, 1914, AO 17:3:81; Barrios to Zapata, San Salvador Cuautenco, D.F., August 3, 1914, AO 16:1:8; and Palafox to Zapata, August 6, 1914, AO 16:2:28. For the near gunfight see Paz Solórzano, *Zapata*, 145–46. Womack, *Zapata*, 187–89 dismisses Carbajal's offer as bogus.

11. Alfredo Breceda to Jacobo Ramos Martínez, Veracruz, July 25, 1914, AO 14:8:47; Dr. Atl to Zapata, August 7, 1914, AO 16:2:27; and Louis M. Teitelbaum, *Woodrow Wilson and the Mexican Revolution (1913–1916)* (New York:Exposition Press, 1967), 143–50.

12. On Robles see Carranza to Zapata, Piedras Negras, May 16, 1913, in Fabela ed., *Documentos históricos,* 21:70–71; Manuel N. Robles to Zapata, San Francisco, D.F., August 4, 1914, AO 16:1:66–67; Manuel N. Robles, "Lo que supe de la muerte del Gral. Emiliano Zapata," *El Campesino,* August 1955; and Magaña, *Emiliano Zapata,* 1:166, 201 and 4:261. For Sala see Barrios to Zapata, August 7, 1913, AO 13:7:103–5; Barrios to Zapata, August 14, 1913, AO 13:7:101–2; and Antenor Sala, *Emiliano Zapata y el problema agrario en la república mexicana* (Mexico City:Imprenta Franco-Mexicana, 1919). See also Palafox to Zapata, Yautepec, July 19, 1914, AO 15:1:8; Palafox to Zapata, Yautepec, July 28, 1914, AO 15:1:136; and Manuel Palafox, "La verdadera intransigencia de Zapata," *El Universal,* August 8, 1933.

13. For the quote see [Palafox?] to Barrios, Yautepec, August [3?], 1914, AO 16:1:129. See also Dr. Atl to Carranza, July 29, 1914, in Fabela, ed. *Documentos históricos,* 21:87–89; the act signed by Atl, Zapata, Barrios, and Santiago Orozco, July 28, 1914, in Ramón Martínez Escamilla, ed., *Escritos de Emiliano Zapata* (Mexico City:Editores Mexicanos Unidos, 1978), 176; Atl to Zapata, August 3, 1914, AO 16:1:55; Atl to Zapata, Mexico City, July 29, 1914, AO 14:8:102–4; and the introduction of Felipe Gálvez to Paz Solórzano, *Hoguera,* 40.

14. For the quote see Atl's August 29th interview with *El Liberal,* cited in Magaña, *Emiliano Zapata,* 5:74. See also Atl to Zapata, August 5, 1914, AO 16:2:25; Atl to Zapata, August 7, 1914, AO 16:2:24, 27; Zapata to Atl, Yautepec, August 14, 1914, AO 17:3:79; Atl to Zapata, August 18, 1914, AO 16:1:17–19; Atl to Zapata, Contreras, D.F., August 10, 1914, AO 16:1:13–16; Atl to Zapata, August 3, 1914, AO 16:1:55; and Atl to Zapata, September 11, 1914, Fabela ed., *Documentos históricos,* 21:121–22. For Serdán's visit, see Zapata to Atl, Yautepec, August 21, 1914, AO 17:3:87; José Guadalupe Palma to Zapata, Yautepec, August 14, 1914, AGM 27:17:397; Alfredo Breceda to Carranza, Veracruz, July 31, 1914, Fabela, ed. *Documentos Históricos,* 21:91–94; and the anonymous report, [August 1914?], in ARD 11:31:32. Finally, for Zapatista anger over the

Treaty of Teoloyucán see Magaña, *Emiliano Zapata*, 4:239–41 and Díaz Soto y Gama, *La revolución agraria*, 167.

15. For the quote see Barrios to Zapata, Milpa Alta, D.F., August 16, 1914, AO 16:3:49. See also Barrios to Zapata, Milpa Alta, D.F., August 16, 1914, AO 16:3:47–48.

16. See Carranza to Zapata, Tlalnepantla, Mexico, August 17, 1914, AGM 27:17:398; John Silliman to the Secretary of State, Mexico City, August 26, 1914, USDS-IAM 812.00/13015; Zapata to Blanco, Yautepec, August 23, 1914, in Zapata, *Cartas*, 56–57; and Magaña, *Emiliano Zapata*, 4:249–55, 264–65 and, for the manifesto, 5:17–21.

17. Anonymous to Zapata, Mexico City, August 18, 1914, AO 16:1:58; Magaña to Zapata, Cuernavaca, August 20, 1914, AGM 27:17:399; Magaña, *Emiliano Zapata*, 2:211–21, and 3:334, 353–56; Zapata to Villa, October 24, 1913, AO 17:2:37; [Magaña] to Zapata, Mexico City, September 17, 1913, AO 11:9:12–13; and Charles C. Cumberland, *Mexican Revolution:The Constitutionalist Years* (Austin:University of Texas Press, 1972), 127–31. For Zapata's two letters to Villa, Yautepec, August 21 and 25, 1914, see Martínez Escamilla, *Emiliano Zapata*, 183–86. For other letters to Constitutionalist figures at this time see Zapata to Antonio Medina, Yautepec, August 25, 1914, AO 17:3:73; Zapata to Calixto Contreras, Yautepec, August 21, 1914, AO 17:3:98; and Zapata to Francisco Múgica, Yautepec, August 25, 1914, in Armando de María y Campos, *Múgica: crónica biográfica (aportación a la historia de la Revolución Mexicana)* (Mexico City:Compañía de Ediciones Populares, 1939), 70. Finally, on Villa's agrarianism see Friedrich Katz, *The Secret War in Mexico:Europe, the United States, and the Mexican Revolution*, portions trans. by Loren Goldner (Chicago:University of Chicago Press, 1981), 280–87.

18. For the quote see Zapata to Blanco, Yautepec, August 21, 1914, AGM 27:17:400. For Blanco's earlier career see Knight, *Mexican Revolution*, 2:48–49. See also Atl to Zapata, Mexico City, August 18, 1914, AO 16:1:17–19; and Armando de María y Campos, *La vida del General Lucio Blanco* (Mexico City:Instituto Nacional de Estudios Históricos de la Revolución Mexicana, 1963), 115–16. It is possible that Blanco had already sent an agent to Zapata by this time—see I. Thord-Gray, *Gringo Rebel (Mexico 1913–1914)*, 2nd ed. (Coral Gables:University of Miami Press, 1960), 380–417.

19. For background on Villarreal and Sarabia see Cockcroft, *Intellectual Precursors.* On Cabrera's agrarianism see Magaña, *Emiliano Zapata,* 2:325–54. For Zapata's letter to Villarreal of August 21, 1914, see the same work, 5:16–17; and for his invitation to the delegation see Juan Sarabia to John Kenneth Turner, January 26, 1915, in Basave del Castillo Negrete, *Notas,* 76–93.

20. On Díaz Soto y Gama see Sarabia in Basave del Castillo Negrete, *Notas,* 76–77; Sarabia's report to Carranza, August 25, 1914, ARD 11:31: 64–66; and Guillermo García Aragón in Diego Arenas Guzmán, *Del Maderismo,* 176–79. Palafox later contended—in an apparent attempt to absolve himself of his share of the blame for this incident—that Zapata did not disappear, but simply hid out nearby and conferred with Palafox in the evenings. For this see Manuel Palafox, "La paz que Carranza propuso a Zapata," *El Universal,* 28 June 1934. For the possibility that Zapata was truly ill see de la O to Zapata, Cuernavaca, August 20, 1914, AO 17:5:8. Finally, some authorities argue that there were coherent groups among the urban intellectuals with conflicting views on these negotiations—see for instance Rodolfo Alanis Boyzo, *Historia de la Revolución,* 61–63. It seems less clear-cut than this to me.

21. For the quote see Sarabia in Basave del Castillo Negrete, *Notas,* 76–93. See also the September 4, 1914, report of Villarreal and Cabrera to Carranza in Magaña, *Emiliano Zapata,* 5:82–90; and Díaz Soto y Gama, *La revolución agraria,* 175. On the arrival of Serratos see Fernando González to Zapata, Mexico City, August 9, 1914, AO 16:1:23; Zapata to Serratos, Yautepec, August 14, 1914, AO 17:3:104; Serratos's report in *La Voz de Juárez,* 22 August 1914, in ARD 11:31:27; and Serratos to Gildardo Magaña, Mexico City, October 1, 1914, AGM 27:7:110. Womack, *Zapata,* 205 suggests that Serratos may have been a Villista agent.

22. For the quote see Villarreal to Zapata, September 5, 1914, ARD 17:3:278. For an early appreciation of northern desires to amend the Plan of Ayala see [Gildardo Magaña] to Zapata, Mexico City, September 17, 1913, AO 11:9:12–13. Zapata's position at this time was that only an official Convention could make such amendments—see [Zapata] to Gildardo Magaña, October 1913, AO 17:2:34. Palafox also understood that the plan was not perfect—see Palafox to Antenor Sala, Cuernavaca, September 3, 1914, in Sala, *Emiliano Zapata,* 29–31. Finally, see Knight, *Mexican Rev-*

olution, 2:252, 285–86; and the Pact of Xochimilco, December 4, 1914, in González Ramírez, *Planes políticos,* 113–22.

23. For the assertion that intellectuals did not manipulate their caudillos see Knight, *Mexican Revolution,* 2:294. For a view that insists on such manipulation of Zapata see Mario Mena, *Zapata* (Mexico City:Editorial Jus, 1959), 183.

24. For the quote see Sarabia in Basave del Castillo Negrete, *Notas,* 76–93. See also the report of Villarreal and Cabrera in Magaña, *Emiliano Zapata,* 5:82–90.

25. For the quote see Sarabia's report of August 25, 1914, ARD 11:31: 64–66. See also Magaña, *Emiliano Zapata,* 5:82–90. Manifestations of Palafox's angling for national power were legion in the following months. See Palafox to Zapata, Mexico City, April 6, 1915, AZ 7:4:46–48; Palafox and Rodrigo Gómes to Roque González Garza, Mexico City, January 27, 1915, Universidad Panamericana, Mexico City, Archivo de Roque González Garza (hereafter cited as AGG) 19:255; and John Silliman to the Secretary of State, Mexico City, January 12, 1915, USDS–IAM 812.00/14188. Finally, see the account of this meeting in Womack, *Zapata,* 202–11. While Womack recognizes that Palafox ran things and had his own agenda, he argues that this had no appreciable effect on the outcome of the talks, because Palafox's agenda dovetailed neatly with the local xenophobia.

26. Villarreal to Zapata, September 5, 1914, ARD 17:3:278; Cabrera to Zapata, Mexico City, September 23, 1914, AGM 27:12:221; and Díaz Soto y Gama, *La revolución agraria,* 264. There were, of course, good tactical reasons for Villarreal and Cabrera to focus the blame on Palafox rather than on Zapata himself:a frontal attack on Zapata would only serve to alienate him irreparably, while criticism of Palafox might sow division among the Zapatistas. Still, the plaints of Villarreal, Sarabia, and Cabrera have the ring of sincerity, and Zapatista sources bear them out concerning the spirit with which Zapata's representatives conducted the conference—see for instance Manuel Palafox, "La paz"; and Magaña, *Emiliano Zapata,* 5:77.

27. For a typical contention that Zapata did not rely on his intellectuals for advice, see Díaz Soto y Gama, *La revolución agraria,* 258–59. Examples of the presence of Zapatista intellectuals during crucial episodes of national politics are, however, abundant. Manuel Palafox, for in-

stance, made a third in Zapata's private conversation with Pancho Villa at Xochimilco—see the Pact of Xochimilco in González Ramírez, *Planes políticos*, 113–22. For another example see the article from *El Monitor*, 22 May 1915, in ACGS 1:1:13. Finally, see Eric R. Wolf, *Peasant Wars of the Twentieth Century* (New York:Harper & Row, 1969), 294.

28. See the Pact of Xochimilco in González Ramírez, *Planes políticos*, 115.

29. Villarreal and Cabrera in Magaña, *Emiliano Zapata*, 5:81; Sarabia's report, August 25, 1914, ARD 11:31:64–66; Zapata to Cabrera, Cuernavaca, September 19, 1914, AGM 27:12:212; and the clipping from *La Voz de Juárez*, 22 August 1914, in ARD 11:31:27.

30. For the quote see Ayaquica to Zapata, AGM 27:7:129–30. See also Zapata's circular, Milpa Alta, August 14, 1914, AO 17:3:105; Zapata to the Constitutionalist Jefe of the Plaza of Tenancingo, August 22, 1914, AO 17:3:91; Herminio Chavarría to Zapata, August 16, 1914, AO 16:1:81; Alanis Boyzo, *Historia*, 37; and Zapata to de la O, Yautepec, August 22, 1914, AO 11:10:75.

31. For the quote see Serratos to Zapata, Topilejo, September 20, 1914, AGM 27:12:235. See also Palafox to de la O, Cuernavaca, September 12, 1914, AO 4:3:19; de la O to Palafox, September 28, 1914, AZ 1:20:66; and AO 4:3:149–51, 153.

32. For Blanco's conspiracy see Guzmán, *The Eagle*, 228–31. See also Blanco to Zapata, September 29, 1914, in Magaña, *Emiliano Zapata*, 5:68–69; Blanco to Zapata, Mexico City, September 10, 1914, CR 3:478; Serratos to Zapata, San Mateo, September 7, 1914, AO 16:4:2; Zapata to Blanco, September 19, 1914, Secretaría de Gobernación, *Exposición homenaje*, 35; Blanco to Zapata, Mexico City, September 11, 1914, CR 3:479; and the clipping from *El Liberal*, 24 October 1914, AGM 26:1:19.

33. For the quote see Felipe Angeles, *Genovevo de la O* (Mexico City:Secretaría de Educación Pública, n.d.), 30. See also the clippings from *El Liberal*, 25 and 26 October 1914, AGM 26:1:21 and 26:1:23 respectively; the photograph in AGM 12:5:14; Paz Solórzano, *Zapata*, 148; Magaña, *Emiliano Zapata*, 5:197–205; and Luis Fernando Amaya C., *La Soberana Convención Revolucionaria*, 1914–1916 (Mexico City:Editorial F. Trillas, 1966), 126.

34. See Díaz Soto y Gama, *La revolución agraria*, 182–83; Womack, *Zapata*, 135, 193–94; and Knight, *Mexican Revolution*, 2:259–60.

35. For the text of this speech see Magaña, *Emiliano Zapata*, 5:218–26. Agustín de Iturbide led the revolt that achieved Mexican Independence, on a conservative footing, in 1821.

36. For the quote see Roque González Garza to Villa, Aguascalientes, October 27, 1914, AGG 3:178. See also Leon Canova to the Secretary of State, October 28, 1914, USDS-IAM 812.00/13619; Womack, *Zapata*, 217; and Ramírez Plancarte, *La Ciudad*, 171–72. For the argument—counter to mine—that the antics of Díaz Soto y Gama were irrelevant to the task of political brokerage, see Knight, *Mexican Revolution*, 2:260.

37. See Díaz Soto y Gama, *La revolución agraria*, 188–89 for how his speech was conceived. See also the documents in Espejel et al., eds., *Emiliano Zapata*, 92–93, 152–57, 196–98, and 206–7; and Magaña, *Emiliano Zapata*, 5:17–21, 108–12. For discussion of changing the Zapatista slogan see Zapata to Francisco Vázquez Gómez, March 31, 1913, AGM 27:6:73; the circular of September 12, 1913, AO 13:8:9; Angel Barrios, *Proposiciones, que, para su consideración y aprobación, presenta a la Convención Soberana Revolucionaria, el suscripto Ing. Angel Barrios . . .* (Mexico City:Imprenta de Roberto Serrano y Cia., 1915), AO 19:5:15–20; and Zapata's circular, Iguala, February 11, 1915, in Fabela, ed., *Documentos históricos*, 21:186.

38. See Robles, "Lo que pensaba Zapata"; the interview with Enrique M. Zepeda, PHO/1/47, p. 96; and Krauze, *El amor*, 98. For the argument that anarchism was consistent with peasant values, see John M. Hart, *Anarchism and the Mexican Working Class, 1860–1931* (Austin:University of Texas Press, 1978), 12. Knight, *Mexican Revolution*, 1:163, meanwhile, contends that Zapata's initial patriotic and liberal ideas were now tinged with anarcho-syndicalism. I agree with Hart that there was some coincidence between Zapata's original popular liberalism and anarchist doctrine, and with Knight that the anarcho-syndicalism of the intellectuals "tinged" the ideas that were already there. I am simply emphasizing that the tinge was not essential.

39. For the use of the flag during the signing of the Plan of Ayala see Reyes Avilés, *Cartones*, 35–36. See also Díaz Soto y Gama, *La revolución agraria*, 203; Robert E. Quirk, *The Mexican Revolution, 1914–1915:The Convention of Aguascalientes* (Bloomington:Indiana University Press, 1960), 249; the interview with Enrique M. Zepeda, PHO/1/47; and *La Convención*, 22 May 1915.

40. See Knight, *Mexican Revolution,* 2:256; Quirk, *Mexican Revolution,* 101–31; Amaya, *La Soberana Convención,* 148–72; Linda B. Hall, *Alvaro Obregón:Power and Revolution in Mexico, 1911–1920* (College Station:Texas A&M University Press, 1981), 76–94; and Magaña, *Emiliano Zapata,* 5:240–43.

41. See Arnaldo Córdova, *La ideología,* 35–39; Knight, *Mexican Revolution,* 2:239, 261–62; and Villa to Zapata, Chihuahua, September 22, 1914, in Secretaría de Gobernación, *Exposición homenaje,* 35–36.

42. For the "logic of the revolution" see Knight, *Mexican Revolution,* 2:5; see also 2:106, 254. I will discuss some of Zapata's less savory allies in later chapters.

43. For troop numbers see Cumberland, *Mexican Revolution:The Constitutionalist Years,* 178–80; and Edwin Lieuwen, *Mexican Militarism:The Political Rise and Fall of the Revolutionary Army, 1910–1940* (Albuquerque:University of New Mexico Press, 1968), 32. Womack, *Zapata,* 213 accepts Sarabia's figure—fifteen thousand—on the number of Zapatistas in the field at this time. Zapatista claims, meanwhile, sometimes reached as high as sixty to seventy thousand. Part of the discrepancy has to do with political motivations, of course, and part with the difficulty of counting members of a loosely organized army that still included many part-time participants.

44. For one of Zapata's most recent attempts to discipline his troops in anticipation of entering Mexico City, see his circular, Yautepec, July 14, 1914, Espejel et al., eds., *Emiliano Zapata,* 211. For a photograph of Zapatistas at Sanborn's see Alba C. de Rojo, Rafael López Castro, and José Luis Martínez, *Zapata:iconografía* (Mexico City:Fondo de Cultura Económica, 1979), 58. See also Leon Canova to the Secretary of State, Mexico City, December 8, 1914, USDS-IAM 812.00/14048; John Silliman to the Secretary of State, Mexico City, November 30, 1914, USDS-IAM 812.00/13939; Cardoso de Oliveira to the Secretary of State, Mexico City, November 29, 1914, USDS-IAM 812.00/139–40; Valverde, *Apuntes,* 155; Quirk, *Mexican Revolution,* 132–33; Taracena, *La tragedia,* 46–47; and Guzmán, *The Eagle,* 326–29.

45. For one eye-witness account, see Leon Canova to the Secretary of State, Mexico City, December 8, 1914, USDS-IAM 812.00/14048. For another version of this meeting, see Berta Ulloa, *Historia de la Revolución Mexicana, periodo 1914–1917:la encrucijada de 1915* (Mexico City:El Colegio de México, 1979) 5:44–45.

46. For the quotes see The Pact of Xochimilco, in González Ramírez, *Planes políticos,* 113–22.

47. For the quote see Krauze, *El amor,* 81. For a cultural explanation of Zapata's aversion to the president's chair, see Romanucci-Ross, *Conflict, Violence, and Morality,* 94, 116.

48. See the photographs in C. de Rojo et al., *Zapata,* 62–68; and Salvador Toscano's film, "Memorias de un Mexicano." See also John Rutherford, *Mexican Society During the Revolution:A Literary Approach* (Oxford:Clarendon Press, 1971), 220; Ramírez Plancarte, *La ciudad de México,* 257–58; Valverde, *Apuntes,* 156; Taracena, *La tragedia,* 47; and Leon Canova to the Secretary of State, USDS-IAM 812.00/14048. Apparently Zapata and Villa again met in the capital in early January—see José Vasconcelos, *Memorias I:Ulises Criollo, La Tormenta* (Mexico City: Fondo de Cultura Económica, 1982), 638–41—but they would otherwise now go their separate ways.

Chapter 6: A Political Whirlwind

1. See Sala to Zapata, Mexico City, November 9, 1914, in Sala, *Emiliano Zapata,* 73–75; and Magaña, *Emiliano Zapata,* 2:140–42.

2. For the quote see Cristóbal Domínguez in Rosoff and Aguilar, *Así firmaron,* 61–62. See also Zapata's amnesty decree, Milpa Alta, August 10, 1914, in Martínez Escamilla, *Escritos,* 177–79; [Jan Leander DeBekker], *De cómo vino Huerta y cómo se fué . . . apuntes para la historia de un régimen militar* (Mexico City:Libreria General, 1914), 239; Ismael Limón to Zapata, Mexico City, January 20, 1915, AZ 4:1:176–77; and [Palafox?] to J.I. Robles, Mexico City, January 5, 1915, AZ 3:2:138.

3. See Argumedo, Aguilar, and José Trinidad Ruiz et al. to Zapata, San Juan Yxcaquistla, Puebla, September 10, 1914, AGM 27:12:198; Zapata to Argumedo et al., Cuernavaca, September 21, 1914, AGM 27:12:199; Almazán's report, Santa María Atexcatl, November 18, 1914, AGM 30:8: 158; González Ramírez, *Planes políticos,* 118; and Carlos Pérez Guerrero, "¿Zapata de acuerdo con el porfirismo?," in *Mujeres y Deportes,* 27 February 1937.

4. Zapata to Villa, Puebla, December 16, 1914, AGM 28:19:808; Zapata to the Minister of War, Puebla, December 18, 1914, in Martínez Escamilla, *Escritos,* 231–32; Miguel A. Sánchez Lamego, *Historia militar de la revolución en la época de la Convención* (Mexico City:Instituto Nacio-

nal de Estudios Históricos de la Revolución Mexicana, 1983), 40; and Eufemio Zapata to Zapata, Cuautla, November 15, 1914, AGM 30:8:152.

5. For the interesting argument that the munitions the United States left Carranza at Veracruz were crucial to his war effort, see John Mason Hart, *Revolutionary Mexico:The Coming and Process of the Mexican Revolution* (Berkeley:University of California Press, 1987), 290–302.

6. For the argument that Zapatista localism would not allow an attack on Veracruz see Knight, *Mexican Revolution*, 2:233, 310; Rueda, "Oposición y subversión," 7; and Federico Cervantes, "Remembranzas Históricas:la entrevista Villa-Zapata," *El Universal Gráfico*, 20 January 1939. It is worth recalling, however, that in the spring of 1911 Zapata offered to send troops as far as Chihuahua to support Madero's revolution. For one Zapatista operating in Veracruz in late December, see Palafox to José Isabel Robles, December 29, 1914, AZ 2:7:69.

7. Guzmán, *The Eagle*, 338–40; El Cronista de la Revolución, "Episodios Revolucionarios. Sobre Veracruz," *Excélsior*, 21 July 1929; Womack, *Zapata*, 222; and Zapata to Villa, Puebla, December 16, 1914, AGM 28:19:808.

8. For the quote see Leon Canova to the Secretary of State, El Paso, December 30, 1914, USDS-IAM 812.00/14131. See also Villa to Zapata, December 27, 1914, AGM 28:19:843; Quirk, *Mexican Revolution*, 144–45; Amaya, *La Soberana Convención*, 181, 183; Cumberland, *Mexican Revolution:The Constitutionalist Years*, 185; Magaña, *Emiliano Zapata*, 5:229; Womack, *Zapata*, 62; Rafael Buelna to Zapata, Hidalgo, December 15, 1914, AGM 28:19:807; Palafox to Zapata, Mexico City, December 18, 1914, AGM 28:19:811; Palafox to Mateo Almanza, Mexico City, December 18, 1914, AZ 2:5:92; AGM 28:19:802; Francisco Cortina to Palafox, Mexico City, December 29, 1914, AZ 2:7:81; Paz Solórzano, *Zapata*, 150–51; and Vasconcelos, *Memorias I*, 636. Some authorities claim that Zapata agreed at Xochimilco that Villa might execute Martínez in exchange for making García Aragón available to him. To me it seems highly unlikely that he would have betrayed Martínez—whom he had probably known since the Leyva campaign of 1909.

9. See Zapata to Palafox, Amecameca, December 10, 1914, in Fabela, ed., *Documentos históricos*, 21:141 and Ramírez Plancarte, *La ciudad*, 302. For other cases of inactive troops during this period see Fortino Ayaquica to Zapata, Tochimilco, March 1, 1915, AZ 6:3:21; and Palafox

to Pacheco, February 3, 1915, AZ 4:3:131. Knight, *Mexican Revolution,* 1:387 suggests that popular rebellions ran the risk of losing their souls when they captured cities. Ironically, Zapata generally behaved as if he understood this, but his own refusal to spend time in the capital did little to protect his jefes from its influence.

10. For the quote see Palafox to Zapata, Mexico City, December 30, 1914, AGM 28:19:853. See also Palafox to Zapata, Mexico City, December 21, 1914, AGM 28:19:818; Palafox to Zapata, Mexico City, December 22, 1914, AGM 28:19:822; Palafox to Zapata, Mexico City, December 23, 1914, AGM 28:19:832; Palafox to Zapata, December 30, 1914, AGM 28:19:853; Mendoza to Zapata, Puebla, December 25, 1914, AGM 28:19:839; and Mendoza to Zapata, Jonacatepec, February 7, 1915, AZ 5:1:44. In general it seems that the intellectuals were more worried about conservative conspiracies than were Zapata or his most prominent chieftains—see, for instance, Dolores Jiménez y Muro to Zapata, Mexico City, December 9, 1914, AGM 28:19:792; and Barrios, *Proposiciones,* AO 19:5:15–20.

11. For the first quote see Barona to Evaristo Fuentes, August 17, 1914, AO 4:2:91; for the second see Serafín M. Robles, "Emiliano Zapata declina el obsequio de un automóvil," *El Campesino,* December 1949. See also Serratos to Gildardo Magaña, October 1, 1914, AGM 27:7:110; Frank Doughty to Zapata, September 28, 1914, AZ 1:20:71; Manuel N. Robles to Zapata, October 12, 1914, AZ 1:21:65; Fernando Solís to Zapata, Mexico City, April 19, 1915, AZ 7:5:76–77; César Prescora Roeves to González Garza, October 24, 1914, AGM 27:7:136; Castillo to Zapata, April 13, 1915, AZ 7:5:25–28; and Sánchez Escobar, *El ocaso,* 133–34.

12. For the quote see Octavio Magaña, "Historia documental," AGM, unnumbered boxes, #348. On the change in everyday life see Rueda, "La dinámica interna," 240–41. See also *The Mexican Herald,* 26 August 1914; Robles, "Segunda celada"; Rosoff and Aguilar, *Así firmaron,* 81; and the interview with Cayetano Hidalgo Salazar, PHO 1/50, p. 130.

13. Paz Solórzano, *Zapata,* 37–38, 125; Anita Aguilar and Rosalind Rosoff, *Emiliano Zapata:hombre de tierra* (Mexico City:Editorial Alhambra Mexicana, 1986), 87, 90; Vanderwood, *Disorder and Progress,* 9; and Francisco Plancarte y Navarrete, *Apuntes para la geografía del Estado de Morelos,* 2nd ed. (Cuernavaca:Imprenta de José Donaciano Rojas, 1913), 87, 89.

14. For the quote see Francisco Franco et al. to Zapata, Anenecuilco,

January 21, 1915, AZ 4:2:6. See also Tomás García and Vicente Rojas to Zapata, November 4, 1914, AZ 2:1:23; the bill from a music store, November 28, 1914, AZ 25:2:1; the Tlaltizapán Festival Commission to [Zapata], AGM 28:5:605; Francisco Mendoza to Zapata, December 9, 1915, AZ 10:10:76; Sabas Piñero to Zapata, Campos de Chinameca, October 12, 1915, AZ 10:5:7; the President of the Junta Patriotica of Cuautla to Zapata, September 6, 1915, AZ 10:1:40; Feliciano Domínguez to Zapata, Villa de Ayala, August 21, 1915, AZ 9:6:3; Eutimio Rodríguez to Zapata, Tlaquiltenango, February 4, 1916, AZ 11:4:14; Porfirio Cabrera to Zapata, Mazatepec, July 30, 1914, AO 15:3:141; Zapata to Pipino L. Valero, Quilamula, September 24, 1914, AO 18:2:47; Díaz Soto y Gama, *La revolución agraria*, 245; Warman, *"We Come to Object,"* 118; Vicente Navarro to Zapata, Mexico City, November 28, 1914, AGM 30:8:171; and Maximo V. Iriarte to Zapata, September 8, 1914, AZ 1:19:13. For an excellent description of local life see also Krauze, *El amor*, 91–96.

15. For the quote see the interview with Gregoria Zúñiga, PHO-Z/1/82. For photographs of some of Zapata's children see AZ 20:26:1–6. See also Palafox to Zapata, Yautepec, July 28, 1914, AZ 15:1:137; Gill, "Zapata," 306–11; Gómez, *Las comisiones*, 160; Herminia Aguilar, "Doña Josefa"; and Policarpo B. Arellano to Palafox, Mexico City, December 11, 1914, AZ 2:5:5.

16. For the quote see Marciano Silva, "El exterminio de Morelos," in Barreto, ed., *Los corridos*, 12. See also Augustina Salazar to Zapata, Anenecuilco, October 23, 1915, AZ 10:6:13; Francisca Z. García to Zapata, Cuautla, October 2, 1915, AZ 10:4:14; Prospero Villegas to Zapata, June 21, 1915, AZ 8:6:7; Lucio Rios to Zapata, Cuautla, August 2, 1914, AO 16:2:43; López González, *Los compañeros*, 251; and Serafín M. Robles, "El Zapatismo y la industría azucarera en Morelos," *El Campesino*, August 1950.

17. For the Ixcamilpa decree, April 30, 1912, see Espejel et al., eds., *Emiliano Zapata*, 119. For the circular of February 11, 1914, see the same volume, pp. 181–82. Since this document refers to an October 25, 1913 law, it may not have been the first time that Zapata ordered the confiscation of enemy holdings. In any event, he authorized such practices earlier than Womack, *Zapata*, 212 recognizes.

18. For the collection of money from haciendas see Zapata to de la O, Tlaltizapán, June 26, 1914, AO 11:10:67; Maurilio Mejía to Zapata,

Cuautla, July 13, 1914, AO 15:1:39; Palafox to Zapata, Yautepec, [July 24, 1914], AA VIII–2, manuscritos, 2:150; Palafox to de la O, Yautepec, July 28, 1914, AO 4:1:141; and Francisco Merelo to Palafox, August 8, 1914, AA VIII–2, manuscritos, 2:160. See also Barrios to Zapata, Milpa Alta, August 16, 1914, AO 16:3:47–48 and the "Decreto de Nacionalización de Bienes," Cuernavaca, September 8, 1914, in Magaña, *Emiliano Zapata,* 5:102–3.

19. Zapata to Antenor Sala, October 25, 1914, in Sala, *Emiliano Zapata,* 49.

20. See Millon, *The Ideology,* 43–44; Warman, "The Political Project," 332; Gómez, *Las comisiones,* 63; [Palafox?] to Jesús Salgado, Mexico City, January 11, 1915, AZ 4:1:28; G. de J. Barrios to Zapata, Mexico City, March 5, 1915, AZ 18:3:68–69; Honorato García to Zapata, Ahuacuotzingo, July 13, [1914?], AO 15:1:32; Julián Ortega to Zapata, Xochitlán, Puebla, November 1, 1914, AZ 2:1:5–6; and Apolonia Avila to Zapata, Tlaquiltenango, November 1, 1915, AZ 10:7:1–2.

21. See Pacheco to Zapata, Huitzilac, October 24, 1914, AZ 1:22:42 and November 4, 1914, AZ 1:22:43–44; Palafox to de la O, September 15, 1914, AO 4:3:155; Palafox to de la O, Cuernavaca, September 9, 1914, AO 4:3:25; and Zapata to Francisco Salgado, November 16, 1915, AGM 31:1: 249. On the de la Torre y Mier case see Ignacio de la Torre y Mier to Zapata, Cuautla, June 7, 1915, AGM 27:1:6; Zapata to Gregorio Zúñiga, Tlaltizapán, January 22, 1916, AGM 30:11:225; the General Delegate of the Red Cross to Zapata, Mexico City, June 1, 1915, AZ 8:4:19–22; Gómez, *Las comisiones,* 122; Serafín M. Robles, "Emiliano Zapata:causa baja como soldado raso a los 48 días," *El Campesino,* January 1952; *La Convención,* 30 April 1915; and Edith O'Shaughnessy, *Intimate Pages of Mexican History* (New York:George H. Doran, 1920), 119.

22. For jefes blocking land reform by various means see Amaya, *La Soberana Convención,* 213; Emiliano Vargas to Palafox, Atlacholoaya, Morelos, November 17, 1914, AZ 2:2:44; Palafox to Zapata, December 29, 1914, AGM 28:19:849; Serratos to Palafox, December 31, 1914, AZ 3:1:26; and [Palafox?] to Ayaquica, January 4, 1915, AZ 3:2:103. See also Gómez, *Las comisiones,* 62–63 and Eufemio Zapata to Zapata, Cuautla, September 19, 1914, AGM 27:12:213.

23. For the first quote see Ayaquica to Zapata, Xochimilco [sic— Tochimilco?], May 10, 1915, Fabela, ed., *Documentos históricos,* 21:218–

19. For the second see "Hace 50 años," in *Excélsior*, 14 December 1964. Also see *La Convención*, 5 January 1915; Paulino Martínez et al. to Zapata, Aguascalientes, November 4, 1914, AGM 30:8:123; and Quirk, *Mexican Revolution*, 143.

24. For the quote see Gómez, *Las comisiones*, 103. See also pages 33–34, 67–68, 85–87, and 112 in that work; Nicolás Mejía to Zapata, May 10, 1915, AZ 19:1:60; Palafox to Zapata, Mexico City, January 11, 1915, in Fabela, ed., *Documentos históricos*, 21:149–52; and Efrén Mancilla to Zapata, Tlaquiltenango, January 3, 1915, AZ 3:2:86. Friction between campesinos and engineers around Xoxocotla continued well into 1916— see Zapata to Lorenzo Vázquez, March 14, 1916, AGM 31:2:378–79.

25. The quote is from Gómez, *Las comisiones*, 77. For an excellent more general account of the land reform process see Womack, *Zapata*, 228–36.

26. See José E. Ponce to Zapata, Huehuetlán, Puebla, July 28, 1914, AO 15:3:151; the citizens of Tixtla, Guerrero to Zapata, August 13, 1914, AO 16:1:99; Domitilo Ayala and Luciano Solis to de la O, Palpan, September 21, 1914, AO 4:3:41; Lucio Zamora to Zapata, Miacatlán, November 3, 1914, AZ 2:1:13; and Fructuoso Acevedo to Palafox, Milpa Alta, December 15, 1914, AZ 17:9:50.

27. See Dolores Damián to Zapata, Tepeji, September 28, 1914, Fabela, ed., *Documentos históricos*, 21:126–27; Lorenzo Vázquez to de la O, December 25, 1914, AO 4:6:12–13; AZ 2:1:8; Modesto Rangel to Zapata, Xochitepec, February 19, 1915, AZ 5:3:113; Mendoza to Amador Salazar, July 1, 1915, AZ 9:1:7; Zapata's decree of November 18, 1914, in Espejel et al., ed., *Emiliano Zapata*, 249–50; Emigdio Marmolejo to Zapata, May 25, 1915, AZ 8:3:36; Gómez, *Las comisiones*, 87, 111–12; Laura Espejel, "El cuartel general órgano rector de la revolución zapatista" (B.A. thesis, Universidad Nacional Autónoma de México, 1985), 52–53, 57; and Robles, "El Zapatismo y la industría azucarera."

28. For damage to many mills see Zapata to Montaño, Tlaltizapán, March 5, 1915, in Cháverri Matamoros, "El archivo de Zapata," *La Prensa*, 27 September 1935. See also Zapata to the citizens of Santa Catarina Huazulco, August 3, 1914, AA VIII-2, manuscritos, 2:156; Graciano Aragón to Zapata, Ticumán, April 20, 1915, AZ 18:4:96–97; Modesto Rangel to Zapata, Cuernavaca, November 19, 1914, AZ 2:2:53; Emigdio Marmolejo to Zapata, February 5, 1915, AZ 4:3:199; Emigdio Marmolejo

to Zapata, Cuautla, February 19, 1915, AZ 5:3:148; Emigdio Marmolejo to Zapata, Hospital, April 16, 1915, AZ 18:4:85; and Womack, *Zapata,* 240–41. It is worth noting that there remained some competition between villages and the cores of the old haciendas, now Zapatista-run, for both land and water.

29. See Encarnación Díaz to Zapata, Iguala, September 14, 1914, AGM 27:12:207; the Municipal President of Huautla to Zapata, January 26, 1915, AZ 4:2:140; F.M. Palacios to Zapata, Cuautla, October 9, 1914, AZ 1:21:51–52; Antonio Galván to Zapata, Huautla, February 8, 1915, AZ 5:1:98; and [Palafox?] to Zapata, Mexico City, December 26, 1914, AZ 2:7:22.

30. For the quote see José Robles and Eduardo López to Zapata, Anenecuilco, January 20, 1915, AZ 18:1:82. For Zapata's concern with schools see F.M. Palacios to Zapata, Cuautla, January 28, 1915, AZ 4:2:175; Zapata to Montaño, Tlaltizapán, March 5, 1915, in Cháverri Matamoros, "El archivo de Zapata," *La Prensa,* 27 September 1935; and Emigdio Acalco to Zapata, Tepalcingo, October 26, 1914, AZ 17:7:90. See also Zapata to Pipino L. Valero, Quilamula, September 24, 1914, AO 18:2:47; the citizens of Villa de Ayala to Zapata, June 4, 1915, AZ 19:2:38; and Miguel Patiño et al. to Zapata, Tejalpa, August 24, 1915, AZ 9:6:32.

31. For the quote see Lorenzo Vázquez to Zapata, Cuernavaca, March 14, 1915, AGM 28:18:781. For elections in Morelos see Zapata to de la O, Yautepec, August 22, 1914, AO 11:10:75; de la O's circular, Cuernavaca, September 5, 1914, AO 19:6:40; de la O's circular, Cuernavaca, September 9, 1914, AO 4:3:52; AGM 28:19:815; Montaño to de la O, Cuernavaca, February 11, 1915, AO 5:2:56; and Lorenzo Vázquez to de la O, Cuernavaca, March 8, 1915, AO 5:3:41. See also Agustín Cordero to Zapata, San Pablo Acatlán, Puebla, December 21, 1914, AZ 2:6:3–4 and Zapata to Montaño, Tlaltizapán, March 5, 1915, in Cháverri Matamoros, "El archivo de Zapata," *La Prensa,* 27 September 1935. Why de la O was replaced in the governorship is unclear. Womack, *Zapata,* 226 says that his military duties were too pressing, but de la O was an angry man in March of 1915, and indirect evidence suggests that the loss of this post may have been a precipitating factor.

32. For the quote see Zapata to Palafox, Cuautla, January 19, 1915, AGM 30:7:104. See also Palafox to Zapata, Mexico City, January 14, 1914 [sic], AGM 27:10:166 and, for a more positive view of Barona, Almazán,

"Memorias," *El Universal,* 13 February 1958. Almazán contends that Barona was slandered by the press during this period, but the reports of his fellow Zapatistas were at least as damning of him as were the newspapers. Finally, for more on Zapata's temper see Antonio Díaz Soto y Gama, "Como era Zapata," in ASyG, roll 3:205–7; and the interview with Jesús Chávez, PHO/1/99.

33. See Palafox to Zapata, December 29, 1914, AGM 28:19:851; Quirk, *Mexican Revolution,* 146–79; Eulalio Gutiérrez et al., January 13, 1915, in Basilio Rojas, *La Soberana Convención de Aguascalientes* (Mexico City, 1961), 189–94; and Palafox to Zapata, Mexico City, January 18, 1915, in Fabela, ed., *Documentos históricos,* 21:152–54.

34. For the ongoing struggle over munitions see the Sub-secretary of War to Zapata, December 22, 1914, AZ 2:6:15; Serratos to Palafox, January 4, 1915, AZ 3:2:112; Serratos to Palafox, Mexico City, January 7, 1915, AZ 3:3:102; and Palafox to Zapata, Mexico City, January 11, 1915, in Fabela, ed., *Documentos históricos,* 21:149–52. See also Quirk, *Mexican Revolution,* 154. While Zapata's movements during early January are unclear, he was apparently in both the capital and the Puebla area. See *La Convención,* 2 and 6 January 1915; and José Vasconcelos, *Memorias I,* 640.

35. See Palafox to Zapata, Mexico City, January 9, 1914 [sic], AGM 27:10:164; Palafox to Zapata, Mexico City, January 11, 1915, CR 3:795; Zapata to de la O, Tlaltizapán, January 11, 1915, AO 11:11:1; Palafox to de la O, Mexico City, January 12, 1915, AO 5:1:29; Sánchez Lamego, *Historia militar . . . época de la Convención,* 153; and Amaya, *La Soberana Convención,* 190, 268. Amaya suggests that the weak defense of the capital reflected Zapatista disinterest in it. I would argue that they were perhaps ambivalent toward it, but certainly not disinterested. It is hard, otherwise, to explain their subsequent efforts to win it back.

36. For the quote see González Garza cited in Montaño to Zapata, Cuernavaca, February 2, 1915, AZ 4:3:96–97. See also González Garza to Zapata, February 2, 1915, AGG 5:447 and González Garza to Palafox, Cuernavaca, February 1, 1915, AGG 5:311.

37. See Roque González Garza to Zapata, February 3, 1915, AGG 7:560 for the quote. See also Zapata to González Garza, February 3, 1915, AGG 7:558; the circular of González Garza, Zapata, and Serratos, February 6, 1915, AGM 30:9:175; and González Garza to Zapata, Cuernavaca,

[early February 1915?], AGG 7:556. Womack, *Zapata*, 172, makes the point that Zapata sought a slightly more formal system of wage payment as early as May 1913. Finally, for the convincing argument that most studies of Zapatismo have missed the crucial theme of salaries see Espejel, "El cuartel general," 88–105. Espejel notes that regular pay might logically have been expected to help professionalize the movement, and thus be supported by such northerners as González Garza, who were anxious to encourage the Zapatistas to fight more along Villista lines.

38. See Heliodoro Castillo to Zapata, Iguala, January 17, 1915, AZ 4:1:114–15; and González Garza to Zapata, February 2, 1915, AGG 5:447.

39. For the quote see [J.M. Rojo?] to Zapata, Iguala, February 14, 1915, AZ 5:2:132. See also [Zapata] to Adalberto Hernández, Iguala, February 9, 1915, CR 3:801; the citizens of Tecalpulco, Guerrero to Zapata, February 12, 1915, AZ 5:2:73–74; and AZ 18:2:203–9.

40. See Zapata's decrees of February 13 and 15, 1915 in Fabela, ed., *Documentos históricos*, 21:189–92. For more on the attempt to change Zapatista organization see also [Magaña] to Zapata, Cuernavaca, February 26, 1915, AZ 6:2:49; *La Convención*, 25 March 1915; [Palafox] to J.M. Carrasco, Mexico City, December 23, 1914, AZ 2:6:25; and Astrolabio Guerra to Palafox, December 31, 1914, AZ 3:1:65.

41. For the quote see Zapata to González Garza, February 9, 1915, AGG 5:445. See also Zapata's appointment of Trinidad Pérez to work the mines for the benefit of the Convention, Iguala, February 12, 1915, CR 3:801; and González Garza to Zapata, February 10, 1915, AGG 5:444. For coinage and Zapata's preference for it see T.V. Buttrey and Adon Gordus, "The Silver Coinage of Zapata, 1914–1915," *Hispanic American Historical Review* 52(1972):456–62; and Serratos to Gildardo Magaña, October 1, 1914, AGM 27:7:110. At least four mints operated in Guerrero in 1914 and 1915.

42. See Zapata to Montaño, Tlaltizapán, March 5, 1915, in Cháverri Matamoros, "El archivo de Zapata," *La Prensa*, 27 September 1935; the conversation between González Garza and Santiago Orozco in AGG 8:377; González Garza to Orozco, February 26, 1915, AGG 6:310; Orozco to González Garza, February 27, 1915, AGG 6:309; González Garza to Orozco, Cuernavaca, March 2, 1915, AGG 6:308; González Garza to Orozco, March 30, 1915, AGG 13:339; and Orozco to González Garza, March 29, 1915, AGG 13:340.

43. For the first quote see Pacheco to Orozco, February 9, 1915, AZ 5:1:147; for the second Pacheco to Zapata, February 8, 1915, AZ 5:1:83; and for the third Pacheco to Zapata, Huitzilac, March 12, 1915, AZ 7:1: 53. Finally, for some of the many complaints of the period about Palafox and other intellectuals see Pacheco to Zapata, Huitzilac, January 31, 1915, AZ 4:2:221; Pedro Saavedra to Zapata, Amacuzac, February 12, 1915, AZ 5:2:49; Astrolabio F. Guerra to Zapata, San Antonio Coapa, D.F., February 26, 1915, AZ 6:2:37; and Pacheco to Zapata, Huitzilac, March 12, 1915, AZ 7:1:53.

44. For the quote see Pacheco to Zapata, Contreras, February 17, 1915, AZ 5:3:56. See also Jesús Aguilar to Roque González Garza, To-pilejo, February 18, 1915, AGG 8:28; González Garza to Zapata, February 18, 1915, AGG 8:528; González Garza to Zapata, February 18, 1915, AGG 8:539; Zapata to González Garza, Cuautla, February 19, 1915, AGG 8:538; González Garza to Zapata, February 24, 1915, AGG 8:527; Magaña to Serratos, Cuernavaca, February 25, 1915, AZ 6:1:111; and Quirk, *Mexican Revolution*, 207–8.

45. For the quote see Zapata's circular, February 25, 1915, ACGS 1:3: 42. See also Zapata to Villa, Cuautla, February 20, 1915, in Fabela, ed., *Documentos históricos*, 21:193–94; Zapata to González Garza, Tlaltiza-pán, February 18, 1915, AGG 8:534; Zapata's orders to various jefes, March 8, 1915, AZ 6:4:73–80; *La Convención*, 21 and 24 February 1915; Hall, *Alvaro Obregón*, 118–19; and Quirk, *Mexican Revolution*, 183–84.

46. See Florencio Barrera Fuentes, ed., *Crónicas y debates de las se-siones de la Soberana Convención Revolucionaria*, 3 vols. (Mexico City: Instituto Nacional de Estudios Históricos de la Revolución Mexicana, 1965), 3:369–86; González Garza to Zapata, Mexico City, April 5, 1915, AGG 9:456; and Quirk, *Mexican Revolution*, 178–79. For three different accounts of this meeting see Ramírez Plancarte, *La ciudad*, 391–95; Ta-racena, *La tragedia*, 52–53; and Quirk, *Mexican Revolution*, 239–40. The accounts of Taracena and Ramírez Plancarte were written earlier, are more similar, and seem more trustworthy, but it is possible that Quirk is right in placing this meeting in May rather than March.

47. See González Garza to Zapata, March 24, 1915, AGG 8:458; Quirk, *Mexican Revolution*, 213–20; Zapata to González Garza, Yaute-pec, March 29, 1915, AGG 19:316; Zapata to Villa, Yautepec, March 29,

1915, ASyG, roll 1:14–15; and Orozco to González Garza, March 29, 1915, AGG 19:233.

48. For the quote see Zapata to González Garza, April 1, 1915, AGG 9:467. See also Palafox to Zapata, Mexico City, March 28, 1914 [sic], AGM 27:10:174; Palafox to González Garza, March 28, 1915, AGG 13: 337; González Garza to Orozco, March 29, 1915, AGG 19:232; González Garza to Zapata, March 31, 1915, AGG 9:468; and Orozco to Zapata, April 1, 1915, AZ 7:4:3. Despite the outcome, it seems that Zapata did plan to let the Convention go—see Palafox to Zapata, Mexico City, March 30, 1914, AGM 27:10:175.

49. For discussions of the ideological differences at play here see Knight, *Mexican Revolution*, 2:307–8; Amaya, *La Soberana Convención*, 187; Córdova, *La ideología*, 159–61; and Richard Roman, *Ideología y clase en la Revolución Mexicana:La Convención y el Congreso Constituyente*, trans. María Elena Hope (Mexico City:Sepsetentas, 1976), pp. 49–50, 54–55.

50. See Palafox to Zapata, Mexico City, April 6, 1915, AZ 7:4:46–48; González Garza to Zapata, April 7, 1915, AGG 19:308; the act signed by González Garza, Díaz Soto y Gama, and Adalberto Hernández, April 9, 1915, AGG 19:224; Palafox to Zapata, Mexico City, April 13, 1915, AGM 30:6:64; and Quirk, *Mexican Revolution*, 233–35, 237–38.

51. For the quote see Zapata to the Convention, Villa de Ayala, May 8, 1915, USDS-IAM 812.00/15085. Quirk, *Mexican Revolution*, 239–40 contends that this is when the meeting between Zapata and González Garza at Los Reyes took place. See also Zapata to González Garza, Jojutla, May 4, 1915, AGG 19:307.

52. See Serratos to Zapata, Mexico City, May 11, 1915, AZ 8:2:2–3; Ramón Aguilar et al. to Zapata, Coyoacán, May 11, 1915, AZ 8:2:5; Barrios to Zapata, Mexico City, May 11, 1915, AGG 11:446; Cardoso de Oliveira to the Secretary of State, Mexico City, May 7, 1915, USDS-IAM 812.00/14994; Ramírez Plancarte, *La ciudad*, 414–16; *La Convención*, 7, 9 and 10 May 1915; and Quirk, *Mexican Revolution*, 241.

53. For the quotes see the reports to the Convention of May 24, 1915, Archivo General de la Nación, Mexico City, Archivo de la Convención Revolucionaria (hereafter cited as ACR) 7:6:9–115. See also *El Monitor*, 22 May 1915, ACGS 1:1:1–3; Quirk, *Mexican Revolution*, 251; and

Díaz Soto y Gama to Zapata, Mexico City, May [17?], 1915, AGM 28:23: 1031.

54. For the quote see González Garza to Zapata, Mexico City, May 27, 1915, AGM 28:6:633. See also González Garza to Zapata, May 26, 1915, AGG 19:303; Zapata to Alberto Piña et al., Tlaltizapán, May 26, 1915, AGG 19:301; Zapata to González Garza, May 29, 1915, AGG 19: 291; González Garza to Zapata, Mexico City, May 31, 1915, AGG 19:288; and Barrera Fuentes, *Crónicas*, 3:617–21.

55. Lagos Cházaro to Zapata, Mexico City, June 10, 1915, AZ 15: 14:5; Villa to Zapata, Aguascalientes, June 12, 1915, AGM 27:1:11; *La Convención*, 5 June 1915; and Quirk, *Mexican Revolution*, 256–65.

56. Gómez, *Las comisiones*, 123; Palafox to Zapata, Mexico City, March 28, 1914 [sic], AGM 27:10:174; Zapata to Palafox, Tlaltizapán, August 23, 1915, AZ 19:4:73; and Zapata to the agrarian commission of Tenango del Valle, Tlaltizapán, August 23, 1915, AZ 19:4:74.

57. See the Citizens of Ocuituco to Zapata, August 3, 1914, AO 16:1: 125; the temporary resolution of the conflict by Zapatista headquarters, Yautepec, August 18, 1914, AO 16:3:77; and Ayaquica to Zapata, Tochimilco, June 17, 1915, in Fabela, ed., *Documentos históricos*, 21: 234–35.

58. Jesús Blancas to Zapata, June 12, 1915, AZ 19:2:85; Modesto Rangel to Zapata, Xochitepec, June 27, 1915, AZ 19:2:49; Benigno Veliz to Zapata, Acatlán, July 18, 1915, AZ 9:2:43; Zapata to Ricardo Reyes Márquez, Tlaltizapán, August 25, 1915, AZ 9:6:36; Zapata to Montaño, Tlaltizapán, March 5, 1915, Cháverri Matamoros, "El archivo," *La Prensa*, 27 September 1935; and Zapata to Gustavo Baz, Tlaltizapán, August 23, 1915, AZ 19:4:71. In sum, it seems safe to say that land reform in Morelos, though fairly successful in the short term, was not the "orderly process" that Womack, *Zapata*, 229 makes it.

59. For other evidence of Mexico City area misbehavior see [Zapata] to Julián Gallegos, undated, AZ 14:20:1; and Magaña to Zapata, Mexico City, June 3, 1915, AZ 8:4:52.

60. For the notion that Zapata was destroyed by power he refused see Octavio Paz, *The Other Mexico:Critique of the Pyramid*, trans. Lysander Kemp (New York:Grove Press, 1972), 58. Córdova, *La ideología*, 153, contends that the Zapatistas were too localist to fight for national power. I am simply pointing out that Zapata did not refuse national

power, and that he certainly did fight for it, though perhaps not tenaciously enough. I think Knight, *Mexican Revolution,* 2:259, is closer to the truth when he suggests that Zapatismo displayed a certain schizophrenia in its efforts to play a national role while remaining true to local concerns. It seems likely, as Womack, *Zapata,* 205, writes, that Zapata himself was rather ambivalent:fighting for national influence, but afraid, deep down, that he might accidentally misuse it.

Chapter 7: Decline and Betrayal

1. See Policarpo B. Arellano to Zapata, Tlaltizapán, July 17, 1915, AZ 19:3:56; and Bibiano A. Trejo to Zapata, Tlaltizapán, April 5, 1915, AZ 7:4:33. For a photograph of the tomb see Alba C. de Rojo et al., *Zapata: iconografía,* 78.

2. For a detailed account of these crucial battles see Hall, *Alvaro Obregón,* 120–39. For another version of the collapse of Zapatismo—the subject of this chapter—see Womack, *Zapata,* 244 ff. Womack covers this collapse in considerable depth, but underplays its extent and significance.

3. See Zapata to Villa, Tlaltizapán, July 24, 1917, AZ, box 26; Villa to Zapata, Irapuato, Guanajuato, April 17, 1915, AGM 28:6:631; Zapata to González Garza, Tlaltizapán, April 3, 1915, AGG 10:492; González Garza to Zapata, April 3, 1915, AGG 10:493; Zapata to González Garza, April 4, 1915, AGG 10:491; and Silliman to the Secretary of State, Veracruz, April 26, 1915, USDS-IAM 812.00/14933.

4. For the quote see Castillo to Zapata, April 13, 1915, AZ 7:5:25–28. See also González Garza to de la O, May 17, 1915, AGG 16:235; Palafox to Zapata, December 21, 1914, AGM 28:19:82; Serratos to Palafox, December 28, 1914, AZ 2:7:42; de la O to González Garza, [March 26, 1915?], AGG 9:269; González Garza to de la O, March 26, 1915, AGG 9:268; González Garza to Zapata, April 4, 1915, AGG 10:478; Leopoldo Reynoso to the Governor of Morelos, Cuernavaca, April 3, 1915, AZ 7:4:15; Lorenzo Vázquez to Zapata, April 4, 1915, AZ 7:4:23; and Palafox to Zapata, Mexico City, April 18, 1915, AGM 30:6:62.

5. For the quote see Palafox to Zapata, Mexico City, March 28, 1914 [sic], AGM 27:10:174. See also Rafael Castillo to de la O, Tacuba, D.F., June 8, 1915, AO 5:6:10; Pacheco to Zapata, Mexico City, May 27, 1915, AGG 19:299; and Zapata to Villa, Tlaltizapán, July 24, 1917, AZ, Box 26.

6. See Teitelbaum, *Woodrow Wilson,* 143–50; Frederick Funston to

the Secretary of State, Veracruz, May 7, 1914, USDS-IAM 812.00/12291;
William Jennings Bryan to Cardoso de Oliveira, Washington, August 28,
1914, USDS-IAM, 812.00/13015; Bryan to Cardoso de Oliveira, Washing-
ton, September 7, 1914, USDS-IAM 812.00/13116; George M. Stephenson,
John Lind of Minnesota (Minneapolis:University of Minnesota Press,
1935), 265–66; Arnold Shanklin to John Lind, May 23, 1914, Mexican
Mission Papers of John Lind, microfilm copy of the original at the Minne-
sota Historical Society (hereafter cited as AJL) 5:196; [Lind] to William
Jennings Bryan, Veracruz, March 23, 1914, AJL 4:311; and Shanklin to
Lind, May 29, 1914, AJL 5:266.

7. For Zapata to Wilson, Yautepec, August 23, 1914, see Magaña,
Emiliano Zapata, 5:104–12.

8. For the quote see Canova to William Jennings Bryan, El Paso, December 30, 1914, USDS-IAM 812.00/14131. For Zapatista efforts to respect foreign property rights, see Eulalio Gutiérrez to Palafox, December
14, 1914, AZ 2:5:25; [Palafox?] to the garrison at Xochimilco, December
30, 1914, AZ 2:7:134–35; Palafox to Herminio Chavarria, Mexico City,
January 7, 1915, AZ 3:2:131; and Palafox to Zapata, Mexico City, December 29, 1914, CR 3:493. On H.L. Hall see Palafox to Hall, Mexico City,
December 21, 1914, CR 3:489; Bryan to Cardoso de Oliveira, Washington,
August 28, 1914, USDS-IAM 812.00/13015; Silliman to the Secretary of
State, Mexico City, August 29, 1914, USDS-IAM 812.00/13040; and Hall
to the State Department, October 31, 1914, USDS-IAM 812.00/13815. See
also Palafox to Zapata, Mexico City, December 18, 1914, AGM 28:19:811;
Palafox to Zapata, December 29, 1914, AGM 28:19:851; Palafox to Zapata, Mexico City, April 15, 1915, AGM 30:6:67; Arnold Shanklin to Bryan,
Veracruz, January 9, 1915, USDS-IAM 812.00/14285; Cardoso de Oliveira
to Bryan, Mexico City, March 11, 1915, USDS-IAM 812.00/14569; Silliman to Bryan, Mexico City, November 30, 1914, USDS-IAM 812.00/
13939; Silliman to Bryan, Mexico City, December 14, 1914, USDS-IAM
812.00/14010; Palafox to Sala, September 28, 1914, in Sala, *Emiliano Zapata,* 63; Serratos' report, August 22, 1914, ARD 11:31:27; Frederick Funston to Bryan, Veracruz, September 28, 1914, USDS-IAM, 812.00/13434;
and Serratos to Magaña, October 1, 1914, AGM 27:7:110.

9. John Silliman to the Secretary of State, Veracruz, May 15, 1915,
USDS-IAM 812.00/15076; and Palafox to Zapata, Mexico City, April 6,
1915, AZ 7:4:46–48.

10. See Eufemio Zapata to R.F. García, April 28, 1915, AGG 19:305; Duval West to Bryan, April 10, 1915, AGM 28:6:627; and Magaña, *Emiliano Zapata*, 5:112–17. For Zapata's claim that it was West who suggested the commission see Zapata to the Convention, Tlaltizapán, April 19, 1915, Fabela ed., *Documentos históricos*, 21:200–201.

11. Eventually Villa and Zapata would agree to make Villista Francisco Escudero preconstitutional president, but the time for such maneuvers had by then passed, and Escudero was never actually appointed. See Zapata to Villa, Tlaltizapán, May 10, 1915, AGM 28:23:1024 and Villa to Zapata, Aguascalientes, June 12, 1915, AGM 27:1:10. For the quote see Zapata to Villa, Tlaltizapán, April 10, 1915, AGM 28:6:630. See also Palafox to Zapata, Mexico City, April 6, 1915, AZ 7:4:46–48; Villa to Zapata, Monterrey, March 19, 1915, AGM 28:6:629; Villa to Zapata, Irapuato, Guanajuato, April 17, 1915, AGM 28:6:631; Quirk, *Mexican Revolution*, 230; and Amaya, *La Soberana Convención*, 406–7.

12. See Quirk, *Mexican Revolution*, 257–58; Zapata to González Garza, June 3, 1915, AGG 19:285; and a translation of Díaz Soto y Gama's address to the Convention, June 5, 1915, in USDS-IAM 812.00/15482.

13. For the quote see Zapata's response, Tlaltizapán, August 26, 1915, USDS-IAM 812.00/16115. See also Palafox to Zapata, Cuernavaca, August 23, 1915, AGM 28:6:639; *The Mexican Herald*, 30 August 1915; Díaz Soto y Gama to Zapata, Toluca, August 17, 1915, AGM 28:6:638; and Zapata's instructions to Antonio Díaz Soto y Gama and Rodrigo Gómez, Tlaltizapán, November 8, 1915, AGM 29:11:587.

14. For the quote see Zapata's circular, June 20–21, 1915, AZ 21:6:12. See also John Silliman to the Secretary of State, Veracruz, June 27, 1915, USDS-IAM 812.00/15318; Cardoso de Oliveira to the Secretary of State, Mexico City, June 30, 1915, USDS-IAM 812.00/15337; Quirk, *Mexican Revolution*, 273–77; Amaya, *La Soberana Convención*, 285–86; and Paz Solórzano, *Zapata*, 154.

15. John Silliman to the Secretary of State, Mexico City, July 28, 1915, USDS-IAM 812.00/15568; Cardoso to the Secretary of State, Mexico City, July 30, 1915, USDS-IAM 812.00/15681; Juan Barragán Rodríguez, *Historia del ejército y de la revolución constitucionalista*, 2 vols. (Mexico City:Editorial Stylo, 1946), 2:358–61, 389, 391; Zapata to Francisco Lagos Cházaro, San Martín Texmelucan, Puebla, July 22, 1915, in Fabela,

ed., *Documentos históricos*, 21:243–44; Francisco Sánchez Peña to Zapata, July 12, 1915, AZ 9:2:4; Almazán to Zapata, San Buenaventura, Puebla, July 15, 1915, AZ 9:2:20–21; Taracena, *La tragedia*, 58; and Paz Solórzano, *Zapata*, 155–56.

16. For the possibility that Zapata was wounded see Carlota López to Zapata, August 20, 1915, AZ 9:5:66. See also Zapata's circular, Tlaltizapán, August 20, 1915, AZ 9:5:55; Zapata to de la O, Amecameca, September 21, 1915, AO 11:11:12; Baltasar Dromundo, *Emiliano Zapata: biografía* (Mexico City:Imprenta Mundial, 1934), 121; and José Angel Aguilar, *La revolución en el Estado de México*, 2 vols. (Mexico City:Instituto Nacional de Estudios Históricos de la Revolución Mexicana, 1976–1977), 2:235.

17. For the quote see Marcial García to Zapata, Taxco, March 2, 1916, AZ 11:7:12. See also Gómez, *Las comisiones*, 111–12; Pacheco to Zapata, December 15, 1915, AZ 10:11:27; de la O to Zapata, December 6, 1915, AZ 10:10:46; Montaño to Zapata, December 7, 1915, AZ 10:10:56; Gonzalo Méndez to Zapata, San Rafael, November 4, 1915, AZ 10:7:12–13; Brígido Barrera to Zapata, Teloloapam, November 5, 1915, AZ 16:3:8–10; Maurilio Mejía to Zapata, Cuautla, November 16, 1915, AZ 16:4:11; F. Cabrera et al. to Zapata, Cuernavaca, October 26, 1915, AZ 10:6:30; Zapata to Luciano Solís, January 23, 1916, AGM 31:2:49; S.M. Robles to Municipal President of Huautla, October 29, 1916, AO 18:4:22; Zacarias Torres to Zapata, Cuautla, April 10, 1916, AZ 12:1:65; Ysidro Evangelista to Zapata, Jiutepec, April 17, 1916, AZ 12:2:91; and Leandro Arcos to Serafín Robles, Jojutla, April 21, 1916, AZ 12:3:7.

18. For the quote see Francisco Mendoza to Zapata, Pizotlán, Puebla, March 25, 1915, AZ 7:3:32. See also Jesús Alcaide to Zapata, September 17, 1915, AZ 10:2:31. I owe the notion that the payment of wages in 1914–1915 may have corrupted Zapatismo to a personal conversation with Laura Espejel in 1990.

19. For the quote see Eufemio Zapata to González Garza, Cuautla, May 8, 1915, AGG 11:433. See also Zapata to González Garza, Tlaltizapán, June 3, 1915, AGG 12:291; "Un Hijo del Pueblo" to Pacheco, Cuernavaca, December 9, 1915, AZ 10:10:77; and Heliodoro Castillo to Zapata, Iguala, September 9, 1915, AZ 10:1:63–64. Womack, *Zapata*, 240–41 argues that there was an abundance of food, but his evidence is not especially compelling.

20. For the quote see Ayaquica to Zapata, December 26, 1916, AZ 20:6:6. See also Fabela, ed., *Documentos históricos,* 21:254–56, 262–64; AZ 20:3; Alanis Boyzo, *Historia,* 41–46, 151–60; Gustavo Baz to Zapata, Toluca, April 20, 1915, AZ 7:5:89–90; Palafox to Zapata, Cuernavaca, August 23, 1915, AGM 28:6:639; AO 5:12, 6:1 and 6:2; and the interview with Leopoldo Alquicira Fuentes, conducted by Alicia Olivera, Tepepan, D.F., July 21 and 31, 1973, PHO-Z/1/3. The assertion in Warman, *"We Come to Object,"* 120, that there were few occasions in which Zapatistas took food against the will of the villagers is wishful thinking. See, for instance, AGM 31:3 generally, and Gregorio Zúñiga to Timoteo Sánchez, Tlaltizapán, April 22, 1916, AGM 31:3:175. For an understanding of how civilians and warriors grew apart, see Womack, *Zapata,* 225. Unfortunately, he then downplays the implications of this split on the pages that follow. For a discussion of the difficulties of separating social bandits from terrorists, see Joseph, "On the Trail," 17; for insight into the use of terrorism by guerrilla movements, see Timothy Wickham-Crowley, "Terror and Guerrilla Warfare in Latin America, 1956–1970," in *Comparative Studies in Society and History* 32 (1990):201–37.

21. For the first quote see Emigdio Marmolejo to Zapata, Cuautla, February 19, 1915, AZ 5:3:131. For the second see the marginal response in Modesto Rangel to Zapata, July 25, 1914, AO 15:3:7. For the third see the marginal note in the citizens of Tepalcingo to Zapata, October 8, 1915, AZ 19:6:11–12. See also Pacheco to Zapata, February 27, 1915, AZ 5:1:110–11; Zapata's circular to municipal authorities, May 31, 1916, Espejel et al, eds., *Emiliano Zapata,* 346–47; the document of August 29, 1915, in AZ 9:6:51–52; Zapata to Huehuetlán, Puebla, September 8, 1915, AZ 19:5:24–25; Ezequiel Herrera to Zapata, Xicotlan, Puebla, April 28, 1915; Modesto Rangel to Zapata, Cuernavaca, November 20, 1914, AZ 19:7:52; the citizens of Tepalcingo to Zapata, October 6, 1915, AZ 10:4: 36–37; and Manuel Arellano Zavaleta, ed., *Pensamiento social de Emiliano Zapata:documentos inéditos* (Mexico City:Editorial Libros de México, 1969), 17.

22. For the quote see Robles, "El Zapatismo y la industria azucarera." See also Zapata's marginal note of August 25, 1915, in AZ 19:4: 84; the various documents of November 15, 1915, AGM 31:1:206–8; Zapata's circular, Tlaltizapán, February 9, 1916, in Fabela, ed., *Documentos históricos,* 21:259–60; F. Mejía to Zapata, Huamuxtitlán, Gro., July

10, 1915, AZ 9:1:79; Palafox et al. to Mendoza, Cuernavaca, February 12, 1916, AGM 27:2:22; the documents of March 11 and 12, 1916, AZ 16:11: 58–61; Crespina Ramírez to Zapata, Yautepec, January 6, 1916, AZ 16:7: 14; and Mejía to Zapata, Cuautla, January 19, 1916, AZ 11:2:27.

23. Palafox to Zapata, Cuernavaca, October 9, 1915, AZ 10:4:46; Maurilio Mejía to Zapata, Cuautla, October 14, 1915, AZ 10:5:15; Palafox to Gabriel Encinas, Cuernavaca, January 7, 1916, AZ 11:1:30–31; Palafox to Zapata, December 3, 1915, AZ 10:10:15; Palafox to Gabriel Encinas, Cuernavaca, March 4, 1916, AZ 16:11:14; Pacheco to de la O, Huitzilac, December 28, 1915, AO 5:12:11; Zapata to Palafox, March 14, 1916, AGM 31:2:405; Zapata to Jesús Dávila, February 10, 1916, AGM 31:2:169; Zapata to José C. Arvizu, November 13, 1915, AGM 31:1:190; Palafox to Zapata, Cuernavaca, December 8, 1915, AZ 19:8:15; Zapata to Palafox, Tlaltizapán, December 20, 1915, AGM 31:1:416; the commission from Palafox and Zapata for Adalberto Hernández, October 30, 1915, AGM 31: 1:134; Zapata to Antonio Gómez, March 15, 1916, AGM 31:2:411; Zapata to Palafox, March 14, 1916, AGM 31:2:415; Eufemio to Zapata, Cuautla, December 6, 1915, CR 3:869; and Palafox to Zapata, Cuernavaca, November 1, 1915, AGM 29:11:583. Palafox to Zapata, Cuernavaca, February 7, 1916, AGM 27:2:19 is a clear statement that even in Morelos the work of land reform was far from over in early 1916.

24. The citizens of San Francisco Xoxitiopan, Puebla, January 29, 1916 to Zapata, AZ 11:3:30–32; Palafox to Zapata, Cuernavaca, December 10, 1915, AGM 29:15:743; Palafox to Zapata, Cuernavaca, February 7, 1916, AGM 27:2:19; Palafox to Zapata, September 28, 1915, AZ 10:3:33; Teofanes López to Zapata, Los Ranchos, Puebla, February 27, 1916, AZ Box 26; and the citizens of Cuaxitlan to Zapata, March 24, 1916, AZ 11: 9:16.

25. For the quote see Zapata to de la O, Cuernavaca, October 15, 1914, AO 11:10:81. For accounts of Barona's death see Ireneo A. Ayala to de la O, Tlaltenango, November 30, 1915, AO 5:11:5–6; Cristóbal Pérez to de la O, Cuernavaca, November 30, 1915, AO 5:11:3–4; and Valverde, *Apuntes,* 168–69. See also Zapata to de la O, August 31, 1912, AO 11:10: 14; the citizens of San Andrés de la Cal, Morelos to Zapata, October 14, 1913, AO 13:9:33–34; Barona to Zapata, February 12, 1914, AO 14:3:58; Victoria Rosas for Soledad Rojas to Zapata, Ahuatepec, December 4, 1915, AZ 10:10:39; and Zapata to Victoria Rosas, January 18, 1916, AGM

31:2:13. Chevalier, "Un factor," 171, writes that Zapata ordered de la O to appear before him after Barona's death, but that de la O never came.

26. See Quirk, *Mexican Revolution*, 289–92; and the act of the Convention's reconstitution, Cuernavaca, October 19, 1915, AGM 28:5:619. It is worth noting that even when the Convention officially ceased to exist in May 1916, the pretense of national government was maintained in the various departments—of War, of Interior, of Agriculture and Colonization—that continued to elaborate on the body of Zapatista legislation.

27. For the Ley Agraria, October 26, 1915, see Espejel et al., eds., *Emiliano Zapata*, 269–75. Womack, *Zapata*, 405–11 gives an English translation of the document. For other agrarian provisions of the period see the instructions to the agrarian commissions, September 10, 1914 [sic—1915?], in Espejel et al., eds., *Emiliano Zapata*, 240–42; and Millon, *Zapata*, 47. Díaz Soto y Gama, *La revolución agraria*, 212, contends that Zapata himself was strongly against the intervention of governors in the land reform process. On this issue see also Zapata to Rafael Espinosa, November 2, 1915, AA VIII-2, manuscritos, 3:202; and Palafox to the Convention, Cuernavaca, September 24, 1915, in Cháverri Matamoros, "El Archivo de Zapata," *La Prensa*, 28 September 1935.

28. The reform agenda was condensed in the Programa de Reformas Político-Sociales of the Convention, a document that Zapatista and Villista delegates had debated throughout much of 1915. With certain purely Zapatista changes, this program was first issued by the executive council from Cuernavaca on October 26, 1915—see Martínez Escamilla, *Escritos*, 256–62. Later the body of the Zapatista Convention reissued it in a slightly different form from Jojutla on April 18, 1916—see CEHAM, *El ejército*, 171–79. See also the legislation in Espejel et al., eds., *Emiliano Zapata*, 278–32, 352–62; Córdova, *La ideología*, 166; Amaya, *La Soberana Convención*, 441–43; and the "Ley sobre la Sujeción de la Ley al Plebiscito," January 8, 1916, in Reyes H., *Emiliano Zapata*, 135–37. For a list of laws passed by the Zapatista Convention between October 22, 1915, and February 14, 1916, see AGM 12:5:24. Some of the provisions on behalf of municipal democracy mentioned here were not enacted until the fall of 1916, several months after the Convention was terminated.

29. In addition to the sources cited in the footnote above, see the "Ley sobre asistencia pública en favor de los incapacitados para el trabajo," November 17, 1915, ACGS 1:2:25–26; and the "Ley sobre funda-

ción de escuelas normales en los estados," December 8, 1915, AA VIII-2, manuscritos, 3:220.

30. For some earlier attention to labor legislation on Zapata's part see Zapata to Pascual Orozco, May 5, 1912, ARD 8:43:1–4. For Zapata's labor constituency see LaFrance, *The Mexican Revolution*, 123; Raymond Th. J. Buve, "Protesta de obreros y campesinos durante el Porfiriato," *Boletín de Estudios Latinoamericanos y del Caribe* 13(1972):2; and Fortino Ayaquica to Zapata, December 25, 1916, in Cháverri Matamoros, "El archivo de Zapata," *La Prensa*, 21 September 1935.

31. For the quotes see the Programa de Reformas Político-Sociales, CEHAM, *El ejército*, 171–79. For the "Proyecto de la Ley General del Trabajo" (General Labor Law) and the colonization law see Espejel et al., eds., *Emiliano Zapata*, 295–98 and 328–32 respectively. For the argument that the Zapatistas now generated a radical class-based plan for the transformation of society see Warman, "The Political Project," 322–24. For views closer to my own see Córdova, *La ideología*, 25, 171–72; Millon, *Zapata*, 67, 69, 99; and Rueda, "Oposición y subversión," 9.

32. For various rumors, plots, and defections see Paz Solórzano, *Zapata*, 156–58; Montaño to Zapata, December 7, 1915, AZ 10:10:56; Zapata to Dolores Damian, November 6, 1915, AGM 31:1:89; Justo Patricio to Domingo Arenas, Santa Justina, Tlaxcala, November 17, 1915, AZ 10:8:32; Melesio Albarrán to Zapata, December 3, 1915, AZ 10:10:18; Rafael Espinosa to Zapata, December 20, 1915, AZ 10:11:57; Andrés Campos to Santiago Orozco, Otumba and Texcoco, Mexico, February 28, 1915, AZ 6:2:99; S.M. Robles to Zapata, Cuernavaca, March 8, 1916, AZ 16:11:40; Rodolfo Rodríguez to Zapata, Tlaltizapán, March 18, 1916, AZ 20:4:18; Palafox to Zapata, Jojutla, April 20, 1916, AZ 12:2:160; José Rivera to Zapata, Jojutla, April 20, 1916, AZ 16:14:37; Gómez, *Las comisiones agrarias*, 93, 134–44; and Rosoff and Aguilar, *Así firmaron*, 44. For Zapata's circular, Tlaltizapán, December 18, 1915, see AGM 31:414.

33. See Victoriano Bárcenas to Zapata, Huitzuco, November 9, 1914, AGM 30:8:129; the circular of Julio Gómez, Tixtla, May 22, 1914, AO 14:6:12; Julio Gómez to Zapata, Zicapa, September 10, 1915, AZ 10:1:72; Encarnación Díaz to Zapata, Iguala, November 15, 1915, AZ 10:8:22; Díaz Soto y Gama to Montaño, Temilpa, January 5, 1917, AGM 30:13:240; Jacobs, *Ranchero Revolt*, 100–101; [David Eduardo?] to the Secretary of State, Acapulco, November 3, 1915, USDS-IAM 812.00/16834; the in-

terview with Victor Valle Lozano, conducted by Laura Espejel, Mexico City, January 30, 1974, PHO-Z/1/27, pp. 31–32; Brígido Barrera to Díaz Soto y Gama, Tlaltizapán, May 3, 1917, AGM 29:10:551; and Zapata to Jesús Salgado, Tlaltizapán, February 11, 1916, AGM 31:194. For the order against Pedro Saavedra see Zapata to Lorenzo Vázquez, January 31, 1916, AGM 31:2:100. This execution was not, however, carried out, presumably because no one had the power to do it.

34. For the quote see Pacheco to Zapata, Huitzilac, August 5, 1915, AZ 9:4:29–32. For Pacheco and de la O see Julián Gallegos to Zapata, Malinalco, November 19, 1915, AZ 10:8:50–51; Pacheco to de la O, Huitzilac, December 28, 1915, AO 5:12:11; Palafox to Pacheco, December 27, 1915, AO 11:9:57; and Palafox to de la O, December 27, 1915, AO 5:12:10. See also Pacheco to Zapata, Huitzilac, October 20, 1915, AZ 10:5:48; Pacheco to Zapata, Huitzilac, December 15, 1915, AZ 10:11:23–25; and Pacheco to [Everardo?] González, Huitzilac, March 11, 1916, AGM 27:3:34. Clearly the fighting had not, as Womack, *Zapata*, 225, contends, brought the people of Santa María and Huitzilac together.

35. Pacheco to Zapata, March 16, 1913, AO 1:6:34; Pacheco to Zapata, February 8, 1914, AO 14:2:4–5; Zapata to Pacheco, Tlaltizapán, January 8, 1916, AGM 31:458; Palafox to de la O, Cuernavaca, March 6, 1916, AO 6:3:49; and Zapata to Pacheco, November 7, 1915, AGM 31:1:122.

36. Isabel Romero to de la O, Cuernavaca, February 21, 1916, AO 6:2:27; de la O to Zapata, Tlaltenango, February 23, 1916, AO 17:9:10; Pacheco to de la O, February 28, 1916, AO 17:9:9; Pacheco to de la O, Huitzilac, May 2, 1916, AO 17:9:11; Zapata to Pacheco, March 3, 1916, AGM 31:2:266; Zapata to Pacheco, March 4, 1916, AGM 31:2:285; Zapata to de la O, Tlaltizapán, March 4, 1916, AO 11:11:22; Pacheco to de la O, March 17, 1916, AO 6:3:86; [Ignacio Ayala Fuentes?] to de la O, Ocuilan, March 17, 1916, AO 6:3:46; Francisco Lamadrid to de la O, Cuentepec, March 19, 1916, AO 6:3:74; unknown to de la O, Las Trincheras, March 19, 1916, AO 6:3:45; and Paz Solórzano, *Zapata*, 158.

37. For the quote see Zapata to Pacheco, March 23, 1916, AGM 31:2:443. See also Pacheco to Zapata, Cuentepec, March 27, 1916, AGM 27:3:38; de la O to Zapata, March 19, 1916, AO 17:5:15; de la O to various, Las Trincheras, March 19, 1916, AO 6:3:73; Zapata to de la O, March 23, 1916, AGM 31:2:445; Rafael Castillo to de la O, Miacatlán, March 31, 1916, AO 6:3:43; Castillo to Zapata, Miacatlán, March 31, 1916, AZ 11:9:

46; Juan Cruz to de la O, Miacatlán, March 31, 1916, AO 17:9:13; AO 17: 9:4; Zapata to de la O, Yautepec, April 1, 1916, AO 11:11:25; Domitilo Ayala to de la O, Cuernavaca, April 2, 1916, AO 6:4:74; Porfirio Romero to Ireneo Albarrán Ayala, Tlaltizapán, no date, AO 6:4:176–177; S.M. Robles for Zapata to de la O, Tlaltizapán, April 3, 1916, AO 6:4:96; S.M. Robles for Zapata to de la O, Tlaltizapán, April 10, 1916, AO 6:4:148; Paz Solórzano, *Hoguera*, 338–51; and Rafael Alvarado, "Zapata intentó asesinar al General Pablo González," *Todo*, 5 November 1942. Finally, for a good overview of these events, see Manuel González Ramírez, "La muerte del General Zapata y la práctica de las emboscadas," *Estudios de historia moderna y contemporánea de México* 2(1967):211–47. There is no evidence that Zapata ordered Pacheco's death, but this is not the kind of evidence he generally left behind.

38. For the quote see Palafox to Zapata, Mexico City, April 6, 1915, AZ 7:4:46–48. See also de la O to Zapata, April 6, 1916, AO 17:5:16; Zapata to de la O, Tlaltizapán, April 28, 1916, AZ 16:14:72; Paz Solórzano, *Hoguera*, 341; Canada to the Secretary of State, Veracruz, May 26, 1916, USDS-IAM 812.00/18256; Womack, *Zapata*, 249–50, 253; Valverde, *Apuntes*, 177; Sánchez Escobar, *El ocaso*, 145–48; Reyes Avilés, *Cartones*, 20; Zapata to Villa, Tlaltizapán, July 24, 1917, AZ, box 26; and Paz Solórzano, *Zapata*, 159–163. For Zapata's order to return to guerrilla warfare see the interview with Severiano Castillo, conducted by Alicia Olivera and Laura Espejel, Santa Cruz Acalpixca, D.F., July 28, 1973, PHO-Z/1/5, p. 20.

39. For the quote see Díaz Soto y Gama, *La revolución agraria*, 225. See also the manifesto of Pablo González, Cuernavaca, July 19, 1916, AGM 28:4:572; Dromundo, *Emiliano Zapata*, 145–46; Taracena, *La tragedia*, 68; Womack, *Zapata*, 254; Porfirio Palacios, "Zapatismo vs. Gonzalismo," *Todo*, 24 December 1942; and the interview with Ignacio Ceballos, conducted by Claudia Canales, Malinalco, Mexico, September 30, 1978, PHO/1/219. Holt Büttner, "Evolución," 31, shows a drastic decline in Tlaltizapán's population that supports the claims of massacres. See also Marciano Silva, "Bola del Sitio de Tlaltizapán," in Barreto, *Los corridos*, 19–20.

40. See the anonymous account of travel to Guerrero, [May 1916], in AGM 27:5:54; and Luciano Solís to de la O, San Gaspar, October 31, 1916, AO 6:10:18. For the quote see Valverde, *Apuntes*, 186.

41. For the quote see Zapata to Vicente Leyva, August 15, 1916, AGM 28:4:581. See also Zapata's decree, August 10, 1916, AGM 28:4:576; Vázquez to Zapata, March 20, 1916, AZ, box 26; de la O to Zapata, April 6, 1916, AO 17:5:16; Vázquez to Zapata, Jojutla, April 21, 1916, AZ 12:3: 14; [Zapata] to Vázquez, Tlaltizapán, April 27, 1916, AZ 12:3:84; *La Convención*, 17 June 1915; Womack, *Zapata*, 262; and the interview with Lorenzo Vergara, conducted by Laura Espejel, Mexico City, July 15, 1973, PHO-Z/1/1.

42. Zapata's manifesto, February 7, 1916, AGM 27:2:20; Zapata's manifesto, May 29, 1916, AGM 27:5:56; Zapata to Heliodoro Castillo, April 25, [1916], in Fabela, ed., *Documentos históricos*, 21:278–79; and the circular of October 9, 1916, AGM 28:2:500.

43. For the quote see Zapata to Mendoza, November 13, 1916, AGM 28:2:518. See also Womack, *Zapata*, 264; Mendoza to Zapata, Jonacatepec, January 23, 1916, AZ 16:8:40; Mendoza to Zapata, January 4, 1916, AGM 29:5:408; Zapata to Mendoza, February 8, 1916, AGM 31:2:160; Zapata to Mendoza, March 17, 1916, AGM 31:2:429; Zapata to Mendoza, Tlaltizapán, June 1, 1916, ADN XI/III/1–274, cancelados, Mendoza, 814; and Mendoza to Zapata, San Miguel Ixtlilco, November 19, 1916, AGM 28:2:523.

44. Paz Solórzano, *Zapata*, 167–70; the Bulletin of the Revolutionary Information Service, January 11, 1917, AGM 30:13:243; Serafín Robles to de la O, Tlaltizapán, November 18, 1916, AO 6:11:14; AO 6:12:30; and Womack, *Zapata*, 263–72.

45. For the quote see Paz Solórzano, *Zapata*, 170. For Zapatista destruction of haciendas see the interview with José Lora Mirasol, PHO-Z/ 1/14, p. 30; Carlos Cedillo to Zapata, August 8, 1915, AZ 9:4:62; Eufemio Zapata to Zapata, Cuautla, May 29, 1917, AGM 28:1:473; and Magaña to Zapata, July 27, 1917, AZ 14:2:10. See also [Zapata] to Paz Solórzano, Tlaltizapán, August 20, 1917, AGM 29:13:635; and the citizens of Huazulco, Morelos to Zapata, March 28, 1917, AZ 20:9:64.

Chapter 8: The Road to Chinameca

1. For the quote see the anonymous report, "En la Meca del Zapatismo," AGM 28:10:659. See also Palacios, *Emiliano Zapata*, 230–31; and Valverde, *Apuntes*, 185.

2. See Díaz Soto y Gama, "Zapata y el Zapatismo," July 2, 1941,

ASyG, Roll 3, 56–58; the act creating the Asociación Defensora for Tochimilco, Puebla, December 12, 1916, AZ, box 26; acts of the meetings creating the Centro Consultivo, Tlaltizapán, January 3–5, 1917, AZ, box 26; Díaz Soto y Gama's circular, Tlaltizapán, January 10, 1917, AZ, box 26; and Díaz Soto y Gama, "Bases a que se sujetará el Centro Consultivo de Propaganda y Unificación Revolucionarias," Tlaltizapán, November 28, 1916, AGM 28:2:525.

3. For the first quote see the Ley de 5 de Marzo de 1917, in Espejel et al., eds., *Emiliano Zapata*, 378–82. For the second see Zapata's circular, Tlaltizapán, March 18, 1917, AGM 28:1:459. See also Zapata's "Decreto Sobre Bienes Nacionalizados," Tlaltizapán, January 30, 1917, AGM 27:18: 406.

4. For the Ley Relativa a los Representantes de los Pueblos en Materia Agraria, Tlaltizapán, February 3, 1917, see Espejel et al., eds., *Emiliano Zapata*, 369–72. See also Eufemio to Zapata, Cuautla, April 9, 1917, AGM 28:21:936; CEHAM, *El ejército*, 159–61; and "De la Necesidad del Fraccionamiento de los Ejidos," [1917?], in [Genaro Amezcua], *Méjico revolucionario a los pueblos de Europa y América* (Habana:Imprenta Espinosa, Ferré and co., n.d.), 54–59. Finally, for the reformed agrarian law of July 5, 1917 see Martínez Escamilla, *Escritos*, 330–41.

5. See the act of February 6, 1917 in AZ, box 26; the legislation in Espejel et al., eds., *Emiliano Zapata*, 363–65, 383–408; and Gregorio Zúñiga's three circulars of March 1917, AGM 28:10:682, 683, 684–85.

6. For the quote see circular #12, Tlaltizapán, April 17, 1917, in Arellano Zavaleta, ed., *Pensamiento*, 85–86. See also Espiridion Pacheco to Zapata, Tlalnepantla, Morelos, February 7, 1917, AZ 13:4:7; the circulars of January 20, March 29, and April 13, 1917 in Fabela, ed., *Documentos históricos*, 21:285–86, 294–96; AGM 28:10:686–94; the unsigned and undated account of the Zapatista education program, AGM 35:1:36; and List Arzubide, *Zapata*, 47–48.

7. For the quotes see the Consultation Center to Salgado, [April 1917?], AZ 14:16:23. See also Palafox, "Pliego de Instrucciones Generales adjunto a la Organización del Ejército Libertador," Tlaltizapán, January 31, 1917, AA VIII-2, manuscritos, 4:286; the act of Zapata's secret meeting with the Consultation Center, April 4, 1917, AZ, box 26; Zapata's circular, November 29, 1917, AGM 29:1:11; Zapata's decree, April 23, 1917, in Fabela, ed., *Documentos históricos*, 21:297–99; Zapata's decree

of January 31, 1917, AGM 28:10:672; and "Medidas de Orden Económico y Financiero . . . ," January 10, 1917, CEHAM, *El ejército*, 180–81.

8. For the quote see Zapata to Mendoza, Tlaltizapán, September 17, 1917, ADN/III.2/1–3m, pensionados, Mendoza, 88. See also Serafín Robles to de la O, Tlaltizapán, August 2, 1917, AO 7:8:73; and Zapata's circular, Tlaltizapán, November 15, 1917, in Arellano Zavaleta, ed., *Pensamiento*, 81–82. My approach to the number of complaints is admittedly impressionistic, but one might compare those of May 1917 in AZ 13:15 with similar groups of documents for other months.

9. Victoriano Bárcenas to Zapata, Huitzuco, May 1, 1917, AZ 13: 13:2; Ponciano Juárez to Zapata, Ahuatepec, May 2, 1917, AZ 13:13:10; the Boletín Extra of the Zapatista Information Service, May 7, 1917, AGM 29:10:577; Brígido Barrera to Díaz Soto y Gama, Tlaltizapán, May 3, 1917, AGM 29:10:551; and Zapata to Victoriano Bárcenas, Tlaltizapán, May 5, 1917, AGM 29:10:554.

10. For the first quote see Zapata to Gregorio Zúñiga, Tlaltizapán, Morelos, May 15, 1917, AGM 29:10:571. For the second see Salazar Pérez, *Otilio Montaño*, 23. See also pages 29 and 45 of this work; the Boletín Extra of the Information Service, Tlaltizapán, May 16, 1917, AGM 29:10: 574; the Boletín Extra of the Information Service, Tlaltizapán, May 18, 1917, AGM 29:10:575; Zapata to Palafox and Gregorio Zúñiga, May 10, 1917, AGM 29:10:566; and Womack, *Zapata*, 284–86.

11. Somewhat suspiciously, the evidence that convicted Montaño apparently no longer exists. For the notion of a Pacheco/Vázquez/ Montaño conspiracy see the preamble to Zapata's "Ley Penal contra los traidores a la Revolución," Tlaltizapán, September 20, 1917, in José G. Parrés, "Zapata y su concepto sobre la lealtad," in *Ofrenda a la memoria de Emiliano Zapata* (Mexico City:n.p., 1938), 25–32. See also Díaz Soto y Gama, *La revolución agraria*, 202, 228–31; José Valero Silva, "El zapatismo ante la filosofía y ante la historia, por Otilio Montaño," *Estudios de historia moderna y contemporánea de México* 2(1967):185–96; Montaño to Zapata, Tlaltizapán, May 1, 1917, AZ 13:13:3; and Paz Solórzano, *Zapata*, 40, 84, 118. For the popular notion that Montaño was the victim of a conspiracy of the urban intellectuals see Miguel R. Delgado, "El testamento político de Otilio E. Montaño:18 de Mayo de 1917," in AA VIII-2, manuscritos, 4:439; the interview with Serafín Plasencia Gutiérrez, PHO-Z/1/59; Valverde, *Apuntes*, 187–90; and Salazar Pérez, *Otilio*

Montaño. Womack, *Zapata,* 285 writes that Montaño may have identified his rebellion with the reactionary Felix Díaz, who was then leading a new uprising in southern Mexico. The evidence for such a contention, however, is weak. If Montaño now invoked the Reform era, he had invoked it many times before as a loyal Zapatista. In fact, a Zapatista document of 1913 contains part of the phrase that Womack cites as incriminating evidence—see Magaña, *Emiliano Zapata,* 3:153.

12. Eufemio Zapata to Emiliano Zapata, Cuautla, May 19, 1917, AGM 29:10:578; Zapata to Melesio Albarrán, April 2, 1916, AGM 31:2: 492.

13. For the quote see William Gates, "The Four Governments of Mexico:Zapata—Protector of Morelos," *World's Work,* 37(April 1919):657. See also Magaña's "Datos Biográficos," ADN XI/III/1–105, cancelados, Magaña, 351–367; Magaña to Zapata, Cuernavaca, August 20, 1914, AGM 27:17:399; Zapata to Villa, Yautepec, August 25, 1914, AGM 27:17:404; Magaña, *Emiliano Zapata,* 2:211–21; Womack, *Zapata,* 288–291; [Magaña] to Zapata, Mexico City, September 17, 1913, AO 11:9:12–13; Magaña to Zapata, Mexico City, June 7, 1915, AZ 8:4:105; Magaña, "Los errores de Madero," Mexico City, August 6, 1912, AGM 28:12:727; and the interview with Octavio Magaña Cerda, conducted by Daniel Cazes, Mexico City, January 1961, PHO/1/14, pp. 1–8, 33–35. For the notion that Magaña's ascendancy was the outcome of a struggle between a group of intransigents led by Palafox and a group of conciliators led by Magaña and Díaz Soto y Gama see for example Espejel et al., eds., *Emiliano Zapata,* 80 and Adolfo Gilly, *The Mexican Revolution,* trans. Patrick Camiller (London:Verso, 1983), 272–73. Again, I find no evidence of such clearly drawn factions among Zapata's intellectuals.

14. Exactly when Magaña officially became chief of Zapata's headquarters in uncertain. His "Datos Biográficos," ADN XI/III/1–105, cancelados, Magaña, 351–67 claim that this happened only in November of 1917. If this date is correct, he was certainly acting in such a capacity much earlier. See also ADN XI/III/1–309, pensionados, Ayaquica, 94 and, for the suggestion that Magaña went to Tochimilco to avoid intrigue, Womack, *Zapata,* 290.

15. See the agreement of Henry Ben Cline and Juan Espinosa Barreda, San Antonio, Texas, July 15, 1916, in Cháverri Matamoros, "El Archivo," *La Prensa,* 13 September 1935; Zapata to Octavio Paz Solórzano, April

15, 1916, AGM 31:3:112; Zapata to Amezcua, Tlaltizapán, May 1, 1916, AA VIII-2, manuscritos, 3:253; Zapata to Amezcua, April 15, 1915, AA VIII-2, manuscritos, 3:250; [Zapata] to Paz Solórzano, Tlaltizapán, January 23, 1917, AZ 13:3:5; Paz Solórzano to Zapata, San Antonio, Texas, January 15, 1917, AGM 29:13:628; Magaña to Zapata, Tochimilco, April 18, 1917, AZ 13:11:14; Paz Solórzano to Zapata, October 27, 1916, AGM 29: 13:626; Paz Solórzano, *Zapata,* 159; and Vice Consul Scott to the Secretary of State, Havana, September 16, 1916, USDS-IAM 812.00/19306.

16. José Inés Dávila and Guillermo Meixueiro to Manuel Martínez Miranda, December 23, 1914, AGM 28:19:831; Eufemio Zapata to Zapata, Cuautla, November 15, 1914, AGM 30:8:152.

17. For the quote see Isidro Vargas to Zapata, February 2, 1915, AZ 4:3:75. See also Miguel Salas to Zapata, Mariscala, Guerrero, February 22, 1915, AZ 5:2:54–55; Dolores Damian to Zapata, Acatlán, Puebla, February 22, 1915, AZ 6:1:25; and R. Reyes Márquez to Zapata, Puebla, February 26, 1915, AZ 6:2:35. In arguing that Zapata never allowed ex-federals like Aguilar into Morelos or coordinated his forces with theirs, Womack, *Zapata,* 264 underestimates Zapata's ties to them, for neither claim is strictly true. For a close examination of Aguilar's curious career, see Garciadiego, "Higinio Aguilar."

18. See Medina to Madero, Toluca, October 25, 1912, AM 2:28:971; Mendoza to Zapata, December 21, 1913, AO 13:11:43; Mendoza to Zapata, Tepalcingo, April 28, 1915, AZ 7:6:46–47; Rafael Reyes Márquez to Zapata, Acatlán, June 10, 1915, AZ 8:4:129; Aguilar to Zapata, Teotitlán del Camino, Oaxaca, September 30, 1915, AZ 10:3:45; Zapata to Aguilar, Tlaltizapán, October 15, 1915, AGM 31:1:15; Juan F. Zorita to Zapata, San Mateo del Río, Oaxaca, November 23, 1915, AZ 10:9:2–5; and Zapata to Aguilar, April 6, 1916, AGM 31:3:22.

19. For Zapata's Veracruz connections see, for instance, Zapata to Marcial Hernández, November 6, 1915, AGM 31:1:103; Zapata to Lauro F. Cejudo, March 23, 1916, AGM 31:2:448; and Zapata to Aguilar, March 10, 1916, AGM 31:2:328. See also Zapata's circular, Tlaltizapán, June 7, 1916, AGM 28:4:571; Paz Solórzano to Zapata, Chautzingo, Guerrero, August 16, 1916, AA VIII-2, manuscritos, 3:265; and Felix Díaz et al., Manifiesto "A la Nación," Ixtlán de Juárez, Oaxaca, August 1, 1916, AA VIII-2, manuscritos, 3:260.

20. For the quotes see the Manifiesto al Pueblo Mexicano, January

20, 1917, in Espejel et al., eds., *Emiliano Zapata,* 366–68. Womack, *Zapata,* 292 puts the beginning of this diplomatic campaign in August of 1917.

21. For the quote see Zapata to Enrique Bonilla, Tlaltizapán, April 14, 1917, AZ 13:11:4. See also Zapata's amnesty decree, Tlaltizapán, March 1, 1917, AGM 28:1:442; Paz Solórzano, *Zapata,* 170; the exchange of April 11–16, 1917, AZ 13:11:9–10; and Magaña to Zapata, April 17, 1917, AZ 13:12:10–13.

22. For the quote see Zapata to Enrique Bonilla, May 12, 1917, AZ 13:14:3. See also Zapata to Bonilla, June 4, 1917, AZ 13:16:16; Magaña to Zapata, May 3, 1917, AZ 13:13:19; Magaña to Zapata, May 14, 1917, AZ Box 26; Zapata to Magaña, June 9, 1917, AZ 13:16:45; Bonilla to Zapata, June 16, 1917, AZ 13:17:9–11; Magaña to Zapata, Cuautla, June 5, 1917, AZ 13:16:21–22; *El Universal,* 27 May 1917; [Zapata] to Magaña, Tlaltizapán, April 25, 1917, AZ 13:12:9; Magaña to Zapata, April 25, 1917, AGM 28:21:960; Ysauro Villarreal, Tlapanalá, April 20, 1917, AGM 28:21:951; and Magaña to Zapata, May 6, 1917, AZ 13:13:31.

23. See Knight, *Mexican Revolution,* 2:465, 470; and Cumberland, *Mexican Revolution:The Constitutionalist Years,* 327–64.

24. For the quote see the Protesta ante el Pueblo Mexicano, Tlaltizapán, May 1, 1917, Espejel et al., eds., *Emiliano Zapata,* 409–11.

25. For the quote see Eufemio Zapata to Rafael Espinoza, Cuautla, June 16–17, 1915, AZ 8:5:86–87. See also José González Ortega, "Como murió Eufemio Zapata," *Todo,* 13 January 1944; Salvador Romero to Zapata, Cuautla, June 18, 1917, AZ 13:17:16; Cristóbal Domínguez and Francisco Mercado in Rosoff and Aguilar, *Así firmaron,* 75; and Rittenhouse, "Emiliano Zapata," 321. For a different account of Eufemio's death see Salvador Martínez Mancera, "Perdura en el sur la leyenda de que E. Zapata no ha muerto," *El Universal Gráfico,* 13 April 1938.

26. For the first quote see the interview with Consuelo Bravo, PHO/1/211, p. 20; for the second see Everardo González to Zapata, Tlalnepantla, Morelos, June 19, 1917, AGM 29:13:615. See also Alfredo Serratos's article, *La Voz de Juárez,* 22 August 1914, in ARD 11:31:27; Trinidad Paniagua to Zapata, Hacienda de Buenavista, July 19, 1914, AO 14:8:126–127; and Díaz Soto y Gama, *La revolución agraria,* 265.

27. For Caraveo and the Felicistas see Zapata to Caraveo, Tlaltizapán, July 3, 1917, AZ 14:1:16; Magaña to Zapata, May 3, 1917, AZ 13:13:

19; Caraveo to Roberto Cejudo, Tochimilco, March 26, 1917, AGM 28:1: 466; Magaña to Zapata, May 19, 1917, AZ 13:14:30; Zapata to Magaña, May 12, 1917, AZ 13:14:1; Magaña to Zapata, May 6, 1917, AZ 13:13:31; Zapata to Paz Solórzano, Tlaltizapán, August 20, 1917, AGM 29:13:635; Peter V. N. Henderson, *Félix Díaz, the Porfirians, and the Mexican Revolution* (Lincoln:University of Nebraska Press, 1981), 116, 129, 140; and Javier Garciadiego Dantan, "Revolución constitucionalista y contrarrevolución (movimientos reaccionarios en México 1914–1920) (Ph.D. dissertation, Colegio de México, 1981), 6, 345. See also Magaña to Zapata, July 27, 1917, AZ 14:2:10; Magaña to Zapata, May 6, 1917, AZ 13:13:31; Zapata to Octavio Magaña, May 22, 1917, AGM 25:3:120; [Zapata] to Ernesto Zorrilla, Tlaltizapán, June 1, 1917, AZ 13:16:3; [Zapata] to Magdaleno Cedillo, Tlaltizapán, July 1, 1917, AZ 14:1:1; Magaña to Zapata, July 29, 1917, AZ 14:3:16; Zapata to Emilio Vázquez Gómez, Tlaltizapán, August 18, 1917, AGM 29:13:638; Paz Solórzano to Zapata, San Antonio, May 23, 1917, AGM 29:13:632; [Zapata] to Villa, Tlaltizapán, July 24, 1917, AZ box 26; and Zapata to Villa, Tlaltizapán, August 18, 1917, AGM 29:13: 637. Finally, on the gradual abandonment of the Plan of Ayala see Womack, *Zapata*, 296, 301, 304.

28. For the quote see Benigno Zenteno to Zapata, Tochimilco, July 25, 1916, AGM 28:4:575. See also Domingo Arenas, "Manifiesto a los Habitantes del E. de Tlaxcala," Calpulalpam, April 26, 1915, AGM 35:1:31; the act of July 7, 1914, AO 15:2:122; Arenas to Zapata, January 7, 1916, AGM 30:11:219; Zapata to Arenas, January 27, 1916, AGM 31:2:77; J.S. Díaz to Zapata, Tlahuapan, February 26, 1916, AZ 11:6:35; Arenas to Zapata, Santa Rita Tlahuapan, March 10, 1916, AZ 11:7:58; Raymond Th. J. Buve, "'Neither Carranza nor Zapata': The Rise and Fall of a Peasant Movement that Tried to Challenge Both, Tlaxcala, 1910–1919," in Katz, ed., *Riot, Rebellion*, 338–75; Hilario Ramos to Zapata, Juchitepec, August 23, 1916, AGM 28:4:583; Everardo González to Zapata, Juchitepec, August 23, 1916, AGM 28:4:584; Arenas to Zapata, August 31, 1916, AGM 28:4:582; J. Sabino Díaz to Zapata, Tlahuapan, August 26, 1916, AGM 28:4:587; and Arenas to Zapata, Chiautzingo, December 21, 1916, AGM 28:2:530.

29. For the first quote see Arenas to Zapata, Chiautzingo, September 15, 1916, AGM 28:2:491. For the second see Arenas to Zapata, Chiautzingo, December 7, 1916, AGM 28:2:527.

30. For the quote see Zapata's order of December 15, 1916, AGM 28: 2:529. See also Arenas's accord with the Carrancistas, Hacienda de San Matías Atzala, December 1, 1916, AGM Box 34; Zapata to Arenas, April 13, 1917, AGM 35:1:49; [Zapata] to Arenas, Tlaltizapán, April 10, 1917, AZ 13:10:12; Magaña to Zapata, May 30, 1917, AZ 13:15:64; Zapata to Magaña, August 1, 1917, AZ 14:4:3; Magaña to Zapata, July 30, 1917, AZ 14:3:18; Zapata to Villa, Tlaltizapán, July 24, 1917, AZ Box 26; and Magaña to Zapata, August 5, 1917, AZ 14:4:12.

31. For the quote see Ayaquica et al. to Zapata, Tochimilco, August 8, 1917, AZ 14:4:25–26. For Zapatista accounts of Arenas's death see *El Clarín* (Cuernavaca), 22 October 1917, AO 19:10:35–36; Ayaquica to de la O, Tochimilco, September 1, 1917, AO 7:9:76; and Fortino Ayaquica, "Como perdió la vida el General Domingo Arenas," *El Hombre Libre*, 4 August through 15 November 1937. For accounts that blame Magaña and Ayaquica see the interview with Pedro L. Romero Cortés, conducted by María Alba Pastor, San Martín Texmelucan, Puebla, June 8, 1974, PHO/1/139, pp. 34–39; Porfirio del Castillo, *Puebla y Tlaxcala en los días de la revolución* (Mexico City:n.p., 1953), 157–60; and *El Hombre Libre*, 26 February 1937. Many Tlaxcalan veterans of the conflict assume that Zapata ordered Arenas killed. Womack, *Zapata*, 293 depends on Ayaquica's 1937 account of Arenas's death, which is highly suspect in that it was presented in defense of Magaña, who was then preparing to run for the presidency.

32. For the quotes see the Decreto Contra los Traidores de la Revolución, September 20, 1917, in Parrés, "Zapata y su concepto," 25–32.

33. For the first quote see Magaña to Zapata, Tochimilco, July 19, 1917, AZ box 26. For the second see Ayaquica et al. to Zapata, Tochimilco, August 8, 1917, AZ 14:4:25–26. See also Mejía to Zapata, "El Platanar," Puebla, July 10, 1917, AZ 14:1:27; the officials of Hueyapan, Puebla to Zapata, July 6, 1917, AZ 14:1:22; Zapata to Magaña, Tlaltizapán, November 3, 1917, in Martínez Escamilla, *Escritos*, 347–48; AO 8:2: 97; Zapata to de la O, Tlaltizapán, November 12, 1917, AO 11:11:51; Zapata to Magaña, November 3, 1917, *Cartas*, 78–80; Zapata to de la O, Tlaltizapán, November 20, 1917, AO 11:11:54; Zapata's manifesto, Tlaltizapán, September 1, 1917, AGM 28:10:707; and Jiménez, *Life and Death*, 143, 159. For the many abuses and complaints see for instance AO 7:9 through 8:1.

34. For the quote see Zapata's manifesto "Al Pueblo," Tlaltizapán, December 27, 1917, Martínez Escamilla, *Escritos,* 365–69. For the second manifesto see the same work, 360–64. Zapata to Magaña, April 15, 1918, AGM 29:3:217 and Magaña to Zapata, May 4, 1918, AGM 27:15:283 concern the use of Zapata's staff. See also Zapata to J. Inés Chávez García, Tlaltizapán, December 25, 1917, AGM 29:1:27; Zapata to Amado Azuara, Tlaltizapán, December 26, 1917, AGM 29:1:29; Zapata to Magaña, December 20, 1917, AGM 29:1:18; Zapata to Hesiquio Barbosa, Tlaltizapán, December 24, 1917, AGM 29:1:21; Magaña to Magdaleno Cedillo, Tlaltizapán, December 25, 1917, AGM 29:1:26; [Magaña] to Saturnino Cedillo, Tlaltizapán, December 25, 1917, AGM 29:1:23; [Zapata?] to Samuel Espinosa de los Monteros, Tlaltizapán, [December 24, 1917?], AGM 29:1:22; and [Zapata] to Manuel N. Robles, Tlaltizapán, December 10, 1917, AGM 29:1:16.

35. For the quote see Magaña to Zapata, February 13, 1918, AGM 29:2:68. See also Magaña to Francisco Coss, Tlaltizapán, January 14, 1918, AGM 29:8:472; Zapata to Magaña, January 26, 1918, AGM 29:8:484; Magaña to Zapata, January 20, 1918, AGM 29:8:476; AGM 29:8:487–88; Zapata to Luis Gutiérrez, January 28, 1918, AGM 29:8:493; Zapata to Francisco Coss, January 28, 1918, AGM 29:8:495; Zapata to Albino Guerrero, Tlaltizapán, February 10, 1918, AGM 29:2:55; [Magaña] to Zapata, Tochimilco, February 12, 1918, AGM 29:2:66; Magaña to Zapata, February 3, 1918, AGM 29:2:38; Magaña to Zapata, February 21, 1918, AGM 29:2:81; [Magaña?] to Eutimio Figueroa, February 28, 1918, AGM 29:2:104; Magaña to Zapata, January 19, 1918, AGM 29:8:475; Womack, *Zapata,* 297–98; and "Un Brindis de Alvaro Obregón," *El Sur,* 1 July 1917, in [Amezcua], *Méjico revolucionario,* 88–89. For Obregón's political maneuvers at this time see Hall, *Alvaro Obregón,* 184–202.

36. For the quote see Magaña to Zapata, Tochimilco, February 2, 1918, AGM 29:2:36. See also Palafox to Magaña, Tlaltizapán, February 3, 1918, AGM 29:2:37; Gates, "The Four Governments"; Paz Solórzano, *Zapata,* 172; Valverde, *Apuntes,* 192; and Womack, *Zapata,* 298–300.

37. Zapata's amnesty decree, Tlaltizapán, March 24, 1918, Espejel et al., eds., *Emiliano Zapata,* 429–31.

38. See the manifesto "A los Revolucionarios de la República," Tlaltizapán, March 15, 1918, in Espejel et al., eds., *Emiliano Zapata,* 425–28; and, for the quote, the manifesto "A los Obreros de la República ¡Salud!,"

Tlaltizapán, March 15, 1918, in Martínez Escamilla, *Escritos,* 393–95. Finally, see Zapata to Magaña, Tlaltizapán, December 8, 1918, AGM 30:19: 317.

39. For the first quote see Zapata to Magaña, April 20, 1918, AGM 29:3:225. For the second see Zapata to Magaña, [April], 1918, AGM 29:3: 209. See also Magaña to Zapata, April 24, 1918, AGM 29:3:233; Boletín #1 of the Information Service, April 28, 1918, AGM 29:3:243; Zapata's form letter, March 15, 1918, AGM 29:4:323; Magaña to Zapata, Tochimilzolco, April 11, 1918, AGM 29:3:208; León-Portilla, *Los manifiestos;* Zapata to Magaña, May 13, 1918, AGM 27:15:307; and Magaña to Zapata, May 16, 1918, AGM 27:15:314.

40. Magaña to Zapata, May 19, 1918, AGM 27:15:331.

41. For the quote see Zapata to Magaña, April 20, 1918, AGM 29:3: 224. See also Zapata to Mendoza, March 9, 1918, ADN X/III.2/1–3m, pensionados, Mendoza, 104; [Magaña] to Zapata, Tochimilzolco, April 11, 1918, AGM 29:3:210; and Magaña to Zapata, January 23, 1918, AGM 29: 8:481.

42. For the quote see Magaña to Zapata, May 2, 1918, AGM 27:15: 270; Toribio Cortés to Magaña, Tochimilco, May 1, 1918, AGM 27:15: 263; Zapata's circular, Tlaltizapán, July 10, 1918, AZ 20:13:9; AZ 13:13: 4–9; Román A. Espinosa, Tlaltizapán, May 16, 1917, AZ box 26; Magaña to Zapata, August 9, 1917, AZ 14:4:30; Palafox to de la O, Tlaltizapán, August 24, 1917, AO 7:8:22; José Alfaro to the Municipal President of Tochimilco, April 1, 1918, AGM 29:3:213; Juan Cruz to de la O, Cuernavaca, October 25, 1917, AO 8:1:107; Francisco Artigas to Everardo González, Mexico City, August 2, 1917, Fabela, ed., *Documentos históricos,* 21:299–300; Espejel, "El movimiento campesino," 36; Federico Córdova to Magaña, Huastepec, February 21, 1918, AGM 29:2:82; Zapata to Caraveo, February 25, 1918, AGM 29:2:96; and Magaña to Zapata, Tochimilzolco, May 23, 1918, AGM 27:15:337. Magaña would eventually accept the argument that pacíficos could not be trusted to bear arms, a sign that the base for Zapata's guerrilla army had been completely destroyed—see Magaña to Mendoza, July 30, 1919, AGM 30:39:625.

43. For the first quote see Zapata to Magaña, Tlaltizapán, August 6, 1918, AGM 30:20:347. For the other two see Zapata to Magaña, Tlaltizapán, August 4, 1918, AGM 30:20:345. See also Zapata to Francisco Vázquez Gómez, Tlaltizapán, August 12, 1918, AGM 30:20:364; and

Zapata to Francisco Vázquez Gómez, Tlaltizapán, August 30, 1918, AGM 27:9:155.

44. For the quote see Magaña to Zapata, June 30, 1918, AGM 30:17: 290. See also Zapata to Magaña, May 16, 1918, AGM 27:15:315; Magaña to Zapata, April 29, 1918, AGM 29:3:247; Zapata to Magaña, Villa de Ayala, April 29, 1918, AGM 29:3:249; the article "Completa Derrota de los Carrancistas," in the Boletín of May 16, 1918, AGM 27:15:318; Magaña to Zapata, May 17, 1918, AGM 27:15:317; Boletín #3, May 18, 1918, AGM 27:15:326; Zapata to Magaña, May 23, 1918, AGM 27:15:338; Zapata to Miguel Díaz Lombardo, Tlaltizapán, May 28, 1918, AGM 27:15:349; and Zapata's "Manifiesto al Pueblo Mexicano," Tlaltizapán, April 25, 1918, in Martínez Escamilla, *Escritos,* 405–9. Finally, for more on Peláez and on Lecona's expedition see Zapata to Magaña, Tlaltizapán, March 19, 1918, in Zapata, *Cartas,* 87–89; Magaña to Zapata, Tochimilzolco, April 9, 1918, AGM 29:3:206; Magaña to Zapata, Tochimilzolco, April 29, 1918, AGM Box 34; Peláez to Zapata, Tierra Amarilla, Veracruz, May 21, 1918, AGM 27:15:334; and Knight, *Mexican Revolution,* 2:201–2.

45. Magaña to Zapata, September 4, 1918, AGM 30:26:465; Lecona to Zapata, Coxcatlán, August 12, 1918, AGM 30:20:353; and Zapata to Lecona, September 1, 1918, AGM 30:26:456.

46. [Zapata] to Angeles, Tlaltizapán, August 11, 1918, AGM 27:9: 151; Zapata to Miguel Díaz Lombardo, August 11, 1918, AGM 27:9:152; Zapata to Mendoza, Tlaltizapán, September 7, 1918, ADN XI/III/1–274, cancelados, Mendoza, 865; and Magaña to Zapata, Alpanocan, September 4, 1918, AGM 30:26:464. For contacts with Obregón and the PLC see Zapata to Obregón, Tlaltizapán, August 17, 1918, AGM 30:20:354; Magaña to Zapata, August 22, 1918, AGM 30:20:355; Zapata to Obregón, August 24, 1918, AGM 30:20:359; Palacios, *Emiliano Zapata,* 253–54; and Octavio Magaña Cerda, *Yo acuso a los responsables:el pueblo que nos juzgue* (Mexico City:B. Costa-Amic, 1961), 26–34.

47. For the quote see Zapata to Magaña, San Rafael, December 13, 1918, AGM 30:19:327. See also Valverde, *Apuntes,* 196–97; Dromundo, *Emiliano Zapata,* 172; Womack, *Zapata,* 312–13; and *Excélsior,* 13 and 28 November 1918.

48. Eduardo Reyes to Magaña, Atlixco, January 10, 1919, AGM 30: 24:423; Magaña to Eduardo Reyes, January 14, 1919, AGM 30:24:425; Zapata to Amezcua, Tlaltizapán, December 25, 1918, AA VIII-2,

manuscritos, 4:346; Magaña to Cesáreo Castro, December 3, 1918, AGM
30:19:313; and Eduardo Reyes to Magaña, Atlixco, December 23, 1918,
AGM 30:19:335.

49. For the quote see Palafox to Luis Cabrera, San Pablo Hidalgo, August 14, 1917, in Fabela, ed., *Documentos históricos*, 21:301–2. For a letter to Carranza of the same date see the same volume, 300–301. See also
Magaña's circular, Tochimilco, Puebla, June 30, 1919, AGM 30:34:555;
Magaña to Zapata, Hueyapan, November 3, 1918, AGM 30:21:375 bis;
Knight, *Mexican Revolution*, 2:369; Palafox to Amezcua, Tlaltizapán,
February 14, 1918, AGM 12:5:33; Zapata to Magaña, May 26, 1918, AGM
27:15:346; Magaña to Zapata, August 7, 1917, AZ 14:4:21; Zapata to Carlos Ariza, December 27, 1917, AGM 29:1:32; the interview with Gregoria
Zúñiga, PHO- Z/1/82, p. 35; Gates, "The Four Governments," 658–59;
and Taracena, *La tragedia*, 81. For some of the hatred Palafox inspired
during his Zapatista career see Emigdio Marmolejo to Palafox, Villa de
Ayala, December 3, 1918, AGM 30:19:310 and the interview with Manuel Sosa Pavón, PHO/1/48. Womack, *Zapata*, 306 claims that Palafox
was gay—or at least bisexual—and that this had something to do with his
disgrace. On that possibility see Valverde, *Apuntes*, 170 and Maurilio
Mejía to Palafox, San Rafael, November 27, 1918, AGM 30:21:387. If
Palafox was gay, it was only a minor factor in his falling out with Zapata.

50. For the quotes see Higinio Aguilar, "Rectificaciones Históricas
#1," January 5, 1919, AA VIII-2, impresos, 1:24. This document cannot, of
course, be taken purely as the confessions of Emiliano Zapata, for a secretary would have given it final form. Still it seems fair to conclude that
the end product had Zapata's approval, because no one else could have
accepted the responsibility for the admissions made in it. For Palafox's
new intrigues see his manifesto in *Excélsior*, 24 January 1919.

51. For the quote see Zapata's "Manifiesto al Pueblo y a los Revolucionarios Mexicanos," February 10, 1919, Espejel et al., eds., *Emiliano
Zapata*, 438–45. See also Emiliano Zapata to Francisco Vázquez Gómez,
Tlaltizapán, February 5, 1919, AGM 30:29:498; Zapata to Magaña, February 4, 1919, AGM 30:29:497; Zapata to Francisco Vázquez Gómez, Tlaltizapán, February 5, 1919, AGM 30:29:499; Zapata to Magaña et al., San
Pablo, Morelos, February 13, 1919, AGM 30:29:507; and Magaña to Zapata, Tochimilzolco, January 31, 1919, AGM 30:24:436.

52. For the quote see AO 12:1:64, March 10, 1919. See also Díaz Soto

y Gama, *La revolución agraria*, 227–28, 231; Díaz Soto y Gama, "Periodo crítico para el zapatismo," May 11, 1955, ASyG, roll 4; Magaña to Zapata, Hueyapan, November 7, 1918, AGM 30:21:377; Magaña to Zapata, Tochimilzolco, February 7, 1919, AGM 30:29:500; Zapata to Magaña et al., San Pablo, Morelos, February 13, 1919, AGM 30:29:506; Zapata to Magaña, March 3, 1919, AGM 30:32:532; Nicolás Rayón to de la O, February 5, 1919, AO 9:4:6; Gregorio Jiménez to de la O, February 6, 1919, AO 9:4:10; Lieuwen, *Mexican Militarism*, 35; and Holt Büttner, "Evolución," 29. Lomnitz, *Evolución*, 97–98 questions the accuracy of the official population count.

53. For the first quote see Zapata to William Gates, March 24, 1919, AGM 30:32:538. For the others see Zapata's "Carta Abierta al Señor Carranza," March 17, 1919, in Palacios, *Emiliano Zapata*, 258–66. See also Gates, "The Four Governments"; Reyes Avilés, *Cartones*, 46; Caraveo to Magaña, San Agustín Atzompa, September 20, 1918, AGM 29:12:601; Zapata to Samuel Espinosa de los Monteros, October 12, 1918, Tlaltizapán, AGM 30:25:447; Zapata to Peláez, January 6, 1919, AGM 30:24:420; and Peláez to Magaña, July 22, 1919, AGM 30:39:623.

54. For the letters containing the quotes see Sánchez Escobar, *El ocaso*, 30–32. On Carranza's role see the interview with Manuel Sosa Pavón, PHO/1/48, pp. 208–9 and "Carranza autorizó la muerte de Zapata, dice P. González," *Novedades*, 28 October 1942.

55. See Sánchez Escobar, *El ocaso*, 32–35; the interview with Gregoria Zúñiga, PHO-Z/1/82, pp. 12–13, 16; and Paz Solórzano, *Zapata*, 176. For one account of Bárcenas's defection see Carlos Reyes Avilés, "Un historiador ingenuo," *El Nacional*, 28 August 1934. Womack, *Zapata*, 323–24 suggests that Zapata wanted Bárcenas because he was the only Zapatista traitor who subsequently fought against him for Carranza. This, however, is not true—Cirilo Arenas and Sidronio Camacho, among others, had also done so.

56. For the quote see Adrián Castrejón Castrejón, "Los últimos instantes de la vida de Emiliano Zapata," *El Campesino*, 1 May 1950. This is one of the most convincing accounts of these events. For other versions see Salvador Reyes Avilés's report to Magaña, April 10, 1919, Fabela, ed., *Documentos históricos*, 21:313–16; José de la Luz Valdés, "El Drama de Chinameca," in Sociedad Chihuahuense de Estudios Históricos, *V Congreso Nacional de Historia de la Revolución Mexicana*, No-

viembre 19–20 y 21 de 1974, Chihuahua, Chihuahua, 182–202; Mario
Huacuja, "Que Zapata tenía fe ciega en la lealtad de Guajardo,"
Novedades, 12 May 1951; José Valero Silva, "Relación de los hechos que
dieron por resultado la muerte de Emiliano Zapata, jefe de la rebelión del
sur," *Estudios de Historia Moderna y Contemporánea de México* 2
(1967):197–203; Cristóbal Domínguez in Rosoff and Aguilar, *Así firmaron,* 85–93; and the interview with Jesús Chávez, PHO/1/99, pp. 28 ff.
Most Carrancista versions claim that Zapata killed Bárcenas's men, as
does the manifesto of Francisco Mendoza, July 15, 1919, in Cháverri,
Matamoros, "El Archivo," *La Prensa,* 1 October 1935. The more widely
accepted story, though, is that he did not. See also F.M. Palacios to Zapata, San Juan Chinameca, April 7, 1919, AGM 30:36:578 and F.M. Palacios
to Zapata, Chinameca, April 3, 1919, AGM 30:36:576.

57. For the quote see Reyes Avilés to Magaña, April 10, 1919, Fabela,
ed., *Documentos históricos,* 21:313–16. On the children see de la O's certification that they were Zapata's, July 22, 1921, AZ 20:26:1–6; and Gill,
"Zapata," 308.

Epilogue and Conclusion

1. See González to Carranza, Cuautla, April 10, 1919, in CEHAM, *El
ejército,* 218; and *El Demócrata,* 11 and 12 April 1919.

2. For the first quote see Rosoff and Aguilar, *Así firmaron,* 91; for
the second see "Al Pueblo Mexicano," April 15, 1919, in Espejel et al.,
eds., *Emiliano Zapata,* 447–51. See also the interview with Jesús Vidales
Marroquín, conducted by Alicia Olivera, Mexico City, November 3, 1972
and January 17, 1973, PHO/1/27, p. 33.

3. For the quotations see Don Leonor of Tepalcingo, cited in Elena
Azaola Garrido, "Tepalcingo:la dependencia política de un municipio de
Morelos," in *Los campesinos de la tierra de Zapata :política y conflicto,*
Elena Azaola Garrido and Esteban Krotz (Mexico City:Instituto Nacional
de Antropología e Historia, 1976), 42.

4. Magaña to de la O, August 16, 1919, AO 9:10:12; Magaña to de la
O, Tochimilco, June 26, 1919, AO 9:8:10; AO 9:13:1; the act of the junta
electing Magaña, Huautla, September 4, 1919, AGM 30:38:598; the manifesto "A los Revolucionarios del Sur," September 5, 1919, Espejel et al.,
eds., *Emiliano Zapata,* 454–55; Everardo González to de la O, Milpa Alta,
May 5, 1919, AO 9:7:3; the Plan of Milpa Alta, González Ramírez, ed.,

Planes, 90–92; Palafox to Arturo Deloy, August 10, 1919, in Cháverri Matamoros, "Archivo de Zapata," *La Prensa,* 7 October 1935; and Palafox to Crispín Galeana, Sierra de Ixtlán, Oaxaca, April 16, 1919, AGM 35:3. For Mendoza's bid to lead the movement see Womack, *Zapata,* 335–45. Womack argues that Mendoza's leadership would have represented a move back to the intransigence of 1914–1915, but I doubt that anyone still considered that a good idea.

5. For the quote see de la O to Gabriel Mariaca, December 1919, AO 9:13:17. See also Magaña's circular, November 30, 1919, ADN XI/III/1–105, cancelados, Magaña, 65; de la O to Magaña, November 11, 1919, AGM 30:4:46; and Womack, *Zapata,* 346–52. De la O's posture sheds considerable doubt on Womack's belief that Magaña spoke for the Zapatistas at this time.

6. For the quote see de la O to Magaña, March 2, 1920, AO 9:15:62. See also de la O to Villa and Peláez, Tepeite, February 24, 1920, AO 9:15:23; Magaña to de la O, undated fragment, AO 10:3:43; Magaña to de la O, Sierra de Puebla, January 31, 1920, AO 9:15:8; and de la O's "Manifiesto a la Nación Mexicana," December 1919, Espejel et al., eds., *Emiliano Zapata,* 458–59.

7. Hall, *Alvaro Obregón,* 203–44.

8. For an excellent summary of the triumphant ideology see Córdova, *La ideología,* 35–37. See also Gill, "Zapata," 305; Warman, *"We Come to Object,"* 135 ff.; Rueda, "Los dos Emilianos," 47; and Womack, *Zapata,* 358–64, 370.

9. For a somewhat fuller examination of the question of inevitability in this case, see Samuel Brunk, "Zapata and the City Boys:In Search of a Piece of the Revolution," *Hispanic American Historical Review* 73 (1993):64–65.

10. This is, of course, counter-factual history. For a lucid discussion of the uses and benefits of such an argument see Knight, *Mexican Revolution,* 1:449.

11. See, for instance, Frank Tannenbaum, *Peace by Revolution:An Interpretation of Mexico* (New York:Columbia University Press, 1933).

12. Womack's *Zapata* is in many respects an early example of revisionism. My point here is simply that neither he nor anyone else submitted Zapatismo to the same skeptical analysis that other regional rebellions have endured.

13. For the historiography of the revolution see Alan Knight, "Interpretaciones recientes de la revolución mexicana," in *Memorias del Simposio de Historiografía Mexicanista* (Mexico City:Gobierno del Estado de Morelos, 1990), 193–221; W. Dirk Raat, *The Mexican Revolution:An Annotated Guide to Recent Scholarship* (Boston:G.K. Hall, 1982), xxiii–xxxviii; David C. Bailey, "Revisionism and the Recent Historiography of the Mexican Revolution," *Hispanic American Historical Review* 58 (1978):62–79; and Barry Carr, "Recent Regional Studies of the Mexican Revolution," *Latin American Research Review* 15 (1980):3–14. For the argument that there was no revolution at all see Ramón Eduardo Ruíz, *The Great Rebellion:Mexico 1905–1924* (N.Y.:W.W. Norton, 1980).

14. Zapatismo was not, of course, Constitutionalism. But they were certainly not polar opposites either, and such an opposition is even less sustainable between the Zapatistas and other regional movements. For two of the many authors that overstate differences between the movements they study and Zapatismo, see Jacobs, *Ranchero Revolt,* and Héctor Aguilar Camín, "The Relevant Tradition:Sonoran Leaders in the Revolution," in *Caudillo and Peasant in the Mexican Revolution,* ed. David Brading (Cambridge:Cambridge University Press, 1980), 92–123.

15. One work that promises to address these issues is Gilbert M. Joseph and Daniel Nugent, eds., *Everyday Forms of State Formation:Revolution and the Negotiation of Rule in Modern Mexico* (Durham, N.C.: Duke University Press, 1994). Unfortunately this book is not yet in print as I finish mine.

16. Tim Golden, "Rebels Determined 'to Build Socialism' in Mexico, *New York Times,* 4 January 1994.

Sources Cited

Archival Collections

Albuquerque, New Mexico.
University of New Mexico.
Zimmerman Library.
Mexican Mission Papers of John
Lind, microfilm copy of the
original at the Minnesota His-
torical Society (AJL).
U.S. Department of State,
Records Relating to the Internal
Affairs of Mexico, 1910–1929,
microfilm (USDS-
IAM).
Mexico City. Archivo Histórico de
la Defensa Nacional (ADN).
Mexico City. Archivo General de
la Nación.
Archivo de Alfredo Robles
Domínguez (ARD).
Archivo de Antonio Díaz Soto y
Gama (ASyG)
Archivo de Emiliano Zapata
(AZ).

Archivo de Francisco Madero
(AM).
Archivo de Genovevo de la O
(AO).
Archivo de la Convención Rev-
olucionaria (ACR)
Archivo del Cuartel General del
Sur (ACGS).
Archivo Fotográfico Díaz, Del-
gado y García.
Archivo Fotográfico Hermanos
Mayo.
Colección Revolución (CR).
Mexico City. Centro de Estudios
de Historia de México,
Condumex.
Archivo de Genaro Amezcua
(AA)
Mexico City. Centro de Estudios
Sobre la Universidad (Universi-
dad Nacional Autónoma de
México)

Archivo de Gildardo Magaña
(AGM).
Mexico City. Colegio de
México.
Luis Muro notes on the
Archivo Histórico de la

Defensa Nacional
(ADN).
Mexico City. Universidad
Panamericana.
Archivo de Roque
González Garza (AGG).

Interviews

Programa de Historia Oral. Insti-
tuto Nacional de Antropología e
Historia and Instituto de Investi-
gaciones Dr. José María Luis
Mora, Mexico City.
Aldana, Carmen. PHO-Z/1/32.
Alfaro, Leonor. PHO/1/100.
Alquicira Fuentes, Leopoldo. PHO-
Z/1/3.
Avila, Andrés. PHO/1/53.
Baz Prada, Gustavo. PHO/4/6.
Bravo, Consuelo. PHO/1/211.
Chávez, Jesús. PHO/1/99.
Chávez Reyes, Nicolás. PHO-Z/1/
17.
Caballero, Ramón. PHO/1/51.
Capistrán, Angel. PHO/1/199.
Castillo, Severiano. PHO-Z/1/5.
Ceballos, Ignacio. PHO/1/219.
Díaz Lozano, Mateo. PHO-Z/
CRMG/1/41.
Espejo, Miguel. PHO-Z/CRMG/
1/65.
Estrada Cajigal, Vicente. PHO/
4/12.

Hidalgo Salazar, Cayetano. PHO/
1/50.
Lora Mirasol, José. PHO-Z/1/14.
Magaña Cerda, Octavio. PHO/1/14.
Padilla Tlapaya, J. Tereso de Jesús.
PHO/1/184.
Peralta, Clemente. PHO-Z/1/20.
Plasencia Gutiérrez, Serafín. PHO-
Z/1/59.
Romero Acevedo, Wenceslao.
PHO-Z/1/23.
Romero Cortés, Pedro L. PHO/1/
39.
Sosa Pavón, Manuel. PHO/1/48.
Tejeda Enríquez, Modesto. PHO/1/
218.
Valle Lozano, Victor. PHO-Z/1/27.
Vázquez Jiménez, Félix. PHO-Z/
1/9.
Vergara, Lorenzo. PHO-Z/1/1.
Vidales Marroquín, Jesús. PHO/
1/27.
Yedra Islas, Domingo. PHO-Z/1/15.
Zepeda, Enrique M. PHO/1/47.
Zúñiga, Gregoria. PHO-Z/1/82.

Newspapers

Diario del Hogar. Mexico City.
1909, 1911–1912.

El Campesino. Mexico City.
1956.

El Demócrata. Mexico City. 1914, 1919.

El Hombre Libre. Mexico City. 1937.

El Imparcial. Mexico City. 1911–1912.

El Monitor. Mexico City. 1915.

El País. Mexico City. 1911–1913.

El Universal. Mexico City. 1917.

Excélsior. Mexico City. 1918–1919, 1964.

La Convención. Mexico City. 1915.

The Mexican Herald. Mexico City. 1911, 1914–1915.

Nueva Era. Mexico City. 1912.

La Prensa. Mexico City. 1964.

La Tribuna. Mexico City. 1913.

México Nuevo. Mexico City. 1909.

Semanario Oficial del Gobierno del Estado de Morelos. Cuernavaca. 1913.

Books and Pamphlets

Aguilar, Anita and Rosoff, Rosalind. *Emiliano Zapata:hombre de tierra.* Mexico City:Editorial Alhambra Mexicana, 1986.

Aguilar, José Angel. *La revolución en el Estado de México.* 2 vols. Mexico City:Instituto Nacional de Estudios Históricos de la Revolución Mexicana, 1976–1977.

Alanis Boyzo, Rodolfo. *Historia de la revolución en el estado de México:los zapatistas en el poder.* Toluca:Gobierno del Estado de México, 1987.

Alonso, Jorge; Corcuera, Alfonso; and Melville, Roberto. *Los campesinos de la tierra de Zapata, II:subsistencia y explotación.* Mexico City:Instituto Nacional de Antropología e Historia, 1974.

Amaya C., Luis Fernando. *La Soberana Convención Revolucionaria, 1914–1916.* Mexico City: Editorial F. Trillas, 1966.

[Amezcua, Genaro]. *Méjico revolucionario a los pueblos de Europa y América.* Habana:Imprenta Espinosa, Ferré and co., n.d.

Angeles, Felipe. *Genovevo de la O.* Mexico City:Secretaría de Educación Pública, n.d.

Ankerson, Dudley. *Agrarian Warlord:Saturnino Cedillo and the Mexican Revolution in San Luis Potosí.* DeKalb:University of Northern Illinois Press, 1984.

Arellano Zavaleta, Manuel, ed. *Pensamiento social de Emiliano Zapata:documentos inéditos.* Mexico City:Editorial Libros de México, 1969.

Arenas Guzmán, Diego. *Del Maderismo a los Tratados de Teoloyucán.* Mexico City:Instituto Nacional de Estudios Históricos de la Revolución Mexicana, 1955.

Aron, Raymond. *Main Currents in Sociological Thought.* 2 vols.

Translated by Richard Howard and Helen Weaver. New York: Basic Books, 1967.

Ayala Anguiano, Armando. *Zapata y las grandes mentiras de la revolución mexicana.* Mexico City: Editorial Vid, 1985.

Azaola Garrido, Elena, and Krotz, Esteban. *Los campesinos de la tierra de Zapata, III:política y conflicto.* Mexico City:Instituto Nacional de Antropología e Historia, 1976.

Barragán Rodríguez, Juan. *Historia del ejército y de la revolución constitucionalista.* 2 vols. Mexico City:Editorial Stylo, 1946.

Barrera Fuentes, Florencio, ed. *Crónicas y debates de las sesiones de la Soberana Convención Revolucionaria.* 3 vols. Mexico City:Instituto Nacional de Estudios Históricos de la Revolución Mexicana, 1965.

Barreto Mark, Carlos, ed. *Los corridos de Marciano Silva.* Cuernavaca:Gobierno del Estado de Morelos, 1983.

Barrett, Ward. *The Sugar Hacienda of the Marqueses del Valle.* Minneapolis:University of Minnesota Press, 1970.

Barrios, Angel. *Proposiciones, que, para su consideración y aprobación, presenta a la Convención Soberana Revolucionaria, el suscripto Ing. Angel Barrios . . .*

Mexico City:Imprenta de Roberto Serrano y Cía., 1915.

Basave del Castillo Negrete, Carlos. *Notas para la historia de la Convención Revolucionaria, 1914–1915.* Mexico City:Editorial Stylo, 1947.

Brading, David, ed. *Caudillo and Peasant in the Mexican Revolution.* Cambridge:Cambridge University Press, 1980.

Brinton, Crane. *The Anatomy of Revolution.* 2nd ed. New York: Vintage Books, 1952.

C. de Rojo, Alba; López Castro, Rafael; and Martínez, José Luis. *Zapata:iconografía.* Mexico City: Fondo de Cultura Económica, 1979.

Camp, Roderic A. *Mexico's Leaders:Their Education and Recruitment.* Tucson:University of Arizona Press, 1980.

Casasola, Gustavo. *Historia gráfica de la revolución mexicana, 1900–1970.* 5 vols. Mexico City:Editorial F. Trillas, 1965–1971.

Castillo, Porfirio del. *Puebla y Tlaxcala en los días de la revolución.* Mexico City:n.p., 1953.

Centro de Estudios Históricos del Agrarismo en México (CEHAM). *El ejército campesino del sur (ideología, organización y programa).* Mexico City:Federación Editorial Mexicana, 1982.

Chávez Peralta, Saúl. *Emiliano Za-*

pata:crisol de la revolución mexi-cana. Mexico City:Editorial Renacimiento, 1972.

Cockcroft, James D. *Intellectual Precursors of the Mexican Revo-lution, 1900–1913.* Austin:University of Texas Press, 1968.

Córdova, Arnaldo. *La ideología de la revolución mexicana:la formación del nuevo régimen.* 7th ed. Mexico City:Ediciones Era, 1979.

Cumberland, Charles C. *Mexican Revolution:Genesis Under Madero.* Austin:University of Texas Press, 1952.

_____. *Mexican Revolution:The Constitutionalist Years.* Austin: University of Texas Press, 1972.

[DeBekker, Jan Leander]. *De cómo vino Huerta y cómo se fué . . . apuntes para la historia de un régimen militar.* Mexico City: Libreria General, 1914.

Díaz Soto y Gama, Antonio. *La cuestión agraria en México.* 2nd ed. Mexico City:El Caballito, 1976.

_____. *La revolución agraria del sur y Emiliano Zapata, su caudillo.* Mexico City:Imprenta Policromia, 1960.

Diez, Domingo. *Bosquejo histórico geográfico de Morelos.* Cuernavaca:Editorial Tlahuica, 1967.

Dromundo, Baltasar. *Emiliano Zapata:biografía.* Mexico City:Imprenta Mundial, 1934.

_____. *Vida de Emiliano Zapata.* Mexico City:Editorial Guaranía, 1961.

Espejel, Laura; Olivera, Alicia; and Rueda, Salvador eds. *Emiliano Zapata:antología.* Mexico City: Instituto Nacional de Estudios Históricos de la Revolución Mexicana, 1988.

Fabela, Isidro and Fabela, Josefina E., eds. *Documentos históricos de la revolución mexicana.* Vol. 21: *Emiliano Zapata, el Plan de Ayala, y su política agraria.* Mexico City:Editorial Jus, 1970.

Figueroa Uriza, Arturo. *Ciudadanos en armas:antecedencia y datos para la historia de la revolución mexicana.* 2 vols. Mexico City:B. Costa-Amic, 1960.

Friedlander, Judith. *Being Indian in Hueyapan:A Study of Forced Identity in Contemporary Mexico.* New York:St. Martin's Press, 1975.

Friedrich, Paul. *Agrarian Revolt in a Mexican Village.* Englewood Cliffs, N.J.:Prentice Hall, 1970.

Fromm, Erich and Maccoby, Michael. *Social Character in a Mexican Village:A Sociopsychoanalytic Study.* Englewood Cliffs, N.J.:Prentice Hall, 1970.

Fuentes, Carlos. *Tiempo Mexicano.* Mexico City:Editorial Joaquín Moritz, 1971.

Gilly, Adolfo. *The Mexican Revolution.* Translated by Patrick Camiller. London:Verso, 1983.

Gómez, Marte R. *Las comisiones agrarias del sur.* Mexico City: Manuel Porrua, 1961.

González Ramírez, Manuel, ed. *Manifiestos políticos (1892–1912).* Mexico City:Fondo de Cultura Económica, 1957.

_____, ed. *Planes políticos y otros documentos.* Mexico City:Fondo de Cultura Económica, 1954.

Gruening, Ernest. *Mexico and its Heritage.* London:Stanley Paul, 1928.

Gruzinski, Serge. *Man-Gods in the Mexican Highlands:Indian Power and Colonial Society,* 1520–1800. Translated by Eileen Corrigan. Stanford:Stanford University Press, 1989.

Gurr, Ted Robert. *Why Men Rebel.* Princeton:Princeton University Press, 1970.

Guzmán, Martín Luis. *The Eagle and the Serpent.* Translated by Harriet de Onis. Gloucester, Mass.:Peter Smith, 1969.

Hall, Linda B. *Alvaro Obregón: Power and Revolution in Mexico,* 1911–1920. College Station:Texas A&M University Press, 1981.

Hamnett, Brian R. *Roots of Insurgency:Mexican Regions,* 1750–1824. Cambridge:Cambridge University Press, 1986.

Hart, John M. *Anarchism and the Mexican Working Class,* 1860–1931. Austin:University of Texas Press, 1978.

_____. *Revolutionary Mexico:The Coming and Process of the Mexican Revolution.* Berkeley:University of California Press, 1987.

Haskett, Robert. *Indigenous Rulers:An Ethnohistory of Town Government in Colonial Cuernavaca.* Albuquerque:University of New Mexico Press, 1991.

Helguera R., Laura; López M., Sinecio; and Ramírez M., Ramón. *Los campesinos de la tierra de Zapata, I:adaptación, cambio y rebelión.* Mexico City:Instituto Nacional de Antropología e Historia, 1974.

Henderson, Peter V. N. *Félix Díaz, the Porfirians, and the Mexican Revolution.* Lincoln:University of Nebraska Press, 1981.

Hernández Chávez, Alicia. *Anenecuilco:memoria y vida de un pueblo.* Mexico City:El Colegio de México, 1991.

Ingham, John M. *Mary, Michael, and Lucifer:Folk Catholicism in Central Mexico.* Austin:University of Texas Press, 1986.

Jacobs, Ian. *Ranchero Revolt:The Mexican Revolution in Guerrero.* Austin:University of Texas Press, 1982.

Jiménez, Luz. *Life and Death in*

Milpa Alta. Translated and edited by Fernando Horcasitas. Norman: University of Oklahoma Press, 1972.

Joseph, Gilbert M., and Nugent, Daniel, eds. *Everyday Forms of State Formation:Revolution and the Negotiation of Rule in Modern Mexico*. Durham, N.C.:Duke University Press, 1994.

Katz, Friedrich, ed. *Riot, Rebellion, and Revolution:Rural Social Conflict in Mexico*. Princeton:Princeton University Press, 1988.

_____. *The Secret War in Mexico: Europe, the United States, and the Mexican Revolution*. Portions translated by Loren Goldner. Chicago:University of Chicago Press, 1981.

King, Rosa E. *Tempest over Mexico*. Boston:Little, Brown and Co., 1935.

Knight, Alan. *The Mexican Revolution*. 2 vols. Cambridge:Cambridge University Press, 1986.

Krauze, Enrique. *El amor a la tierra: Emiliano Zapata*. Biografía del poder, no. 3. Mexico City:Fondo de Cultura Económica, 1987.

LaFrance, David G. *The Mexican Revolution in Puebla, 1908–1913: The Maderista Movement and the Failure of Liberal Reform*. Wilmington, Delaware:SR Books, 1989.

Langle Ramírez, Arturo. *Huerta contra Zapata:una campaña desigual*. Mexico City:Universidad Nacional Autónoma de México, 1981.

León-Portilla, Miguel. *Los manifiestos en nahuatl de Emiliano Zapata*. Mexico City:Universidad Nacional Autónoma de México, 1978.

Lewis, Oscar. *Life in a Mexican Village:Tepoztlán Restudied*. Urbana:University of Illinois Press, 1951.

_____. *Pedro Martínez:A Mexican Peasant and His Family*. New York:Vintage Books, 1964.

_____. *Tepoztlán:Village in Mexico*. New York:Holt, Rinehart and Winston, 1960.

Lieuwen, Edwin. *Mexican Militarism:The Political Rise and Fall of the Revolutionary Army, 1910–1940*. Albuquerque:University of New Mexico Press, 1968.

List Arzubide, Germán. *Zapata*. 8th ed. Mexico City:Federación Editorial Mexicana, 1973.

Lomnitz, Claudio. *Evolución de una sociedad rural*. Mexico City: Fondo de Cultura Económica, 1982.

López de Rodríguez, Alicia. *Emiliano Zapata:biografía*. Cuernavaca:Talleres Gráficos de Impresores de Morelos, 1982.

López González, Valentín. *Los compañeros de Zapata*. Cuernavaca:Gobierno del Estado Libre y Soberano de Morelos, 1980.

Luz Valdés, José de la. *El mito de Zapata*. Saltillo:Editorial Espigas, 1974.

Madsen, Douglas, and Snow, Peter G. *The Charismatic Bond:Political Behavior in Time of Crisis*. Cambridge, Mass.:Harvard University Press, 1991.

Magaña, Gildardo (and Pérez Guerrero, Carlos). *Emiliano Zapata y el agrarismo en México*. 5 vols. Mexico City:Editorial Ruta, 1951–1952.

Magaña Cerda, Octavio. *Yo acuso a los responsables:el pueblo que nos juzgue*. Mexico City:B. Costa-Amic, 1961.

María y Campos, Armando de. *La vida del General Lucio Blanco*. Mexico City:Instituto Nacional de Estudios Históricos de la Revolución Mexicana, 1963.

_____. *Múgica:crónica biográfica (aportación a la historia de la Revolución Mexicana)*. Mexico City:Compañía de Ediciones Populares, 1939.

Martin, Cheryl English. *Rural Society in Colonial Morelos*. Albuquerque:University of New Mexico Press, 1985.

Martínez Escamilla, Ramón, ed. *Escritos de Emiliano Zapata*. Mexico City, Editores Mexicanos Unidos, 1978.

Mazlish, Bruce. *The Leader, the Led, and the Psyche:Essays in Psychohistory*. Hanover and London:Wesleyan University Press, 1990.

Melgarejo, Antonio D. *Los crímenes del zapatismo (apuntes de un guerrillero)*. Mexico City: Editora y Distribuidora Nacional de Publicaciones, 1979.

Melville, Roberto. *Crecimiento y rebelión:el desarrollo económico de las haciendas azucareras en Morelos (1880–1910)*. Mexico City:Editorial Nueva Imagen, 1979.

Mena, Mario. *Zapata*. Mexico City: Editorial Jus, 1959.

Mendieta Alatorre, María de los Angeles. *Juana Belén Gutiérrez de Mendoza (1875–1942):extraordinaria precursora de la revolución mexicana*. Mexico City:Impresores de Morelos, 1983.

Mexico. Secretaría de Gobernación. *Exposición homenaje nacional a Emiliano Zapata en el centenario de su nacimiento (1879–1979)*. Mexico City:Secretaría de Educación Pública and Instituto de Bellas Artes, 1979–1980.

Meyer, Michael C. *Huerta:A Political Portrait*. Lincoln:University of Nebraska Press, 1972.

_____. *Mexican Rebel:Pascual Orozco and the Mexican Revolu-*

tion, 1910–1915. Lincoln:University of Nebraska Press, 1967.

Meyer, Michael C., and Sherman, William L. *The Course of Mexican History*, 2nd ed. New York: Oxford University Press, 1983.

Migdal, Joel S. *Peasants, Politics, and Revolution:Pressures toward Political and Social Change in the Third World*. Princeton: Princeton University Press, 1974.

Millon, Robert P. *Zapata:The Ideology of a Peasant Revolutionary*. New York:International Publishers, 1970.

Moore, Barrington. *Social Origins of Dictatorship and Democracy: Lord and Peasant in the Making of the Modern World*. Boston:Beacon Press, 1966.

O'Shaughnessy, Edith. *Intimate Pages of Mexican History*. New York:George H. Doran, 1920.

Palacios, Porfirio. *Emiliano Zapata:datos biográfico-históricos*. Mexico City:Libro Mex, 1960.

Parkinson, Roger. *Zapata*. Briarclift Manor, N.Y.:Stein and Day, 1980.

Paz, Octavio. *The Other Mexico: Critique of the Pyramid*. Translated by Lysander Kemp. New York:Grove Press, 1972.

Paz Solórzano, Octavio. *Hoguera que fue*. Edited by Felipe Gálvez. Mexico City:Universidad Autónoma Metropolitana, 1986.

_____. *Zapata*. Tres revolucionarios, tres testimonios, vol. 2. Mexico City:Editorial Offset, 1986.

Peña, Guillermo de la. *A Legacy of Promises:Agriculture, Politics, and Ritual in the Morelos Highlands of Mexico*. Austin:University of Texas Press, 1981.

Pinchon, Edgcumb. *Zapata the Unconquerable*. New York:Doubleday, Doran and Co.:1941.

Plancarte y Navarrete, Francisco. *Apuntes para la geografía del Estado de Morelos*. 2nd ed. Cuernavaca:Imprenta de José Donaciano Rojas, 1913.

Quirk, Robert E. *The Mexican Revolution, 1914–1915:The Convention of Aguascalientes*. Bloomington:Indiana University Press, 1960.

Raat, W. Dirk. *The Mexican Revolution:An Annotated Guide to Recent Scholarship*. Boston:G.K. Hall, 1982.

_____. *Revoltosos:Mexico's Rebels in the United States, 1903–1923*. College Station, Texas:Texas A&M University Press, 1981.

Ramírez Plancarte, Francisco. *La Ciudad de México durante la revolución constitucionalista*. 2nd ed. Mexico City:Ediciones Botas, 1941.

Redfield, Robert. *Tepoztlán, A Mexican Village:A Study of Folk Life*. Chicago:University of Chicago Press, 1930.

Reina, Leticia. *Las rebeliones campesinas en México (1819–1906)*. Mexico City:Siglo Veintiuno, 1980.

Rejai, Mostafa. *The Comparative Study of Revolutionary Strategy*. New York:David McKay, 1977.

Reyes Avilés, Carlos. *Cartones Zapatistas*. Mexico City:n.p., 1928.

Reyes H., Alfonso. *Emiliano Zapata:su vida y su obra (con documentos inéditos)*. 2nd ed. Mexico City:Libros de México, 1963.

Ribot, Héctor. *El Atila del sur*. Mexico City:Imprenta 1a de Humboldt, [1913?].

Richmond, Douglas. *Venustiano Carranza's Nationalist Struggle, 1893–1920*. Lincoln:University of Nebraska Press, 1983.

Rojas, Basilio. *La Soberana Convención de Aguascalientes*. Mexico City, 1961.

Roman, Richard. *Ideología y clase en la Revolución Mexicana:la Convención y el Congreso Constituyente*. Trans. María Elena Hope. Mexico City:Sepsetentas, 1976.

Romanucci-Ross, Lola. *Conflict, Violence, and Morality in a Mexican Village*. Palo Alto:National Press Books, 1973.

Rosoff, Rosalind, and Aguilar, Anita. *Así firmaron el Plan de Ayala*. Mexico City:Secretaría de Educación Pública, 1976.

Ross, Stanley R. *Francisco I. Madero:Apostle of Mexican Democracy*. New York:Columbia University Press, 1955.

Ruíz, Ramón Eduardo. *The Great Rebellion:Mexico 1905–1924*. New York:W.W. Norton, 1980.

Rutherford, John. *Mexican Society During the Revolution:A Literary Approach*. Oxford:Clarendon Press, 1971.

Sala, Antenor. *Emiliano Zapata y el problema agrario en la república mexicana*. Mexico City:Imprenta Franco-Mexicana, 1919.

Salazar Pérez, Juan. *Otilio Montaño*. Cuernavaca:Ediciones del Gobierno del Estado Libre y Soberano de Morelos, 1982.

Sánchez Escobar, Rafael. *El ocaso de los héroes:como murieron algunos connotados revolucionarios*. Mexico City:Casa de Orientación para Varones, 1934.

_____. *Episodios de la revolución mexicana en el sur*. Mexico City: Talleres Tipográficos de la Casa de Orientación para Varones, 1934.

Sánchez Lamego, Miguel A. *Historia militar de la revolución en la época de la Convención*. Mexico City:Instituto Nacional de Estudios Históricos de la Revolución Mexicana, 1983.

_____. *Historia militar de la revolución mexicana en la época maderista.* 3 vols. Mexico City: Instituto Nacional de Estudios Históricos de la Revolución Mexicana, 1976–1977.

_____. *Historia militar de la revolución zapatista bajo el régimen huertista.* Mexico City:Talleres Gráficos de la Nación, 1979.

Sedano P., Miguel Angel. *Emiliano Zapata:revolucionarios surianos y memorias de Quintín González.* Mexico City:Editorial del Magisterio, 1970.

Sinkin, Richard N. *The Mexican Reform, 1855–1876:A Study in Liberal Nation-Building.* Austin: Institute of Latin American Studies, University of Texas, 1979.

Skocpol, Theda. *States and Social Revolutions:A Comparative Analysis of France, Russia, and China.* Cambridge:Cambridge University Press, 1979.

Sotelo Inclán, Jesús. *La escuela de Anenecuilco.* Cuadernos Zapatistas. Cuernavaca:Gobierno del Estado Libre y Soberano de Morelos, 1979.

_____. *Raíz y razón de Zapata.* Mexico City:Editorial Etnos, 1943.

_____. *Raíz y razón de Zapata.* 2nd ed. Mexico City:Comisión Federal de Electricidad, 1970.

Stephenson, George M. *John Lind of Minnesota.* Minneapolis:University of Minnesota Press, 1935.

Tannenbaum, Frank. *Peace by Revolution:An Interpretation of Mexico.* New York:Columbia University Press, 1933.

Taracena, Alfonso. *La tragedia zapatista.* Mexico City:Editorial Bolívar, 1931.

_____. *Zapata:fantasía y realidad.* 2nd ed. Mexico City:B. Costa-Amic, 1974.

Teitelbaum, Louis M. *Woodrow Wilson and the Mexican Revolution (1913–1916).* New York:Exposition Press, 1967.

Thord-Gray, I. *Gringo Rebel (Mexico 1913–1914).* 2nd ed. Coral Gables:University of Miami Press, 1960.

Tutino, John. *From Insurrection to Revolution in Mexico:Social Bases of Agrarian Violence, 1750–1940.* Princeton:Princeton University Press, 1986.

Tweedie, Mrs. Alec. *Mexico as I Saw it.* 2nd ed. London:Thomas Nelson and Sons, 1911[?].

Ulloa, Berta. *Historia de la Revolución Mexicana, periodo 1914–1917, V:la encrucijada de 1915.* Mexico City:El Colegio de México, 1979.

Valverde, Custodio. *Julián Blanco y la revolución en el Estado de Guerrero.* Mexico City:Imprenta de J. Chávez y Hno., 1916.

Valverde, Sergio. *Apuntes para la historia de la revolución y de la política en el estado de Morelos, desde la muerte del Governador Alarcón, pronunciamiento de los Grales. Pablo Torres Burgos y Emiliano Zapata mártires, hasta la restauración de la reacción por Vicente Estrada Cajigal impostor.* Mexico City:n.p., 1933.

Vanderwood, Paul J. *Disorder and Progress:Bandits, Police, and Mexican Development.* Lincoln: University of Nebraska Press, 1981.

Vasconcelos, José. *Memorias I: Ulises Criollo, La Tormenta.* Mexico City:Fondo de Cultura Económica, 1982.

Vázquez Gómez, Francisco. *Memorias políticas (1909–1913).* Mexico City:Imprenta Mundial, 1933.

Warman, Arturo, *Los campesinos: hijos predilectos del régimen.* 7th ed. Mexico City:Editorial Nuestro Tiempo, 1979.

_____. *"We Come to Object":The Peasants of Morelos and the National State.* Translated by Stephen K. Ault. Baltimore:Johns Hopkins University Press, 1980.

Weber, Max. *On Charisma and Institution Building.* Edited by S.N. Eisenstadt. Chicago:University of Chicago Press, 1968.

Wickham-Crowley, Timothy. *Guerrillas and Revolution in Latin America.* Princeton:Princeton University Press, 1992.

Wolf, Eric R. *Peasant Wars of the Twentieth Century.* New York: Harper & Row, 1969.

Womack, John, Jr. *Zapata and the Mexican Revolution.* New York: Vintage Books, 1970.

Zapata, Emiliano. *Cartas.* Edited by Chantal López and Omar Cortés. Mexico City:Antorcha, 1987.

Articles and Unpublished Manuscripts

Adame Medina, Eduardo. "De Villa de Ayala a Chinameca, 1909–1919." *El Campesino,* May to July 1958.

Aguilar, Herminia. "Doña Josefa Espejo Vda. de Zapata." *El Campesino,* May 1958.

Aguilar Camín, Héctor. "The Relevant Tradition:Sonoran Leaders in the Revolution." In *Caudillo and Peasant in the Mexican Revolution,* 92–123. Edited by David Brading. Cambridge:Cambridge University Press, 1980.

Almazán, Juan Andreu. "Memorias del General Juan Andreu Almazán." Serialized in *El Universal,* 1957–1958. (Bound photocopy at the Colegio de México).

Alpuche y Silva, Fernando. "El General Emiliano Zapata:apuntes." *El Nacional,* 20 July 1941.

Alvarado, Rafael. "Zapata intentó asesinar al General Pablo González." *Todo*, 5 November 1942.

Andonegui, Juan Angel. "Cuando imperaba el zapatismo." *El Universal*, 18 April 1948.

Arías Gómez, María Eugenia. "Algunos cuadernos históricos sobre Emiliano Zapata y el Zapatismo." In *Emiliano Zapata y el movimiento zapatista*, 181–280. Mexico City:Secretaría de Educación Pública and the Instituto Nacional de Antropología e Historia, 1980.

Ayaquica, Fortino. "Como perdió la vida el General Domingo Arenas." *El Hombre Libre*, 4 August through 15 November 1937.

Azaola Garrido, Elena. "Tepalcingo: la dependencia política de un municipio de Morelos." In *Los campesinos de la tierra de Zapata III:política y conflicto*, 13–186. Elena Azaola Garrido and Esteban Krotz. Mexico City:Instituto Nacional de Antropología e Historia, 1976.

Bailey, David C. "Revisionism and the Recent Historiography of the Mexican Revolution." *Hispanic American Historical Review* 58 (1978):62–79.

Brunk, Samuel. "Zapata and the City Boys:In Search of a Piece of the Revolution." *Hispanic American Historical Review* 73 (1993): 33–65.

Buttrey, T.V. and Gordus, Adon. "The Silver Coinage of Zapata, 1914–1915." *Hispanic American Historical Review* 52 (1972):456–462.

Buve, Raymond Th. J. "'Neither Carranza nor Zapata':The Rise and Fall of a Peasant Movement that Tried to Challenge Both, Tlaxcala, 1910–1919." In *Riot, Rebellion, and Revolution:Rural Social Conflict in Mexico*, 338–75. Edited by Friedrich Katz. Princeton:Princeton University Press, 1988.

_____. "Protesta de obreros y campesinos durante el Porfiriato." *Boletín de Estudios Latinoamericanos y del Caribe* 13 (1972):1–20.

B.V. "Emiliano Zapata." *El Popular*, 11 April 1932.

Calderón Ramírez, Salvador. "'La Bachillera' madrina de Zapata." *Todo*, 20 June 1940.

Carr, Barry. "Marxism and Anarchism in the Formation of the Mexican Communist Party, 1910–1929." *Hispanic American Historical Review* 63 (1983):277–305.

_____. "Recent Regional Studies of the Mexican Revolution." *Latin American Research Review* 15 (1980):3–14.

"Carranza autorizó la muerte de Zapata, dice P. González." *Novedades*, 28 October 1942.

Castrejón Castrejón, Adrián. "Los últimos instantes de la vida de Emiliano Zapata." *El Campesino,* 1 May 1950.

Cervantes, Federico. "Remembranzas Históricas:la entrevista Villa-Zapata." *El Universal Gráfico,* 20 January 1939.

Cháverri Matamoros, Amado. "El Archivo de Zapata." *La Prensa,* September 12 through October 11, 1935.

Chevalier, Francois. "Un factor decisivo de la reforma agraria de México:el levantamiento de Zapata (1911-1919)." *Cuadernos Americanos* 113 (1960):165-87.

Cosío Robelo, Francisco. "Dígale a Zapata que ya acabe el circo." *Mujeres y Deportes,* 6 February 1937.

Crespo, Horacio, and Frey, Herbert. "La diferenciación social del campesinado como problema de la teoría y de la historia, hipótesis generales para el caso de Morelos, México." *Revista Mexicana de Sociología* 44 (1982):285-313.

El Cronista de la Revolución. "Episodios Revolucionarios. Sobre Veracruz." *Excélsior,* 21 July 1929.

Cutierrez [sic?] y González, Luis. "Hoy visita a la viuda de Zapata." *Hoy,* 28 March 1953.

"Emiliano Zapata iba corneado cuando se fue a la revolución." *La Prensa,* 15 April 1932.

Espejel, Laura. "El cuartel general órgano rector de la revolución zapatista." B.A. thesis, Universidad Nacional Autónoma de México, 1985.

———. "El movimiento campesino en el oriente del estado de México:el caso de Juchitepec." *Cuicuilco* 2 (January 1981):33-37.

Figueroa Uriza, Arturo. "Como surgió caudillo maderista Emiliano Zapata." *El Universal,* 24 March 1956.

Flores Vilchis, Othón. "El problema agrario en el estado de Morelos." Thesis, Facultad Nacional de Jurisprudencia, Universidad Nacional Autónoma de México, 1950.

Garciadiego Dantan, Javier. "Higinio Aguilar:milicia, rebelión y corrupción como *modus vivendi.*" *Historia Mexicano* 41 (1992):437-88.

———. "Revolución constitucionalista y contrarrevolución (movimientos reaccionarios en México 1914-1920). Ph.D. dissertation, Colegio de México, 1981.

Gates, William. "The Four Governments of Mexico:Zapata—Protector of Morelos." *World's Work,* 37 (April 1919):654-65.

Gill, Mario. "Zapata:su pueblo y

sus hijos." *Historia Mexicana* 2 (1952):294–312.

Golden, Tim. "Rebels Determined 'to Build Socialism' in Mexico," *New York Times*, 4 January 1994.

González Navarro, Moisés. "Zapata y la revolución agraria mexicana." *Cahiers du Monde Hispanique et Luso-Brésilien* 9 (1967): 5–31.

González Ortega, José. "Como murió Eufemio Zapata." *Todo*, 13 January 1944.

González Ramírez, Manuel. "La muerte del General Zapata y la práctica de las emboscadas." *Estudios de historia moderna y contemporánea de México* 2 (1967):211–47.

Hall, Linda B. "Alvaro Obregón and the Politics of Mexican Land Reform." *Hispanic American Historical Review* 60 (1980):213–38.

Holt Büttner, Elizabeth. "Evolución de las localidades en el estado de Morelos según los censos de población (1900–1950)." *Anuario de Geografía* 2 (1962):9–126.

Huacuja, Mario. "Que Zapata tenía fe ciega en la lealtad de Guajardo." *Novedades*, 12 May 1951.

Joseph, Gilbert M. "On the Trail of Latin American Bandits:A Reexamination of Peasant Resistance." *Latin American Research Review* 25 (1990):7–53.

Knight, Alan. "Interpretaciones recientes de la revolución mexicana." In *Memorias del Simposio de Historiografía Mexicanista*, 193–221. Mexico City:Gobierno del Estado de Morelos, 1990.

———. "Peasant and Caudillo in Revolutionary Mexico, 1910–1917." In *Caudillo and Peasant in the Mexican Revolution*, 17–58. Edited by David Brading. Cambridge:Cambridge University Press, 1980.

López, Hector F. "Datos para la historia de la revolución mexicana:cuando fue consignado Emiliano Zapata." *El Hombre Libre*, 5 April 1937.

López Méndez, Sinecio. "Hueyapan:un pueblo de la tierra fría." In *Los campesinos de la tierra de Zapata I:adaptación, cambio y rebelión*, 15–100. Laura Helguera R., Sinecio López M., and Ramón Ramírez M. Mexico City:Instituto Nacional de Antropología e Historia, 1974.

Luz Valdés, José de la. "El Drama de Chinameca." In Sociedad Chihuahuense de Estudios Históricos. *V Congreso Nacional de Historia de la Revolución Mexicana*, 182–202. Chihuahua:n.p., 1974.

Macias, Anna. "Women and the Mexican Revolution, 1910–

1920." *The Americas* 37 (1980): 53–82.

Mallon, Florencia E. "Peasants and State Formation in Nineteenth Century Mexico:Morelos, 1848–1858." *Political Power and Social Theory* 7 (1988):1–54.

Martínez, Paulino. "Causas de la revolución en México y cómo efectuar la paz." In *La cuestión de la tierra*, 1913–1914, vol. 3:219–35. Edited by Jesús Silva Herzog. Mexico City:Instituto Mexicana de Investigaciones Económicas, 1961.

Martínez Mancera, Salvador. "Perdura en el sur la leyenda de que E. Zapata no ha muerto." *El Universal Gráfico*, 13 April 1938.

Martínez Martínez, Guillermo. "El Gral. Emiliano Zapata y el movimiento zapatista en el Estado de Guerrero." In *Emiliano Zapata y el movimiento zapatista:cinco ensayos*, 329–73. Mexico City: Instituto Nacional de Antropología e Historia, 1980.

Martínez Medina, Héctor Gerardo. "Génesis y desarrollo del maderismo en Oaxaca." In *La revolución en Oaxaca*, 1900–1930, 88–158. Edited by Víctor Raúl Martínez Vásquez. Oaxaca:Instituto de Administración Pública de Oaxaca, 1985.

McNeely, John H. "Origins of the Zapata Revolt in Morelos," *Hispanic American Historical Review* 46 (1966):153–69.

Mentz, Brígida von. "La región morelense en la primera mitad del siglo XIX:fuentes e hipótesis de trabajo." In *Morelos:cinco siglos de historia regional*, 131–47. Edited by Horacio Crespo. Mexico City:Centro de Estudios Históricos del Agrarismo en México and Universidad Autónoma del Estado de Morelos, 1984.

"México:los viejos soldados de Zapata." *Cuadernos del Tercer Mundo* 11,2 (1977):92–112.

Muñoz Cota, José. "El Partido Liberal Mexicano y Zapata." *El Nacional*, 6 December 1965.

O, Genovevo de la. "Memorias." *Impacto*, 14 January 1950.

Olivera, Alicia. "¿Ha muerto Emiliano Zapata? Mitos y leyendas en torno del caudillo." *Boletín INAH*, época II, 13 (1975):43–52.

Páez, Joaquín. "Cuatro meses de vacaciones con Zapata." *El Sol de Puebla*, March 26 through April 28, 1951.

Palacios, Porfirio. "Revolucionarios del sur:el sordo Felipe Neri." *El Campesino*, 15 May 1967.

———. "Revolucionarios del sur: Francisco Mendoza Palma." *El Campesino*, 30 November 1967.

———. "Revolucionarios del sur: Gabriel Tepepa." *El Campesino*, April 1967.

_____. "Zapatismo vs. Gonzalismo." *Todo,* 24 December 1942.

Palafox, Manuel. "La paz que Carranza propuso a Zapata." *El Universal,* 28 June 1934.

_____. "La·verdadera intransigencia de Zapata." *El Universal,* August 8, 1933.

Parrés, José G. "Zapata y su concepto sobre la lealtad." In *Ofrenda a la memoria de Emiliano Zapata,* 23–34. Mexico City:n.p., 1938.

Pérez Guerrero, Carlos. "Porque el General Zapata no atacó Jojutla en 1911." *El Hombre Libre,* 8 September 1937.

_____. "¿Zapata de acuerdo con el porfirismo?" In *Mujeres y Deportes,* 27 February 1937.

Piña, Joaquín. "Zapata y el yerno de Don Porfirio." *Ultimas Noticias,* 9 March 1960.

"Por que existe y como se desarrolla el zapatismo en el Estado de Morelos." *La Tribuna,* 4 June 1913.

Rausch, Jr., George J. "The Early Career of Victoriano Huerta," *Americas* 21 (1964):136–45.

Reyes Avilés, Carlos. "Un historiador ingenuo." *El Nacional,* 28 August 1934.

Rip-Rip. "Una cena trágica iluminada por las llamas del incendio." *Gráfico,* 17 June 1930.

Rittenhouse, Floyd. "Emiliano Zapata and the Suriano Rebellion:A Phase of the Agrarian Revolution in Mexico, 1910–1920." Ph.D. dissertation, Ohio State University, 1947.

Robles, Manuel N. "Lo que supe de la muerte del Gral. Emiliano Zapata." *El Campesino,* August 1955.

Robles, Serafín M. "Como surgió el Plan de Ayala." *El Campesino,* November, 1950.

_____. "Cunde la revolución de Madero en Morelos." *El Campesino,* February 1952.

_____. "El caudillo se casa en la Villa de Ayala, Morelos." *El Campesino,* November 1954.

_____. "El General Zapata, agricultor y arriero." *El Campesino,* October 1951.

_____. "El niño va a la escuela y concluye la primaria." *El Campesino,* March 1953.

_____. "El jefe suriano combate en Amayuca, Morelos." *El Campesino,* May 1952.

_____. "El Zapatismo y la industría azucarera en Morelos." *El Campesino,* August 1950.

_____. "Emiliano Zapata:consecuencias de la conferencia Díaz-Creelman." *El Campesino,* April 1954.

_____. "Emiliano Zapata:con su amigo Sánchez combate con federales." *El Campesino,* January 1954.

_____. "Emiliano Zapata:causa baja como soldado raso a los 48 días." *El Campesino*, January 1952.

_____. "Emiliano Zapata declina el obsequio de un automóvil." *El Campesino*, December 1949.

_____. "Emiliano Zapata fue siempre fiel a su doctrina." *El Campesino*, November 1949.

_____. "Emiliano Zapata no fue fanático." *La Prensa*, 26 June 1936.

_____. "Emiliano Zapata sienta plaza como soldado el año 1910." *El Campesino*, December 1951.

_____. "Emiliano Zapata:ya hombre, es el paladín del campo." *El Campesino*, August 1953.

_____. "Lo que pensaba Zapata sobre el comunismo." *El Campesino*, October 1949.

_____. "¿No crees que esto es una injusticia?" *El Campesino*, February 1953.

_____. "Segunda celada para dar muerte al jefe suriano." *El Campesino*, December 1954.

_____. "Se incorpora Jesús Morales:toma de Chietla, Puebla." *El Campesino*, June 1952.

_____. "Se levantaron al grito de ¡Viva Madero! ¡Muera Díaz!" *El Campesino*, March and April 1952.

_____. "Semblanza del Plan de Ayala." *El Campesino*, January 1950.

_____. "Temararia hazaña del pundonoroso y valiente General Mucio Bravo." *El Campesino*, July 1950.

_____. "Verdadera personalidad de don Emiliano Zapata." *El Campesino*, January 1951.

_____. "Zapata, desde niño era un gran charro." *El Campesino*, December 1950.

Romero Flores, Jesús. "Mil biografías en la historia de México." *El Nacional*, 14 December 1946.

Rueda Smithers, Salvador. "Administración política y utopía hacendada:la lucha por el poder en el estado de Morelos (1869–1913)." *Historias* 13 (1986):95–116.

_____. "Emiliano Zapata, los signos de un caudillo, biografía de un símbolo." In *Estadistas, caciques y caudillos*, 133–51. Edited by Carlos Martínez Assad. Mexico City: Instituto de Investigaciones Sociales, 1988.

_____. "La dinámica interna del zapatismo:consideración para el estudio de la cotidianeidad campesina en el area zapatista." In *Morelos:cinco siglos de historia regional*, 225–

49. Edited by Horacio Crespo. Mexico City:Centro de Estudios Históricos del Agrarismo en México, 1984.

———. "Las causas del movimiento zapatista en Morelos: desniveles históricos en el origen de un conflicto agrario." In *Memorias:la revolución en las regiones*, 261–88. Guadalajara:Universidad de Guadalajara, 1986.

———. "La zona armada de Genovevo de la O. *Cuicuilco* 2 (January 1981):38–43.

———. "Los dos Emilianos Zapata, concepciones clasistas en torno a una figura." *Boletín del Centro de Estudios de la Revolución Mexicana "Lázaro Cárdenas"* 3 (April 1980): 43–51.

———. "Oposición y subversión: testimonios zapatistas." *Historias* 3 (1983):3–32.

"Siete meses de gobierno de Benito Juárez Maza." In *Oaxaca en México* 46:3 (April 1939): 9–15.

Taracena, Alfonso. "Madero quiso refugiarse con Zapata." *Revista de Revistas*, 22 September 1957.

Valero Silva, José. "El zapatismo ante la filosofía y ante la historia, por Otilio Montaño." *Estudios de historia moderna y contemporánea de México* 2 (1967):185–96.

———. "Relación de los hechos que dieron por resultado la muerte de Emiliano Zapata, jefe de la rebelión del sur." *Estudios de historia moderna y contemporánea de México* 2 (1967):197–203.

Van Young, Eric. "To See Someone Not Seeing:Historical Studies of Peasants and Politics in Mexico." *Mexican Studies/Estudios Mexicanos* 6 (1990):133–59.

Warman, Arturo. "The Political Project of Zapatismo." Translated by Judith Brister. In *Riot, Rebellion, and Revolution:Rural Social Conflict in Mexico*, 321–38. Edited by Friedrich Katz. Princeton: Princeton University Press, 1988.

Waterbury, Ronald. "Non-revolutionary Peasants:Oaxaca Compared to Morelos in the Mexican Revolution." *Comparative Studies in Society and History* 17 (1975):410–42.

White, S.J., Robert A. "Mexico: The Zapata Movement and the Revolution." In *Latin American Peasant Movements*, 101–69. Edited by Henry A. Landsberger. Ithaca,

N. Y.:Cornell University Press, 1969.

Wickham-Crowley, Timothy. "Terror and Guerrilla Warfare in Latin America, 1956–1970," in *Comparative Studies in Society and History* 32 (1990):201–37.

Womack, John, Jr. In *Jornadas de historia de occidente*, 119–22. Jiquilpan de Juárez, Michoacán:Centro de Estudios de la Revolución Mexicana "Lázaro Cárdenas", A.C., 1978.

_____. "The Mexican Revolution, 1910–1920." In *Cambridge History of Latin America*, 5:79–153. Edited by Leslie Bethell. 7 vols. Cambridge:Cambridge University Press, 1984–1990.

"Zapata, ¿Bandido o Apostol?" *Hoy*, 14 February 1948.

Film

García Videla, Adolfo. "Testimonios Zapatistas." Programa de Historia Oral (PHO), Instituto Nacional de Antropología e Historia.

Toscano, Salvador. "Memorias de un Mexicano."

Index